BATTLEFIELD CHAPLAINS

BATTLEFIELD CHAPLAINS

Catholic Priests in World War II

Donald F. Crosby, S.J.

Foreword by Martin Blumenson

University Press of Kansas

98/0055

Published by the University Press of Kansas (Lawrence, Kansas 66049), which was organized
by the Kansas Board of Regents and is operated and funded by Emporia State University,
Fort Hays State University, Kansas State University, Pittsburg State University, the University
of Kansas, and Wichita State University

Library of Congress Cataloging-in-Publication Data

Crosby, Donald F., 1933–
    Battlefield chaplains / Donald F. Crosby ; foreword by Martin
  Blumenson.
      p.   cm. — (Modern war studies)
    Includes bibliographical references and index.
    ISBN 0-7006-0662-9 (cloth)   ISBN 0-7006-0814-1 (pbk.)
    I. Title. II. Series.
  D810.C35C76 1994   93–39804
  940.54'78'0973—dc20

British Library Cataloguing in Publication Data is available.

Printed in the United States of America
10 9 8 7 6 5 4 3 2

The paper used in this publication meets the minimum requirements of the American
National Standard for Permanence of Paper for Printed Library Materials Z39.48–1984.

To

Norman F. Martin, S.J.,
with gratitude

CONTENTS

ILLUSTRATIONS

FOREWORD

Father Donald F. Crosby, a Roman Catholic priest and a member of the Society of Jesus, through his impeccable research and brilliant writing, tells a story both authentic and stirring. The subject, never explicitly stated yet always present, is the intensity of devotion and care given by the chaplains to their charges, the men and women in the army and navy during World War II. The setting is the marvelously described and painted battlefield—on land and sea—in the major overseas combat zones of the war. There the chaplains shared the risks, the dangers, and the sufferings of those whom they served.

Although Crosby focuses on the activities of the Catholic chaplains, he extends his coverage to those of other faiths. Never parochial, he is ecumenical in his outlook. The army (which included the Air Corps) and the navy (including the Marine Corps) commissioned priests, ministers, and rabbis as chaplains for the purpose of enhancing morale among servicemen and women. The chaplains' duties were a regular part of military life. Serving in the chain of command, chaplains were subject to the wishes of their military commanders, who supervised and evaluated their activities and who recommended promotions.

For example, General George S. Patton, Jr., who attended church—as he informed a group of visiting clergymen—"every goddam Sunday," believed the chaplains' work to be important. He routinely inspected the work of his chaplains of all faiths, as he did the work of other specialists. Those whose performances he judged less than excellent had immediate word of his dissatisfaction.

Chaplains fostered good morale in a variety of ways. They held religious services for soldiers and sailors and preached to them. They counseled and advised those who sought help. They were everywhere they deemed their presence to be necessary—in battle, that meant with the combat troops, and there the chaplains often acted above and beyond the call of duty. Under hostile fire, they risked their lives. They sought the wounded, the dying, and the dead who lay exposed and helpless. They succored them, rescued them, brought them back to medical aid stations, and prayed over them. They buried bodies and wrote to the families of the deceased.

They were terribly overworked, for there was always too few of them to attend to all the tasks they felt it necessary to perform. A few, of course, failed to measure up, and Crosby, without moralizing, tells about these unfortunate individuals. He also admonishes the religious bodies at home for their reluctance to furnish adequate numbers of clergy to the armed forces. He gives us the truth of some celebrated occurrences related to chaplains, for example, the real story of "Praise the Lord and Pass the Ammunition" and how General Patton's Christmas prayer came into being.

Often, soldiers, sailors, airmen, and marines who were not religiously inclined became enthusiastic supporters of chaplains. Chaplains kept spirits up and gave the men in combat a firm anchor. In the postwar years, when combat veterans have met to commemorate their wartime exertions, they have venerated their chaplains. They regard the padres—the priests, ministers, and rabbis who shared their perils—with equal amounts of awe and affection. For the chaplains traveled over battlefields under fire and through the flaming interiors of stricken battleships to look for and rescue those in danger. The chaplains did so for two reasons: This was their duty, and they were concerned, genuinely and sincerely, for the safety of their charges.

Crosby's words will bring lumps to the throat, tears to the eyes, and a sense of wonder and joy at how men of the cloth took part in the war.

Martin Blumenson

ACKNOWLEDGMENTS

I fear that most readers will skip the next two paragraphs as soon as they spot the dreaded list of the names of people "without whom I could not have written this book," as some authors like to say. Nevertheless, I would be boorish in the extreme if I failed to acknowledge, in some way, the many generous individuals who have assisted my work. Blame for lapses of any kind rests on me; credit for anything I may have accomplished clearly must be shared with them. Paul Goda, S.J., heroically read every draft of every chapter, applying his lawyer's mind to errors of both logic and fact, as well as suggesting ways to shorten the military background of each section. Others whose wise and careful reading of the manuscript led to numerous improvements were Martin Blumenson, Lieutenant General Leo A. Dulacki (USMC, Ret.), Joseph and Gloria Whelan, M.D., William L. Hutchison, and Robert Senkewicz, S.J.

Among my superiors in the Society of Jesus who provided the time and support necessary for my work, I am especially grateful to John Clark, S.J., Terrence Mahan, S.J., William F. Donnelly, S.J., and Thomas F. McCormick, S.J. To my former students at Santa Clara University who suffered through my course in World War II, I owe continued gratitude for their enthusiasm for the study of the conflict. No teacher was ever more buoyed by his students. Richard Buchter meticulously proofread the entire text without complaint. Among the many physicians who kept me healthy enough so that I could complete the project, I am especially indebted to Joseph Giansiracusa, M.D., Seymour Grossman, M.D., William McGann, M.D., Julius Heuscher, M.D., Jerome Goldstein, M.D., and above all, H. Theodore Freeland, M.D. The 280 former chaplains whom I contacted gave generously, not only their recollections of the war, but of their untiring interest in the topic as well. Most have since entered into the celestial Chaplain Corps. One hopes that this volume does them justice. Finally, William Rewak, S.J., will understand why I so appreciate his unfailing support during the decade that it took to complete this volume.

INTRODUCTION

Somewhere in the Pacific, in the second year of World War II, a navy chaplain watched a plane take off from a carrier. Although separated in age by more than ten years, the chaplain and the pilot had formed a deep friendship during their brief time together in the service. "He was the only boy I ever spent a leave with outside of my priest friends," the chaplain said later. Above all, the young pilot's devotion to his religious practice had awed the priest, and that same morning the pilot had attended Mass and received communion.

The priest watched as the frail craft took off from the carrier on a patrol, what the navy called "a routine mission." Suddenly the engine began sputtering erratically and pouring out long plumes of smoke. A few seconds later, the plane fell into the ocean. The priest watched helplessly as it floated up and down in the waves 500 yards away. Gradually it filled with water, then slowly sank out of sight. The chaplain later wrote:

> I ran aft to be a little closer, as our ship had to maintain her course and under no conditions alter speed. The bridge already had signaled an escort destroyer to the crash. I prayed running down the deck, then spoke absolution.
>
> Reaching out as far as I could I gave the blessing; I repeated the form a couple of times; then I took the ritual from my blouse and began the prayers for the dying. I couldn't see: tears jammed my eyes, blurring the words. I said them from memory. His plane was his casket, the sea the cemetery, his shipmates standing helplessly about became his mourners.
>
> But he needed a grave marker. I felt in my pocket for my rosary. I had that rosary from seminary days and intended to keep it for life; I looked at it once more; kissed the crucifix for the last time and threw it overboard to make a Christian grave. A tiny spot in the Pacific holds the remains of a

loved one, marked with the Sign of the Cross, fresh from God's Communion table, ready to meet his Maker. A good pilot, a grand shipmate, a true Catholic.[1]

The names of the pilot, the chaplain, and the carrier will never be known, since all record of the incident, save for this description, has been lost. In some ways, however, it little matters. The story vividly illustrates two of the most important themes of this volume: the friendships that so often developed between chaplains and servicemen and the manner in which the wartime chaplains shared fully in all the sufferings and other experiences of the men they served.

When the surviving chaplains were asked in 1983 to fill out a questionnaire regarding their wartime experiences, they were asked whether they had found their work with the men "rewarding." Of those responding, 98 percent said "yes"; only 2 percent said "no." The 98 percent also reported that their wartime ministry had been among "the most rewarding" of their lives. When asked about their work with non-Catholic servicemen, they reported much the same, with only 1 percent saying they had encountered "difficulty" in their dealings with them. My own interviews with the surviving chaplains revealed the same views, as they repeatedly made statements like, "The GIs were among the best friends I've ever had," and "I lost my closest friend in the service, a young officer, who died in combat."

The lot of the American fighting man was equally the fate of his chaplain. Wherever the troops went, the Chaplain Corps followed—to the icy wastes of the Aleutians, to the deserts of North Africa, to the jungles of the South Pacific, to the crumbling cities of Europe. Both endured the same perils in combat, the same long stretches of boredom, the same difficulties with other officers, the same homesickness, and the same unpalatable food; both also encountered many of the same joys and achieved the same successes.

The chaplains of World War II served in a body that had its origins in colonial times, when ordained clergymen first accompanied Americans into battle. The highly structured chaplaincy of today, however, with its professional schools and specialized offices, did not emerge until the present century. World War I saw the establishment of the army's Chaplain School, as well as the naming of the first chiefs of chaplains for both the army and the navy. (The navy did not authorize its own Chaplain School until just after the start of World War II.) The air force's chaplaincy service emerged full-blown as a result of the National Security Act of 1947, which carved a separate Department of the Air Force out of the wartime Army Air Forces. Like every branch of the armed services, the corps had developed their own structures, by which they directed the work of their personnel. To outsiders, the military chaplaincies might look baffling and complex. To the chaplains themselves, however, their organizations seemed simple enough, and the hierarchy of offices and bureaus seldom gave rise to confusion. Based on a cooperative scheme with the churches, by World War II, both Chaplain Corps had developed a high degree of efficiency and carried out their tasks with a minimum of disturbance.

Each religious body contributed its own candidates for the chaplaincy. A clergyman interested in military service first applied to his denomination's endorsing board, which decided whether it would recommend him or not. Catholic priests contacted an office in their church's hierarchy called the Military Ordinariate (since resoundingly renamed the Archdiocese for the Military Services, USA). A Protestant minister approached the board that his own denomination had designated for the same purpose. (For instance, clergy from the Protestant Episcopal church consulted the Army and Navy Commission of the Protestant Episcopal church. Similarly, Jewish rabbis dealt with the Jewish Welfare Board.)

Throughout this book, I have used the term "Protestant" as precisely as possible, since "Protestantism" is an umbrella that includes hundreds of discrete denominations. Unfortunately, missing records in the National Archives have sometimes made it impossible to determine the denominational affiliation of some World War II army chaplains; when this problem has arisen, I have indicated that fact in a note.

The requirements for entry into a chaplaincy? Nothing more than a certification of ordination and evidence of two years of successful work in the active ministry. The recommending agencies presented their candidates to the armed forces, giving them their "endorsement," as the Chaplain Corps called it. The services then examined each candidate, just as all the branches of the army and navy did. After a series of tests, the corps would pronounce each man fit or unfit. Once admitted, he ceased answering to church authorities and submitted himself to military jurisdiction. If the service experienced difficulty with a chaplain, however, the corps might well consult the man's endorsing board before deciding what to do with him.

From this point on, the clergyman took his orders from his local commanding officer, just like everyone else in the armed forces. Instead of entering boot camp, however, he reported to the Chaplain School (two weeks for the navy, a month for the army) where he learned the essentials of his new trade. The highly programmed (and by general consensus, almost fatally boring) course of studies taught all the fledgling chaplains the same subjects: laws governing the services, customs, drill, the use of equipment, physical fitness, and history of the corps. Above all, they learned how to work in close cooperation with chaplains and servicemen of other denominations.[2]

Both the army and the navy viewed religious conflict as highly destructive and inculcated the virtues of collaboration and teamwork. The chiefs of the two corps would quickly call a fractious chaplain to account, telling him to get along or get out. Following a slogan of "cooperation without compromise," the two schools tried to make collaboration a practical matter by treating Catholics, Protestants, and Jews as one group. Although each denomination received time during the day for its own religious services, everyone ate, slept, drilled, and shared recreation time together, and members of differing denominations were mixed up as much as possible. Many Catholic priests found that for the first time in their lives, they had the experience of talking to Protestant and Jewish counterparts—and vice versa.

In a later period, this kind of close-meshing activity would come to be known as "ecumenism," one of the most revolutionary developments in recent American religious history. The wartime chaplaincy gave the idea an enormous impetus by making it a principle for every chaplain to follow wherever he went, whatever work he undertook. During the war, it was a matter of the simplest possible expediency, a result of necessity rather than of a progressive theology within the churches themselves. In the postwar decades, theologians from Catholic, Protestant, and Jewish ranks would extensively develop the idea.

Although each group practiced its own religious celebrations and followed its own rituals and traditions, every chaplain learned how to conduct the services of the chaplains of other denominations, doing as much as his own religion and the practice of the other religions would allow. For instance, Catholic priests learned how to lead "general services" for the Protestants, receiving instruction in how to combine singing, scripture readings, and a homily of their own composition. They also learned how to preside at Seder services for the Jewish servicemen. Out of deference to Catholic belief, Protestant and Jewish chaplains were told not to hear confessions or preside at the Catholic Mass; nor were Catholic or Protestant clergy to attempt to direct Jewish services, over which only a rabbi could preside. Protestant and Jewish chaplains learned how to lead the rosary for their Catholic men and how to read the church's prayers for the dying.

Throughout the war, most chaplains ministered nearly as often to men of other religions as to those of their own because the armed services, laboring

Bishop John F. O'Hara administers the sacrament of confirmation to Catholic soldiers at Fort Leonard Wood, Missouri. (Source: National Archives)

under a chronic shortage of chaplains, could assign only one chaplain to every 1,200 servicemen. With less than a third of the soldiers, sailors, and airmen calling themselves "Catholics," a priest-chaplain soon found himself acting as a kind of "universal minister" who took care of everyone's religious and personal needs as best he could.

After the training at the Chaplain School (called "indoctrination") had been completed, each man was commissioned a second lieutenant. He reported (sometimes timorously, sometimes eagerly) to his first duty station, usually a large army post or naval base somewhere in the forty-eight states. After a few months he might be sent overseas—indeed, a large majority of the Catholic chaplains in World War II eventually served in either the European or the Pacific theater of war.

Jurisdiction over chaplains was simple enough: While they were in the service, their superiors and bishops at home had nothing to say about what they would do, and like all service personnel, they answered to their local commanding officers. The allocation of chaplains to particular posts, however, was a complex one. Since army and navy regulations stipulated how many chaplains each unit (such as a division, regiment, or ship) would have, the chief of chaplains often sent a chaplain to a place simply because he was needed there to fill the unit's allotment. On other occasions, if a vacancy arose somewhere, a commanding officer might ask the chief to send him a particular chaplain whom he knew and especially admired or he might ask for a chaplain from a particular denomination. The chiefs always did their best to oblige.

Filling every vacancy became increasingly difficult as the war spread across the globe. Further complicating an equitable distribution of chaplains was the failure of some denominations to contribute enough candidates to the services. Among the religious bodies represented in the two corps (thirty-seven in the navy, forty in the army), the worst offender in this respect was the Roman Catholic church, as it never filled its informal "quota." Within the church itself, the Archdiocese of Philadelphia and the Society of Jesus (the Jesuits) contributed the smallest percentages, sending a smaller proportion of their available priests than the other archdioceses, dioceses, and religious orders. Judaism, by contrast, sent the military chaplaincies half of all the rabbis in the United States.[3]

If a chaplain carried out his tasks properly and rang no alarm bells, he remained in the military for the duration of the war. If he caused problems for his unit, the chief of chaplains might ask the man's recommending board to revoke its endorsement. In such a case, he left the military chaplaincy, sometimes under what the armed services called "less than honorable conditions" or "for the good of the service." Causes for complaint included habitual sloth, chronic failure to obey orders, inability to work smoothly with other chaplains, difficulty in dealing with officers or enlisted men, habitual violation of army or navy regulations, and causing a public scandal of any kind. Examples of such impolitic behavior included womanizing, public drunkenness, gambling, profanity, black marketeering, insubordination, and flagrant abuse of the chaplain's status as a noncombatant. (One man stationed at a tank training school got himself certified first as a tank driver, then a tank gunner—both entirely illegal, not to mention imprudent.)[4]

Another cause for reprimand was the act of leaving one's post without permission. Catholic chaplains especially had a tendency to "discover" groups of men (more often than not Catholics) who had not had attended religious services in a long time and felt impelled to abandon their assigned posts without orders of any kind. What usually followed was not only a rebuke from the local commanding officer but a blistering letter of censure from the chief of the Chaplain Corps if he heard about the incident, as he usually did.

The best available evidence, however, shows that despite their lapses and indiscretions, only a few clergymen (both Catholic and non-Catholic) left the service for reasons of health, temperamental unsuitability, or disgraceful conduct. In 1943 (the middle of the war), the army studied its rate of "separation," as it called the process of removing men from the service, and reported that out of the 5,200 chaplains on its rolls, only 23 had been forced to leave. The navy announced at the end of the war that it had discharged only 5 out of a total of 2,900 who had served during the conflict. The number of chaplains from specific denominations who left under pressure remains unknown, but it is clear that the total number of failures was small indeed.[5]

The Chaplain Corps also assigned supervising chaplains, with an appropriately high rank, for each major unit. Thus, General Patton's Third Army had a Third Army Chaplain as well as chaplains at the head of each division and regiment; the navy assigned its chaplains to districts, fleets, squadrons, and other units. The function of these supervisory chaplains was to oversee and coordinate the professional performance of their subordinates. They issued regular reports to the Office of the Chief of Chaplains in Washington, D.C., and at stated intervals (usually every six months), they wrote evaluations of each chaplain, as did each man's local commanding officer. (The federal government has maintained all of its written reports for army chaplains in the Washington National Records Center, a branch of the National Archives in Suitland, Maryland, and they proved invaluable for this study.) A supervising chaplain might also recommend that a chaplain move to another station, receive more chaplains to help him, undergo medical treatment, or go away for a brief rest.

It was precisely at this point in the structure of the corps—where supervisory chaplains dealt with the chaplains in the ranks—that the worst conflicts between Catholic and Protestant chaplains took place. For instance, if a supervising chaplain happened to be a Catholic and the lower-ranking chaplain a Protestant (above all a fundamentalist one), one could almost expect sparks to fly. The same was true if a fundamentalist held rank over a Catholic. Why so much difficulty? The reasons seem apparent enough now: differences in ideology (priests were marginally less rigid and right wing), in geographical origin (Southern Baptists tended—not surprisingly—to come from the South, priests from the Northeast and the Great Lakes states), and finally, the stereotypical views that each had of the other (priests complained that some Protestants treated them as if they had horns on their heads, while some Protestants charged that Catholic chaplains regarded them as "heretics" and "schismatics"). Gen. William Arnold, the army's chief of chaplains and a Catholic monsignor, said at one point that the battle within the Chaplain Corps between the different churches was almost as fierce as the one against the enemy. His thoroughly challenging task was to keep the peace among the chaplains, an assignment that might well have broken a less resilient, resourceful, and patient man.

Lack of earlier contact with clergymen of other faiths was also a part of the problem. Many Catholic priests reported after the war that they had never even talked to a Protestant minister until they entered the military chaplaincy. After the shock of the first meeting, and perhaps a few tense encounters, many priests and ministers learned how to get along with each other—even to enjoy the other's company. A clear majority of Catholic chaplains, 65 percent, later said they had found the experience of working with non-Catholic chaplains during the war a positive and growth-producing one and expressed gratitude for the opportunity. Of the 31 percent that dissented, most complained of painful and distasteful episodes with the more traditionalist Protestant ministers.

Even if some conflict between denominations was almost inevitable, the chaplains could at least take comfort in the belief that debate over church-state issues had adjourned for the duration of the war. Or so they thought. Even though the churches and the government went out of their way to accommodate each other during the war years, conflicts between the two groups continued, especially in the military.

The most vexatious disputes turned on questions of sexual morality. Priests, ministers, and rabbis all fought prostitution (many brothels carried on a flourishing business near camps and bases) as well as the widespread availability of condoms to protect the men if they engaged in sexual contact. The military's practice of issuing condoms to the men before they left their posts and the establishment of "cleansing stations" for them to visit when they returned angered the chaplains, especially the Catholic priests and the more fundamentalist ministers. (This was one of the few times the interests of Catholics and fundamentalists coincided.) Similarly, many Catholic and Protestant chaplains vehemently protested the military's practice of selling what they called "pornography" in its stores. One must, however, note in all frankness that pornography as we know it today had no counterpart in the war years, and one is tempted to wonder what the fuss was all about. But a fuss there was.

The events of the war had a numbing effect on even the chaplains, leading them to support—or at least not object to—government policies that may seem strange today. Few chaplains, for instance, raised serious objections about the removal of Japanese-Americans from their homes, the massed bombings of German and Japanese cities, or the use of the atomic bomb against the Japanese at the end of the war. To be sure, few Americans entertained substantial doubts about such policies, and the chaplains simply reflected the views of the American people at the time—except on issues of sexual morality, in which they marched resolutely to their own drummer.

Not withstanding their lapses and failures, the chaplains (both Catholic and non-Catholic) enjoyed marked success in their wartime ventures. Their greatest achievement was undoubtedly the high quality of their dedication to the care of the men and women they served, both at home and overseas. They paid a terrible price, however. Many perished in combat, suffered injury, or spent long years in prisoner-of-war camps, all as a result of their attempts to bring succor to wounded sailors, soldiers, and airmen. Twenty-five Catholic chaplains were killed (out of a total of 100 for all the denominations in the two Chaplain Corps), 90 were wounded (from a total of 275), and 12 detained as prisoners of war (out of 42). The Army Chaplain Corps announced late in the war that it had suffered a larger percentage of casualties than any other branch of the services except the infantry and the Army Air Corps.[6]

It would seem that the Catholic priests who served in the armed forces during the war—and the Protestant and Jewish chaplains as well—acquitted themselves uncommonly well and did so despite facing daunting obstacles, despite their own personal lapses, and despite a troubling number of conflicts among themselves and their non-Catholic counterparts. That many of them functioned at times in a truly heroic manner is abundantly clear.

Sadly, this work is the only full-length study of any of the denominations that sent chaplains into the wartime ministry. (Alex Grobman's recent examination of the work of American Jewish chaplains with Jewish refugees in Europe discusses only that aspect of their activity.) Although clergymen of every persuasion have written autobiographies (as did many Catholic priests), we still have no systematic account of the work of the chaplains from the major Protestant bodies or from Judaism. One hopes that such studies will appear soon, since they could tell us much about both the lives of the uniformed clergy and the larger American wartime experience. An indispensable paradigm for any examination of military chaplains is Gardner Shattuck, *A Shield and a Hiding Place: The Religious Life of the Civil War Armies* (Macon, Ga.: Mercer University Press, 1987).[7]

One laments the dearth of scholarly writings about non-Catholic chaplains, but one can nevertheless apply the Catholic experience to other denominations since all the chaplains shared the same life. By military law and the practice of the services, all of them performed many of the same duties, which led them to encounter the same problems, enjoy much the same success, and submit to the same military organization. From their first days at Chaplain School to the day of their discharge from the military, they lived under the same regimen. No matter what their religious affiliation, they all worked with anyone who needed their help (whether sharing their religion or not), they carried out the same works of support and mercy, and they experienced the same kinds of problems with overbearing officers and irritable enlisted personnel. They also counseled everyone in need of succor, no matter what the problem. In short, they administered assistance to men and women of every religion and of none at all. What they had in common far outweighed what made them different from each other.

In combat, every chaplain experienced the same terrors—the threat of sudden annihilation or severe injury, the death of one's closest companions—the same crushing burden of labor, and hardships of weather and terrain. At the same time, chaplains who remained in the United States during all of the war (many of whom resented having to stay at home while "the boys" were suffering overseas) suffered from boredom and frustration.

In this book, I say little about the war in the "outposts," such as Alaska, the Middle East, China-Burma-India (commonly known as "CBI"), Greenland, and Iceland, and since chaplains did not work in (and seldom even visited) American submarines, I also do not discuss the battles for the Atlantic and the Pacific. My intent was, not to slight the labors of the chaplains who served in those often forgotten regions, but to concentrate on the principal theaters of conflict. A number of topics not discussed in this volume, or only in passing, will be included in the next volume of a projected three-volume treatment of Catholic chaplains during World War II. The next book will discuss their work on the home front, examining such subjects as ecumenism and interfaith conflict, sexual morality, women in the military, the shortage of Catholic chaplains, the role played by bishops and religious superiors, minorities and racism, the two chaplain schools, problems arising from medals and

promotions, pacifism and conscientious objection, and chaplains as noncombatants. The third volume will describe the work of the largest group of Catholic chaplains to serve in the conflict, the Jesuits.

My goal here has been to present the whole story of the Catholic chaplains
in the war, both their triumphs and their darker moments. I should be gravely
disappointed if what I have produced sounds, in the end, like an exercise in
hagiography, but I would be unfaithful to the evidence if I failed to note that
their successes far outweighed their failures, which is to say that I found rather
more to praise than to condemn. Still, I have tried to describe the structural
difficulties that beset their work as well as the personal conflicts in which they
sometimes found themselves engaged.

In sharp contrast to the vast majority of books on the war, this book does
not describe either battles or military leaders. Instead, I describe the viewpoint and experiences of a group of men who held a unique position in the
American war machine. That is to say, they had one foot inside the military
and one outside. As commissioned officers of the army and navy, they occupied official positions in the military, but as ordained clergymen, they were, in
a sense, outside the command structure. Even though they obeyed orders
from superior officers and followed the laws governing the armed services,
they still maintained an allegiance to their own religious bodies, to which almost all of them would return after the war ended.

This unique position meant that the chaplains had an opportunity to observe both the working of the military command structure and the lives of the
enlisted men who had submitted to it. Often bonded by close ties to their fellow officers and the enlisted personnel, they nevertheless stood apart from
both. They had a special vantage point from which they could see the successes and achievements of the military people they served, their sufferings
and ordeals, and their religious and psychological states of mind. From the
chaplains' reports, letters, and oral recollections, one can piece together a description of the life of the foot soldier that is available nowhere else. These
men of God become men of war had an independent viewpoint, and their
harrowing and sometimes deeply moving descriptions of what they saw seem
worthy of serious examination. For example, the letters of the Jesuit chaplain
James Deasy, who served on Iwo Jima, are a treasury of first-hand descriptions
of the battle, including not only his own agonies but also those of the marines
whose lives he shared so closely. His harrowing narrative has remained hidden
from public view for too long.

I decided to write this work while teaching a course on the war at Santa
Clara University. The enthusiasm of my students for the study of the war fired

my own, and as I looked through the Catholic press for the war years, it became increasingly clear to me that the story of the Catholic American chaplains needed telling, not only because it seemed inherently interesting but because it yielded insights into the life of the American fighting man not found elsewhere. What emerged from my research is a mosaic of lights and shadows, of successes and failures, of leaps ahead and unsettling reverses, of cooperation and conflict, of generosity and selfishness. These seemingly contradictory elements combine to tell the story of the Catholic chaplains in World War II.

1

PEARL HARBOR

We're in it. We're in it. God help us, we're in it.
—Chaplain William Maguire, December 7, 1941

He had never seen the harbor look as lovely as it did that early Sunday morning. "Joe, this is one for the tourist," he said to the young sailor standing next to him on the pier. Later he would remember the blue-green waters of the lagoon, the pink clouds skirting the tops of the mountains that ringed the bay, and the rich green plantations along the shore. Above all, he would recall the sight of the great gray ships of war as they lay quietly along Battleship Row, floating so silently and majestically on the ebbing tide.[1]

He waited impatiently for the small boat that would take him to the battleship *California* where he would offer Sunday Mass. A stiff trade wind was blowing from the west, he noted, and he reminded himself that since he would be saying Mass on the open deck, he should tell the ship's crew to put a windbreak behind the altar so that his chalice and books would not blow over the side. It really was a bright and fresh morning he told Yeoman Joe Workman again. Finally the staff motorboat arrived at the Officer's Club landing where they had been standing, and the two men stepped aboard.

At precisely the same moment, he heard the sound of distant airplanes and looked toward the northwest to see who could be flying into the harbor at such an hour. "I spied a flock of light carrier planes that resembled our own," he remembered later. Suddenly, they began diving almost straight down, dropping what looked alarmingly like bombs on the ships moored along Battleship Row. He told Workman, "They're phony bombs, full of flour or something." Nevertheless, it seemed to him bizarre in the extreme that a "sham battle" would be scheduled for such a time.

1

A plane suddenly spun out of the sky and shot across his right shoulder. It carried a thin, glistening torpedo. The plane leveled out about twenty feet above the water headed for a battleship. It "dropped the torpedo and pulled up sharply, nearly hitting the upper works of the ship. Following instantly came another plane." Looking carefully at its markings, the two men could see a round patch of red paint on the plane's fuselage—these were Japanese aircraft, they realized with a start, not their own. Then came the sound of bombs exploding nearby, and moments later a huge geyser of water erupted near the battleship. The shock made him strangely sick. All he could say was, "We're in it. We're in it." He braced himself against the railing of the craft, which was now pitching wildly in the waves sweeping the harbor. "God help us, we're in it." He was William A. Maguire, Pacific Fleet Chaplain of the Chaplain Corps, United States Navy, in the Hawaiian Islands. The time was 7:55 A.M., December 7, 1941, and the place was Pearl Harbor.[2]

Maguire had weathered the first of many close calls he would experience that Sunday morning. It suddenly occurred to him that if he had left the shore only a minute earlier, the Japanese planes might well have blown him to pieces, but there really wasn't time to think about such possibilities now. Japanese airplanes continued to swarm over the harbor, torpedoes skimming only forty feet above the water, while still more aircraft streamed in from the west and northwest. Peering intently through the billowing haze, Maguire could see the dim outlines of an appalling scene: dozens, perhaps hundreds of men were swimming in the harbor trying frantically to escape the savage fires now gutting the *California* and its sister ships the *West Virginia* and the *Arizona*. A few sailors, the lucky ones, had climbed onto rafts, and motor launches had picked up a few others. Most, however, bobbed up and down like corks in the fire-swept waters, and there would be many who would not be able to escape a terrible death in the lagoon. Maguire could do little for them except impart a general absolution.

Once he had managed to board the *California*, his home ship, Maguire headed toward the officers' wardroom, where a large number of seriously wounded men were waiting for treatment. As he looked at them, they seemed so courageous in the face of their suffering and uncertain fate: Most lay quietly on the floor, asking no favors, making no complaints. Navy corpsmen moved quickly among the injured, quietly administering morphine and blood plasma and bandaging open wounds. The priest first administered the Last Rites to the dying, then gave them to everyone else who asked for them.[3]

Meanwhile, the grim business of war went on. From the ammunition rooms below deck, a steady stream of sailors, black with oil, carried boxes of ammunition up the ladders to the anti-aircraft guns. At the same time, motor launches from the ship ferried wounded personnel to the shore, where waiting trucks sped them to the dispensary at nearby Hickam Field. No one doubted that the *California* was in deep trouble. Four torpedoes had slammed into the side of the ship, causing it to list sharply. Sensing that the end was near for the dying vessel, Maguire moved as rapidly as he could among the wounded men lying on the deck and in the corridors, but he could not keep up with the growing tide of burned, lacerated, and dying sailors. They made a "grim tableau," he would recall years later; still, none would complain. He heard as many confessions as he thought there was time for and then imparted a second general absolution, this time to the ship's entire company.

All too soon, he heard a grim-faced young officer give the dreaded command, "Abandon Ship." The *California* had started to go under. Maguire felt another crunching blow against the side of the ship, followed by an increased tilting. He ran to the top deck and joined the men who were moving the wounded into launches and lifeboats. A few minutes later, the situation became even more perilous: The *California* lurched again, and it looked now as if the capsizing of the ship were only a few moments away. Soon the whole deck was ablaze, the fire racing wildly out of control. Working against time, the rescue parties succeeded in loading the last of the wounded into a waiting boat, then jumped into another one and sped across the debris-strewn harbor.

From the safety of the shore, Maguire looked back at the *California*. It was blazing fiercely but was still afloat, and fire tugs were still pouring streams of water on its flaming, bulging hull. The flagship was not the only vessel struggling for life, however. He could see that the "whole of Battleship Row had become a great inferno." To Maguire, a career navy man who had spent most of his life as a Catholic priest in the chaplaincy service, it must have seemed as if his whole life were burning up before him.[4]

A few minutes later, Maguire and his men arrived at the Hickam Field dispensary. Inside he found dead and dying men lying all over the floor, but their number did not appear to be overwhelmingly large, and the doctors and corpsmen seemed to have the situation in hand. Again, he moved quickly with the wounded, doing for each as the religious and personal circumstances of each individual man seemed to require.

Soon word reached him that the marine barracks near the harbor had also suffered heavy damage in the enemy attack. Having done what he could at Hickam Field, he hurried to the barracks. A catastrophe had overtaken the post, turning it into chaos. All afternoon wounded men poured into the facility's dispensary, soon filling it beyond capacity. Since no other officer was free to lead the evacuation of the remaining injured to nearby hospitals in Honolulu, Maguire did it himself. First, however, he needed to find transportation. After a long and frustrating search, he finally located several vehicles and was able to direct the removal of the wounded. By sundown, an exhausted and harried Chaplain Maguire could report that all the navy and marine casualties he had seen had received treatment.[5]

At the end of the day, as the sun slipped over the mountains to the west of the bay, he looked again at the devastation. "Battleship Row was a sight to break a sailor's heart," he wrote sadly. The *Arizona* was still burning fiercely, despite swarms of fireboats pumping streams of water into the ship's open hatches. No one could predict what would happen next to the stricken vessel. As he looked at the wreckage, he worried above all about the chaplains who might still be on board the flaming ships; as senior chaplain, he felt a heavy measure of responsibility for them. He wondered about his longtime Protestant friend, Chaplain Stanton Salisbury, a Presbyterian minister on the battleship *Pennsylvania*. Had he escaped? So far Maguire had heard nothing about him. He wondered also about another Protestant chaplain, young Thomas Kirkpatrick, stationed on the ill-fated *Arizona*. With the wreckage of that vessel sinking toward the bottom of the harbor, Maguire wondered how he could possibly have survived. Finally, his thoughts went to Aloysius Schmitt, a Catholic chaplain the same age as Kirkpatrick, assigned to the battleship *Oklahoma*. The prospects of his survival also seemed terrifyingly remote.[6]

The navy was not the only Japanese target that day. The army's ground and air forces on Oahu also underwent their own ordeal before the day finally came to a disastrous end, and caught in the middle of the Japanese strike was one of the chaplains on Hawaii, Terence F. Finnegan (also a Catholic) of the 25th Infantry Division. Finnegan, too, would witness the full shock of the attack, but he would come much closer than Maguire to joining the 2,325 service personnel who perished at Pearl Harbor.

While Maguire was standing on the dock of the Officers' Club waiting for the launch that would take him to the *California,* Finnegan was preparing to offer Mass at the army's Schofield Barracks, directly north of the harbor. He thought that before going to the barracks, he would stop by a small chapel near his quarters to pick up some new altar candles. He, too, noted the hushed beauty of the early December morning, and he also thought that the planes flying in were American, probably returning home from a recent maneuver. Suddenly he saw the planes diving on the ships lying at anchor in the harbor and then on nearby Hickam Field. A minute or two later, several smaller aircraft turned away from the bay and began flying directly over him, swooping so low he could see the faces of the pilots. With a start, he saw that the flyers were Japanese, not American.[7]

He jumped into his 1931 Buick and drove frantically toward the barracks. His only thought was to get to the Assembly Hall before the Japanese did so that he could quickly dismiss the men who were waiting for Mass. He would tell them to run for their lives. Along the way, however, a Japanese fighter strafed his car, the bullets splattering the side of the road like silver dollars hitting a hard floor. Somehow they missed him, and he prayed his luck would hold until he reached the hall. It was only a five-minute drive, but the road seemed to go on forever. He hit a sharp turn in the road, then felt the car go into a wild skid. He gripped the steering wheel as hard as he could, somehow drove the vehicle into a ditch, then got it back onto the road. He raced down the lane as fast as he could, reaching the hall with almost no time to spare. So far no bombs had fallen, but minutes later Japanese planes began diving at the field, strafing it from one end to the other. Finnegan dashed into the hall, looked frantically about for the commanding officer but could see only enlisted men. He decided to take command himself and shouted, "Get out and go to your stations at once."

Inside the barracks, there was a rectangular yard that was used for reviews and inspections. By now most of the men were milling about in the enclosure, wondering what was happening. A number had concluded that a show of some kind was going on. Before Finnegan could command them to disperse, a bomb fell in the middle of the yard, instantly blowing six men to pieces. Seconds later a young sergeant fell lifeless to the ground next to Finnegan; bullets had struck him in the forehead, killing him at once.

Finnegan and several corpsmen who had rushed to the scene began carrying the bodies of the dead and wounded into a building nearby where army doctors began attending their injuries. Meanwhile, he ministered to everyone who asked him for his help. With the Jewish and Protestant men, he recited prayers taken from their faiths, speaking whatever comforting words seemed appropriate, and then gave each man a final blessing. The Catholic soldiers received confession and absolution if they were conscious; if not, he gave them the Last Rites.

All morning and afternoon, Finnegan struggled against time to take care of the dead, the dying, and the gravely wounded. So exhausting was the work that he lost track of the men he had already seen, which led to a moment of humor in the chaotic situation. Late in the morning, he knelt beside a young Catholic soldier whose face was so covered with blood and dirt that the priest could not make out the wounded man's features. "Let's go to confession, son," Finnegan suggested. The boy nodded, made his confession, and received absolution. Later, Finnegan came back again to the same soldier but failed to recognize him because corpsmen had cleaned the blood and the grime from his face, thus giving him an entirely different appearance. "Let's go to confession, son," he said again. The boy smiled, nodded, repeated his confession for a second time, and received another absolution. Still later in the day (and now stumbling wearily from litter to litter), Finnegan came upon the same soldier a third time. Again he failed to recognize him because by now the doctors had completely covered his face with bandages. "Let's go to confession, son," Finnegan said for the third time. "Now look, father," the boy protested, "don't you think twice is enough for one day?" Finnegan agreed that twice in one day was more than adequate.

Not until five o'clock in the afternoon did Finnegan finally have time to eat his breakfast. That night and all of the following day he received so many urgent calls from families asking about their sons that he could not go to bed, nor could he find time to change his clothes until a full three days after the attack. The other army and navy chaplains in the area were fully as harried and equally exhausted at the end of their ordeal.[8]

Meanwhile, Thomas Kirkpatrick on the *Arizona* and Aloysius Schmitt on the *Oklahoma* found themselves caught in the fury of the enemy's assault. Neither would survive December 7, 1941. The first wave of Japanese torpedo planes and bombers attacked the *Arizona* with a spread of torpedoes and armor-piercing bombs, scoring a series of direct hits on the ship's ammunition hold. Within a single minute of the first bombing, violent detonations ripped the ship from stem to stern, dooming it to certain destruction. Walls of flame raced through the hull; collapsing bulkheads trapped a thousand men below the waterline, giving them no chance to escape. Despite the ship's hopeless situation, crew members fought desperately to save it, but to no avail. Soon the loudspeaker rasped out an order to abandon ship. The time was 10:32 A.M. Out of the 1,400 officers and enlisted men on board the *Arizona*, 1,103 died in the tragedy. Among them was Chaplain Thomas Kirkpatrick, whose body, along with those of so many others, remains entombed in the sunken hull.

The same wing of Japanese planes also attacked the *Oklahoma*, lying at anchor in the southernmost corner of the harbor. Three torpedoes tore into the ship's side, and it quickly listed at a perilous angle. Within five minutes, the senior officer aboard the vessel ordered "Abandon Ship," and ten minutes later it rolled over completely. Flung to their deaths were 415 of the officers and enlisted men of the 1,354 on board the battleship that day. Among them was the Catholic chaplain, Aloysius Schmitt of Dubuque, Iowa. No one knows whether Thomas Kirkpatrick or Aloysius Schmitt died first. One can only say that Kirkpatrick was the first Protestant chaplain to fall in the war and Father Schmitt was the first Catholic chaplain to suffer the same fate.

Schmitt quickly became the American Catholic church's first war hero, thanks to the sailors who witnessed his courageous last hours and related the story afterward. A native of Lucas, Iowa, he had taken his theological studies at the North American College in Rome, where he also received ordination to the priesthood. Assignment to study at "the North American," as American clerics generally called the college, usually meant that the seminarian's bishop thought the young man had enough talent to become a bishop later in his life. In Schmitt's case, his superior's confidence in his abilities seems justified. After returning to Iowa, Schmitt worked in several Catholic parishes but soon volunteered for the Navy Chaplain Corps. In the next three years, he became one of the most popular chaplains in the service, quickly gaining both the respect and the friendship of the service's personnel and demonstrating a talent for dealing equally well with both Catholics and non-Catholics.

Not long before Pearl Harbor, the navy sent Schmitt to the *Oklahoma,* which soon set sail for Hawaii. Like every true sailor, he rejoiced at the granting of his greatest wish— assignment to a ship at sea. When his ship docked at Pearl Harbor, William Maguire had the opportunity to meet the young Catholic chaplain from the Midwest that he had heard so much about from other chaplains. Maguire recalled his first impressions of Schmitt: a tall, impressive man who "had all the earmarks of a young junior officer" fresh from the navy's chaplaincy training school in Norfolk, Virginia. He thought that Schmitt would give a fine accounting of himself in the navy.

Although uncommonly bright, Schmitt was far more than a priest-intellectual. From the first day of his new assignment, he demonstrated a natural gift for communicating with the young sailors on the vessel. He organized social activities for his seamen and also arranged for transportation to take them to the shore parties he had arranged. (The navy called such festivities "legitimate entertainments," as opposed to "illegitimate" ones such as barhopping and consorting with women of low moral estate.)[9]

On the morning of December 7, 1941, Schmitt set out for the ship's recreation room, where he planned to offer an early morning Mass as he did every Sunday. He had hardly begun preparations for the service when three Japanese torpedoes slammed into the side of the battleship, which heeled quickly to twenty degrees, then thirty degrees, as tons of water crashed into the hold. Within a few minutes, hundreds of men were trapped in their cabins far below the waterline. Schmitt and several crew members made their way to a compartment below deck where a large group of men awaited rescue.[10] When they reached the room, it was pitch-black, save for a little light coming in from a single porthole, and sea water was pouring into the room while the ship continued to tilt at a sickening angle. Since the open porthole offered the only means of escape, Schmitt began frantically pushing and shoving the men through the narrow opening.

When all of the men inside had finally escaped, Schmitt asked them to pull him through the aperture. He could not squeeze his way through the tiny opening, however, no matter how hard he struggled or how vigorously the men outside pulled at him. One sailor recalled what happened next: "Boys, I'm having a tough time getting through," Schmitt said. "So we all got together and tried to pull him out," but no amount of effort could move him through the tight passage. Seeing the hopelessness of the cause, Schmitt told the men, "You are endangering your lives," and he asked them to stop trying to rescue him. The men protested: "Chaplain, if you go back in there, you'll never come out." Schmitt's reply was, "Please let go of me, and may God bless you all." Soon he fell back into the darkened ship. Meanwhile, still more men had crawled into the compartment, and Schmitt helped maneuver them through the porthole until, inevitably, water filled the blackened chamber. An electrician's mate remembered hearing Schmitt splashing around in the water, but soon the splashing stopped. The chaplain was gone. Had he lived just one more day, he would have celebrated the seventh anniversary of his ordination to the priesthood.[11]

His selfless, heroic death inspired a flood of accolades and tributes. Later in the war, the navy would name a destroyer after him, and the Marine Corps dedicated a new Catholic chapel at its training base at Camp Lejeune, North Carolina, to the lost chaplain. A year after his death, the navy awarded him the Navy and Marine Corps Medal, citing his courageous efforts to save his men: "Calmly urging them on with a pronouncement of his blessing, he remained behind while they crawled out to safety. . . . He gallantly gave up his life for his country."[12]

Perhaps the most touching tributes came from the men who knew him best—the sailors, the officers, and his fellow chaplains. Several months after the attack on Pearl Harbor, a Jewish sailor spoke to a Protestant church audience in San Francisco and described how Schmitt had given up his own life so that he might live. The audience listened intently, riveted by the story. In addition to a description of heroism, the young man's address was also an example of ecumenism: A Protestant audience heard a Jewish sailor praising a Roman Catholic priest whose example had moved him profoundly on a day when he had nearly lost his life. Indeed, one of the leitmotifs of World War II was a growing respect among Americans for the religion of others.[13]

Within minutes of the bombing of Pearl Harbor, word of the attack had spread across the globe. Some 4,800 miles (and five time zones) away, the chief of army chaplains was sitting in his quarters at Fort Myer, Virginia, just outside Washington, D.C. Brig. Gen. William R. Arnold (a Catholic) had decided to spend Sunday at home, though Sundays had long since ceased to be a day of rest for him. Two years of mounting international crises with Germany and Japan had led to an unprecedented increase in the size of the armed forces, with a parallel rise in the size of the chaplaincies of both the army and the navy. He worked six days a week now in the Munitions Building in downtown Washington, putting in twelve-to-fourteen-hour days at his office.

On the afternoon of December 7, as the radio buzzed softly in the background, he was working quietly on his papers. Suddenly a voice broke in: "We interrupt this program to bring you a special announcement. The Japanese have attacked Pearl Harbor." Only a minute or two later, his office in Washington was ringing his home. Yes, he had heard the news, the general said. Yes, he would report to his office immediately.[14]

As he sped across the Arlington Memorial Bridge, he doubtless thought about the safety of his seven army chaplains at Pearl Harbor. He wondered also about his men in the Philippines, at Wake Island, and on Guam. Would the Japanese strike there, too? He had chaplains stationed not only in all of those endangered locations but in all the other army outposts in the Pacific that the Japanese might be likely to hit. As he sped through the streets of the capital, he worried about the dozens of army chaplains who might soon be caught in the disaster. He would not soon forget December 7, 1941—the first day of a new era for the United States.

Around the country, Catholic priests, Protestant ministers, and Jewish rabbis all listened to the news. Many asked themselves the same questions: Should I volunteer now for a military chaplaincy? Am I needed with the service people overseas? Can I be spared from my work here at home? Am I too old to join the service? One priest, assigned to a parish in the Midwest, was sitting quietly in his room in the rectory working on his parish books and records and listening to classical music on the radio when the music stopped abruptly. "Flash. Pearl Harbor has been bombed. An act of war has been committed against the United States," the announcer said. "An act of war!"

Brigadier General William R. Arnold, chief of army chaplains during the war, at his desk in Washington, D.C. Presiding over the largest military chaplaincy in history, he was known for his hard work, fair-mindedness, and vehement opposition to the use of chaplains in nonchaplaincy activities. (Source: National Archives)

Chaplain Florimond Vanholme talks with two privates in a hospital at an army camp in South Carolina. On the home front, chaplains served at facilities such as boot camps, ports of embarkation, and hospitals. (Source: National Archives)

he thought to himself. "I sat frozen in my chair. My brain whirled madly, 'Act of war! Act of war!' like a stuck phonograph record."[15]

He forgot his parish books, even his supper. Far into the night he listened to fragmentary reports of the attack as they filtered through the radio waves. By early the next morning, he had made his decision. "God and superiors willing, I would offer myself to the military endeavor as a chaplain; I would forsake the shelter of parish life to attach my fate to the military way of life." Before the conflict had ended, nearly 3,000 other Catholic priests would do the same.

The nineteen army and navy chaplains at Pearl Harbor could have used his help. Their first tasks, burial of the dead and notification of the next of kin, took up so much of their time that they had little opportunity to visit the thousands of injured men now lying in the military and civilian hospitals scattered around the city. The work was urgent: 2,330 people had died in the attack—all but 70 of them military personnel—and those not already entombed on the *Arizona* had to receive decent interment before their remains began to decompose. Afterward, their personal effects had to be gathered together, examined, and sent home. The task was exhausting and profoundly distressing, but it had to be done, and without delay.

The chaplains and their assistants began the day after the attack, on Monday, December 8. Even the weather seemed to reflect the tragic scene around Honolulu: heavy gray clouds covered the sky, and sheets of rain lashed the city and the harbor. December 8 was a religious feast day for the Catholics, the observance of the Immaculate Conception of the Blessed Virgin Mary, but the Catholic chaplains stationed in Hawaii would have little time to celebrate the occasion.[16]

In addition to burials, many other tasks awaited: visiting the sick and the dying, finding temporary lodgings for the homeless, calling on the dozens of military and naval positions scattered around Hawaii—the list of responsibilities to be met seemed endless, daunting. On top of all else, confusion reigned everywhere. Families wanted to know immediately whether their loved ones were still alive, soldiers wanted to send urgent messages to their parents back home saying that they were all right, and anxious friends wanted to know where evacuated service people and civilian families had been located. Everyone wanted information and help immediately. The telephones in the chaplains' quarters in Honolulu and nearby posts never stopped ringing. At any hour of the day or night a chaplain might receive a phone call from a nurse in a hospital asking him to rush to the bedside of a dying sailor; or from anxious husbands in Hawaii who wanted to pass emergency messages to their wives; or from the media, the government, and even other chaplains. All the chaplains soon found themselves pushed to the limit of their endurance, and each wondered how long he could hold out.

The hardest task of all was the interment of the dead. Many bodies could not be identified because the fires aboard the ships had charred them beyond recognition, and any record of religious affiliation had often been obliterated as well. Thus, groups of Protestant, Catholic, and Jewish chaplains began working together as teams. One Jewish chaplain has described the scene that occurred over and over in the island's cemeteries. The flag flew at half-mast, casting a long, thin shadow across the rows of simple white crosses. On one side stood a military guard of honor. On the other stood the three chaplains—Protestant, Catholic, and Jewish. First the Protestant chaplain would read the simple prayers of committal and then recite a set of prayers that would be familiar to his fellow Protestants. After a moment of profound silence, the Catholic chaplain would read his church's liturgy, first in Latin, then in English. Last, the Jewish chaplain would intone the Kaddish, the ancient Hebrew prayer for the dead. Their ceremonies finished, the three clergymen would then stand aside as an honor guard fired volleys in tribute to the fallen. The sound of the shots echoed off the surrounding hills. A bugler sounded taps, and the brief but touching ceremony had come to an end. Day after day the burials went on, until at last, all of the dead at Pearl Harbor had been buried, save those who would rest forever inside the *Arizona*.[17]

The Japanese assault on Pearl Harbor gave birth to many legends, of which a few remain alive and well. One myth still says, for instance, that President Roosevelt "knew" that the Japanese were advancing on Hawaii but did nothing to prevent the attack because he so desperately wanted the nation to enter the war. The story usually implicates the top members of Roosevelt's cabinet as well, asserting that they too had prior knowledge of the assault but said nothing. The army and navy chiefs had also received advance warning—so the story goes—but they, too, failed to take action because they wanted to be able to go to Congress with a blank check for future military spending.[18]

An equally enduring story is a tale linking the Pacific Fleet chaplain, William A. Maguire, with the war's most famous fighting song, "Praise the Lord and Pass the Ammunition." The account says that on the morning of December 7, 1941, Maguire had begun offering Mass on the deck of the *California* when Japanese planes suddenly flew over the top of the ship. Seeing the opportunity of a lifetime (so the tale has it), he stopped the Mass, turned around to the sailors assembled on the deck, and shouted in a most unpriestly fashion, "Praise the Lord and pass the ammunition!" He then fired an anti-aircraft weapon at the diving planes, causing them unknown and somewhat vague damage. It is an arresting account, and one that has endured the passage of fifty years. Where did it all begin?

The story originated in the mind of a popular young songwriter. Shortly after the strike on the harbor, the American composer Frank J. Loesser, moved by the tragedy of the event, began work on a song with the title, "Praise the Lord and Pass the Ammunition." It described the exploits of a heroic but unnamed chaplain (whom he called "the sky pilot") who fought back against the Japanese using not only prayer and homily but bullet and gunbarrel as well. As Loesser put it:

> Down went the gunner, and then the gunner's mate.
> Up jumped the sky pilot, gave the boys a look,
> And manned the gun himself as he laid aside the Book, shouting,
>
> "Praise the Lord, and pass the ammunition!
> Praise the Lord, and pass the ammunition!
> Praise the Lord, and pass the ammunition!
> And we'll all stay free!"

The ballad quickly became the first of the war's great fighting songs, and it made its author an instant celebrity. Before the conflict had ended, it had sold 2 million records and another million copies of sheet music.[19]

Who, however, was the intrepid "sky pilot" whose exploits on the firing platform far overshadowed his accomplishments at the altar and in the pulpit? Loesser stoutly refused to say, insisting only that his inspiration for the song came from his sense of the enormity of the tragedy and the nation's consummate courage in responding to it. For the rest of his life, he would have no further explanation to offer, but much to Chaplain Maguire's displeasure—and as a result of a bizarre set of circumstances—the song became inextricably associated with his name.

Maguire's connection with the song began in September 1942, nine months after the attack. The navy's Office of Public Relations had sent Maguire to Los Angeles to take part in a radio dramatization of his life in the chaplaincy before the war began. After the show had finished, Maguire happened to meet Kay Kyser, whose radio program, "the Kollege of Musical Knowledge," was a popular music and quiz show of the day. In a college-classroom format, Kyser (known as "Professor Kyser") would wear an academic cap and gown and address the audience as "students." The "professor" invited Maguire to attend the next broadcast of the show, but apparently he said nothing about Maguire himself appearing on the show. Maguire told Kyser that he would be delighted to attend; little did he guess how much he would regret his decision.

About halfway through the program, Kyser announced dramatically: "Students, we have in the studio tonight, Father Maguire, the chaplain who was at Pearl Harbor on December 7th. He left his altar, grabbed a gun, and fired at the Japs, yelling, 'Praise the Lord and pass the ammunition.' "* Maguire was stunned. Asked later whether Kyser's story was true, he insisted emphatically that it was not and said that he had been sitting too far away from the microphone to deny the story at the time. Later in his life, Maguire insisted that he had issued a public denial of the story immediately after the program but that the press had ignored it.[20]

All too soon, the tale had become an imperishable part of the folklore of the war, and Maguire found that all across the country he was being touted as the "chaplain-gunner" and "the author of the war's best slogan." From this

---

*In quotations, the word "Japs" appears exactly as the chaplains and others used it during the war years. Although we have since come to deplore the use of such ethnic slurs, it was part and parcel of the racist language that prevailed at the time.

point on, as he traveled on a speaking assignment for the navy, audiences would want, above all, to hear about his exploits at Pearl Harbor instead of learning about his day-to-day work in the navy. And worse was yet to come.

His first appearance on his speaking tour was to be at the University of Notre Dame. He arrived on the campus the day before the most important football game of the season, the annual contest with its school's arch-rival, the University of Michigan. When invited to speak to the students at a pregame rally, Maguire made a foolish statement that only served to strengthen his association with Loesser's song. Speaking in what he thought was an informal, off-the-cuff setting, he told the students, "Fellows, I have a new one for you: 'Praise the Lord and make it tough for Michigan.'" The students whooped with joy, shouting: "He's a Notre Dame man! Chaplain Maguire, Chaplain Maguire, Chaplain Maguire! Rah! Rah! Rah!" The result? Both Notre Dame and Maguire lost: Michigan trounced the Fighting Irish, and Maguire succeeded only in strengthening his reputation as the gun-toting chaplain from Pearl Harbor. By the time Maguire reached the East Coast, he had become such a folk-hero that his photograph appeared on the front cover of *Life* magazine.[21]

Maguire made repeated efforts to quash the story, but everything he said seemed only to magnify it. Finally, the navy and army chaplaincies, and the American bishops, entered the controversy, hoping to stop the story from gaining further currency. The damage, however, had been done, and the more Maguire and the authorities denied it, the larger the legend became. It endures to this day.[22]

However ambiguous his role in the affair might seem to us today, Maguire gave no one the slightest pretext for thinking that he wanted anything out of the war except an overwhelming victory against the Japanese. Speaking at a memorial service for naval personnel held shortly after the attack, he first saluted the dead: "Shipmates, in our simple way we have paid honor to our departed friends." Now, he said, it was time to "keep our spirits high and carry on with all our heart and soul in this fight for victory."[23] The possibility of an incongruity between the peaceful goals of his profession and his heartfelt desire for the triumph of American arms in battle seems not to have crossed his mind. Nor would it occur to the other army and navy chaplains who served during the war and who prayed with equal fervor for the annihilation of the enemy. If it is true, as is often alleged, that *inter arma leges silent* ("laws are silent during time of war"), then one wonders if much the same thing was true with respect to the collective consciences of the nation's uniformed clergy. Most of them simply parroted, in an entirely uncritical way, the inflammatory rhetoric of the Allied propagandists.

If a tragedy lies in the continued association of Maguire's name with the nation's most famous war song, perhaps it rests in the fact that it succeeded in distracting the public's attention from the real story of the chaplains at Pearl Harbor—a record of accomplishments against almost impossible odds. Moreover, what they achieved on December 7 and in the days following they would repeat countless times during the war, no matter where the fighting took them. They would follow the men and women of the armed services to every theater of the conflict, to every continent except Antarctica, to all the seas of the world, and even (in a few cases) into the submarines that waged the war under the seas. All that was missing in Hawaii from the larger war experience was the suffering the chaplains would share with their fellow inmates in German and Japanese prison camps. As they soon learned to their horror, Japanese-run camps would prove to be far worse than those of the Germans. As prisoners of Japan, theirs would be a story of continuing martyrdom, of anguish and of misery almost beyond description. In the Pacific, this story would begin in the Philippines, Japan's first target for invasion.

2

THE FALL OF THE PHILIPPINES

There are no atheists in foxholes.
—Statement attributed to Chaplain William T. Cummings

Pearl Harbor was only the beginning. As the convoy of Japanese carriers wheeled north from Hawaii, four other task forces struck at targets far to the south and west. The Japanese had shrewdly timed their attacks so their convoys would hit all of their remaining victims—Hong Kong, Malaya, Thailand, and the Philippines—at the same time. Their closest goal, and the one most prized by the Japanese, was the Philippine Islands. Capture of that 7,000-island chain had become an essential part of Japanese strategy because Japan needed both oil and rubber if it were to survive as a modern industrialized empire. The only oil and rubber within reach, however, lay in Malaya, and between Japan and Malaya stood the Philippines. They would have to be secured for Japan or the empire would die for lack of fuel and raw materials.

Japan had still another reason for coveting the Philippines: The islands had long served as an outpost of American influence in the Pacific. As long as the Americans called the Philippines theirs, and stationed army and navy forces there, the Philippines threatened every hope the Japanese had of establishing a hegemony of their own in the western Pacific, a "greater East Asia Co-prosperity Sphere" as they called it. By the early 1940s, tension between the United States and Japan had been mounting for over two decades, and in the final months of 1941, the Japanese became convinced that the Asian coast, and the island chains that dotted the middle and the western reaches of the Pacific, properly belonged to them alone. They decided to throw the Americans out and take the Philippines for themselves.

Despite unmistakable signs of Japan's growing truculence, the Americans had done little more than begin the development of the islands' defenses. Gen. Douglas MacArthur, who was in charge of American operations in the Far East, commanded a mere 31,000 American troops, and he had made little attempt to build a defensive network around the Philippine archipelago, one capable of stopping the Japanese on the shoreline so the Americans would have time to resupply their troops. But even if he had done so, he would have found himself thwarted from the start by American policy toward the Japanese.

Its wartime policy would be one of "Europe first," which meant that the primary claim on the nation's resources would be first the defense of Great Britain and then the recovery of the European Continent from the Nazis (a strategy that continued even after the attack on Pearl Harbor). Thus, MacArthur could expect no emergency relief from home, and his superiors in Washington had told him that in the event of a Japanese invasion of the Philippines, he would probably have to fight on alone. The Philippines, therefore, lay open for conquest, and no one knew it better than the Japanese war lords in Tokyo who now dictated the nation's policies.[1]

The attack on the Philippines began at almost exactly 11:30 A.M., December 8 (Manila time). A squadron of 108 Japanese bombers, protected by 84 of the new and much-feared Zero fighters, smashed Clark Field, located some sixty miles north of Manila. Luck seemed to be on the side of the Japanese, as their strike force arrived just after a group of American B-17 bombers (MacArthur's chief hope for defending the islands) had returned home after searching for a Japanese fleet purportedly bringing an invasion force to the Philippines. Failing to locate the Japanese ships, they had come back to Clark Field, and the flight crews had just begun lunch when the Japanese planes appeared overhead. In the carnage that followed, the Japanese destroyed every one of the eighteen B-17 bombers on the field and most of the American fighter force as well. In one well-timed blow, the Japanese had destroyed virtually all American air power in the Far East. Worse still, 55 American servicemen had died in the wreckage, and over 100 more had received serious wounds.

Caught in the middle of the attack was Chaplain John A. Wilson, a priest of the Society of the Precious Blood. Since Catholics are required to attend Mass on December 8 (the Feast of the Immaculate Conception), Wilson had risen at 5:00 A.M., to prepare for early morning Mass at the field's chapel. He recalls that it was an idyllic, quiet, and cool morning, but as he walked toward the chapel for the 6:00 A.M. Mass, the post's commanding officer drove up in his car and asked Wilson where he was going. When Wilson told him that he was on his way to the chapel, the officer said, "Get back to your quarters and get ready to leave because there will be an alert sounded within minutes. The Japs have bombed Pearl Harbor." Wilson dashed back to his quarters, and a few minutes later an alarm did indeed go off, shattering the blissful silence of the early morning.[2]

Taking his Mass kit and a small parcel of personal belongings, he ran to the base's headquarters. When all of the officers on the post had finally assembled, the commanding officer told them, "You can believe what you want but I think it is a false alarm because the Japs would simply not be that stupid as to attack the U.S." But just in case he might have guessed wrong, he ordered that Clark Field be placed in a state of readiness. When the men at the field tried to execute an air raid drill, however, the effort was a miserable failure. Confusion reigned in all quarters. The cavalry, for instance, had just received 1,500 horses from the west coast, and no one seemed to know what to do with them. The Medical Corps operated a 500-bed hospital on the post, and the doctors wanted to know if they should evacuate the patients. No one seemed to know. The Signal Corps and the Quartermaster Corps both had large stockpiles of equipment on the base, but no one in charge had any idea whether such provisions should be moved to a safer place or left where they were. Wilson saw hundreds of men "milling around" trying to figure out what to do next. Some even talked of fleeing Clark Field and running into the jungle. Eventually a squadron of B-17 bombers took off from the field, circled overhead, then disappeared into the sky. They returned several hours later with the seemingly reassuring news that the enemy was nowhere to be found.[3]

The sense of relief that settled on the base fell apart a few minutes later when Japanese planes suddenly appeared out of nowhere and began to rake the field with machine-gun bullets and high-explosive bombs. Wilson was on the parade grounds when the attack began. He counted 81 of the 108 bombers that the Japanese sent that day, noting that they were grouped 9 planes to a wing. They first hit the B-17s lined up on the runway, then attacked the barracks where the pilots and mechanics were eating their noon meal. As soon as the Japanese finished their first assault, Wilson ran to the post hospital, knowing that a flood of wounded men would soon begin arriving. Ambulances, their sirens screaming, were already racing toward the barracks.

As casualties arrived at the hospital, Wilson helped unload them and gave the worst cases the Last Rites. As the hospital's wards began to fill, he moved down the rows of beds, anointing the men who would not survive, talking quietly to the men who needed calming, and giving cigarettes to those who asked for them. All afternoon ambulances kept bringing more wounded men to the hospital; Wilson believes that he gave the Last Rites to at least 400 wounded. He remained at the hospital until dark, then joined the other men in his unit who had already gone into hiding in the thick brush surrounding Clark Field. He would remain there for several months before finally making his way south to the Bataan Peninsula west of Manila, where he would join the American forces fighting a last-ditch battle against the advancing Japanese.[4]

Three other army chaplains were also serving at Clark Field on the day of the Japanese attack. Two of them, John Curran and Joseph V. LaFleur, were Catholics, and the third, Ralph Brown, was a Methodist. All three distinguished themselves. During the hour and thirty minutes of the attack, LaFleur labored almost without stop, tending the wounded and dying, helping move them away from areas under attack, and assisting them on the way to the hospital. After the attack, the army awarded him the Distinguished Service Cross, commending him for carrying out his work without flinching despite the "intensive attacks of the enemy dive bombers and strafing airplanes . . . when the taking of shelter would not have caused censure." Both Joseph LaFleur and John Curran would perish later in the war. Chaplain Brown demonstrated the same kind of unstinting courage. All during the attack, he repeatedly put his life in grave danger by refusing to take shelter and insisting on helping injured men reach the base hospital. The army would later give formal tribute to his valor by bestowing the Distinguished Service Cross on him as well.[5]

Two days after their overwhelming victory at Clark Field, the Japanese bombed Manila and initiated a series of terror attacks designed to unnerve the populace and weaken its power to resist. The Jesuit weekly *America* condemned the bombings as a "barbaric act" inflicted against a people "utterly unable to defend themselves."[6] Chaplains stationed in Manila and its suburbs had to minister as best they could to the victims of the bombings, knowing they would receive no help from the United States. An army chaplain who was later to gain much notoriety on Bataan, William T. Cummings of the Maryknoll order (an American missionary group), worked day and night at the army's Sternberg Hospital in Manila, which had started receiving civilian as well as military casualties. In one especially hectic week, he visited over 800 patients in the hospital, sent hundreds of telegrams to relatives at home, and assisted the local Red Cross in its efforts to bring relief to the victims of the bombings. Most of the other chaplains in the vicinity were fully as hardpressed.

As the bombings increased in tempo and the situation in Manila deterio-

Army Chaplain William T. Cummings of the Maryknoll order at the rail of a troop transport on the way from San Francisco to Manila in 1941, just before the Japanese attack on Pearl Harbor. (Source: National Archives)

rated, MacArthur ordered more and more of his forces to withdraw to the Bataan Peninsula located twenty-five miles across Manila Bay from the city. One of the last to leave was Cummings, who late one night boarded an army barge filled with exhausted and dispirited American soldiers. As the vessel pulled away from the pier, he could see fire sweeping across large parts of the city. Buildings exploded, sending sparks flying high into the sky and then falling into the bay like Roman candles. He wondered how soon enemy soldiers would arrive.

When the barge docked at a native village on Bataan, the soldiers jumped out of the boat, walked up a short dusty road, and waited for orders. Soon an officer drove up and gave them their assignments. Cummings would report to the supervising chaplain on Bataan and begin work immediately. He knew only that the need for his services was far more urgent on Bataan than in Manila, since so many men stationed there had suffered injury in Japanese bombardments.[7]

On December 22, just two weeks after the bombing of Clark Field, the Japanese landed 43,000 troops in the Lingayen Gulf, only 120 miles north of Manila. Opposing them would be Douglas MacArthur's makeshift army of American and Filipino soldiers. Though they outnumbered the Japanese at the start of the campaign, they were poorly trained and equipped. Moreover, earlier American losses to the Japanese had severely demoralized their ranks. Making the defense of the islands all the more difficult was the near-absolute command of the air and the sea that the Japanese had achieved; even if the Roosevelt administration did decide to reinforce MacArthur's troops, getting any supplies and reinforcements to them would be almost impossible.

Soon a second Japanese force landed south of Manila, putting the city in grave danger of encirclement. Despite heroic resistance by the American defenders in the Lingayen Gulf, led by Gen. Jonathan Wainwright, the Japanese quickly advanced toward the embattled capital. MacArthur had foreseen the possibility that the enemy would take such a route from the north and had prepared a defensive line some twenty miles long at the base of the Bataan Peninsula. He hoped to stem the Japanese tide at that point, while waiting desperately for reinforcements from the United States.

On Christmas Eve—a black, cheerless night—MacArthur's troops fought a delaying action to the north of the city but had to fall back under heavy pressure toward Bataan. On the same desolate night, MacArthur, accompanied by his family and members of his staff, moved to the island of Corregidor. Located a mile off the tip of Bataan, heavy guns on the island guarded the entrance to Manila Bay. On the day after Christmas, MacArthur declared Manila an open city, hoping that the Japanese might thus spare it further destruction. With Manila now in the hands of the enemy, how long would the defenders of Bataan and Corregidor, now under fierce siege, be able to hold out? No one knew.[8]

In the final days of the battle for Manila, as Americans and Filipinos fled the doomed city, U.S. Navy vessels remained in the city's harbor in order to harry Japanese shipping in the area. One of them, the USS *Canopus,* was a submarine tender. On December 29, 1941, Japanese planes attacked the vessel. As the ship maneuvered wildly to avoid the bombs, one scored a direct hit on the magazine, setting off a furious explosion that killed six men instantly and severely wounded six others. With a raging fire now engulfing the tender, Chaplain Francis J. McManus dashed into the engine room where most of the dead and wounded lay unattended. After giving first aid to the injured, and administering the Last Rites to the Catholic men, the chaplain helped rescue parties evacuate the ship. With the whole vessel in danger of blowing up at any minute, he worked at great peril to himself. The navy found his work on the *Canopus* that day so impressive that it awarded him the Silver Star.

In the weeks that followed, McManus made frequent trips between the ship and the soldiers defending Corregidor, who were now coming under increasingly heavy bombardment from the Japanese. Years later, McManus's supervising chaplain on Corregidor praised his work on the island, saying that in effect, he had done the work of two chaplains at the same time—and had done so under the most trying circumstances possible. McManus, however, would not live to collect his medal or hear his praises sung. He would die as a prisoner of war.[9]

On January 2, 1942, the Japanese marched triumphantly (and not a little arrogantly) into Manila. As the troops paraded down the main thoroughfares of the city, many of the residents turned their backs on them in silent protest. Meanwhile, the American and Filipino armies, together with a large number of civilians, prepared to defend Bataan.

No one could have predicted the disaster that would follow. MacArthur's forces had stored up enough food, ammunition, and other supplies to support themselves for perhaps a month, but certainly no longer. To their shock, they found that besides the 80,000 troops on the peninsula, they also had to care for 26,000 civilian refugees. Worst of all, the siege would not end in a month. It would last for nearly three. The battle for Bataan would turn into a campaign of starvation, disease, and horror. In terms of the volume of suffering that occurred there, it has few parallels in the history of the war.

The situation did not appear entirely hopeless at the beginning. MacArthur had prepared a stout defensive line anchored by a 4,000-foot peak in the middle of the peninsula. A stretch of treacherous, malaria-filled jungle also stood menacingly between his forces and the Japanese. Problems soon began to mount, however. The mountain peak frustrated communication between MacArthur's two armies, placed on opposite sides of the peninsula. Far more serious, the malarial swamps hurt the Americans and Filipinos more than the enemy, since the former could no longer replenish their slim supplies of quinine, a task the Japanese could carry out at their leisure. Soon less than a third of the American soldiers were combat-effective.[10]

As the siege of Bataan wore on, more and more of the soldiers and civilians on the peninsula fell ill with malaria or grew weak from lack of food, and stocks of medicine and ammunition dwindled to alarming levels. As the weeks went by, the realization dawned on the peninsula's defenders that they would never receive the supplies they needed to survive. Although word of their plight soon reached the American people via shortwave radio, the nation found itself unable to assist. Chief of Army Chaplains William Arnold may well have expressed the feelings of the nation best of all. He wrote a friend in Illinois, "I really wish I were there now to help the boys with those slimy Japs." As a career military man, however, he knew that the fate of the men and women on Bataan was entirely out of his hands.[11]

The twenty-one Protestant and Catholic chaplains on the peninsula now faced a herculean task. Morale sagged lower and lower as the battlefield situation steadily deteriorated. They walked long miles through hot, fetid jungles and matted undergrowth trying to reach soldiers in isolated and endangered units. Using shortwave radio, the chaplains relayed messages from the men on the lines to their families at home. They registered and marked the graves of the dead, sometimes taking mementoes from the bodies of the fallen such as rings or photos to send home at a later date. They comforted the sick, the grieving, and the soldiers whose nerves had fallen apart under the relentless pressure of the Japanese artillery and aerial bombardments. And as always, they held religious services wherever soldiers or civilians could safely congregate—in dripping caves, in musty and darkened tents, in jungle clearings. One of the first pictures to come out of Bataan showed a priest offering Mass at a temporary chapel deep in the Philippine jungle. He called it "the Catholic chapel of Lourdes," in honor of the famous shrine in southern France. After about a month, the army was able to provide more suitable areas for religious services, though none were truly safe or even remotely comfortable.

Just as at Clark Field, several chaplains distinguished themselves by the unstinting service they rendered to the people serving on Bataan. John Curran, who had earlier assisted the victims of the attack on Clark Field, received the Distinguished Service Cross for his services on the peninsula. During one particularly fierce artillery bombardment on an American-held valley, he worked for eight hours without interruption trying to extricate the injured of his battalion from the murderous Japanese fire. Although exposed to enemy shelling the whole time, he refused to seek cover. When he finally found a small ravine that offered a little shelter, he began carrying the wounded into it. He tended their wounds himself, since medical personnel were unable to reach the place because of the intensity of the bombardment. All morning and afternoon he crawled back and forth between the ravine and the open area, dragging the bodies of the dead behind him and ministering to the injured. Somehow, he survived.[12]

Like the other chaplains on the peninsula, Curran found that the campaign took a massive toll on his health. An army nurse who had worked with him earlier at Clark Field saw him on Bataan and was shocked at the change in his appearance. While at Clark, she remembered, he had looked the "picture of health," with rosy cheeks and fine, strong limbs. Now he had no color, and his weight had dropped precipitously; in the two months since the war had started, he had lost fifty pounds.

By the beginning of 1942, Bataan was the only American-held territory left in the Philippines, and many of the chaplains who had gone into hiding in other areas as the Japanese swept by decided to try to pick their way through the dense jungle and attempt to reach the peninsula. One of these was John Wilson, who had earlier survived the bombing of Clark Field. Three months later, he left his men in the hills surrounding the field, slipped past Japanese lines, and reported for duty on Bataan. Shortly after his arrival there, he was able to tell his superiors in far-off Ohio that despite the malaria-infested jungles, his health remained "perfect."[13] He could see, however, that the defense of the peninsula was a lost cause. The soldiers had reached the end of their tether: All were desperately underweight, and most suffered grievously from malaria, dysentery, and other jungle-related illnesses. Wilson thought it remarkable that the American and Filipino defenders had held out as long as they had. They had performed extraordinarily well under circumstances so appalling that he would not have believed it had he not seen it himself.

Without question, the best-known of all the Catholic chaplains on Bataan was William Cummings, who had earlier served in the army hospital in Manila. Week after week, he worked almost without stopping among the men and women of Bataan, becoming a true legend in his own lifetime. He was older than most of the other chaplains and was in frail health, yet somehow he managed to withstand the long days of interminable rounds in the wards, the violent pounding from Japanese bombers and artillery, and the hellish living conditions that prevailed everywhere on Bataan. To those who knew him well, it was apparent that he drew his strength from his deep and abiding faith.

Above all, he had reservoirs of courage, which helped him rise to any occasion, no matter how intimidating. One incident stands out. Early one morning, just a few days before the Americans surrendered Bataan, Japanese bombers began a devastating attack on the hospital in which Cummings was working, pounding it to its foundations. At the height of the barrage, some patients panicked and began screaming in terror, fearful that the whole building would collapse on top of them. Cummings immediately raised his voice: "All right boys, everything's all right. Just stay quietly in bed or on the floor." Then he invited them to pray with him. The screams quickly died down, and a deep calm seemed to settle over the men in the ward. Enemy bombs continued to explode on top of the building, and hospital beds swayed and buckled, but Cummings stood resolutely in the middle of the ward, his hands raised in the air, his clear voice carrying over the din. Suddenly a bomb fell only a few yards away, breaking his arm and shattering his elbow at the same time. Undaunted, he kept on praying. Not until the raid had finally stopped did he finish his prayer. Then he turned to one of the other chaplains standing beside him, and said, "All right, partner, take over. I'm wounded."[14]

The story of Cummings's calming of the panic-stricken men in the hospital, and his almost frivolous view of his own wounds, became one of the classic tales of the Philippine campaign. Cummings also received credit for coining one of the most famous phrases to come out of the war, "There are no atheists in foxholes." Legend has it that he uttered the phrase, probably with no idea that it would attain immortality, during a sermon he delivered at Easter Sunday Mass on Bataan. The evidence for the story is tenuous at best: Gen. Carlos P. Romulo, a prominent Filipino military leader, attributed it to Cummings, but the general was careful to say that he had never actually heard Cummings say it. Other survivors of Bataan also reported hearing stories about his making such a statement, but none of them were present when (and if) he said it. The simple fact is that no one ever said they actually were present when Cummings made the remark, either on Bataan or anywhere else. Nevertheless, the statement became inescapably linked to Cummings, and it has remained securely connected with him ever since.

Few adages received wider use during the war, or caused more controversy. American politicians quickly learned the virtues of repeating it, especially in the middle of patriotic orations before constituents or in state assemblies and the federal legislature. It had a nicely pious, yet military, ring to it and was suitable for any occasion where either patriotism or piety (or the two together) had to be invoked. Most of the chaplains in the army and navy vehemently disagreed with the statement and were skeptical about the lasting value of what many called "foxhole piety," the tendency of some men to become intensely religious when the bombs were falling and the bullets were whizzing by but to forget that tendency immediately after the battle was over. Most chaplains insisted that there were, indeed, atheists in the foxholes during World War II.[15]

William Cummings spent the rest of the war trying to patch up the shattered lives of the men and women of Bataan. When the peninsula fell, he accompanied the troops and their officers to a prison camp north of Manila. (Fortunately, the Japanese allowed him to travel by bus, otherwise he would almost certainly have perished.) While a prisoner of war in various camps in the Philippines, he continued to serve the troops in a generous and uncomplaining manner. He impressed even his fellow chaplains, who quickly learned that he was the man who never said "no" to anyone. He would die on a Japanese prison ship, only eight months before the war ended.[16]

By the end of March, the Bataan defenders had been reduced to a daily ration of eight ounces of rice and only two ounces of fish or tinned meat, and nearly a thousand people were succumbing to malaria every day. On Good Friday, April 3, the Japanese began their final and most devastating offensive of the campaign. After two days of nonstop enemy attack, the Americans and the Filipinos on Bataan decided that they could endure no more. Fearful of a mass slaughter if the fighting continued, the American command asked the Japanese to set terms for a capitulation.

At eleven o'clock on the morning of April 9, 1942, Maj. Gen. Edward King, Jr., surrendered his entire force of 80,000 men to the Japanese. It was the largest, and certainly the most humiliating, defeat for American arms up to that time. King had asked for a twelve-hour reprieve so he could collect his wounded men, but the Japanese general, Motoo Nakayama, had coldly refused. "Will our troops be well treated?" King had asked. "We are not barbarians," Nakayama had replied. (In view of the atrocities that followed the surrender, one feels tempted to paraphrase Winston Churchill and say that seldom in human history has so little been promised to so many.) Weary of the three-month siege and believing that he had no other choice, King finally placed his sidearm on the table.[17]

Although the defense of Bataan had ended in tragedy, it was clear that the military chaplains had carried out their duties in an exemplary manner. Of the thirty-one chaplains who served in the peninsular campaign, six from the army and one from the navy received decorations for their heroism and remarkable endurance while under fire. Certainly the chief of army chaplains had every reason to laud their courage, and he took pains to do so on many occasions in the months that followed.[18]

On April 10, the infamous Bataan Death March began. Few incidents in the history of the war equal it for sustained suffering and brutality. Quite deservedly, it occupies a tragic place all of its own in the annals of the conflict. The Japanese had planned to take all of their captives from Bataan to Camp O'Donnell, a rude confinement sixty-five miles north of the peninsula. They had expected to have to transport about 25,000 prisoners, but their intelligence had grossly underestimated the size of the defending forces, as well as the number of civilian refugees who had sought shelter on Bataan. As a result, the Japanese found that they had nearly 80,000 prisoners on their hands, with not nearly enough trucks or trains to carry them and food and medicine for only about a third of that number.

Most of the prisoners had to walk the whole distance, suffering horribly because of the tropical sun, starvation rations, foul water, and an almost total lack of medical care. Many perished along the way—the estimates of the number of dead range from 7,000 to 10,000—and the vicious behavior of many of the Japanese guards added another dimension of horror to the march. A few treated their prisoners well, caring for them as best they could, but most acted in an unspeakably cruel and barbarous manner, passing up no opportunity to wreak havoc on their hapless charges. Some guards clubbed and stabbed their captives unmercifully; others forced prisoners to bury their dying comrades alive, even as the victims themselves struggled to dig their way out of their makeshift graves.[19]

Five Catholic chaplains were a part of the Death March, among them John Wilson, who doubts he will ever forget what he saw in those terrible seven days. Fortunately for the prisoners, the Japanese chose to begin the march at night. "It was cool then," Wilson remembers, "and we didn't fare too badly, except that we were all dead tired." The next day, however, the situation rapidly disintegrated. After a short break in the middle of the day ("we just dropped where we were and fell asleep"), the ghastly procession began anew. "In the heat of the day it was just terrible. The men were dropping like flies." After being cooped up inside Bataan's caves and tunnels for three months, many of them had almost forgotten how to walk. For the rest of the march, if a man dropped, a Japanese soldier simply bayoneted him on the spot, kicked his body to the side of the road, and went on as if nothing had happened.[20]

The Japanese changed guards about every five miles (they found the trip so grueling that they refused to march any further), but the frequent changes in personnel failed to improve their mood. Many were also the most rapacious of thieves, grabbing everything in sight from the bedraggled prisoners. Wilson, for instance, lost not only his watch, for which he cared little, but also his rosary, for which he cared deeply.

For seven terrible days, the marchers wound their mournful way through the jungle and the bushy hills on the way to the camp. To make their own task easier, the Japanese divided the prisoners into groups of 1,000 each. Wilson cannot be certain how many of the 1,000 in his group died during the trip. "They just disappeared," he said. Some were bayoneted, some simply lay down and died, and others staggered out of the line and were never seen again.[21]

One day, while stopping for a brief rest along the side of the road, he stumbled upon the prostrate body of his friend, Chaplain John Curran. Fortunately, a friendly Filipino had given him an egg several hours earlier. Wilson bent down, put some water in the cup he carried with his canteen, and mixed the water with the raw egg. With the help of an American soldier, he pried open the priest's mouth and poured the mixture down his throat. Curran revived a little, and later was able to complete the walk to O'Donnell. Wilson had undoubtedly saved Curran's life, because the Japanese guards would not have made the slightest attempt to restore him had they found him lying on the ground. But even though he had survived the Bataan Death March, Curran would perish later in the war, like so many other Protestant and Catholic chaplains, on a Japanese prison ship bound for Japan.

Another priest on the trek was not so fortunate. A Filipino Jesuit, Juan Gaerlan, had served for several years as a chaplain in the Philippine Army. A young man with a young man's daring, he had begun the march with the men of his unit, but when he and 100 other Filipinos found an opportunity to escape, they bolted away into the jungle. The Japanese, however, caught up with them a short while later, and the punishment they meted out to Gaerlan and his companions was, by all accounts, one of the more atrocious episodes of the Philippine campaign. They proceeded to bundle all of the men into small groups, fastened baling wire tightly around them, and then bayoneted each one until they perished in agony. Gaerlan's body was never recovered, but he is still widely revered by Filipinos as one of the greatest of the many martyrs of the Death March.[22]

As the survivors of Bataan wended their grim way toward Camp O'Don-nell, a small band of American troops on the rocky island of Corregidor, just off the Bataan Peninsula, continued to hold out against stiffening enemy at-tacks. With Bataan now firmly in their hands, the Japanese could concentrate all of their heavy artillery and bombers on "the Rock," as the island was com-monly called. The Protestant and Catholic chaplains on Corregidor began to encounter increasingly difficult obstacles as they attempted to bring assistance to the island's harried defenders. The Japanese now began pounding the rocky fortress twenty-four hours a day, knowing that the Americans would never be able to replenish their supplies or reinforce their lines, and although the troops had dug themselves deep into the long, winding tunnels of Corregidor, the continuing bombardment was so heavy that the tunnels began to cave in. Soon their available stocks of food, medicine, ammunition, and water began to run out. Anxiety mounted daily as the situation on Corregidor became ever more desperate, and finally a young army radio operator from Brooklyn tapped out Corregidor's last message: "Everyone is bawling like a baby. They are piling dead and wounded in our tunnel. The jig is up."[23]

Fearing that continued resistance would result in the destruction of his re-maining men, Gen. Jonathan Wainwright sued for peace on May 6, 1942. The Japanese forced him to accept humiliating terms of capitulation, yielding not only Corregidor but all of the Philippines as well. (Before he left for Aus-tralia, MacArthur had authorized him to relinquish the whole island chain, if nothing else could be done to defend it.) A Japanese censor stood next to Wainwright, now deeply emaciated, as he broadcast the news of the surrender. It was one of the most shocking moments in American history.

True to form, the Japanese refused to show mercy. For a week they kept their 13,000 captives sealed up in the steamy tunnels on the island, allowing no supplies of food, water, or medicine to reach them. Nor were they any less pitiless toward the island's chaplains. When the supervising chaplain on the is-land asked the Japanese authorities permission for his men to minister to the soldiers, many of whom had been unable to attend religious services for three or four months, he received a curt refusal. Several of the chaplains, however, pulled a trick on the Japanese so they could minister to the men anyway. They dressed up as litter bearers and carried a number of wounded men into the is-land hospital. Once inside the building, they promptly identified themselves as chaplains and began to take care of the religious needs of the men, free from Japanese interference.

When the Japanese finally decided to allow the Americans to leave Corregi-dor, they drove them like cattle through the streets of Manila, bayoneting those who fell and bullying them whenever the whim struck. Later the same day, they put them on trains bound for a prison camp at Cabanatuan sixty miles north of the city. Now they were prisoners of war and would be at the mercy of the Japanese until they were liberated in 1945.[24]

With the subjugation of the Philippines complete, the Japanese now herded some of their prisoners into two new camps, one at Cabanatuan, to the north of Manila, and the other at Davao, to the south of the city on the island of Mindanao, where they would remain for the duration of the war. In many ways, Davao and Cabanatuan were an improvement over the prison camps in which the Japanese had incarcerated them before. To their relief, the Americans found that the Japanese guards, earlier brutal beyond measure, now treated them a little better than they had up to then. Stragglers who could not walk the whole distance were often able to hitch rides in Japanese trucks. Though the guards had their bayonets fixed on the tips of their rifles during the whole of the trip, most chaplains saw no acts of outright brutality. "I can report no acts of cruelty," said one of the most virulently anti-Japanese chaplains, speaking just after the Allied forces had freed him from confinement three years later.[25] Despite the small improvements, however, prisoners continued to die of starvation and disease. At Cabanatuan, thirty to forty prisoners succumbed each day.

Chaplain John Dugan, a Jesuit from Boston, recalled that on days when he went to the cemetery at Cabanatuan to bury the prisoners who had perished the previous day, only "a single sentry came along with us." Sometimes, he noted to his astonishment, a guard would "pick a few wild flowers and lay them on the grave after it was filled in."[26] More than once, a guard lay down and fell fast asleep while Dugan and his men scooped out a grave, remaining in a deep slumber until Dugan woke him and told him it was time to return to the enclosure. Nor did the Japanese authorities at Cabanatuan object when the chaplains asked formal permission to build a chapel on the grounds of the encampment, as well as for materials to use in its construction. The commandant gave both permissions without delay or difficulty.

Moreover, the Japanese could prove merciful if they thought mercy a worthwhile policy. They decided, for instance, that it would be best to leave the prison hospital at Little Baguio, another smaller camp, to supervision of the Americans. Although Japanese inspectors (usually noncommissioned officers) occasionally examined the facility, no guards molested the patients or their physicians. The idea of letting the Americans take sole responsibility for the place seems to have come from the Japanese officers themselves, not the

Americans. The reason? The chaplains thought that they knew it: During the earlier days of the battle, the Japanese had noted that when their own soldiers fell into the hands of the Americans, they had received medical treatment as good as that the American troops received. The generosity of the Americans had paid off handsomely.[27]

The army and navy chaplains imprisoned on Luzon, Leyte, and the other islands all shared the same dismal fate as their men. After the Japanese took over the chain, thirty-seven chaplains found themselves incarcerated in the prison camps that the Japanese had scattered across the Philippines; twenty-one of them were Catholic and sixteen Protestant. Twenty would perish, giving what the military quite properly calls "the supreme sacrifice."[28]

The priests and ministers who survived the camps, however, also made their own sacrifices. Life was an unending series of harrowing shocks, of endless hunger and exhaustion, of nights filled with terror and despair. None of them would ever forget what they had lived through. None could ever blot from their minds the horrors that they saw visited so often, and with such ferocity, upon their fellow prisoners. In their darkest hours, it seemed as if the war with Japan would never end and that they had no support except their common faith in a benevolent Almighty and their friendship with one another. At times, they lived almost without hope. They had become prisoners for the duration of the conflict. They were at the mercy of the Japanese.

3

GUADALCANAL

From a distance, Guadalcanal seemed almost to float on top of the ocean like a dark green jewel. A column of razor-sharp mountains ran the length of the island, their deep ravines covered with dense rain forests falling away to the edge of the shore. The ocean curled and foamed along the beaches, and towering coconut trees nodded gently in the trade winds blowing from the east. For hardy vacationers who made the long trip to the Solomon Islands, Guadalcanal was a novelist's dream, a photographer's delight, and a ninety-mile-long equatorial paradise.

Suddenly, in the summer of 1942, it turned into a green hell. Why Guadalcanal? Few people in either the United States or Japan had ever heard of the island, so remote was its location, so obscure its history. It seemed the least likely place on earth to have become a turning point in world history. With the onset of the global conflict, however, Guadalcanal quickly took on a meaning far beyond its small size and remote position. The reason? Its location. It lay only 1,000 miles off the northeast corner of Australia, and just 1,400 miles from Sydney, that country's largest city. As the Japanese swept across the Pacific, they realized that if they could occupy Guadalcanal, they could bomb Australia and attack Allied shipping to the country—and thus cut off its supply lines. An isolated and unsupplied Australia would mean a helpless Australia, and an Australia that could not be supplied could never become a base for a future Allied offensive against Japan.

In July 1942, American intelligence uncovered a shocking piece of news: The Japanese had taken over Guadalcanal and had begun building an airfield there. The threat was unmistakable. Allied operations in the Pacific were heavily dependent on Australia, and if Australia were open to air attack from Guadalcanal, the huge island-nation would be in grave danger. An accident of

Navy Chaplain William McCabe offers Mass for native tribesmen on Guadalcanal.
(Source: U.S. Marine Corps)

geography thus meant that Guadalcanal would be the site of the first major
land battle in the South Pacific.[1]

Spanish explorers discovered the island in 1567 and had given it its name.
(The Japanese pronounced the rather difficult name "Gadaruanaru," but to
the marines, it would always be "the Canal.") In time, Guadalcanal developed a flourishing Catholic mission, which ministered to the island's natives,
as well as a profitable copra industry. After several changes in ownership (no
country seemed enthusiastic about claiming Guadalcanal), it finally became a
British protectorate in 1893. The Catholic missionaries remained on the island
and were still running their mission at the time of the Japanese occupation in
June 1942.

Though the island looked lush and inviting from a distance, the marines
about to land on it found that it became distinctly less inviting the closer they
drew to it from the sea. Guadalcanal stank. Though blessed with an abun-
dance of exotic birds, lush vegetation, and cloud-garlanded mountains, it was
also a rotting, festering mess. One marine veteran who survived the battle for
the island recalled bitterly that the place was "sour with the odor of her own
decay," its breath so "hot and humid, so sullen and still" that he cursed it.
Everywhere he went he found a "mass of slops and stinks and pestilence," of
"scum-crusted lagoons and vile swamps." The island was a tropical chamber
of horrors.[2]

To add to their discomfort, it never seemed to stop raining on Guadalcanal. Neither the Japanese nor the Americans had ever seen anything quite like the violent downpours that drenched the island every day. It rained during the night, and it rained during the day. It rained when the jungle streamed with water and when it merely dripped. It rained until the dirt turned to mud, then to mush, then to a primordial ooze that sucked trucks and jeeps to a standstill and made the simple act of walking an exercise requiring almost superhuman strength. Occasionally it stopped raining, and then the mud quickly turned into a hot, choking dust so thick that the marines sometimes prayed that it would start raining again, which it invariably did. (It rains over 200 inches a year on Guadalcanal.)[3]

The downpours and humidity produced a wild luxuriance of animal life that would have enraptured a zoologist—but not a fighting man. Spiders dropped silently from the trees to spread their nets inside the tents of soldiers, stringing thick webs across jungle trails, stinging the unwary, or ending up squashed "in gory clods beneath an unsuspecting hand," as one marine morosely put it.[4] Ants occupied their own special place in the kingdom of Guadalcanal: One of them had a bite that felt like "a live cigarette against the flesh," complained a Jesuit chaplain who survived the battle and the Japanese, but not the ants. Of all the creatures living on Guadalcanal, however, the one that the men came to hate the most was the lowliest of all—the humble mosquito. Guadalcanal's numberless pools, pits, swamps, and sumps bred some of the most voracious mosquitoes on the planet. Chaplain James Dunford of Boston said that in the evening they attacked him "like dive bombers."[5] No matter how tight he pulled his netting about him, a few always managed to sneak inside. They often kept him awake all night, even after he had become used to the sound of Japanese artillery shelling the camp.

The Americans could hardly have picked a more noxious site for their first offensive strike against the Japanese: a choking climate, fierce terrain, and a witch's brew of tropical diseases. The problems that nature posed for the marines on Guadalcanal would not be unique to that island, however. Much of the fighting in the Pacific would be jungle warfare, most of it in places dismayingly similar to Guadalcanal. Before long, a string of battles would turn the islands of the Pacific into a furious succession of green hells.

The chain of mountains that formed the spine of the island rose so precipitously that military operations were nearly impossible. The Japanese had therefore built their primitive airstrip on the only possible site (and also the most likely place for warfare), a narrow strip of flat plain and rolling hills fronting the northern coast of the island. Nearly all of the fighting on Guadalcanal would take place on this narrow patch of land, about nine miles long and five miles deep.

When the navy learned that Japanese and Korean construction workers had begun building an air base on the island, American leaders quickly perceived the threat to the Allied campaign in the Pacific. Although hampered by the small pool of available troops and enormous supply problems, they decided nevertheless to make maximum use of what they had, committing every available marine and every spare weapon to a Guadalcanal offensive.

In mid-July 1942, Task Force 61 left Norfolk, Virginia, passed through the Panama Canal, and headed across the Pacific for New Zealand. The 19,000 marines of the 1st Marine Division, plus a small element of the 2d Marine Division, crowded into nineteen barely seaworthy transports. It took seven weeks for the convoy to reach New Zealand, and the troops were in a less than holiday mood. Though they sang the popular songs of the day (such as "Blues in the Night" and "Chattanooga Shoeshine Boy"), they spent most of their time complaining about the food, the heat, the oppressive humidity of the central Pacific in mid-summer, and the island with the unpronounceable name their country was sending them to. Besides sharpening their bayonets (they had heard they would have to use them) and cleaning their rifles, they listened to Know Your Enemy lectures from marine officers who, when pressed hard, admitted that they knew little more about the Japanese than anyone else.[6]

Accompanying the marines were six chaplains, two of them Catholic. One hot Sunday morning, while still in the mid-Pacific, Chaplain Francis W. Kelly of Philadelphia (known to all as "Nose Kelly" because of his prominent proboscis) offered up Mass for the Catholics on the ship and then conducted Protestant services for the non-Catholic men. A marine correspondent on the same ship described him as "a genial smiling fellow with a faculty for plain talk." Before the war, he had served as a parish priest in a Pennsylvania mining town and had developed a direct, simple way of preaching. He would use that blunt style during the coming campaign. By all accounts, he was one of the more successful "GI preachers" in the Marine Corps.[7]

The other Catholic chaplain was Thomas Reardon of New Jersey, and the marines took to his easygoing ways, addressing him affectionately as "Padre." He would be the first chaplain to set foot on Guadalcanal and would see the worst fighting of the campaign. When weather permitted, he held Mass on the fantail of the ship. Forty years later near the end of his life, he would say that he counted those celebrations among his most satisfying experiences. The men would gather behind him, sometimes a thousand or more, as he cele-

Marine Chaplain Thomas Reardon says Mass for the men of the 1st Marine Division during the critical early days of battle on Guadalcanal. A short time later, he stopped wearing vestments during ceremonies, since he realized that the large cross on his back made an excellent target for Japanese snipers. (Source: U.S. Marine Corps)

brated the liturgy under the open skies of the Pacific. After he had read several passages from scripture, he would preach briefly, trying to apply the Bible's teachings to the conditions in which the men now found themselves. If he failed to get across to them, he knew that he would have only himself to blame, since he had found that the marines were invariably attentive, respectful, yet unpretentious. "The boys were great," he remembers. "They treated me wonderfully."[8]

After nearly two months at sea, the convoy finally arrived in New Zealand, and the troops immediately set up their tents along the coast. The New Zealanders expected a Japanese invasion at any moment, but the marines quickly took on a holiday mood. Fed up with shipboard life, they delighted in the food, the drink, and of course, the women of the country. The people of New Zealand, in turn, welcomed the Yanks as if they had just liberated them from the Japanese.

The revelry ended quickly, however, when the marines got an idea of what lay in store for them. One morning an American troopship steamed into Wellington harbor, and the marines received orders to help unload the vessel. It happened that the ship was carrying home a group of New Zealand troops who, along with British and Australian forces, had just suffered a disastrous defeat on Crete at the hands of the Germans. The marines gasped at what they saw: "This was the first time they had looked at amputees," Reardon relates, and at men blinded in battle. "You could see a change come over them. Until then, it had been a great adventure—no sweat, no blood, no tears, and all of a sudden, overnight, they had become so very serious."[9]

All too soon their time in New Zealand came to an end, and they filed back onto the lumbering troop transports for the final leg of the voyage to Guadalcanal. On August 2, 1942, the last Sunday before the invasion of the island, Reardon celebrated Mass in the ship's mess hall. War correspondent Richard Tregaskis, author of *Guadalcanal Diary*, the classic account of the battle, watched the scene intently from the back of the room. He noted that Reardon's face looked pale in the flickering light of the candles on the altar. At one point, the priest knelt, then rose slowly, his eyes half shut, his lips moving quietly. The marines attending the Mass seemed equally rapt and solemn. After the liturgy had ended, they filed silently out of the hall. Tregaskis was impressed by the devotion of the men, and he remembered what Reardon had told him just before the Mass began: The marines were going to Mass today because they wanted to be prepared for "at least the possibility of death."[10]

At 9 A.M. on August 7, the American fleet began bombarding the shoreline of Guadalcanal, scattering some 2,000 Japanese and Korean construction workers into the jungle. An hour later, 16,000 American marines charged ashore. To their astonishment, they met no opposition. Not a single hostile shot was fired, not a single artillery barrage, not even a strafing attack from a Japanese airplane. The enemy was nowhere to be found. The only casualty of the day's outing, it seemed, was a clumsy marine who cut his hand with a knife when he tried to slice open a coconut. The only target in sight was a pack of wild pigs who snorted aggressively at the Americans—from the safety of the brush ringing the edge of the landing beaches.

Thus began—unimpressively, almost disappointingly—one of the longest and most bitter campaigns of the war in the Pacific. Before the island would fall to the Americans, they would have to endure seven major naval battles, more than twelve major land clashes, innumerable smaller skirmishes, and bombardments from the land, the air, and the surrounding waters.[11]

Early the next day, the marines seized the half-constructed airfield without incident and named it Henderson Field in honor of a Marine Corps pilot killed in air combat six months earlier. With the capture of the field, however, summer vacation in the Solomons abruptly ended. Early on the morning of the following day, a naval action took place only a few miles north of the island that would have a grave impact on the destiny of Guadalcanal's marines.

Learning of the marines' presence on the island, a Japanese naval force attacked the American fleet assigned to the protection and supplying of the troops. The surprise assault took place at Savo Island, an ugly volcanic outcropping eight miles north of Guadalcanal. (To the marines and sailors who had to live with it, Savo Island looked like a primeval monster thrusting its vile head out of some primordial sea.) While it was still dark, a Japanese task force encountered an American fleet anchored quietly in the ocean, expecting no problems of any kind. It would pay bitterly for its lack of alertness. In a brief firefight lasting exactly thirty-two minutes, the Japanese destroyed four American cruisers while losing no ships of their own. Reardon watched the battle from the narrow perimeter that the marines had established on the edge of Guadalcanal. After it had ended, the bodies of the American dead and wounded started to wash up on the shoreline. "Some of them came in without any torsos on them. They just had their life jackets on," he remembers. He first helped the marines pull the few survivors out of the water, then began collecting the mangled parts of what had once been the bodies of American sailors.

The battle of Savo Island was a humiliating defeat for the Americans, and one for which they could blame only themselves. Rear Adm. Richmond Kelly Turner, in charge of operations on both Guadalcanal and in the surrounding seas, then compounded the peril of the men on the island: Afraid of losing the rest of his fleet to the Japanese, he chose to flee the area, leaving the marines stranded, dangerously undersupplied, and almost totally defenseless. They would grow increasingly bitter at their lonely fate and wonder why the navy had left them unaided when they so desperately needed its help.

Thus began a period of crisis on Guadalcanal, a time of trial and hardship that would test the mettle of the marines beyond anything they could have imagined. Less than half the supplies they needed had been unloaded from the ships, and since they had only enough food to last for thirty days, meals fell to two a day. Further, they had less than half the ammunition they needed. Forced now to defend a five-mile perimeter along the edge of the island, they found that they had almost no barbed wire to build a defensive line against the Japanese, should they attempt to drive them off the island. Seeing that the Americans had no naval or air protection of any kind, Japanese warships bombarded the marines at will, steaming brazenly into full view even in broad daylight. Virtually defenseless, the marines could do nothing but curse the enemy.

Thomas Reardon lived through all of the Japanese bombardments and the furious land battles that followed. For the next 125 days he would never leave the beach, affectionately calling it his "parish." He tried to maintain as optimistic an attitude as he could, though he had concluded, in his own mind, that they had lost Guadalcanal. "We had almost no medicine, almost no food except Japanese food. At times we had no pills for malaria. We were all alone." In the four months that followed, he lost fifty pounds, lived in the same clothes for eighty-five days, and had virtually no time to himself for rest or even for prayer. Most of the time he was sick like everyone else with malaria or streptococcal infections, but he stubbornly refused to go to the hospital, arguing that he had too much work to do. The havoc of the fighting would finally take its toll on him, and near the end of the campaign, he would have to be evacuated from the island, unconscious and close to death. A long recuperation would follow before he could return to duty with the corps.[12]

After the marines had finally established a set of precarious defensive lines around their meager forces, Reardon decided that he would build a chapel for the men. Taking the task to heart, the marines first built an open-air structure and then fashioned an altar from empty ammunition boxes. Next they designed a cross, assembling its parts from empty shell casings, and used other empty casings to serve as flower vases. The religious fervor of the men amazed Reardon. He never failed to be moved by the sight of his rough, aggressive marines, who after returning from battle, would pick flowers from the jungle and put them gently on the rude, homemade altar that they had built for themselves. It was a simple place, this chapel on Guadalcanal, but to Reardon it quickly became "the most beautiful church in the world."

"I think that my happiest moments on Guadalcanal were when I was saying Mass," he says. "I felt really close to God. It was as if the war didn't exist. Only the Mass existed." Again, as on the troopship, the men would gather around him, and he would draw strength both from their obvious faith and from his own religious convictions. On Sundays he sometimes had to offer Mass as many as seven times, since he wanted to reach as many of the men scattered around the beachhead as he possibly could. After his last Mass, he would lead a general service for the Jewish and Protestant men of the division. One Protestant marine was so deeply impressed at finding a priest in such a forlorn and faraway a place that he told Reardon: "The Catholic Church is like the Standard Oil Company. It has stations wherever you go."[13]

In the Pacific, where chaplains often had to build their own altars and chapel equipment, navy Chaplain Alfred Kammler fashions a tabernacle from native wood. (Source: U.S. Marine Corps)

On the night of August 18, just eleven days after the Americans had arrived, the Japanese landed a contingent of troops on Guadalcanal, and from this point on, the marines had to cope with the Japanese army as well as its navy. Grievously underestimating the size of the American force on the island, however, the Japanese landed fewer than 1,000 men. Though the group was a small one, it nevertheless succeeded in wreaking havoc, and it demonstrated the savage tenacity that would characterize the Japanese fighting forces for the rest of the war. Eventually the Japanese would lose nearly all of their men on Guadalcanal in the many suicide charges they would hurl at the marines.

Meanwhile, the Japanese had achieved complete control at night over an all-important naval passage called "the Slot" (a narrow channel of water separating the island from its closest neighbors). For the next three months, the American and Japanese navies would wage a series of furious battles for domination of the channel: Before long it had become so filled with the wreckage of sunken ships that it acquired the ominous nickname of "Ironbottom Sound." The Japanese dominance of the Slot at night allowed them to land troops and supplies under cover of darkness, while at the same time their airplanes bombed the Americans on the beach. Worst of all for the marines, Japanese warships shelled the beachhead with their heavy guns, killing hundreds of Americans and throwing terror into the hearts of the rest. Every attempt by the U.S. Navy to break the Japanese control of the Slot at night would fail until November 1942, when the Americans would finally succeed in besting the Japanese in a series of nighttime engagements. Until then, the Japanese attacked the American forces after dark with impunity, raining death and destruction on them until, finally, the first rays of the morning sun streaked the eastern sky and the enemy ships would withdraw. Daytime meant a brief respite from the Japanese ships, though Japanese troops on the island continued to try to drive the Americans into the ocean.

Reardon describes a typical day in those terrible weeks of August when the marines had to carry on alone. After a night of bombing by the Japanese, he rose wearily at dawn and offered his first Mass of the day at 6 A.M. Next came the first of the day's two meals, both consisting of rice and fish, most of it abandoned by the Japanese when they fled to the hills. It would be the only cooked meal of the day because the marines dared not light a fire except in the early morning hours lest the smoke give away their position. After breakfast, he made the first of several visits to the island's hospital, a cluster of hastily erected tents next to a cluster of foxholes where the wounded could be taken quickly if the Japanese started shelling or bombing the area. In the hospital he tended to the seriously wounded, the dying, and the men suffering from the ravaging diseases so endemic to the island.[14]

At noon, the second and final meal of the day consisted of the monotonous rice and fish plus a tin of the dreaded meat product called "Spam," which the marines came to detest because they had to eat it for so long. (In fact, it was a nourishing provision that probably helped save the lives of many of them.) As the weeks went by, the marines became increasingly obsessed with food. One man remembered that eggs became a forbidden subject on Guadalcanal: "The time came when fried eggs could no longer be mentioned. The thought was too painful."[15]

In the early afternoon, Reardon would walk up the muddy road leading to the marine cemetery and bury all those killed in the previous twenty-four hours. No respecters of places, the Japanese sometimes even bombed the cemetery while he was conducting burials. More than once, he and the other marines working in the graveyard had to leap into newly dug graves and lie down next to the corpses to save their own lives. Before they arrived on the island, the marines had called Reardon "the marrying parson" because of the large number of weddings at which he had officiated at their training base in New River, North Carolina. Now he found himself conducting the final obsequies for many of the same men. "Whenever I buried one of those Marines, I felt I was putting in that grave the heart of the girl back home." Just before pronouncing a final blessing on a married man's remains, he would remove the rings from his fingers and search through his pockets and wallet for personal mementos. He would keep them until the time when he could mail everything home, hoping that they might somehow bring some measure of consolation to a wife who would never see her marine husband again.

Sometimes the marines had their own ideas about how to inter their "buddies," as they always called them. One afternoon, as Reardon was burying a young marine, he and another soldier found an American flag wrapped carefully inside the jacket of the dead man. It seemed that he had wanted desperately to protect the flag, probably to keep the enemy from deliberately violating or profaning it. Reardon asked, "Why don't we save the flag?" His young assistant responded quickly, "Oh no, Padre, he died for this flag." So they wrapped the body of the young marine in the flag that had come to mean so much to him and lowered him gently into his final resting place.[16]

Readon found that the hardest part of his work was helping marines who were grieving the death of their friends. One example would always stand uppermost in his memory. Two brothers, Andrew and Bernard Fetchko of New Jersey, had landed on the island at the same time. Reardon had taken a special interest in them, in part because he, too, came from New Jersey but in part because he found them so friendly and likeable. One morning, Andrew became so ill with malaria that he could not report for duty at the front. His brother went out, however, and shortly afterward died on a patrol. Later that same day, the marines wrapped young Bernard Fetchko's body in a blanket and carried it to the cemetery. After Reardon had finished reading the prayers of interment, Andrew slowly unwrapped the blanket to take one final look at his brother. Then he carefully wrapped the blanket around the body again and helped lower it into the earth. For a moment, he stared at his brother's grave, stupefied with grief. Then he suddenly fell to the ground, grabbed Reardon's legs, and held them tight, his body convulsed with sobs. Reardon did his best to comfort him, but he realized the total inadequacy of his words. After a time, young Andrew Fetchko raised himself up and walked with determined stride out of the cemetery, resolved now to avenge the death of his brother.[17]

Late in the afternoon, after completing his work in the cemetery and visiting the base hospital one more time, he would walk back to Henderson Field and offer the second and final Mass of the day. He often wondered as he stood by the altar how many of the men with him on that late afternoon would survive the coming night's bombing and how many would be present for Mass the next morning or alive the next afternoon. He often wondered, too, how long he himself would survive the death-infested island. Like the other marines, his primary emotion in battle was the instinct for self-preservation: "You forgot whom you were fighting. You were trying to preserve your own life." Though he felt no personal hatred for the enemy, he was above all aware of a driving need, deep inside his soul, to keep himself alive. He experienced many close calls. Once, as he was talking to a doctor standing next to him, a sniper's bullet spun through the medic's skull, killing him instantly. A few weeks later, the same thing happened to another doctor. Neither man had stood more than a foot or two away from Reardon. He often asked himself, as did everyone on "the Canal," when his own turn would come.

Like all the marines on Guadalcanal during that crisis period of early August, he constantly feared that at any moment the Japanese would overwhelm the frail defensive lines and pin the Americans into tiny pockets so they would be incapable of repelling a major assault. "We were afraid of being thrown into the sea. We had no place to go to. We never thought that we would get out," he remembered with a shudder. For the rest of his life he would wonder how he had made it off Guadalcanal alive.[18]

The island's most celebrated chaplain was probably Frederick P. Gehring, who served on Guadalcanal from the middle of September 1942 until late February 1943. By the time he arrived, American troop strength had increased from 16,000 to 19,000, but the Japanese had also reinforced their own numbers by quietly landing small groups of reinforcements during the night. The Americans still outnumbered the Japanese, but the enemy made up for its small size with its cunning, audacity, and unique talent for night fighting.

Gehring quickly learned that no place was safe on the island, not even the tiny chapel in which he offered Mass every day. One morning, just after he began a service, a Japanese sniper suddenly fired two shots at the congregation. He had climbed into a tree overlooking the marine encampment and was shooting at the men with a high-powered rifle. For a moment, no one moved. Taking a deep breath, Gehring continued the Mass. Then one of the men kneeling in the rear of the chapel, a young lieutenant, quietly moved away. A few minutes later Gehring heard the loud report of a rifle shot, then a heavy thud on the ground. It was the sniper's body toppling out of the tree. "I let out a deep sigh and resumed the Mass," he said.[19]

Nor was the island's cemetery any safer for him than it was for Reardon. One day, when Gehring and his men went to the cemetery, they took along a Japanese prisoner to help them with the grave digging. No sooner had they finished shoveling their trenches, however, than a Japanese Zero swooped down on the marines. "He just peppered us with machine gun bullets," Gehring remembers. "Thank God he didn't hit anybody." The marines and the Japanese prisoner all tumbled into the nearest graves. One marine was so angry at the Japanese planes for shooting at them while they were burying their dead that he wanted to shoot the Japanese prisoner. Gehring had all he could do to calm the young marine and prevent another tragedy from occurring that day.[20]

As the grim weeks slowly dragged by, the Japanese intensified their attacks on Henderson Field. One evening two huge battleships, the *Kongo* and the *Haruna,* dropped anchor close to the island and began pounding Henderson Field with their fourteen-inch guns. For an hour and a half the Japanese pummeled the field and the surrounding areas, hurling over 900 high-explosive shells at the Americans. Gehring and his comrades threw themselves flat against the bottom of their foxholes and wondered if the Japanese attack would ever stop. When it finally ended, forty-one Americans lay dead, with many more seriously wounded. Yet the Japanese had even more unpleasant surprises in store for the marines on Guadalcanal. In early September, a force of 6,000 Japanese troops landed along the coast, one group north of Henderson Field and the other south. The plan was to squeeze the American perimeter from both sides, cut it in half, then drive the marines into the sea. It came perilously close to succeeding.[21]

The hardest fighting took place along an escarpment immediately south of the field, named (quite appropriately) Bloody Ridge. As usual, the Japanese did most of their fighting at night, staging repeated suicide charges and infiltrating the American lines almost at will. One afternoon, a young major approached Gehring and asked him if he would visit the marines manning the artillery pieces on the Ridge, explaining that the Catholic men there had been without Mass and confession for several weeks. Early the next day, the major drove Gehring to Bloody Ridge. After parking their jeep under a banyan tree, Gehring held Mass on the hood of the vehicle for all of the Catholic men free to leave their positions. When he had finished, he heard the confessions of the Catholic officers and enlisted men, then followed the major as he led the way along the twisting trail connecting the American gun emplacements. Each one held three to five men. The major would bring the men out to Gehring one at a time, and each man would make his confession, receive absolution, and then receive Holy Communion from a little gold box Gehring carried with him.

Gehring had visited perhaps three-fourths of the batteries when Japanese artillery began a savage assault on the Ridge. Gehring recalls that he and the marine major "just hugged the side of the Ridge and did a lot of praying." In a brief pause between rounds, an enlisted man dashed down the hill to Gehring, shouting, "Padre, there's been a direct hit on one of the gun emplacements." Gehring and the major ran after him and found that a large gun position manned by five men had indeed been hit. Three of the men had died instantly, and the other two had suffered fatal wounds. Gehring had just talked to three of the five. Acting quickly, he gave everyone the Last Rites. As they drove back to Henderson Field, the major appeared badly shaken. Soon Gehring could hear him sobbing, then he saw tears rolling down his cheeks. When they arrived back at the field, Gehring turned to him and said softly: "Major, you did a great thing today. You went out of your way to give our boys the opportunity to go to confession and communion. Suppose that this had happened, and they didn't have the opportunity? You made it possible for them to do that."[22]

The Americans had no way of knowing it, but the Japanese situation on Guadalcanal was growing increasingly desperate, and in the middle of September, their fortunes began a long decline, one that would culminate in a withdrawal five months later. The Japanese were unable to provide adequate provisions for their men, and many began starving to death. Most of them moved to the mountains where they would be out of reach of American artillery and the increasingly aggressive marine patrols—but out of food as well. Many had nothing to eat except the bark of trees, some mosses and roots, and thin leather straps, at which they gnawed frantically in search of sustenance. Not without reason, the Japanese troops began to call Guadalcanal "the Island of Death."

The Americans, however, were unaware of the increasingly desperate Japanese situation, largely because the Japanese were now resorting to increasingly desperate suicide charges, which gave them an illusory appearance of strength. The marines, naturally, interpreted the attacks not as a sign of Japanese desperation, but as a sign of the enemy's increasing confidence in its ability to win the campaign; moreover, U.S. intelligence apparatus on Guadalcanal was in a primitive state of development and had no way of discovering the true facts.

Late one evening in early October, the Japanese succeeded in landing another contingent of troops on the shore, not far from the American perimeter. Gehring and his men could see them coming, but nothing could be done to stop them because the Japanese still controlled the sea and the air at night. At midnight, Japanese infantry and navy launched a coordinated attack on the marines. From his trench, Gehring could see "shell after shell thunder into our positions and explode with such shuddering impact it seemed impossible that any of us would survive." Although the marines succeeded in beating off repeated Japanese banzai (suicide) attacks, the cannonading from the Japanese warships continued all that night, the next day, and the night following. The second straight night of shelling was "almost more than I could bear," Gehring remembered. When it finally ended, his nerves felt so shattered that he could barely stagger back to his tent. To Gehring, it seemed as if the American position was becoming increasingly hopeless. The constant naval bombardments and the unnerving suicide charges had turned increasing numbers of marines into what he called "raving, wide-eyed shock cases." The deadly combination of frenzied fighting, blazing heat, torrential rains, mud, and dust seemed more than many of the men could bear. He wondered how long they could hold out. He worried, too, about how long he would last.[23]

In mid-October, a new commander arrived on the scene, and he seemed to bring a new sense of hope with him. Tough-tempered, aggressive Vice Adm. William Halsey replaced an enervated Rear Adm. Robert L. Ghormley. Halsey quickly announced that the Americans would now go on the offensive, helped by the reinforcements that a surging American war machine could finally begin supplying to the embattled island. When Gehring told him that many marines feared that Guadalcanal would turn into a second Bataan, Halsey grew furious and told him, "This won't be another Bataan, dammit. We're going to win, and you and I will both see Yamamoto in hell!" (Adm. Isoroku Yamamoto had planned the Japanese attack on Pearl Harbor.)[24]

Not even Halsey's determination to win and a strengthened American presence could prevent the Japanese from giving him a bracing introduction to combat, Guadalcanal-style. In a series of violent clashes around the Matanikau River (a small stream to the west of Henderson Field), they stormed the American lines with shouts, screams, and fixed bayonets, hoping they might score a knockout blow before the Americans could reply in force. But the marines now had an overwhelming preponderance of tanks on their side and fresh units of army infantry to reinforce their battle-hardened units, and they managed to subdue the Japanese attack, killing 1,700 of the enemy in one ghastly nighttime clash along the banks of the stream.

That same night, the Chaplain Corps sustained its only injury on

Guadalcanal. Matthew F. Keough, a diocesan priest from Philadelphia, received the Purple Heart for wounds suffered during a Japanese bombing raid
along the Matanikau. He also received the Bronze Star for volunteering the
same night to act as a guide for a reserve battalion when it received orders to
march forward to the front lines. More familiar with the territory than anyone
else in his unit, he succeeded in getting his men into their foxholes even before the medical teams arrived to assist the battalion's casualties. He also put
himself in violation of the Geneva Convention, which forbade such a clearly
aggressive action by chaplains.

In every battle on Guadalcanal, Keough always managed to show up where
the fighting was at its worst. He seemed to have an instinct for where the Japanese would strike next—and where he would therefore be needed the most.
During the daytime hours he patrolled the front lines looking for wounded
men, and at night he visited patients in the island's hospital. The men in the
regiment wondered if he ever slept. Besides ranging up and down the lines, he
offered Mass for the marines every weekday and said three or more Masses on
Sundays. Keough was also one of the most aggressive chaplains in the entire
South Pacific. Too aggressive, in fact, in the opinion of many. Despite regulations explicitly forbidding chaplains to carry firearms, he habitually stalked
around the island with a loaded pistol and a cartridge of extra bullets. One veteran of the battle has several photographs of him, each showing him brandish-
ing his weapon and his loaded cartridge belt. He also carried his gun into combat, though no evidence has emerged that he actually fired his weapon in
battle. All of this behavior, of course, was contrary to both the Geneva Convention and the explicit instructions that he and every other navy chaplain
had received many times from the Chief of Navy Chaplains. It is not known
whether he ever received a reprimand for his patent violations of these regulations.

Not surprisingly, the marines thought him magnificent. He was what they
called a "gung-ho marine," a man among men. "The boys loved him, because he was a real man," Reardon recalls. It helped greatly that he stood over
six feet tall and weighed 190 pounds, thus giving every appearance of being
the aggressive fighting man. Perhaps without realizing it, however, he crossed
over the fine line separating the marine's chaplain from the marine's marine.
The truth is, he never seemed to realize the difference.[25]

By early December 1942, the situation of the Japanese forces on Guadalcanal
had become desperate in the extreme. Weakened by starvation and ravaged by
disease, they awaited the end without hope. On December 7, 1942, the

Americans staged a "hate shoot" on the remaining pockets of Japanese resistance in memory of their comrades who had fallen at Pearl Harbor the year before. Two days later, the 1st and 2d Marine Divisions began leaving the island, replaced by fresh army units that had begun arriving. The Americans clearly had gained the upper hand, though much mopping-up remained.

On the last day of 1942, a ceremony took place on the island marking the formal end of the marines' role in the battle for Guadalcanal. Early in the morning, as the sun rose shimmering across the quiet water of Ironbottom Sound, the marines held a memorial service in their cemetery. Near the beach, American troop transports stood at anchor waiting to leave with the marines of the two divisions. In the middle of the cemetery, the Seabees (the navy's engineers) had built a massive platform constructed of coconut logs. On top, they had placed a large, imposing altar and framed it with candlesticks fashioned from Japanese ammunition shells. A catafalque, symbolizing all the marines who had perished on the island, stood in front of the platform. A marine guard of honor stood stiffly at attention around its sides. Surrounding the altar in every direction were long rows of plain white crosses (and some Stars of David) marking the graves of the 1,400 marines who had fallen in the campaign. Standing in long rows around the edge of the cemetery were 7,000 battle-weary marines, carrying all of their gear in backpacks, ready to leave Guadalcanal forever.

Three of the Catholic priests on the island—chaplains Keough, Dunford, and Thomas J. Tracy—celebrated a Solemn High Mass of Requiem. When they had finished, a Protestant chaplain spoke, then a Jewish chaplain, and then Frederick Gehring. Each paid a short, moving tribute to the marines who had given their lives in the struggle for Guadalcanal. Then came what was perhaps the most touching moment in the service: From each platoon, a single marine stepped forward, carrying a palm frond. Quietly, reverently, he placed the frond next to the cross of a fallen comrade, then returned to his place. When the last of the platoons had taken part, a bugler sounded taps in the distance. The lonely song echoed around the cemetery, across Henderson Field, to Ironbottom Sound, and back from Bloody Ridge. The ceremony finished, the long line of marines and their chaplains made their way slowly toward the ships in the harbor waiting to take them to a richly deserved rest in Australia. Few would ever return.[26]

In the weeks that followed, the Japanese soldiers on Guadalcanal showed a steely determination to resist fanatically even against hopeless odds, but their effectiveness continued to decline. After several months of continued but fruitless struggle, the Japanese High Command in Tokyo concluded it had lost

Three Catholic chaplains offer a Requiem Mass for the men of the 1st Marine Division just before leaving Guadalcanal in December 1942 (left to right: Thomas Tracy, navy; James Dunford, army; Matthew Keough, marines). Palm fronds cover the bodies of the dead, the crucifix and candlesticks are made of empty shell casings, and the altar platform is constructed from coconut logs. (Source: U.S. Marine Corps)

the battle and reluctantly made the decision to abandon the island. American commanders in charge of the army troops (which had replaced the marines) had no knowledge of the decision, but they could see an appreciable weakening in the Japanese resistance.

As the American forces on Guadalcanal grew in power, making the island seem a little more secure, distinguished visitors began to arrive from the United States. Some were anxious to see what the island looked like, others hoped they might be able to assess the morale of America's men overseas. The First Lady, Eleanor Roosevelt, was among the first to come. For some unaccountable reason, the military authorities on Guadalcanal chose Marine chaplain John J. O'Neill, a Catholic priest from Philadelphia, to act as her escort. They could hardly have picked a more unlikely tour guide. A tough-talking, cigar-chomping priest from one of Philadelphia's large Catholic communities, O'Neill had little use for Eleanor Roosevelt—and had often said so (he primarily objected to her open advocacy of birth control). Moreover, he vehemently opposed letting female celebrities visit Guadalcanal, since he thought that the

Marine Chaplain James Fitzgerald, veteran of Guadalcanal, stands next to a blackboard in his office in Australia. The signs "Crying Room" and "Towels for Rent" reflect the common attitude that someone with a problem should "tell it to the chaplain." (Source: U.S. Marine Corps)

men who would have to provide for their protection should be left free to fight the enemy instead of acting as a visitor's bureau. O'Neill also shared the feeling, common among male chauvinists of the period, that Mrs. Roosevelt left something to be desired in the way of good looks and attractiveness. The long months of living in an all-male environment on Guadalcanal, however, had taken their toll even on O'Neill. "I had been there so long on the island that even she looked good," he remarked ruefully fifty years later.[27]

Still, he did as he was ordered, and minded his manners as he accompanied Mrs. Roosevelt on her tour of the island's hospital, airport, spanking new docks, and now-famous marine cemetery. During the tour, a surprising change began to take place in the grizzled marine chaplain from Philadelphia: By the time she had finished her visit, she had won his grudging approval. On her last day on Guadalcanal, she turned to O'Neill and asked him, "Who are your relatives back in the States?" He told her that his mother had long since passed away but that his father was still living in Philadelphia. She asked him for his father's name and address, and when she returned to the White House, she wrote a letter to the elder O'Neill saying that his chaplain-son on faraway Guadalcanal was doing "a beautiful job" and that she had been "delighted" to meet him. Since O'Neill's father had heard nothing from his son in several months, he was thrilled to hear that he was alive and thriving in his new assignment. Concludes O'Neill: "She did a good job out there. She was most congenial, and didn't give me a bad time at all." Eleanor Roosevelt had won herself a convert from the ranks of the priest-chaplains assigned to Guadalcanal.[28]

In the last months of the fighting on the island, a Catholic chaplain stationed there began to have serious second thoughts about the war, and indeed about the possibility of ever having a morally justifiable armed conflict. Chaplain John P. Daly of Philadelphia, a mild, soft-spoken man who serves today as the pastor of an all-black parish in one of the poorest ghettos of America, the Mill Creek area of West Philadelphia, in a quiet but determined way has become an impassioned critic both of war itself and of the American capitalistic system. Capitalism, he has come to believe, has worked not only to deepen the impoverishment of his beloved black parishioners but to keep the world at war with itself. Though his ideas form neither a new criticism of capitalism nor a new position for an American Catholic priest, they come as a surprise when we hear them from Daly, a bona fide war hero.

How did he arrive at—for him—so radical a position? It all started on Guadalcanal. Daly, like most other priests, had entered the chaplaincy service as an ardent patriot, convinced that the American way of life was grievously imperiled by the Japanese and the Germans. After several brief assignments at army posts in the States, he received orders to report to Guadalcanal, arriving there several months after the Japanese had evacuated the bulk of their troops. Since enemy soldiers remaining on the island still posed a continuing threat, the army sent patrols around the island to look for stray Japanese. One afternoon, while walking along a jungle trail, Daly stumbled across the bodies of two Japanese officers. When he asked what had happened, he was told that the day before an American officer had run into the two Japanese and had gunned them down, even though they were ready to surrender. He remembers the feeling of despair he had at that moment: The local commanding general had programmed all of his men into hating the enemy, an attitude that, as he puts it today, was "totally opposed to what Jesus tried to tell us."[29]

A few days later, he had a second experience that eventually revolutionized

his attitudes toward war, human relations, and even life itself. One tense afternoon, as he accompanied another patrol in the jungle, a GI found the body of
a young Japanese soldier. When Daly examined the man's personal effects, he
found that he had kept a diary in which he had meticulously recorded the
events of each day. Daly picked it up, and when he returned to camp he had a
Japanese prisoner translate it for him. He would never forget what the diary
said. The Japanese soldier had written at great length about his girl friend in
Japan, about the happy times they had shared in the past, and about the future life they would enjoy when the war finally came to an end. Daly was
thunderstruck. None of these things would ever happen now. The young Japanese soldier would never marry, never have children, never have a home he
could call his own. A family had been destroyed even before it had come into
being. The priest began to think about the futility of war, of the folly of even
this particular war, which he and most Americans believed was among the
most justifiable wars in American history.[30]

At this stage in his life, Daly was still far from the universal pacifist that he is
today. For the rest of the war he would remain a loyal soldier, continuing to
follow orders and enjoying remarkable success in the army. By the end of the
war he had attained the rank of colonel and had piled up medals, citations,
and the highest possible recommendations from his superior officers. So outstanding were his leadership abilities that the Chaplain Corps begged him to
remain in the service after the war, offering him a commission in the Regular
Army and a career as a chaplain in the peacetime force. Daly, however, had
seen more than enough of war and military life and had come to the conclusion that all war was a useless, barbaric, and utterly futile endeavor. He would
have no more of it, though for a long time he kept his antiwar feelings strictly
to himself.

In the postwar era, as the fragile peace of the Cold War years grew increasingly unsteady and as the nation slipped repeatedly into a series of vicious local
wars, Daly's ideas came to fruition. He decided it was time to separate himself
from the capitalistic system as much as he could and asked for a transfer from
one of Philadelphia's wealthiest parishes to one of its poorest, located in the
middle of a violence-prone black ghetto. He has remained there ever since. A
war hero had become a pacifist of deep conviction, a soft-spoken but determined opponent of the American free-enterprise system and something of an
enigma to his fellow veterans of the war who shared the same experiences as
he. It all started on Guadalcanal. "War produces nothing," he says today,
"and it never does bring real peace."[31]

One who never entertained even the slightest doubt about the morality of the war was Frederick Gehring. The role of the United States in World War II had no more ardent supporter in the army's Chaplain Corps than he, or anyone else who wrote more voluminously about the conflict. Or about himself. He described his own role on Guadalcanal at such length that a controversy arose, and it lingers still. No one has ever questioned his personal courage or his devotion to his men, but both the Military Ordinariate and several of the chaplains who served with him on Guadalcanal believe that he was, to use their phrase, "a publicity hound." [32]

In a sense, they are right. He took the greatest pains to make sure that the record of his activities on Guadalcanal made its way into print, and as one examines his considerable body of writings, two things stand out: He rarely mentions other chaplains, and he makes rather annoyingly frequent references to the famous people he met on Guadalcanal and elsewhere. In recent years, two of his fellow chaplains have taken exception to what they believe was Gehring's excessive self-advertising, one leveling what is probably the most serious criticism of Gehring, which is that he gave the distinct impression in his writings that he was the only chaplain on Guadalcanal. There were, of course, many others, but they are seldom mentioned—even in cursory fashion—in his written accounts from the island. Worst of all (continues the same chaplain), Gehring's dispatches gave readers the impression that he was a *marine* chaplain rather than a navy chaplain assigned to the Seabees. He did, of course, minister to many marines, because the grievous shortage of chaplains on Guadalcanal made it necessary for him to do so, but marines vehemently dislike any nonmarine calling himself one of their own. [33]

In fairness to Gehring, it must be said that the marines themselves recognized him as an outstanding chaplain, giving him their highest praise even when he himself discouraged it. When a Jewish friend, Barney Ross, told him during the battle that after he got back home he would tell the world about him, Gehring replied, "You will do me a favor if you just don't say anything about it." Ross, however, ignored Gehring's request, and a few months later, while recovering from wounds at a hospital in San Diego, he took pains to tell everyone within earshot how much he admired his favorite Catholic chaplain. Said Ross from his hospital bed: "All the boys on the 'Canal' look up to Father Frederick Gehring. They think he is the greatest thing next to God Almighty that there is." He cited Gehring's repeated forays into the front lines, his work as a volunteer litter bearer, and his ceaseless ministering to the wounded, the dead, and the dying of every faith. [34]

Justice to Gehring also demands noting the fact that he never made even a veiled reference to the two medals that he received while serving on the island.

In the more prestigious of the two, the Legion of Merit, he was described as an officer who had been consistently "brave under fire, cheerful in the face of discouragement, and tireless in his devotion to duty." The other award was the Navy and Marine Corps Medal, which the navy bestowed on him for giving "the maximum in energy and zeal" and for his "cool and courageous example under fire, enemy bombings, strafing and shelling." In a remarkably short time, he had become, in the words of the citation, "a rallying point for all hands." During my own interview with him, Gehring repeatedly and successfully evaded my questions about his awards, preferring instead to talk about the bravery of the marines on the island and the trials that all of them had endured together. Gehring also had admirers other than the navy's "brass." The enlisted men and the younger officers also held him in the highest esteem and often said so. When the American Red Cross in New Guinea completed a recreation center for the navy men on the island, the men insisted on calling it "Gehring Hall." When someone asked a young lieutenant, not a Catholic, what he thought of Gehring, he replied, "He was a leader, teacher, friend of men." A tough, battle-hardened marine from Brooklyn perhaps put it best: "The guy is only terrific."[35]

The battle for Guadalcanal ended not with a bang, nor even a whimper, but with a silent stealing away in the night. During the first week of February 1943, the Japanese evacuated almost all of their 13,000 remaining troops from the island, accomplishing the complex operation in a series of brilliant maneuvers that cost them only one destroyer. The success of the action came not only from their outstanding execution of the plan but also from the Americans' continuing ignorance of the strength and moves of the Japanese forces on the island. The Japanese succeeded in executing, under cover of darkness, the Dunkirk of the Pacific. The enemy soldiers who had escaped from Guadalcanal would go on to fight other, equally fierce, battles for the emperor and for Japan.

How did the fighting men of Guadalcanal—the sailors, soldiers, airmen, and marines—get along with the Catholic men of the cloth who attempted to minister to them in the midst of the battle for the island? The evidence seems unmistakable: The hardships and danger of the campaign drew them all closer together. On Guadalcanal, just as earlier in the Philippines and repeatedly until the war finally came to an end, deep bonds of friendship developed between the priests in the military and the men they served, with some friendships lasting long after the war was over. The chaplains, for their part, had few complaints about their men, and most were emphatic in their praise of them.

"The officers and men have been grand to me," wrote Chaplain John Scannell to his family in Denver. Forty-five years after the battle, Thomas Reardon would say the same, and John J. O'Neill of Philadelphia agreed enthusiastically: "The Marines were the greatest guys in the world you would want to work with."[36]

If a chaplain developed a warm relationship with his men, he sometimes found that the men greeted him in a friendly, bantering manner that at once showed their affection for him but sacrificed none of the respect they felt for his position. Reardon remembers that when he arrived at Wellington, New Zealand, and first walked down the gangplank of the ship, the marines hooted and booed at him because he was wearing a navy uniform. "Since when do navy men take free rides on Marine ships?" they shouted at him. It seems that he had left the United States in such a hurry that he had forgotten to pack his marine uniform. Reardon, ever ready with a riposte, told his young charges to mind their own business, which only encouraged them to heckle him all the more. When he returned to the ship at the end of the day, however, he found to his surprise that a crisp new marine uniform was waiting for him in his cabin. It fitted perfectly. A hastily scrawled note read, "To our favorite *marine* chaplain." Concludes Reardon: "The marines always went out of their way to take good care of me."[37]

The most vivid memory that the chaplains of Guadalcanal would take away with them was the remarkable religious fervor that they found in so many of their men. No one ever denied, of course, that much of their piety came from the rigors of combat and above all, from the threat of sudden annihilation. "It was the presence of death that got to the men," remarks Reardon. The troops on Guadalcanal, both the marines and the army draftees, were all such young people, he notes. Few of them had ever thought seriously about death, least of all about the possibility of their own demise. "They all thought they were going to live forever, and then all of a sudden death came to the guys around them." He suggests that "the presence of death had a sobering effect on them" and made them more interested in religion. "Courage is fear saying its prayers," said Gehring after the battle for the island had ended. Few of the priests, ministers, or rabbis who served on Guadalcanal would have disputed his claim.[38]

Yet it seemed to many chaplains that the piety of many of the men also had deeper roots: a discovery of God as a Father, a realization that the church was an ally and a source of comfort, and a love for Catholicism's sacraments that they acquired simply by receiving them more often than they had done before. Whatever the motivation for their zeal, the religious fervor of so many of the men on Guadalcanal gave the chaplains an inspiration that they would never forget. Army Chaplain Terence Finnegan noted that whenever he conducted services in the mud of Guadalcanal, he asked the men not to kneel, but they did so anyway.[39] Perhaps the religious experience of the American fighting man on Guadalcanal is best summed up by an epitaph a war correspondent found on a headstone in the marine cemetery on the island. It reads:

> And when he gets to heaven,
> To St. Peter he will tell:
> One more Marine reporting, sir—
> I've served my time in hell.[40]

The American triumph on Guadalcanal marked a turning point in the war for the Pacific. Although it was not quite "the end of the beginning," as Winston Churchill said about the battle of El Alamein in North Africa (the clear turning point in the campaign on that continent), it unquestionably signified the start of a new phase of the war against the Japanese. The Americans had finally taken the offensive and had begun to move decisively against the enemy. They would suffer no more Pearl Harbors, or Bataans, or Corregidors. If an Allied victory in the Pacific was not yet in sight, it was at least well on the way.

For the first time in the war, the Allies had thrown the Japanese off an island that they had earlier lost to them. After a string of defeats in the Pacific, which had transformed the western Pacific into a veritable Japanese lake, the tide had turned irrevocably. Events would continue to move, inexorably, in the same direction, culminating on the morning of Sunday, September 8, 1945, when the imperial Japanese government would finally surrender unconditionally to the Allies on the battleship *Missouri* in Sagami Bay.

That final moment of triumph, however, was still two and a half years and 3,400 miles away. Before victory could be complete, the Americans, the British, and the Australians would first have to remove the flag of the rising-sun from the other Japanese-occupied islands in the Pacific. Doing so would involve a repetition of much of the Guadalcanal experience, in the same kind of relentless terrain and climate. The next big clash would take place on the second-largest island in the world, New Guinea. To the men who fought there, it was the worst of "the green hells" of the South Pacific. Only the veterans of Guadalcanal would have disagreed.

4

FORWARD IN THE PACIFIC:
NEW GUINEA AND TARAWA

God bless you, and God have mercy on the Japanese.
—Chaplain Frank Kelly

At the same time that the struggle for Guadalcanal was approaching a climax, in late 1942, a combined Australian-American force was locked in fierce combat with the Japanese in a second major campaign in the Pacific. It took place on an enormous island 1,200 miles to the west of Guadalcanal, and would be not only the longest battle in the war with the Japanese but a deeply frustrating one as well. In the end, the Americans and their Australian partners would bring the operation to a conclusion by using the easiest of all possible strategies: They would simply walk away, leaving the Japanese remaining on the island to dwindle down to nothing. Before they achieved that grim success, however, the battle would be as violent as any yet seen in the Pacific war. The name of the island? New Guinea.

The second-largest island in the world (surpassed in bulk only by Greenland), New Guinea stretches 1,300 miles from southeast to northwest. Its 309,000 square miles contain some of the world's densest and most dangerous jungle swamps, and a mountain range rising to 16,000 feet crowns its spine. Why a major confrontation over so preposterously intimidating a territory? The Allies feared that if the Japanese succeeded in wrenching it away from them, Australia would be in danger of enemy aggression, which would gravely imperil all future Allied operations in the southern reaches of the Pacific. They dared not lose Australia, but if New Guinea fell, that might well happen.

Thus began a two-and-a-half-year campaign for New Guinea that would become known in later years as the struggle for the "Green Hell." From a distance, it looked charming enough: steep, deeply crevassed hills sparkling green and fresh in the eastern trade winds while mountain peaks, the loftiest in the Pacific Basin, cradled towering cumulus clouds. Close up, however, the true New Guinea quickly revealed itself. In many ways, it seemed less an island than a horror of nature: a cauldron of bugs, snakes, bats, leeches, ants, and scorpions all thriving in the island's soupy humidity.

Chaplains serving in New Guinea made no attempt to hide their loathing for the place. "We ought to give it to the Japs and make them live there," a Catholic chaplain from Cleveland complained. Another argued that they should simply leave the enemy's troops trapped on the island and let them suffer all of its ravages to the fullest, thus receiving a fitting punishment for the crimes they had visited upon the human race. A third summed up what virtually every chaplain thought about the island: New Guinea was a "hole," and he vowed that he would never set foot on it again after the war had ended. He kept his promise. New Guinea's insect life boggled the mind. Insects of all varieties swarmed over the island in vast, churning clouds, apparently convinced that they owned it. One career chaplain who had seen much of the world, but nothing even as remotely noxious as New Guinea, complained vehemently that "our major enemy just now is . . . bugs, insects, beetles, locusts, ants, mosquitos, bats and every dam[n] thing that crawls or flies." Many times when he tried to write letters, "a cloud of these pests" would swarm all over him, "slither around on the paper, block the pen, zoom into your eyes, ears, mouth." He grew to detest New Guinea and all its rapacious wildlife.[1]

The struggle for New Guinea began in March 1942 when the Japanese landed a small band of soldiers on the northern coast of the island. In a few short weeks, they succeeded in building up a mobile striking force of more than 11,000 troops, most of them stationed in camps located not far from the towns of Buna and Gona. The Americans and Australians launched a drive on the two villages on November 16, 1942, having been told that the area was only "lightly" held. They walked into a hail of Japanese fire that tore viciously into their ranks from unseen bunkers on every side. Confused and badly shaken, the Americans withdrew and tried to piece their shattered forces together. Furious at the collapse of the troops, MacArthur sent one of his field generals, Lt. Gen. Robert Eichelberger, to the scene. MacArthur's orders seemed clear enough: "Bob, I want you to take Buna or not come back alive."[2]

Eichelberger quickly reorganized the dispirited American forces and then hurled a series of attacks at the entrenched Japanese. For the next two months, the two sides flailed wildly at each other in the jungle, with both sides sustaining heavy losses. Any chaplain who served the men in the lines did so at appalling risk to his own life. Once, while conducting a burial service in the jungle, a Japanese sniper fired at Chaplain Edward Connolly from close quarters, and the bullet missed his head by only a few inches. Another time, a Japanese plane strafed him while he was walking down a jungle trail, and he was hit as he tried to take cover. Asked about the incident afterward, he reported that the Japanese pilot had merely "grazed" him with a "stray shot."[3]

After five weeks of heavy fighting, the Australians and Americans finally gained the upper hand at Buna. Helped greatly by their superiority in supplies, they were able to begin a sustained assault on the Japanese perimeter at Buna beginning on December 31, 1942, and three weeks later, it fell to the Allies. A month later, the Americans closed a vice around the rapidly collapsing Japanese lines and succeeded in taking all of the vital Buna-Gona area. They had won only the opening round in the long campaign to clear the Japanese from the northern coast of New Guinea, and a protracted struggle to seize the rest of the island would follow. Nevertheless, the crisis point in the New Guinea campaign was past.

With Buna and Gona safely locked up, MacArthur began a series of amphibious assaults on the northern coast of New Guinea. In the first eight months of 1943, his forces would dash 1,400 miles along that coast, then sweep across the sea just south of the equator, finally landing on the island of Morotai, only 300 miles away from the Philippines. At long last he stood within reach of keeping the promise he had made when he had fled the Philippine Islands two years before, the pledge that every American school child used to know, "I shall return."[4]

Nearly 700 miles up the coast from Buna and Gona lay the harbor city of Hollandia, taken by the Allies in April 1943, which would act as the principal staging point for the rest of the campaign. It was also the scene for one of World War II's noncombat tragedies, one that had little to do with either the war or its terrors but was dreadful nonetheless. I refer to the role assigned to black troops in the war. Most of the black soldiers who served in New Guinea spent their time at the base in Hollandia where they performed menial and humiliating chores that the army, as a matter of policy, relegated to blacks only: The men of the all-black 93rd Division built and cleaned latrines, maintained ammunition dumps (where accidental explosions accounted for most of the black fatalities in the Pacific), worked as stevedores on the docks, and manned warehouses. They did everything except go to battle, save on the rare occasions when the army assigned them to security patrols in areas long since removed from combat.

The army routinely assigned black soldiers to the kind of degrading labor that no fighting white man would have accepted as his permanent work in the Pacific. The services' racial policies, however, simply reflected the nation's racial attitudes at the time, and the army had determined not to give blacks any other kind of work partly because it believed (as did the navy) that blacks were incapable of standing up to the rigors of combat. Few of the black soldiers of the 93rd Division made any complaint, and most quietly obeyed their orders. The division made a good record for itself because the men who served in it did what the army assigned them with a quiet steadiness and hard application to their tasks. Moreover, the division had an admirable sense of esprit de corps, and the men in it generally cooperated with their mostly white officers.[5]

Fortune smiled on the Catholics in the division because of the black priest assigned to the 93rd. John W. Bowman, the thirteenth of fourteen children, had spent his boyhood years in Maryland, where his parents (slaves before the Civil War) had raised him and his siblings in a strictly Catholic atmosphere. After his early schooling, he entered the Society of the Divine Word, a religious order devoted to the spiritual and social welfare of black Catholics. When the American bishops began looking for a black priest to serve the growing number of black troops in the military, they asked Bowman if he would volunteer. The offer delighted him, and he entered the service a short time later, the first black Catholic priest to be formally a part of the Chaplain Corps (five black priests had served earlier as chaplains in the army, but none had received a commission).

Bowman spent most of his time in the 93rd Division serving non-Catholics, since the division was 98 percent Protestant. That was, of course, the situation that prevailed almost everywhere throughout the war: Most chaplains spent the vast majority of their time ministering to men and women of other denominations—or of no religious affiliation at all. It was ecumenism born of necessity, but true ecumenism, nonetheless, and Bowman's work in the Pacific with the 93rd Division was a good example of it.

Arriving at Hollandia at the end of October 1944, Captain Bowman's first challenge would be to make his peace with the division's officer corps, 50 percent of which was white. He recalls no difficulties in dealing with any of them, either in New Guinea or anywhere else, and remembers with special affection a white colonel from Alabama who served his early morning Mass nearly every day. Nor did he encounter any special problem with the black troops. The same was true of his work with the other eleven clergymen in the division, all non-Catholic. No chaplain ever lodged a complaint against Bowman, not even after he became the supervising chaplain for all of the 93rd Division. When the army awarded him the Bronze Star shortly before he left New

Army Chaplain John W. Bowman of the Divine Word Fathers was the first black Catholic priest to receive a commission in either the Army or the Navy Chaplain Corps. (Source: National Archives)

Guinea, he received praise not only for the long and dangerous trips that he had often made to supervise the many units in his far-flung territory but also for the "unflagging . . . zeal and enthusiasm" with which he ministered to American soldiers, Australian troops, and even the natives of New Guinea. The citation concluded that John Walter Bowman had set "an example for other chaplains to follow."[6]

Reflecting on his wartime work forty-five years later, Bowman concluded that his wartime ministry in New Guinea had been one of his "most rewarding years" in a lifetime spent in the Catholic priesthood. Still, not all went smoothly. As the division's ranking chaplain, he had to accompany the provost marshal whenever the army decreed that an extraordinary punishment had to be visited upon a soldier guilty of a serious crime. On one particular occasion, Bowman had to attend the execution of a young black GI. After speaking quietly to the boy, he read the prayers for the dying to him, then blessed him one last time. Then he stepped back, and the execution, which was death by hanging, was carried out. This incident seems to have bothered Bowman profoundly, and its memory remained fresh nearly a half-century later. Nor was his own career in the service without its problems. When the time came for the 93rd to leave New Guinea and move on toward the Philippines, the army left Bowman behind in an administrative position. Whatever it was that it had given him to do (details of the task have been lost), he detested it and finally called on the chief of chaplains in Washington to remove him from the post. He left the army in 1946 and returned (no doubt with considerable relief) to his work with black Catholics in the South. He described his return to civilian life as an exceptionally "easy" one and said that he never experienced any desire to return to military life.[7]

Shortly after the Americans had secured Hollandia (and before Chaplain Bowman took up his duties there), they moved to counteract Japanese air power in the region. Included in that effort was the struggle for the island of Biak. Located just off the coast of New Guinea, almost 1,000 miles beyond Buna-Gona, Biak is a tiny speck of land in the Pacific, smaller even than Rhode Island. Nevertheless, it held enormous potential for damage to the Allied cause, since the Japanese had built three airfields on the island and could use them to raid American sea-traffic in the vicinity. Moreover, the bases would prove invaluable to the Allies if they could ever seize them from the enemy, since Biak could act as a jumping-off point for further campaigns in the Pacific. No one could have predicted after the first day of the battle how maddeningly difficult it would be for the Americans to wrest the island from the Japanese. Landing unopposed on May 27, 1944, the first twenty-four hours of the operation went so smoothly that just a few days later, MacArthur grandiloquently announced "the practical end of the New Guinea campaign." The general's announcement proved disastrously wide of the mark: The Japanese had simply conceded the beaches to the invaders and were waiting for them behind the coastline.[8]

What the Americans did not know was that a seasoned force of 3,000 Japanese troops, led by the brilliant and resourceful Col. Kuzume Naoyuki, was waiting to defend the island. Taking advantage of the hundreds of deep caves that honeycombed the island, Naoyuki had connected the deepest of them with twisting tunnels and placed his heaviest artillery far inside. Expecting a long battle, he had also built up huge stocks of food, ammunition, and water. Supplies of water, he knew, would be critical to the course of the campaign, since the coral that made up the island quickly soaked up all the rain that fell on it. The Japanese had enough water to last at least four months.

As American infantrymen moved across the island, they stumbled repeatedly into Japanese ambushes. The defenders succeeded in blowing so many American units to pieces that the American position on the island quickly deteriorated into chaos. Field commanders, fearing that the Japanese might annihilate their men, begged MacArthur for permission to retreat. His response was always the same: Attack, attack some more, then attack again. Retreat, he insisted, was out of the question. At first he also turned a deaf ear to his generals' repeated requests for more troops. The Americans, sensing the near-hopelessness of their situation, dug in for a long fight.

The battle was a touch-and-go affair from beginning to end. Despite the almost unendurable heat and humidity, many of the American troops had to last twenty-four hours on only one canteen of water. Some died of thirst; others perished as they crawled toward water cans that the Japanese had placed within range of their weapons. Japanese artillery raked every American position, all day and all night, without stopping. Japanese sharpshooters popped their heads out of caves, fired, then ducked back into their holes, leaving the Americans shocked and bewildered at an enemy that could track their every move yet themselves remain invisible. All the usual methods of attack failed miserably. Finally, after nearly two weeks of unsuccessful attempts to take the Japanese caves, aerial reconnaissance flights began to locate hidden entrances of the dens. Soon army engineers began climbing up cliffs toward them. Once in place they poured gasoline and TNT inside a cave, and then ignited it. Wild screams would indicate if they had cleared the Japanese out of the cave; if not, they would have to try again.[9]

Few battles in the Pacific theater so tested the stamina and endurance of the chaplains as the struggle for tiny Biak. One chaplain in a field hospital on the island watched in stupefaction as army surgeons labored at their operating tables twenty-four hours a day, some of them working as long as a week without rest. Enemy bombers pounded the island so often that after a while the doctors and nurses no longer even paused in their work when they heard the air-raid sirens. So many people died that one day the chaplain interred twenty-three bodies in one grave. After two weeks of nonstop labor with the wounded at the island's aid stations, he had acquired a gruesome, if useful, talent: "I can now take the scattered parts of the body and put them together, and go for dinner without the slightest hesitation." Although his remark might seem callous to some, it at least demonstrates how the ferocity of the fighting on Biak eroded the sensitivities of even the chaplains.[10]

Since the Japanese hidden in the island's caves and tunnels could fire at any point on the island, no one was safe, including the men of the cloth. One day a Japanese marksman hidden in a cavern fired on Chaplain James J. Moran of Cleveland and his assistant as they drove across the island. The sniper hit the vehicle four times, wounding the assistant (though not seriously) but somehow missing the priest. Moran took a cheerfully macabre view of the incident. After the battle he wrote a friend, "I thought I was getting old, but you should have seen me go over the foot of the car to a safe point." He wondered half-seriously if he might enter the all-Catholic track meet in Cleveland when he returned home after the war.[11]

Although it is clear that the vast majority of the chaplains who served on Biak more than met the challenges the battle thrust upon them, at least one of them did not. He was a Catholic priest from Buffalo and a "career army man," as the military liked to say, which meant that he had entered the chaplaincy before the war. Now, gifted with rank and seniority, he held the position of supervisory chaplain over all the other chaplains on Biak. The army could hardly have chosen a more ill-suited man than Roman C. Nuwer. He had shown rare generosity toward his men in the earlier battles at Buna and Gona, but at Biak, he appeared to take little more than a passing interest in the welfare of his chaplains, all of whom were in grave danger. During the battle, he spent little time in the field, staying as much as possible in a well-protected command post deep under ground.

Even though he was almost completely removed from the rigors of the fighting, he complained that the trials of life on Biak had pushed him to the limits of his endurance. "I have had no beer since last Christmas," he wrote pathetically to a friend at home. "This dam[n] chlorinated water is getting monotonous and would make a prohibitionist vote wet." He vowed that when he got back to Washington, "You are going to do some very wet entertaining, if and when I ever get into your apartment again." Almost as useless as the water, in his view, were the Japanese prisoners, but it is worth noting that most chaplains (both Catholic and non-Catholic) shared the country's widespread hatred of the Japanese.[12]

The intensity of the fighting charred Biak down to its coral foundations, and its ghastly appearance astounded visitors seeing it for the first time after the battle had ended. Weeks after the campaign, two Catholic chaplains toured the remains of the battlefields in a jeep. The high point of their tour, not surprisingly, was a visit to the island's celebrated caves. One man, a navy chaplain serving on a troopship, reported that he saw "where the nips [Nipponese] had dug in and there were still skulls, jawbones, thighbones etc. with wrecked nip equipment in them. A ghastly sight. The nips wouldn't surrender so they were burned out." Burned out at terrible cost to both sides, he might have added.[13]

One would have thought that the intense fighting would have brought an end to the religious divisions that had characterized American life before the war. Sadly, it did not. Even during the long battle against the Japanese in New Guinea, fresh squabbles between antagonistic clergymen broke out with dismaying frequency, especially in the parts of the island where the fighting had ceased, where combat was sporadic, or where it had never occurred at all. Chaplains with no enemy to fight sometimes fought each other instead. In one backwater outpost on the island, angry bickering ended only when the Catholic chaplain succeeded in getting his Protestant counterpart transferred to another post.

The fracas began in early April 1944. Chaplain Benjamin Knowles, a Methodist, had put up a sign outside his office quoting the scripture passage, "I am the resurrection and the life." When the Catholic chaplain saw the sign, "he acted very ugly about it," reported Knowles to his wife. Apparently the priest was mainly upset because the sign said nothing about the role of organized religion in salvation. As a result of the pressure the priest put on the local commanding officer, the sign was torn down. Knowles said that he did not mind the fact that "these Catholics have their own way" so often. What he detested was that so often "the Catholic way" seemed to become "the army way." To add to Knowles's unhappiness, he had long since given up smoking, drinking, playing cards, gambling, and profane language, and as a result, most officers would have nothing to do with him—apparently they thought him "too religious." Knowles did have a constituency among the enlisted men, but the officers treated him like a pariah. They would not even help find a jeep for him to use in his ministry; he noted bitterly that the Catholic chaplain never seemed to want for proper transportation.

The dispute ended in a fully predictable way: Knowles received a letter from his commanding officer telling him he was about to move to another post. "It came as no surprise to me," he admitted. He resented having to leave because another chaplain had exercised undue influence over him, but he nevertheless sensed that perhaps it was best for him to go elsewhere. Fortunately, his new assignment proved more amicable in every way. The Catholic chaplain at the new post proved fully cooperative, and Knowles felt so much at ease with his new associate that he began to hope that the army would soon make him his supervising chaplain.[14]

On another island not far from Knowles, tension between another Protestant chaplain, Watt N. Cooper (Presbyterian), and a Catholic chaplain went on even after the campaign had ended. When the priest returned to Detroit, his home town, he had a stack of photographs of a chapel that he said he had built in New Guinea with the help of the Catholic men on the post. "That just burns me up," lamented Cooper, because he and his Protestant men had built the chapel. "The Protestant does the spectacular thing and the Catholic jumps in and takes credit for it," he protested vehemently.[15]

But there were also many outstanding examples of interfaith cooperation. When Chaplain John Young, a Presbyterian, sailed for New Guinea in the summer of 1942, he and a chaplain-friend, John Hurley, landed on the beaches together in the opening hours of the battle for the port city of Lae, 150 miles northwest of Buna and Gona. It was good that they had done so, since all but five of the men who had come ashore in the same boat had perished. "The Lord spared us," said Young, "for the work that lay ahead."[16]

With the American conquest of Biak finally achieved, MacArthur moved swiftly in a last series of amphibious operations to seize the remaining Japanese enclaves on New Guinea, taking first the beaches that he planned to use for the invasion of the Philippines. Noemfoor, Sansapor, and Morotai in the Moluccas all fell in quick succession. In under three months, MacArthur's American and Australian armies sped 1,400 miles from the Admiralty Islands to the western tip of New Guinea. As the Allies fought their way across the island, they also cleared the Japanese off several smaller islands located well to the east. Hardly known before the war, the obscure places where these battles took place suddenly became household words to Americans at home: Bougainville, Makin, Kwajalein, Eniwetok, and above all, a tiny coral island named Tarawa.[17]

Stretching 1,600 miles across the Pacific was a vast network of Japanese-held islands that one historian aptly called a "giant tropical spider."[18] The navy and its land-going arm, the marines, would have to break through this far-flung tangle of islands or Japan would never fall to its knees. Few people questioned the necessity of routing the enemy from its strongholds in the mid-Pacific, since the Japanese presence there imperiled all future westward operations. Although the Americans discovered they could safely sidestep some islands—using a "leap-frogging" strategy, which meant that they invaded some islands and merely sealed off others—a few places were of such strategic value that they had to be seized. Some had excellent air strips or good locations for future air strips; others simply stood directly in the line of march to Tokyo. For a variety of reasons, each would have to fall.

The campaigns to take the Solomon, Gilbert, and Marshall islands, which began in July 1943 and continued without pause until February 1944, encompassed some of the stiffest fighting in the whole Allied campaign for control of the Pacific. The shocking casualty rates gave abundant proof of the intensity of the island war: In conquering a land area only 4,000 square miles in size (smaller than the state of Connecticut), the Americans and Japanese together lost 2,500 people (1,000 Americans, 1,500 Japanese). Some of the hardest fighting took place during the effort to take a series of atolls (coral reefs) located 900 miles northeast of New Guinea. The battle for the first of these atolls was one of the bloodiest struggles of the whole Pacific war. Its name was Tarawa.

"If God had not given me His special protection I would have been wounded or killed at least a dozen times," said Chaplain Joseph Wieber about the horrors of Tarawa.[19] He would remain forever grateful for his delivery from death, but he would also wonder why the battle had spared him when so many others had perished. Probably every chaplain who served on Tarawa, and lived to talk about it, felt the same way—and with good reason. Tarawa still stands as one of the most violent battles in the 200-year history of the U.S. Marine Corps. The ferocity of the Japanese defense of the island and the heroism of the men of the 2d Marine Division have given the struggle an almost legendary character, the stuff of myths and marvels. Yet the battle was no myth. It was an incredibly violent seventy-four-hour contest for a tiny Pacific atoll, one that, by the time it had ended, would take the lives of over 1,000 Americans and more than 4,700 Japanese and result in nearly 8,000 casualties for both sides. Put another way, one can say that the battle cost 194 lives per acre, of which 34 per acre were American marines.

The battle took place in a terrain entirely different from Guadalcanal and New Guinea. The atoll was a place of spectacularly beautiful inlets formed by coral reefs enclosing lagoons of every possible size. The Tarawa atoll encompasses forty-seven islands, of which the largest, Betio, is only 291 acres in size, less than half the area of Central Park in New York City. It was on this tiny sand spit, and in the terrible lagoon that lay next to it, that the horrendous battle of Tarawa would take place. Nature favored the Japanese because all of Betio lay within 300 yards of the beach; thus the Japanese defenses (the most formidable the Americans had yet seen) could come to bear on an invading force attempting to land anywhere on the island. Long, narrow, and curving like an Australian boomerang, Betio squatted menacingly on the southwest corner of the atoll, and the Japanese were prepared not only to throw back the American invaders but to protect their vital airfield as well.[20]

The Japanese commander on Betio, Rear Adm. Keiji Shibasaki, is said to have boasted that "a million men" could not take Betio "in a hundred years."[21] He had good reason to feel such unbounded confidence in his fortifications, since the island bristled with superbly fashioned defenses. His men had heavily mined the ocean side of the lagoon to force the Americans to approach the island through its middle, and the water had been studded with underwater obstacles designed to funnel American landing craft into the firing lanes of the Japanese guns located on the shore. Admiral Shibasaki had 200 large-scale weapons at his disposal, of which his eight-inch artillery pieces formed the centerpiece. His men had also constructed a sea wall four feet high on the lagoon side, through which 100 machine guns could pour fire onto the oncoming waves of marines. The atoll, in short, was a giant hornet's nest, ready to explode into action.

Vastly complicating the plans for the invasion of Tarawa were vexing questions concerning its tides. Would they be high enough to carry the landing craft over the coral reef at the edge of the lagoon? If not, would the marines have to climb out at the edge of the reef and wade the 100 yards across it, running straight into the enfilading fire of the Japanese? The marine command pleaded for a delay in the invasion until a full moon would guarantee the highest possible tide. The navy listened but decided to take a gamble on the tide. It lost, or rather, the Marine Corps lost. When the landing came, the assault craft stalled against the coral reefs, and the men had to wade through the water, much of it so deep they had to swim their way across, carrying heavy packs all the way.[22]

As the navy's professionals tried to piece together what little information they had about the atoll, the convoy carrying the attack force bore down on the island chain. The largest collection of ships yet seen in the Pacific war, it encompassed nearly 200 vessels destined for Makin (another atoll that the army would attack) and Tarawa (left to the marines). After splitting off from the Makin force, the Tarawa convoy made a final, four-day lunge at its target. The weather was hot and humid, and the marines used the daytime hours to

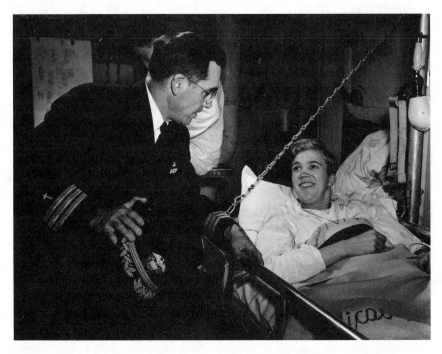

An unidentified chaplain visits a young patient in the sick bay of the USS *Alabama* before the invasion of Tarawa. (Source: National Archives)

play cards, talk, smoke, and toss baseballs and footballs at each other. Evenings, however, were altogether different—and decidedly grim—as that was the time for officers to brief the young marines about the island, describing its formidable defenses and warning them to expect alarmingly high casualty rates.

During the first two days, morale remained high. Some of the marines even took a boasting, arrogant attitude toward the Japanese; others feared the whole campaign was a hoax—that it was just another marine training exercise, though perhaps a bit more realistic than most. They told Chaplain Frank Kelly of Philadelphia (who had earlier served on Guadalcanal) that they hoped a few Japanese would still be left on the atoll when they arrived. As the ships drew closer to the target, however, they became less boastful, noticeably more quiet and serious, and above all, more interested in religion. Protestant and Catholic services took place whenever space became available—usually on deck because the weather was so hot and sticky—and the corps made every possible attempt to leave the men free to attend. Frank Kelly remembered that men came to him virtually around the clock for confession.[23]

Both Kelly and his Protestant counterpart, Malcomb J. MacQueen (Northern Baptist), soon found that the artificial barriers that had earlier tended to separate them from marines of other denominations quickly melted away. Although his battalion was 73 percent Protestant (and, indeed, many of the men had never seen a priest before), Kelly found that in a day or two no marine showed the slightest hesitation about seeing him. The famed war correspondent Robert Sherrod, sailing on the troopship the *Blue Fox,* believed that Kelly became "as popular with the Protestants" as McQueen was "with the Catholics." In a single sentence he summed up the ecumenical dimension of the war: "Denominational distinctions did not mean much to men about to offer up their lives."[24]

On the last afternoon of the trip, Chaplain John V. Loughlin of Rochester, New York, held his final Mass before the attack. A physician who was also a close friend directed the choir, shepherding the men through the familiar Catholic hymns. The next day, the doctor would be among the first marines to hit the beach and also one of the first to perish. (He would not be the only physician to perish on Betio. Seventy-eight percent of the medics and corpsmen would die or suffer serious wounds in the two-and-a-half-day struggle for the island.) In the late-night hours, Kelly celebrated his own final Mass. He used the severely cramped, dimly lighted officers' mess, since it was the only space available, and the room and the passageway outside it filled quickly with men of every faith. At the end of the Mass, Kelly turned toward the men, gave them a final blessing in Latin, and then said in plain English, "God bless you, and God have mercy on the Japanese." As he was removing his vestments, he received word that Col. Dave Shoup, the young marine officer who had planned the operation and would lead it, wanted to see him. "Padre, I want you to pray for me," Shoup said. "What sort of prayer, Colonel?" Kelly asked, surprised at the request because he knew that Shoup was a Protestant. "I want you to pray that I don't make any mistakes out on that beach; no wrong decisions that will cost any of those boys an arm or a leg or a hand, much less a life. I want you to pray for that, Padre." Kelly promised him that he would.[25]

The landing came on Saturday, November 20, 1943. On the transports approaching the island, reveille sounded at 12:45 A.M. to begin what would be one of the longest days in the history of the Marine Corps. At 2:50 A.M., lookouts spotted the low silhouette of Betio on the horizon. At 4:00 A.M., the marines clambered down cargo nets to the landing craft. At 4:30, the landing craft reached the line of departure and maintained their positions while waiting for orders to race toward the coral reef surrounding the lagoon.

At 6:30, a massive shelling from the navy's battleships and cruisers clattered over the heads of the men in their boats, exploding with violent fury on the tiny island. Many of the marines wondered how the Japanese could possibly survive such an onslaught. The order of the day had called for the marines to hit the beach at 8:30 A.M., but mishaps and inevitable confusion delayed the landing. At 9:13, the first groups reached the coral reef, followed in short order by the second and third waves. They would suffer lighter casualties than the marines who followed them because they rode in large "amtracs" (amphibious tractors), which easily rode over the top of the reef rimming the lagoon.

The landings that followed on the rest of that day and on the next two days did not go well. Most of the smaller craft crashed into the coral reef; viciously accurate Japanese fire tore into the little vessels; pools of blood spread around the boats and across the 100 yards of lagoon that lay between the reef and the beach. Hundreds of marines had to struggle, as best they could, through the shoulder-high water. Some fell into deep pools and drowned; others got caught in Japanese cross fire. Bodies and parts of bodies bobbed grotesquely in the water. In one battalion, the first wave succeeded in landing only 30 percent of its men on Betio, the second brought in slightly fewer, and the third wave had virtually no survivors. The only safe area turned out to be a long pier jutting out 500 yards from the shore, past the reef, and into the deep open water beyond. Men struggled to make it to the pier, then clung to it in desperation, knowing that any attempt to leave it for the beach would mean certain death.[26]

The first chaplain to reach the shore was Douglas Vernon, a Presbyterian; the second, Joseph Wieber, was a Catholic from Michigan; John V. Loughlin and his Protestant colleague, W. Wyeth Willard, followed shortly after. Wieber had the dubious distinction of serving as chaplain to the command boat of the first assault wave. After a Japanese shell smashed into the vessel, killing all the other officers, Wieber became the highest-ranking officer on the craft, but since the regulations of the Chaplain Corps forbade him to take command, the next-ranking marine took over. "We considered wading in," said Wieber, "but decided it was too far and waited for another tractor. That little wait probably saved our lives. They were so far away from the shore, wading across the lagoon would have meant certain death by drowning or annihilation by artillery fire."[27]

Loughlin came even closer to death than Wieber. Assigned to a medical unit, he rode in a craft that carried two ambulance jeeps, large amounts of medical supplies, several doctors, and a number of corpsmen. As it approached the lagoon, it crashed into the coral reef and stopped dead in the water. In a single second, it had become a perfect target for Japanese machine guns and mortars. What to do? Running the gauntlet across the lagoon meant almost certain death. Should they stay put and try to protect the medical supplies so desperately needed on the beaches, or was it too risky to remain where they stood? They decided to stay because there were wounded marines floating all around them, most of them desperately injured. Loughlin and the medics began pulling the men out of the water and administered drugs and blood plasma as quickly as they could. The tiny craft became a makeshift hospital and somehow managed to stay in one piece, despite continued shelling from the Japanese. For the next twenty-four hours, the priest and his medical comrades remained on the reef. They worked desperately to save the lives of the marines floating in the surf around them, as well as some of the most seriously wounded on the beach that a small craft occasionally succeeded in reaching. The chaplain and the doctors did what little they could in a situation that grew increasingly desperate by the hour.

When word reached the medics that no more medical supplies remained on the shore, they decided to make a dash toward the beach, four men running abreast. They moved as fast as they could, floundering in the deep water, but Loughlin was the only one to make the beach. He was carrying his Mass kit and wondered if the Japanese had guessed that he was a chaplain and had decided to spare him. Once on the shore, he ministered to the wounded and dying who were lying everywhere and began the grim task of helping to carry dead marines, and parts of unidentified marines, into one place. His remarkable service under fire would earn him the Legion of Merit.[28]

In the middle of the morning on that first day, Chaplain Frank Kelly and his assistant somehow reached the long pier. Lulled into complacency by the seeming safety of the dock, they had failed to notice that the Japanese had turned the pier into a death trap. They learned soon enough, however, for after walking only 200 yards toward the beach, a burst of gunfire forced them to dive into the water. Somehow Kelly reached the marine command post on the island where Col. Dave Shoup (later the commandant of the Marine Corps) was struggling against vicious odds to stem the disaster. Kelly and the regimental surgeon began interring the bodies in makeshift fashion, doing what little they could in near-impossible conditions. Soon they had set up a temporary cemetery behind the post, and marines began carrying in the bodies of their dead comrades, covering them with ponchos.[29]

The deeply distressing task of interring the dead would continue for the next seven days, with chaplains and burial details often in immediate peril of their lives. The first cemetery, located near the command post, stood only fifty yards behind the lines, and Japanese snipers in nearby coconut trees fired on the clergymen as they went about their errand of mercy. If the firing came too close, they would drop to the ground and wait; when it lessened a little, they would return to their tasks. At times, as many as six chaplains conducted burials at once, and often as many as twenty-five to thirty bodies had to be placed in the same trench. Frank Kelly, it was widely believed, had buried more than 100 marines. It was not an impossible figure.[30]

By the end of the first day, 5,000 marines had made it to the beaches, but 1,500 of them had died or suffered injuries. The marines' situation was perilous in the extreme, and an all-out Japanese counterattack during the night could well have pushed the entire force back into the lagoon. Fortunately for the marines, it never came.

William O'Neill spent much of the battle crawling from foxhole to foxhole assisting the men who needed to see a priest or were suffering from severe wounds. Marines saw him jumping repeatedly into craters and foxholes in order to hear the confession of a dying man or to pray quietly with him while his life ebbed away. A physically powerful man who stood over six feet tall, the marines of his regiment had given him the nickname "Big Joe." He evacuated many of the wounded himself, carrying them in his arms or draping them over his shoulders. A marine correspondent wrote that O'Neill was "worth as much to the boys of his regiment as a trainload of ammunition."[31]

Most of the men on Betio, including the chaplains, were probably too busy to notice that by noon of the second day of the battle, the Americans had begun to gain the upper hand. First and most important, the tide in the lagoon had turned, and at long last, the navy could use its smaller craft to bring desperately needed supplies and reinforcements over the reef to the beaches. More good news soon followed. In the early afternoon, marine units on the island began dividing the remaining Japanese troops into isolated sections, then forcing them into even smaller pockets from which they would have no escape. At four in the afternoon, Shoup triumphantly radioed his superiors on the battleship *Maryland*, "We are winning." An hour later, the first fighter plane touched down on the pockmarked Betio airfield, and at precisely 6:30 P.M., the first two jeeps moved slowly down the long pier pulling two artillery pieces behind them. More difficult fighting still lay ahead, but the men of the 2d Marine Division had turned a corner, and the worst at last seemed over.

The next day, the third of the battle, reinforcements arrived, more of the wounded left the island that they had come to hate, and the marines continued to tighten their stranglehold on the Japanese forces. Late on the evening of the same day, the Japanese staged the first of three furious counterattacks. The marines, not surprised, blew the Japanese assault apart with artillery, grenades, machine guns, rifles, and fixed bayonets. The last enemy charge came at 5 A.M., November 23, the final day of the battle. By the time it had spent itself, it was clear to the Americans that the Japanese had nothing left. As the sun rose in the east, the marines discovered a scene of frightful carnage: They counted 325 Japanese bodies lying in the sand while their own casualties numbered only 3 dead and another 25 wounded. After seventy-six hours of some of the most desperate fighting seen in the war to that point, the battle of Betio had ended. At 1:30 P.M., Gen. Holland Smith, in charge of the operation, announced the end of organized resistance on Tarawa.

Only 17 of the 500 Japanese still on the island chose to surrender, out of an original force of nearly 4,900. The rest either died during the fighting or willingly spilled their own blood, the latter apparently believing that in doing so they had given their last full measure of devotion to the nation of their destiny and to their emperor. The same would occur in all of the battles to come in the Pacific: The closer the Allies drew to Japan, the more fanatic the Japanese resistance, the smaller the percentage of Japanese who yielded themselves up to their conquerors, and the larger the number of Japanese suicides.

The battle for Tarawa meets every possible definition of the word "slaughter." The marine losses were 1,085 killed and 2,233 wounded, for a total casualty rate of 17 percent. The figures surpassed those for Guadalcanal, and only the struggle for Iwo Jima, fifteen months later, would prove costlier. The chaplains who were a part of the battle, however, saw the figures not as mere casualty statistics, but as a testament to the heroic and awesome men they had come to know so well.[32]

Burying the American and Japanese dead proved no easy task in the foul, stifling humidity, and to speed up the process of digging trenches, the marines sometimes resorted to using bulldozers. Hundreds of bodies lay stacked like cordwood along the beaches and sand dunes; one war correspondent described the stench as "almost unbearable . . . the sickening smell of death seeped into the earth, into your clothes, into your food, and floated out over the ocean." He heard men curse and shout in revulsion as they pulled the decaying corpses from holes, using long wires and ropes to slide them onto stretchers. Some stared in horror as they recognized the disfigured remains of their closest friends, with whom they had shared the most important days of their lives.[33]

After the burial crews had carried the bodies to Betio's permanent cemetery, the chaplains took over. First they had to remove the dog tags from the corpses, making sure that each received proper identification. Some had died as much as five days earlier and stank horribly. The chaplains, with the greatest gentleness possible, reverently placed the remains in the waiting grave. "We therefore commit this body to the ground; earth to earth, ashes to ashes, dust to dust," they said over each marine. Danger still lurked: Mines sometimes went off, forcing chaplains and burial parties to "hit the dirt," as they said, and wait until demolition teams had cleared out the remaining explosives. Once the bodies had been buried, the chaplains wrote letters of condolence to the next of kin. William O'Neill wrote until his hands ached. He refused to use impersonal form letters, especially since he had known most of the deceased intimately. A marine friend of his who saw several of his messages testified that "each one he wrote was an individual letter and straight from the heart." Undoubtedly one could have said the same about the other priests and ministers who shared the same sad, grim duty.[34]

Besides caring for the dead, the chaplains also assisted with the wounded—hundreds lay maimed and bleeding in the hospital ships off the island or in temporary hospitals set up on the atoll itself. O'Neill visited the wards day and night answering calls for help but also visiting the men even when he had not received a call. One marine sergeant wrote that O'Neill spent "just as much if not more time with a Protestant or a Jewish boy than he did with a Catholic, and I often wondered when he ever got time to sleep." Many others asked the same question.[35]

In recognition of extraordinary devotion to both the living and the dead, the navy singled out an unusually high number of chaplains for special recognition. To three of the clergymen who had served on Tarawa—Frank W. Kelly (Catholic), John V. Loughlin (Catholic), and W. Wyeth Willard (Northern Baptist)—it awarded the Legion of Merit. Letters of Commendation went to Gordon V. Tollefson (Lutheran) and William O'Neill (Catholic), with both men receiving warm praise for conducting religious services under fire, for ministering to the wounded and the dying, and for taking a leading role in the daunting task of burying the dead. Many other chaplains, unrewarded by medals or commendations, had carried out the same tasks.[36]

Loughlin nearly missed receiving his medal. Four months after the battle, while recuperating on a nearby island, he offered Mass early one morning at the post chapel and then happily tumbled back into bed thinking he had nothing else to do until noontime. Promptly at 9 o'clock, however, the sound of a Marine Corps band awakened him. "I drew the covers over my head and was dozing off again when the phone rang. It was the Sergeant Major to tell me that Admiral Nimitz was waiting on the field to give me a medal. I threw some cold water on my eyes, put on my pants and shirt and dashed over. Sure enough, I got a medal. If I had more time, I even might have shaved."[37]

Loughlin played down the battle—and the award—when he returned home to Rochester, but other chaplains gave explicit descriptions of their harrowing experiences on the island. One priest who had served on a destroyer located just off the coral reef said the battle was something he could never wipe out of his memory.[38] His two most vivid images were of the desperately wounded men he had dragged out of the water on the first day and the remarkable courage of the marines throughout the battle. His respect for the corps became something that "nothing will ever diminish." Frank Kelly believed that the religious devotion of the Catholic marines on the atoll had given him an inspiration almost beyond measurement: "I found a lot of solid Catholics in my marines," he said, and though they were "professional fighting men," their religious faith took second place to none. Most of his Catholic and non-Catholic confreres would have agreed emphatically with him.

Kelly had an exceedingly low estimate of the Japanese, however. (He was not, of course, the only chaplain—or American—on Betio to share the same harsh view.) Quick to recognize their cunning in battle and what he called their "toughness," Kelly noted that Japanese captives just sat on the ground and stared vacantly into space, doing nothing and apparently thinking the same. The reason for their passivity, he believed, was a simple absence of brain power: "They didn't seem to be a very intelligent lot."[39]

With the capture of Tarawa and Makin, the Americans had succeeded in wresting the Gilberts from the Japanese and had breached the southern flank of its outer defensive ring. No one could doubt that the Americans had put together a string of vastly impressive victories in the central and southern Pacific, and Japan's leaders knew they now faced an increasingly desperate battle for survival.

While the Americans were fighting the Japanese in New Guinea, the Americans and the British were making a vast commitment to the destruction of German hegemony in North Africa in the European theater of war. This campaign, too, would not be an easy one, and as in the Pacific, the Allied leaders expected heavy losses, intense German resistance, and victory only after a protracted struggle. In the first week of November 1942, the Americans landed on the west coast of Morocco, and the British simultaneously hit the beaches further to the east in Algeria. Though the war in the Pacific continued as before, the eyes of most Americans were riveted on North Africa because the Allied world was clamoring for a historic, massive victory over Adolf Hitler. It would have to come in North Africa or not at all.

5

NORTH AFRICA AND SICILY

> I could write pages and never get said all I want to say—so, my darling
> mother and good dad—"au revoir" and "adieu"—until we meet again
> with God.
> —A chaplain's last letter home

Winston Churchill had a problem. It was the summer of 1942, and the Americans had yet to fire a shot at a German soldier. Preoccupied by the attack on
Pearl Harbor, the United States seemed to have forgotten about its commitment to a strategy of Europe First (a policy formulated after a series of informal
meetings between British and Americans and made public in August 1941 at
the Atlantic Conference held off the coast of Newfoundland). The Americans
in general, and President Roosevelt in particular, seemed increasingly locked
into a policy of Japan First—or perhaps Europe Second. Churchill could
hardly contain his frustration. The German submarine campaign in the Atlantic threatened to strangle Great Britain, his forces had suffered a series of disastrous reverses in the Far East, and a prolonged war with the Germans in North
Africa had suddenly turned sour, with Germany's Erwin Rommel driving the
British Eighth Army out of territories it had earlier wrested from the enemy.

What to do? He decided that he would use a tactic he had earlier pursued
with great success: He would appeal directly to his old friend, President
Franklin Roosevelt, hoping to impress on him the urgency of the British situation and that country's desperate need for an immediate American move
against Nazi Germany. Pressuring Roosevelt as intensively as he dared, Churchill finally managed to convince the American president of the need to move
as quickly as possible against the Germans. Churchill's second task was to per-
suade Roosevelt that the best target for attack was North Africa, where Rom-

mel's vaunted Afrika Korps continued to bring humiliation to British forces and deepening despair to Churchill's embattled citizens at home.

Following a series of exchanges between the American Joint Chiefs of Staff (who argued for a quick invasion of northern Europe) and the British Joint Chiefs (who desperately wanted an assault on North Africa), Roosevelt agreed at the end of July to a combined Anglo-American amphibious invasion of North Africa in November 1942. The Americans would land on the western coast of Morocco while the British seized a series of beaches in Algeria, 850 miles to the east. The attack was to take place while the Americans continued to fight the Japanese on Guadalcanal.

The convoy carrying the American landing force of 69,000 American troops left Norfolk, Virginia, in the dark of night, October 23, 1942, maintaining strict secrecy. By all accounts, the clandestine aspects of the operation worked exceedingly well; the Germans would not catch word of the invasion force until it was only thirteen hours away from North Africa, and even then, they would fail to guess which beaches the Americans would land on.[1]

The Americans had put together a massive gray fleet of battleships, cruisers, carriers, and over forty destroyers to surround the twelve troopships that formed the heart of the convoy. A vast canvas of somber-shaded vessels twenty miles long and thirty miles wide, the convoy plowed slowly through mounting seas toward its target, the Atlantic beaches of Morocco and the rich port city of Casablanca. A Jesuit chaplain from New England described the convoy as it churned its way across the ocean: "As far as the eye can see, ships are still in Indian file. We make a hard turn to port, turn and count. Now in all there are 14 ships in our convoy—2 battlewagons, and 11 others. We are growing!" Later that same evening, as the fleet moved under cover of darkness, he leaned on the rail of the deck, silently admiring the breathtaking majesty of the flotilla. The troopships looked to him like "greyhounds straining to cover the distance that separates us from our destination." Off his starboard side, a "lane of hammered silver runs from our ship to the little destroyer directly under the moon." In the dim light of the wintry night sky, the procession looked like a "ghostly galleon."[2]

Stuffed into tight, humid compartments, the men spent most of their time waiting in endless chow lines. A chaplain on the troopship *Leedstown* described the dismal experience of trying to eat on a ship carrying 3,000 men when the ship had only one tiny mess hall in which to serve them. The troops could be served only two meals a day, which took from 4 A.M. until 11 P.M. "The chow line," he reported, was "like Stonewall Jackson's foot cavalry, always on

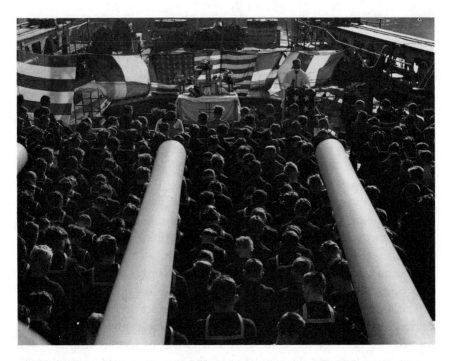

Navy Chaplain Daniel Burke directs services on board the cruiser USS *Philadelphia* in a North African port. Two of the ship's fourteen-inch guns serve as a frame for Burke and the altar. (Source: U.S. Navy)

the move." At the end of the line waited the navy's usual vile offerings, a glutinous gray mass of uncertain origin and uninspired preparation.[3]

Chaplains scheduled religious services whenever possible, ignoring periods of rough weather, their own problems with seasickness, or submarine warnings. One morning, John Foley's transport received reports of four German submarines lurking only twenty-five miles directly ahead. He had scheduled Mass for 10:30, after which he had planned to hold a catechism class for men interested in becoming Catholics. Despite the announcement of the presence of German submarines in the vicinity, he went ahead with both, reasoning that the immediate danger only made religious services all the more necessary. Those who attended, much to their credit, followed both the liturgy and the lecture attentively. Foley thanked the God of the oceans for their deliverance, saying that He had been "with us when we zigged and when we zagged."[4]

Other priests, however, had the misfortune to experience the terrors of a submarine attack. Henry Ford, of Denver, Colorado, was sleeping in his bunk when he heard a torpedo slam into the side of his ship. He threw on his clothes and somehow managed to make his way in the darkness to his assigned station, where he waited for the loudspeaker to deliver further instructions. None came, and the ship began to list alarmingly. After a few terrifying minutes, however, it seemed to stabilize, and it looked as if the danger had passed. The captain spoke reassuringly over the intercom, announcing that the crew had managed to contain the damage from the torpedo and that no one need panic. A destroyer soon appeared alongside the crippled transport and took it under tow.

For the next eight hours, the ship seemed to remain in balance, but the improvement turned out to be little more than the calm before the storm. Suddenly, a junior officer, acting in a moment of panic and with massive imprudence, shouted over the public address system, "This ship is on fire!" Amazingly, everyone remained calm. Since no instructions about abandoning ship followed, Ford decided to take matters into his own hands and calmly slid down a rope ladder to the destroyer, which was now next to the transport. In the process, he lost everything—his Mass kit, his personal papers, and all of his clothing. "All I had was what I had on and a few toilet articles in my hand," he said later. Once safely aboard the destroyer, he looked back sadly on the "black burning mass" that had brought him so close to the shores of Morocco. "It made me heartsick to see that magnificent ship," which only a few days before had won a terrible battle with "an angry sea," now swallowed up unmercifully by the same ocean. He felt fortunate that the Atlantic had not swallowed him up also.[5]

On all the transports, men stood in line for hours at a time to go to confession, despite the constant listing of their ships as the ocean tossed them first one way, then another. Nor could the bitter cold keep them from attending Mass when it was held on the open deck. (Few transports had large rooms that were free long enough for Mass to be offered out of the wind and cold.)[6]

The plan of the invasion called for the American troops to land on the Atlantic beaches of the northwestern coast of Morocco, near the cities of Fedala, Safi, and Mehedia. The British would stage a later incursion near Oran and the city of Algiers further east in Algeria. The primary goal was to capture Casablanca, and after its fall and those of the cities in Algeria, Allied leaders expected that the final drive of the North African war would begin. A large British force and a smaller American one would plunge eastward from Algiers into Tunisia to seize Bizerte and Tunis, arriving there before the Germans could reach them.

In the early morning hours of November 8, 1942, as the troops clambered down the sides of the ships, chaplains stood next to the rails to shake their hands just before they hoisted their heavy packs, then shouted their blessings after them. They must have wondered how many of their youthful charges they would ever see again. At 5:15 A.M., the first line of landing craft hit the beaches, and the battle for North Africa, the first of a long series of massive struggles with the Axis powers, had begun. Despite the rough seas and a series of accidents, the Americans succeeded in landing 3,500 troops in the first hour of the assault. By sunrise, they had taken most of their principal objectives and had a large swath of the Moroccan coast well under control.

Death came to many Americans on the beaches of Morocco that morning, among them a much-admired Catholic chaplain from the Middle West, Clement Falter. Two months earlier, as his unit was leaving its camp in the United States to head for a port of embarkation on the East Coast, he had stood next to the troop train as it boarded the young men of the 7th Infantry Regiment. As each soldier entered the train, he received a "bear hug" from the priest, who then walked among the crowd standing alongside the train trying to meet as many parents of the soldiers as he could. By common account, he was an unusually gregarious man who asked nothing of life except a chance to care for the men entrusted to him.

On the day of the invasion, at exactly 6 A.M., Falter and his soldiers climbed into their landing craft as it bounced up and down next to the troopship, then hung on tight as it plowed through heavy seas toward the shore less than a mile away. Just as the vessel approached the halfway point between the troopship and the shore, an enemy fort behind the beach unleashed a crushing bombardment on the American assault forces. Low-flying German bombers added to the chaos, greatly delaying the landing of the first waves of infantry. The closer Falter's boat came to the land, the heavier the fort's artillery seemed to grow.

At 8 A.M., an enemy shell landed on top of Falter and a small band of men running up the beach alongside him. A sergeant standing nearby saw Falter and several others fall to the ground, and he could see that enemy fire had hit the chaplain across the head and face, snuffing out his life at once. His death came as no great surprise to the other men who had run up the beach toward the same artillery post. One said that when he landed, he knew that the enemy's gunners "had a line" on him because they seemed to see his every move.[7]

A Protestant chaplain, Charles B. Brown of San Antonio, Texas, carried the priest's body to a collecting spot on the beach, and a few hours later Brown and several other chaplains risked their own lives to bury Falter in a temporary cemetery. While digging a trench for his remains, a squadron of German bombers began smashing up the beach where the burial party was working, and Brown wondered if perhaps he were digging his own grave as well. Fortunately none of the bombs scored a direct hit on the cemetery, though Brown said later that they had come close enough to cause him to think far more seriously about the next life than the present one.

A few days later, burial parties moved Falter's body to a permanent American cemetery at the foot of the fort that earlier had taken his life. The ranking Catholic chaplain for North Africa celebrated a Requiem Mass for him, after which both Catholic and Protestant chaplains joined in blessing his grave. A generous man who had made as many friends among Protestants as among his fellow Catholics, it seemed somehow appropriate that in death, just as in life, he had joined Catholics and Protestants together. When the army later awarded Falter the Purple Heart, his most voluble supporters, the soldiers of the regiment, enthusiastically seconded the bestowing of the medal. "If any man ever deserved it, he did," said a sergeant who had been the last person to speak to him. "It will be a long time before I shall forget him. He meant much to us Catholic boys, and also to the non-Catholic boys in the battalion."[8]

As the invasion of North Africa progressed, the American lines drove steadily forward, despite heavy machine-gun and artillery fire. A chaplain from San Francisco recalled both the sight of the wounded men he had to prepare for death and the men he had to carry to the nearest aid station. During the fighting on that first day, he had his initial encounter with a problem that would bring him his greatest moments of frustration: the need to be everywhere at once, "in forced marches, in darkness, in open spots, in hiding, waiting, moving." No matter how hard he tried, he never seemed able to reach all of the men who called for his help.[9]

In the first two months after the landings, British and American columns raced across the desert, seizing Morocco, then Algeria, and finally—two weeks before Christmas—reaching the western edge of Tunisia where the bulk of the German and Italian troops had gathered behind formidable defensive lines. The Allies planned first to push the enemy forces into the Tunisian peninsula, jutting north out of the continent into the Mediterranean, and then force them up its length until finally, with no more land left for further retreat, they would have to surrender. Unfortunately, hardly anything worked out as the Allied leaders had envisaged.

As the American and British troops moved slowly toward the eastern sector of Tunisia, they encountered stiffening resistance, which led inevitably to mounting casualties. The wounded men streamed slowly back from the front, their injuries giving bitter evidence of the intensity of the fighting. A priest riding a train across North Africa later recalled that as he and his battalion waited on a railroad siding one day for a train with American wounded to pass by, the men had been joking happily, telling bawdy stories, playing poker, and arm wrestling with each other. All at once, as the hospital train started rolling by, the smiles vanished and the kidding stopped as the men gawked open-mouthed at the maimed and twisted bodies they could see lying on cots inside. The vast ugliness of war had suddenly thrust itself upon them: "Sightless eyes stared emptily into ours, burned faces and bodies wrapped in smelly yellow bandages"—they could see it all. "No one spoke. . . . No one trusted himself to speak." Finally the train passed into the desert, and an eerie silence fell over the men as they watched it shrink into the distance. The chaplain, Louis B. Kines, would himself suffer injury two months later, though unlike many of the men on the train that had just passed by, he would survive.[10]

The horrors of combat were the worst, but bureaucratic meddling and nit-picking sometimes harassed the hard-pressed chaplains as well. No sooner had John Wise and his battalion survived a furious armored attack by the Germans than he received an urgent communication passed down from division head-quarters. The purpose of the emergency missive? The Office of the Chief of Chaplains in Washington wanted to know if he had yet made his annual retreat! As Wise commented to a friend: "I had to smile a little. Gosh, it's been a solid month of retreat days—and nights, too. I never prayed so much in my life. . . . Did I make my retreat days! The best ever."[11]

Christmas would bring a brief respite from the growing horrors of the North African campaign to some of the discouraged Americans fighting in it, and to some of them, it would seem almost an act of Divine Providence, a gift from the heavens, that this first Christmas for the Americans in Europe should take place in a desert environment. All the chaplains noted the similarities between their circumstances and those of the Holy Family in the first Christmas in Bethlehem: stark poverty everywhere, an arid setting not unlike ancient Israel itself, and even a few groups of Arabs and camels present in the area to add an authentic touch to the scene.

A priest from California assigned to a field hospital set up camp on Christmas Eve in the middle of the gentle, rolling hills outside Casablanca. Ironically, there had been no room for them in the city's inns, and since no one had thought to throw their sleeping bags off the troopship, they slept on bales of hay that the army had given them. When Christmas Day came, the priest

An unidentified marine chaplain offers Mass on Christmas Eve on Bougainville in the Solomon Islands on the edge of a cemetery filled with marines killed in recent fighting. (Source: U.S. Marine Corps)

conducted an impromptu Christmas Mass, making it as celebratory as the straitened circumstances would allow. He placed four bales of straw on top of each other for an altar and invited his men to kneel around him for a Mass commemorating the birth of Christ. Quite by chance, a dozen Arabs came by during the liturgy and sat on the edge of the group, adding what seemed to him the perfect, natural touch to a Christmas Day liturgy in war-ravaged Morocco.[12]

For another chaplain in North Africa, however, Christmas brought, not the joy of the season, but the grief of capture by the enemy. The first Catholic chaplain that the Germans would seize in the European war, Stanley C. Brach, began two and a half years of imprisonment that day after a German panzer (armored) division ambushed his unit near the city of Mateur in northern Tunisia. Like so many of the other American chaplains taken by the Germans during the war, he simply had the misfortune to be in the wrong place at the wrong time, as he helped evacuate a group of badly wounded soldiers. His captors treated him well enough at the start, but in subsequent days, imprisonment at the hands of the enemy would prove an ordeal almost beyond his powers of endurance. After several weeks of moving from camp to camp, the Germans finally transferred him to a prisoner of war installation in Poland, where he would remain until the Russians liberated the camp near the end of the war. Stanley Brach, too, had experienced an unforgettable Christmas.[13]

As the African campaign progressed, it became increasingly clear not only that the American troops were fighting in a chaotic manner but that they were severely hampered by poor leadership, and Rommel decided to take immediate advantage of their weakness. In late January 1943, he began plotting a dashing maneuver that, if successful, might well have sent the hapless Americans reeling back across the desert all the way to Algeria and perhaps even Morocco. Thus ensued the battle of the Kasserine Pass, a most inglorious chapter in American military history.

A sweet indifference had taken over at Kasserine Pass where the 34th Infantry Division stood guard. American intelligence had repeatedly ignored signs of a German buildup a few miles away. Like everyone else in the American lines, the chaplains saw no reason to listen to reports of a German rout of the French at nearby Faid Pass or even of American losses at Fondouk Pass only sixty miles away. One priest from Rochester had nothing more serious on his mind than the wretched quality of the alcohol the army was issuing its officers. "Sigh!" William O'Brien wrote to his family. "I guess we won't get another shot of White Horse [until] the war is over." He bemoaned the hopelessness of his situation: "There is lots of wine, but we are not getting the good wine." Worst of all, "the cognac is pretty well gone too." And Chaplain Edward Farley, who had earlier protested bitterly about the lack of high-quality American cigarettes available on the troopship to Morocco, found the tobacco situation little improved in Tunisia. "American cigarettes just about ain't [around]," he lamented one day. It seems that he had bought three cartons of "Marvels" in Cairo at a price that was far more than he could easily afford. Lest others misinterpret him, however, he insisted that he was not "complaining." His cigarettes would arrive eventually, he firmly believed, and then "we will have luxury again."[14]

Despite their preoccupations with the comforts of life, both men would later rise to the occasion when the Germans counterattacked in force in the middle of February. William O'Brien would distinguish himself by his selfless assistance to the victims of the battle. The maimed, the shell-shocked, and the dying would all find in him an unfailing source of support. He would continue his remarkable work during the remaining years of the war as he accompanied his men through the clearance of the Germans from North Africa, the mountains of Sicily, then finally the length of the Italian peninsula. Edward Farley would prove fully as courageous in bringing comfort to his own men during the Kasserine disaster and in the trying weeks that followed. One best explains their behavior on the eve of the battle not so much as laziness or self-indulgence but as a reflection of the listless spirit of all the American forces in the area. Like the other Americans serving in North Africa, the chaplains, too, had somehow come to the fantastic conclusion that winter was a time to enjoy oneself in the desert; serious fighting would wait, surely, for the coming of spring. They all would pay bitterly for their lack of alertness.

At 6:30 A.M. on February 14, 1943, German infantry and armor suddenly crashed into the town of Sidi bou Zid where the center of the American line was located. Racing columns of tanks carried the brunt of the charge, throwing the Americans' forward lines into chaos. Somehow the Americans managed to regroup, then mount a small counteroffensive the next day, but although they inflicted heavy damage to the German tanks and 88-millimeter guns, they lost still more tanks. The weakness of the American counterattack surprised the Germans, since they had expected a far more vigorous response from the enemy, whose numbers were much greater than their own. Knowing now how truly feeble the enemy was, the Germans decided to launch an all-out assault immediately.

Late afternoon of February 20 marked the high point of Rommel's Kasserine Pass campaign. At 4:30, surveying the battlefield with his binoculars from a nearby mountaintop, he could see his 10th Panzer Division take the pass, then sweep across the basin lying on the other side, where his tanks encountered little resistance. Although the west now lay open, Rommel wisely stopped where he was, because his intelligence had told him that the British and Americans were bringing up heavy reinforcements. He knew that despite his recent success, he lacked the resources that would be necessary to break the Anglo-American-French defenses. The Afrika Korps had passed its zenith, but Rommel had succeeded in driving the Allies back fifty-five miles, setting them back for months.[15]

Most chaplains responded well to the German challenge as it rolled across the plains, though the army thought fit to decorate only one of their number. Chaplain Orville Lorenz, a Protestant, received the Silver Star for rescuing wounded men while surrounded on every side by enemy fire. During one heavy German artillery attack, he heard a distant voice calling from a foxhole and could see that a soldier had been injured. Lorenz scrambled out of his own foxhole and began running in the direction of the injured man, clambering over huge piles of rocks and deep artillery craters. Twice, the concussion from artillery shells exploding nearby knocked him to the ground, but somehow he escaped injury. Finally he reached the wounded man, but a quick examination revealed that the soldier had suffered such massive injuries that he would probably die if Lorenz attempted to take him to the aid station. Without hesitation, he dashed back toward the American lines, again under enemy fire the whole way. He talked a doctor and several corpsmen into going back with him so they could carry the wounded soldier back, moving carefully to avoid further injury. Once they had returned with the man to the aid station, Lorenz stood by and comforted him as medics tried to save his life. His fate remains unknown. Lorenz's remarkable courage, however, is a matter of record.[16]

Only one chaplain fell wounded in the campaign, a Jesuit from Maryland named L. Berkeley Kines. The embarrassing location of his wound would occasion amusement among his fellow chaplains for years to come. After the war, Kines himself would relate the story of his injury, usually with a rueful smile on his face. It seems that during the struggle for the Kasserine Pass, he was crawling across a field covered by heavy enemy fire. Kines hugged the ground as close as he possibly could, but the stream of bullets whizzed closer and closer. Finally his luck ran out; a German sniper spotted a rumplike object creeping stealthily across the ground and hit it square in the middle. A priest-friend described the incident in verse:

> Poor Berk fell hard and wounded alas—
> For he got shot in the Kasserine Pass.

Or, as Kines himself put it:

> I got shot in the ass
> In Kasserine Pass.

Although his frolicsome ditty would cause many a snicker later, his experiences in the war brought him to a state of exhaustion, the result of enervating fevers and an eye infection. His combined illnesses would leave a heavy mark, and only the best of medical care and the passage of time would heal him completely.[17]

After the Kasserine catastrophe, the Americans had to take careful stock of themselves. Their inexperience, lack of proper training, and muddled leadership had cost them dearly, and their heavy casualties caused amazement both in army circles and at home. Neither the British nor the Americans could suffer such heavy losses and expect to beat the Axis powers in North Africa. Not surprisingly, the American forces in Europe underwent a major rebuilding, and the result was a far more effective fighting force. The improvement in the performance of the Americans soon brought the Allied campaign to a major turning point: A historic linkup occurred on April 7, 1943, when English and American forces met near the coastal town of Sfax, 150 miles south of the city of Tunis.[18]

Two days later, Archbishop Francis Spellman, the American Catholic church's Military Ordinary (the bishop who acted as liaison between the church and the military chaplaincy) arrived in Sfax. He had been touring American army camps in North Africa, having previously visited military installations in Alaska, the Aleutians, and the United States. He spent most of his day in Sfax with a bomber group, speaking to the men, offering Mass, and writing down the names of the men who wanted him to write to their families when he returned to New York City. At the end of a hectic day, he sat down with the local Catholic chaplains to a dinner of tea and Spam. It was the archbishop's first experience with GI rations. Ever the diplomat, he refrained from either praising or criticizing the food that the troops ate daily.[19]

While Spellman was at the front, the Americans continued to make headway against the Axis forces, which had been squeezed into an ever-shrinking perimeter at the head of the Tunisian peninsula. On May 7, 1943, the Americans seized Bizerte, and an Anglo-French force took Tunis, the two principal port cities in northern Tunisia. Since the two harbors provided the only means of escape for the beleaguered Germans and Italians, their fate was sealed. The Germans refused, however, to yield the two cities without a spirited battle. Bizerte was especially hard hit by the fighting, as the combination of heavy Allied bombing and the determination of the Germans to leave a leveled city behind them reduced the once-beautiful coastal city to a smoldering pile of wreckage. "Bizerte is a shambles," said a chaplain who rode with the first tank column to enter the city. "Nearly every building hit, roofs fallen in, rubble, debris. A handful of civilians left." When the Americans found snipers shooting at them, "they didn't bother to send infantry in—they just shelled it."[20]

On May 12, all Axis resistance ended, and Col. Gen. Jürgen von Arnim, the commander in charge of Axis operations in the area, formally accepted the Allies' terms of unconditional surrender. Some 275,000 troops surrendered to the Allies, making this one of the greatest disasters in German military history.[21]

With the fall of the Axis forces in Africa, some chaplains found themselves in bizarre and unexpected situations. Edward R. Martin of New York City happened to be present at American headquarters for the capitulation of Maj. Gen. Willibald Borowietz, commander of the 15th Panzer Division. Martin had just finished morning Mass when Borowietz and his aides arrived at the command post. They clicked their heels impressively, then smartly saluted the American commander, Maj. Gen. Omar Bradley. Bradley needed an interpreter and, knowing that Martin was fluent in French, Spanish, and German, ordered Martin to translate as he dictated the terms of the capitulation. When the brief ceremony ended, Martin told Borowietz and his three aides that the Russians were now chasing the fleeing Germans on all three of the fronts in Russia. The news stunned them, because the German High Command had kept them completely ignorant of the growing debacle in the east.[22]

The brief period of rest that followed the seizure of North Africa proved both a blessing and a curse for the army's chaplains, because it brought a return of the usual vices that afflict armies with too little to do. Not only did prostitution thrive around the camps, but even Arab women who refused to engage in prostitution sometimes fell victim to the Allied soldiers. One priest, assigned to an army air force squadron, complained that his airmen were teaching filthy English to the local women. He described, for instance, a stunning young belly dancer who had just become one of his converts. When the chaplain asked the new Christian one day if she would like to see him at 10 o'clock the following morning for her next instruction in religion, she replied, "Yes, Chaplain, goddam right I'll come!" That was too much, even for so seasoned and experienced a shepherd of souls as Chaplain Alfred Schneider of Green Bay, Wisconsin.[23]

American participation in the desert war in North Africa had lasted only seven months, yet a revolution had taken place in the American military during that time. It had evolved from an inexperienced army into a highly mobile and well-organized one that was capable of taking on the most difficult assignments and giving an admirable account of itself. At last prepared to do battle with the Nazis on their own terms, the question now was, where would the Americans strike next? It quickly became apparent to everyone, even Adolf Hitler himself, that Sicily would be the next Allied target. Even though most of the Afrika Korps had been removed from participation in further battles, no one expected the campaign to be an easy one. An island of rugged mountains and few valleys, Sicily would tax the resources of the Allies to the limit.

The prospect of more war weighed heavily on the minds of the Catholic priests serving the Americans, and one of them expressed the fears of all. "We all hope that this awful war will be over soon. At times we think it will soon be over. But when I look at the map of Europe I have different thoughts." The fall of Berlin looked many campaigns away. The chaplains would not enter the fray without hope, however. As always, they clung to the belief that the God who had walked with them in North Africa would do the same in Sicily.[24]

The U.S. Army, at least, would enter the fray considerably stronger than before, thanks to the bloodying of its troops and a corps of remarkably skilled leaders, above all the vaunted George Smith Patton, Jr., who now provided the dashing sort of leadership that the Americans had earlier so conspicuously lacked. Despite their enormous resources and new leaders, however, the Allies expected no easy campaign, believing that the combination of mountainous terrain and battle-tested German troops would make the operation a difficult and prolonged one. Their prebattle assessment proved correct: The fighting in Sicily lasted almost five weeks and resulted in a high number of casualties.

On the night of Friday, July 9, 1943, an enormous attack fleet bore down on the beaches of southern and eastern Sicily. It carried the largest number of men ever landed in an amphibious operation anywhere in the war in a single day. In terms of sheer magnitude, it dwarfed even the Normandy invasion fleet, which set sail from England just eleven months later.

At the heart of the convoy were twenty-eight combat transports, each crammed with British and American soldiers primed for battle. The immense, complex invasion plan called for 150,000 men to land on the first day and 150,000 more on the next two days. Eventually a total force of 478,000 troops would set foot on the island. With Eisenhower in charge of the operation, the British Eighth Army would attempt to take forty miles of beaches on the eastern side of Sicily, and the Americans would sweep ashore on the southern coast. Eisenhower put Patton in command of American forces in the field, a skillful move that would greatly accelerate the campaign.

The Germans had 30,000 soldiers stationed on Sicily and a much larger force of almost 200,000 in Italy. The two groups would give continued anxiety to both American and British leaders. German strength on the island would almost certainly grow as the campaign progressed, bringing with it the nightmarish possibility of a bloody and protracted struggle against Hitler's formidable veterans.[25]

In the early morning hours of July 10, an airborne force swept over the island, preceding the invasion troops who would assault the beaches several hours later. Despite rough weather, high winds, and the loss of many paratroopers in the sea, the American and British jumpers managed to seize a number of key bridges and road junctions behind the beaches. Their success would soon prove vital. Four chaplains, two of them Catholic, landed in Sicily with the American paratroopers. One of them, a Franciscan named Edwin Kozak, held the honor of being the first Catholic priest in the army to qualify as a paratrooper. In the predawn hours of the invasion, he added to his distinctions by earning the Bronze Star for his work with the wounded men of his battalion who landed that night. His fellow priest-paratrooper, Matthew S. Connelly, had entered the service from a Benedictine monastery in Colorado, and it was said of him that he had taken to jumping from airplanes like a monk to prayer.[26]

At daylight, infantrymen swept onto the beaches in the British and American sectors, arriving in wave after inexorable wave. Chaplain Joseph Barry of the University of Notre Dame had to swim for his life through the lashing surf, floundering under a heavy backpack the whole distance from his landing craft (which had tipped over) to the shore. "I always wanted to swim in the Mediterranean," he told his superior, but he didn't exactly relish the idea of being "dumped in, bag and baggage." He also brought his love of Notre Dame football along with him, describing the Seventh Army's landing in terms reminiscent of the Fighting Irish against Michigan State: "First we'd hit center, then smash the tackle and now and then we'd make an end run." After the opening game against Sicily, Barry accompanied his regiment to Italy, where it would continue to make "end runs" and "off-tackle smashes" as it fought its way up the Italian peninsula, into France, then finally into Germany. The men of his regiment would have to survive twenty-three major battles before the war ended.[27]

On that same invasion day, another Catholic priest received special praise for the risks he took to assist the wounded and to bury the men already lost in the invasion. While digging a grave in a makeshift cemetery for a soldier who had perished only a few hours before, navy chaplain Francis J. Keenan nearly became a casualty himself. As he scooped out a hole, German planes and artillery began attacking the cemetery. Enemy shrapnel lacerated his arms and legs, but he continued digging, much to the consternation of troops working nearby who urged him to flee and get medical aid for himself. Instead, he finished excavating the trench and calmly read the burial service over the man's grave before walking to a launch that took him to a troopship standing just off the shore. Once aboard, he continued to refuse medical attention until the doctors had taken care of all the men he thought more seriously injured than he. The navy honored him with a Purple Heart, the Silver Star, and the Legion of Merit.[28]

As the American Seventh Army advanced beyond the beaches into the hills and mountains, Patton drove his forces furiously toward Palermo, a city of critical importance because of its magnificent harbor. From there, he hoped to stage a quick dash to the greatest prize of all in Sicily, the fabled city of Messina. In a brilliantly executed series of maneuvers, his three divisions covered 100 miles of mountainous territory in just four days, and on the eve of July 22, 1943, Patton formally accepted the surrender of Palermo—and became America's newest war hero.

A tragic death in the Chaplain Corps marred the fall of the city, however. Just two days before the Americans seized it, one of the Seventh Army's most loved and widely respected priests perished in the village of Castrofilippo, fifty-five miles south of Palermo. On the morning of Sunday, July 18, James P. Flynn of the 30th Infantry Regiment celebrated Mass for the officers and men of his battalion, using the town's small church, and then spent the rest of the morning discussing the progress of the campaign and addressing the needs of the GIs who dropped by to see him. He knew them well, for he had been with them since the invasion of North Africa eight months earlier and had accompanied them on the long march from Morocco to Tunis. By now, he understood them as well as he had known his former congregation in Crookston, Minnesota.

At noontime he stopped work, joined an army dentist and an officer friend, and headed for the home of the local chief of police, who had invited them to lunch. On the way to the house, they passed a drunken soldier standing next to a well, shouting crazily at the passersby and making a general nuisance of himself. Hoping to prevent him from hurting someone, Flynn's officer-friend took the man's pistol away from him. The three then continued walking down the street. Unknown to them, the soldier went back to his tent, picked up his M-1 rifle, and began hunting for Flynn and his two companions. When he found them at the chief's house, he smashed down the front door and charged into the room, blazing away at the group with his rifle. Flynn ran toward a back door, but two shots struck him in the back, slamming him to the floor. The officer who had earlier disarmed the soldier shot him on the spot with his own pistol, killing him instantly. Flynn breathed his last a few minutes later, surrounded by army medics and the local parish priest, who had run at top speed to the house as soon as he had heard of the shooting.[29]

News of his tragic passing shocked everyone in the regiment, and Flynn's commanding officer reported that his loss would be "deeply felt" for a long time to come. A colleague in the army chaplaincy, Denis Moore of San Francisco, said simply, "He was one of my best friends." Why the outpouring of grief over his death? The men in the regiment reported that no one had equaled him in kindness, dedication to their needs, or determination to be the best Catholic priest and army chaplain that he could be. While in North Africa, he had ministered diligently to his regiment during the harrowing days of the landing on the Moroccan beaches and as it fought its way through Algeria to the tip of the Tunisian peninsula.[30]

One day, near the end of the campaign, as he faced the coming invasion of Sicily, he wrote a friend that he had already decided where he would want to be located when the assault forces began touching down on the island: He would use all of his influence to make sure that he was in the "advance wave." He knew full well that his chances of death or injury were greatest in the first line of landing craft, but that, he believed, was where he belonged. "If I get clipped while helping someone else—well that's just fine, for I can't imagine any better stepping stone . . . from this life than just that."[31]

Shortly before the invasion, he shared with his parents in Crookston his reflections on the war, the men in the army, and the meaning of the priesthood in his life. His letter stands out not only as a credit to Flynn, but also as a moving tribute to all of America's men of the cloth who followed their destiny overseas into the no-man's land of combat.

> If losing my life should happen to be the price I pay for the position I hold—then it's certainly a cheap price—for after all I'm probably better prepared to meet God as my Judge now than I ever have been and if death must come—then far better for it to come when I'm shoulder to shoulder with these men who are fighting to preserve our country. I'd a lot rather have it come when I'm giving my absolution to dying men— than to have it come by a heart attack in my sleep or in an auto accident. I'd a lot rather have it happen when other men are going to know that in spite of being "scared as hell" like the rest of them, a Catholic Priest is still going ahead and doing his work . . . .
>
> Funny thing about this letter, if I'm alive two weeks from now—you won't receive it. In other words, if you get this letter, it will mean that Almighty God had decided I've been on earth long enough and He wants me to come up and take the examination for permanent service with Him. It's hard to write a letter like this—there are a million and one things I want to say, there are as many that I'll remember when it's no longer possible to write you . . . .
>
> It's a funny thing about this operation—but I don't really believe I'll come out alive. Call it an Irishman's hunch, or a presentiment or what-

ever you will. I believe it's Our Lord and His Blessed Mother giving me a tip to get prepared. Naturally I'll go to Confession before we sail and get absolution. . . . Furthermore, in the event I get killed, you can have . . . [the] consolation of knowing that it was "in the line of duty" not only for my country but especially for the work of Almighty God.

I could write pages and never get said all I want to say—so, my darling mother and good dad—"au revoir" as the French say, and "adieu"—until we meet again with God. We'll never split up—for through our prayers we'll always be together and God willing, we'll be united at His throne some day. And why not—for that's the only reason He put us in the world after all. Good luck, God bless you—and don't cry, just pray, and God will see to it that everything works out for His honor and glory and your and my eternal welfare.[32]

Flynn survived the attack on the south coast of Sicily and nearly two weeks of fighting in the mountains, only to perish while accepting the hospitality of a grateful Sicilian host. What German bombs, artillery, tanks, and land mines had failed to do, a drunken American soldier accomplished in a single second. After a Requiem Mass, Flynn's chaplain friends interred him in Plot B, Row 3, Grave 34, of a temporary American cemetery near the city of Licata, thirty miles south of Castrofilippo. A few weeks later, his family in Crookston heard the news, grieved deeply, then doubtless went on with their lives as best they could, like every American family who lost a child in the war. No other record of Flynn survives, save in the memories of the friends in the 30th Infantry Regiment, the 3d Infantry Division, the Seventh American Army, whom he served with such unstinting devotion. Without question, he achieved his life-long desire: He had compiled a remarkable record both as an army chaplain and as a Catholic priest.[33]

With Palermo now in American hands, Patton lost no time in mounting a major drive to Messina. He pushed his divisions furiously, and in just twenty-six days of intense combat, they covered the 165 miles from Palermo to Messina. As the Seventh Army followed Patton into battle, its chaplains found themselves overwhelmed with work. Denis Moore saw the war in Sicily at its worst and nearly lost his life twice while attempting to rescue American wounded from German mine fields. The first time was in early August while his regiment was trying to cross the Furiano River under heavy artillery fire. He had heard that several injured American soldiers were trapped in a nearby ravine, and though warned that the area was heavily mined, he decided to attempt to reach them. Leading a crew of six litter bearers, he carefully pushed a mine detector ahead of him, but soon found that a carpet of shell fragments made the device useless. He spotted four mines straight ahead and told the men behind him to take another path. A moment later, an explosion behind him killed three of the litter bearers immediately and fatally wounded a fourth. The remaining two emerged unscratched. Uninjured himself, Moore summoned a pair of medics from a nearby hill and helped them evacuate his comrades. He was heartbroken. He had lived with these men since the invasion of North Africa, and he felt like they were his own sons.

Just four days later, in a vicious contest for a German defensive redoubt called the San Fratello Line the same events repeated themselves. In an almost exact replay of the earlier tragedy, Moore heard again that the bodies of several soldiers lay in an area filled with booby traps and mines. Just as before, he led a rescue party to the spot, the men following at what they believed was a safe distance. Near the edge of the field, Moore cautiously stepped over a series of vicious mines that the American and British soldiers called Bouncing Bettys (so called because when stepped on, they bounded several feet into the air and then exploded violently, unleashing a storm of metal fragments in every direction). He thought he had located all of them, but two of the men behind him accidentally stepped on one. The unthinkable had happened yet again, and Moore made no attempt to hide his horror of German mines: "I came too close to meeting my demise," he wrote a friend. "I was really shaken up. . . . You better keep those prayers in action. It must of been someone's good prayers that kept me from hitting a mine."[34]

Occasionally a chaplain would have an opportunity to help the war-stricken Sicilian peasants who suffered so grievously during the campaign. During one tense nighttime battle for the coastal city of Cefalu, Chaplain Anthony de Laura of Brooklyn left his tent to see if the local Catholic church had survived a recent enemy shelling. To his consternation, he found a group of American soldiers and Sicilian peasants huddled inside. Shocked by the German shelling, they had formed a tight body of humanity and were crowded together against the walls of the tiny chapel. De Laura went to work immediately, anointing the dying soldiers and civilians, assisting the wounded with first aid, and calming those who fell into a panic every time they heard German shells screaming overhead. When he had restored a semblance of order, he led the Catholics in the chapel in the recitation of the rosary. Eventually he had settled the group enough so he could even tell a few jokes, for which he had a considerable reputation in his regiment. He then regaled them with several of his celebrated imitations, of which the best-known were his characterizations of Benito

Mussolini, Josef Goebbels, and a certain egotistical American general whose dashing exploits in battle almost equaled his flamboyant descriptions of the same. One soldier said later, "He kept [us] all hoping and praying until relief arrived."[35]

On the evening of August 17, 1943, Patton triumphantly entered Messina. Standing in the back of a jeep, he graciously accepted the thunderous plaudits of the citizens of the city. Distracted by their success, the Allies failed to notice the withdrawal of the remainder of the German Army to Italy. By the time they realized what was happening, nearly 100,000 soldiers had evacuated the island from the northeastern corner and moved quietly across the water to ports in the southernmost part of Italy. The escape of three German divisions, two of them armored units, would mean a bloody and frustrating prolongation of the war in Italy.[36]

After a brief rest (too brief for the enlisted men, too long for the Allied strategists who worried about a possible German buildup in southern Italy), assault divisions began gathering in North Africa, Sicily, and the United States. Their chaplains would accompany them on the troopships heading for a landing in southern Italy, at the city of Salerno, on September 9. Many of the chaplains in the convoy had already served in North Africa and Sicily and longed for nothing so much as a quiet assignment back home. Like the men they served, however, they would follow their orders and go wherever their units went.

6

ITALY

They had become the men of the forgotten front.
—Chaplain Karl Wuest

"Mud, mountains, and mules"—thus did the American soldiers describe, in terms of unalloyed loathing, the Allied campaign for Italy. No one would ever put it better. The Italian campaign evolved into one of the most difficult and frustrating operations of World War II. It would force American and British troops to fight a winter war in the blizzards of the Apennines, against brilliantly constructed German defenses, and suffer casualties that would reach into the tens of thousands by the time they succeeded in routing the Germans out of Italy twenty-one months later.

Less than a month after the surrender of the Axis troops in Sicily, the Americans and the British launched two invasions of Italy, one at its southern end and the other one hundred miles north on the western side. The two assaults marked the beginning of one of the bloodiest phases of the war. Few places in the Mediterranean have so captured the heart of mankind as the ancient harbor of Salerno, the target of the combined Anglo-American thrust. The bay looked as exquisite as ever on that fateful morning in September 1943 when the American and British force swept up its broad, elegant beaches. None of the men on the ships, however, would have time to observe the beauty of the harbor or the villas of the city lying just in back of it. A new campaign was about to begin, and in less than two days, the 100,000 British and 70,000 American troops on the beaches would find themselves faced with the grim possibility that they might have to leave Salerno precisely the same way they had arrived—by sea.

The invasion began on September 9, 1943, with the landing craft pulling

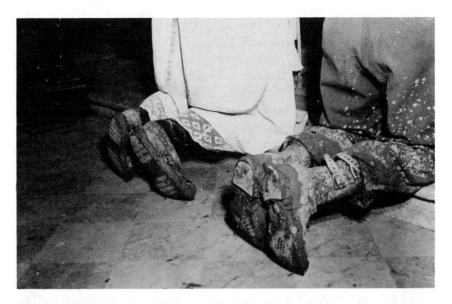

The mud-encrusted shoes belong to an unidentified chaplain kneeling at a Mass for the men of the Fifth Army in northern Italy in the winter of 1944. (Source: National Archives)

away from the transports at 3:30 A.M. The men in the light, pitching craft could see the coast of Italy just a few miles away. The crowded LCIs (Landing Craft, Infantry) and LSTs (Landing Ship, Tank) slowly plowed their way through the rising swells toward the line of departure, then executed a final, well-coordinated swing toward the mainland. Soon the first wave of infantrymen were jumping into the breakers and sloshing their way toward the shore. So far, so good: The water was shallow, the sea calm, and the enemy gave no sign of its presence. Suddenly, brilliant flares exploded, illuminating the night and casting an eerie glare over the men battling the crashing waves and running up the beaches. Mortar shells and machine-gun blasts raked the oncoming waves of infantrymen, and many fell. What had resembled only another practice landing had quickly turned into a death trap.[1]

The chaplains carried on as best they could in the face of enemy mortar and artillery fire exploding all around them. One incident illustrated the perils they faced from every side. A Catholic chaplain had just begun celebrating Mass for a small group when a German fighter plane swooped down and began strafing the little band. The famed wartime cartoonist Bill Mauldin saw the attack and watched in amazement as the priest dived into a muddy ditch, white vestments and all, the plane's tracer bullets missing his hurtling body by only a few feet. When the plane had disappeared, the chaplain returned to his liturgy "as if nothing had happened," Mauldin observed. The incident inspired one of Mauldin's better cartoons, showing a chaplain reading from his prayer book, his hand cupped to his ear. Suddenly he says to his men: "Forever, Amen. Hit the dirt!" Not religiously inclined himself, Mauldin nevertheless became an enthusiastic supporter of the army's chaplains: "I have a lot of respect for those chaplains who keep up the spirits of the combat guys. They often give the troops a pretty firm anchor to hang onto."[2]

Despite a few minor Allied successes on the first day, German artillery on the peaks of the mountains lying behind the harbor continued to fire with unnerving accuracy at the men crouching on the plains below, leaving no one in the Salerno perimeter feeling even remotely safe from attack. As fatalities mounted hourly, chaplains had to bury the dead under terrifying conditions, often while standing in the open without the slightest protection. On the second day, the Germans decided to attempt a knockout blow at the enemy squeezed onto the beaches below, hoping to throw the Americans and the British back into the sea. In the first few hours of the attack, Chaplain Francis J. Keenan anointed twenty soldiers, gave communion to the Catholics among them, and helped prepare all of them for evacuation to a hospital ship in the harbor. German fire grew ever more dangerous as he ministered to the men. He saw fighter planes strafing the sand dunes and low-flying bombers blasting foxholes and hastily constructed bunkers. Crouching low, he tried to reach as many dying men as he could.

Enemy fire finally hit Keenan himself. While he was burying a soldier, a German shell exploded only a few yards away, knocking him to the ground and nearly blinding him. For the rest of his life, he would suffer from profoundly impaired eyesight, but he would call his handicap his "badge of honor" because he had received it while serving on the blood-soaked beaches of Salerno. The navy granted him the Purple Heart, the Silver Star, and the Legion of Merit in recognition of his valor and his injury.[3]

The Allies succeeded in gradually enlarging their beachhead, but they still remained locked in a precarious position. Finally, on September 18, they broke out of their narrow perimeter. To their astonishment, they found that the Germans had quietly withdrawn during the night, moving quickly to set up another defensive line further to the north. With the establishment of the enemy's new defenses, the basic structure of the rest of the Italian campaign had been established. For the next twenty months, the Allies would have to assault one German line after another, with the enemy almost always holding the high ground or the opposite bank of the river. Only the names of the lines, the rivers, the peaks, and the valleys would change. The army's chaplains would accompany their units all the way, but only the strongest and most durable among them would survive until the end. Some weaker and older men would have to return home—the war in the mountains had been too much for them. A few would breathe their last in the embattled land of the ancient Romans. Italy would become a recipe for hell.

After a brief but bitter struggle for Naples, the British and Americans began preparing for the long drive on Rome. That task would take them nine months and would bring the hardest fighting of the peninsular war. The names of the battles read now like synonyms for Armageddon: Monte Cassino, Anzio, San Pietro, the Gustav Line, the Rapido River, and the Volturno River. The fighting took place in the most rugged European mountains south of the Alps and during the most severe winter in recent memory. The campaign also led to the destruction of some of the most ancient and honored structures in the Mediterranean world.[4] Given the length of the action and its ferocity, it was inevitable that chaplains, too, would suffer grievously in the fray. One priest had his left leg blown off, another died instantly when a 500-pound German bomb demolished his tent, a German shell tore the body of another to pieces, and a fourth perished from a massive heart attack brought on by weeks of exhaustion without rest. Dozens fell prey to frostbite, disease, and overwhelming fatigue. In terms of the number of Catholic chaplains killed or wounded, the nine-month march from Naples to Rome was the most costly anywhere in the war.

The Allied drive on the ancient Roman capital began early in the morning of Wednesday, October 13, with a quick thrust at the Volturno River, the scene of violent combat for the next ten days. The Germans had constructed a series of interlocking defenses that overlooked the most likely places for a crossing, and heavy rains, mud, and slippery roads all added to the hazards of the operation. The Americans finally achieved a permanent crossing only when their engineers succeeded in placing a strong but flexible bridge across the roiling Volturno. At the cost of more heavy losses, infantry squads beat off a series of furious German counterattacks. Drenching storms, meanwhile, had turned the Volturno battlefield into a water-logged purgatory. One Franciscan chaplain described the miseries of the fighting: "Our clothes never dried, our shoes were soggy, our beds were laid in the mud for we had no cots, the food was miserable. We had lived on C-ration hash ever since we had come to Italy, and now it became C-ration hash soup."[5]

Denis Moore, who had earlier seen combat in both North Africa and Sicily, found living conditions in Italy far more difficult than anything he had seen so far. More than once, he asked himself how anyone could "sleep restfully in a blanket and shelter halve [half]" covered with water. "I can now say with authority that it can't be done." Like every chaplain who suffered through the wintry struggle, he found that the farther his division advanced up the mountains, the worse the mud and the rain became, until it seemed that all the world consisted of a gooey, flowing muck from which he had no possible escape.

The worst cannonades seemed to come after dark. The Germans would try to keep the Americans awake all night, hoping to make them so disoriented and demoralized that they would find it impossible to fight the next day. Although deeply unnerving, the attacks nonetheless had what many chaplains thought a salutary effect: They literally "scared the hell out of the men." The hell got scared out of not a few chaplains, also. Joseph Barry, stationed near the mountain village of Sesto Campano, found to his consternation that "every night on this battle-front is a constant reminder of Death." On the previous evening, the Germans had shelled the town from midnight until three in the morning. "Each shell came a little closer and . . . each prayer became a little more fervent. When you are crouched against a thick wall while the air splits and the earth quakes there is one and only one thing to do: Pray boys, pray," he wrote a friend at home.[6]

For the chaplains in the Seventh Army, the campaign meant the carrying out of one task above all, the care of the dead. At night they crept into battle-fields, climbed up mountain ravines, and clambered down steep hillsides looking for the victims of the previous day's fighting. The Italian campaign was leaving a growing mass of shattered bodies in its wake. Karl Wuest found that though he spent months serving on what the army called its "graves registration detail," he never got used to the work. "With each succeeding burial service, instead of becoming accustomed to it, I shrank from it with greater dread." What bothered him most was not so much the burying of so many American men, as their tragically youthful age. Some had become, in all too short a time, among the best friends he had ever made. Now they had disappeared from his life, their breath stifled in a split second by an enemy mortar shell or a sniper's bullet.[7]

His first day of work in a gray, desolate, army cemetery left a memory that would haunt him for the remaining days of his life. The first truck rolled in, its pile of bodies stacked "like cordwood." Most had lain on the battlefield for a week or more, since constant enemy shelling had made it impossible to reach them, and some had already started to putrefy, giving out a sweet, nauseating odor that sickened him. The truck's crew put the men's remains gently on the ground, laying them out in long, neat rows. What to do when they had found only parts of bodies to collect? The army had a procedure. The crew piled the "odd legs and arms" next to bodies "lacking their own extremities."

Wuest's first task was to locate the personal effects of each man and set them aside so he could mail them later to the next of kin. Then he and his assistants fingerprinted each body, a grisly job that the fierce cold made all the more demanding. The fingers of many of the bodies had frozen solid, making it exceedingly difficult to retrieve a usable fingerprint from them. Often he had to soak a finger in warm water, then massage it until some semblance of warmth returned. It was a grim, dismaying task that often left him in a profoundly distressed state.

Finally the burial crews began preparing the remains for interment. They first wrapped each corpse inside a large mattress sack, tying it securely at each end. "As I watched, it seemed as if a part of my heart disappeared with the covering of each body," he recalled years later. After he had blessed each body, the crew carried it to its final resting place just a few yards away. Before they could lower the bodies into the trenches, however, they had to bail out the icy water that had collected inside. When this had been done, Wuest read a brief service over each grave and the burial detail then threw a canvas covering over each so the rain would not fill it up again.

When Wuest had finished burying a group of men, he would hurry back to his cold, soaking tent to write letters to the families of the young men he had just interred. Sometimes he found himself unable to write, so overwhelmed was he by the enormity of the tragedy unfolding all around him. He would stare vacantly into space, thinking about what was happening and praying for the strength to repeat his duties all over again the next day. At times he could get nowhere with the letter writing, "for tears blurred my vision." The futility of mere words staggered him. "What could I say to compensate them for the loss of their loved ones in the inanity of war?" he asked himself repeatedly.[8]

In the campaign for the Volturno River, the most decorated of the war's chaplains reached the end of his work in Italy. Albert Hoffman, who had received several commendations after the earlier fighting in North Africa and Naples, suffered a wound that would bring his wartime career, and nearly his life, to an abrupt conclusion. Hoffman's unflinching devotion to the injured men on both sides of the line ended on November 4, 1943, when he stepped on a German land mine, a device he believed was the most terrifying menace he faced in combat because he could hardly ever see them or feel them at

Army Chaplain Albert J. Hoffman of Dubuque, Iowa, was the most decorated chaplain of World War II. Serving in both the North African and Italian campaigns, he lost a leg during heavy fighting south of Rome, then worked in army hospitals helping other amputees learn how to use their artificial limbs. (Source: National Archives)

night, when he did most of his hunting for American and German casualties.[9] On this particular evening, while the men of the 133d Infantry Regiment were attempting to root the enemy out of the northern reaches of the Volturno valley, Hoffman noticed what looked like a German soldier lying in a wet field near the village of Santa Maria Olivetta. He had heard that the area, though covered with water and harmless looking, held many enemy mines. Aware of the danger, he waded slowly through the mud, moving carefully to avoid what he thought were telltale signs of hidden explosives. A group of medical personnel followed at what they hoped would be a safe distance.

An explosion ripped through the night sky, smashing Hoffman down and sending a piece of shrapnel searing across his face. Except for the cut on his brow, however, he remained unhurt and was able to pick himself up and continue walking gingerly across the swampy field. A few minutes later, a second mine went off. This one exploded directly underneath him and threw him backward into the swampy muck. Unfortunately for Hoffman, the device was the dreaded Bouncing Betty mine. Eventually he would lose his entire left leg above the knee; he was fortunate not to have lost his life.

"Stay where you are," the medics behind him shouted. "Don't move. You may set off another mine. We're coming for you."

"I'm all right," he shouted back. "Watch out for yourselves. There must be mines all around us."

A second later, a third one went off, blowing one doctor to pieces and leaving another in a heap on the ground. Back in Santa Maria Olivetta, the men of the company heard the roar from the three mines and, knowing that Hoffman and a medical team were working in the area, dashed toward the field. When he saw them coming, Hoffman shouted, "Stay back! You want to be killed? Get the [mine] sweepers in here. The whole terrain is mined." In the confusion of the moment, Hoffman seemed unable to discover which of his legs had suffered injury. "The funny thing is," he said, "I thought I had lost my right leg. I couldn't move it." Then he lifted his left leg and saw that its lower half had disappeared. "It had been cut off just below the knee. I picked it up and looked at it, and put it down again. It was only then [that] I saw I still had my right leg. I thought I was dying, all right—in fact, I was pretty sure of it." Still, he felt no pain, just "very weak. And tired." He lay on the field for nearly four hours before help finally arrived.

His next memory was of a bed in a clean, warm hospital room well to the rear of the Volturno battlefield. Suddenly a dismaying thought flashed through his mind. He had planned to "show the boys all through Rome" when they finally reached the city. He thought he would have done a good job of it, too, since he had studied theology there before the war. "I had been planning to show them Rome as only a native could show them. And there I was, flat on my back, with a lot of other amputees all around me."[10]

Told of Hoffman's injury, a Jesuit chaplain familiar with his work declared emphatically, "There will never be another like him." In the days following his injury, dozens of commendations about Hoffman came from the regiment's infantrymen and officers. Most believed that he was the most extraordinary soldier any of them had ever seen. All of them had known that if they ever suffered injury or died, he would somehow find them—and he would also bring them out. Praise came not only from the men at the front but also from the commander of the Fifth Army, Gen. Mark Wayne Clark. In a letter to Archbishop Spellman, Clark praised Hoffman for representing, in a truly exceptional manner, "the qualities that make a chaplain valuable to our Army." Clark noted that months before his regiment entered the war zone, Hoffman had studied "the art of the infantryman," so that he might be "better fitted to serve his men." In Hoffman's person, he said, one found "skill, courage, and understanding of the splendid possibilities of spiritual work among our troops." The sheer volume of work that "this exemplary priest" accomplished had made a major contribution to the American victory in the bloody Volturno River campaign. During Hoffman's stay in the Mediterranean, he won the Distinguished Service Cross, the Silver Star, the Bronze Star, the Purple Heart, and the Italian government's Medal of Valor, making him the most highly decorated American chaplain of World War II.[11]

Hoffman himself, however, took a skeptical view of his war medals. "In combat, no one stands out as doing anything heroic. Out there acts of heroism are commonplace. Probably the only reason that anyone gets a medal is that his deed happens to be noticed and reported." Most of the other chaplains who served in combat heartily agreed. They found that thousands of men committed untold acts of heroism, but most of their deeds went unrewarded because too few people had seen them occur. To the day of his death, Hoffman considered himself no hero at all, just a simple "infantryman's chaplain," as he often liked to put it.[12]

As grueling as the Volturno operation had proved to be, worse was yet to come. The most bitter fighting of the Italian campaign would come three months after the landing at Salerno, when combined British and American forces tried to smash through the Germans' formidable Gustav Line, thirty miles north of the Volturno valley. It would take five months for them to accomplish the task and would result in the largest number of casualties of the Italian campaign.

The fortifications that made up the Gustav Line were a triumph of German military engineering. Stretching across the whole peninsula, the linchpin was the fabled mountain mass called Monte Cassino. Its ridges bristled with some of the most awesome fortifications that the Allies would see in Europe. Its summit was also the site of one of the oldest and most revered monasteries in

Army Chaplain Stanley J. Kozlowsky stands in the mud and rain to hear the confessions of the Catholics in a tank-destroyer battalion during winter fighting along the Gustav Line. (Source: National Archives)

western Christendom, and its destruction at the climax of the operation began a controversy that has lasted to this day.

The Germans used their positions on the top of the peaks to excellent advantage, aiming their barrages with stunning accuracy at the Allied troops located in the valleys far below. Chaplain William O'Brien, assigned to a tank company, reported wearily that the Germans had been firing in his direction with such dismaying accuracy that he had the feeling they were looking right at his camp. He was right. They were. One day O'Brien learned from a soldier who had just returned from scouting the German lines that with their superb field glasses, "they could see ants."[13] The soldier exaggerated only slightly. With their unparalleled views of the terrain, the Germans could choose their targets with precision, waiting patiently for the proper moment to fire their long-range weapons. The result? In less than a month, Chaplain O'Brien buried 1,600 men in a nearby cemetery. The American situation along the Gustav Line would remain virtually the same for the rest of the winter.

Christmas brought no pause in the battle, but it was a reminder of better, earlier times at home. It also carried with it the promise of a redeemer who would someday lead the soldiers out of the sorry, ice-clad land in which they had become locked in endless combat. Chaplain Ernest Miller, assigned to a field hospital at the foot of a German-held peak, had the pleasure of offering his Christmas Eve Mass in an abandoned castle that his men had found earlier in the day. The building provided a warm, safe place for the liturgy that few Americans fighting along the Gustav Line would enjoy that evening. At midnight, the hospital's Catholic officers, soldiers, and army nurses packed themselves into the castle's little chapel. Although the celebration that followed bore little resemblance to a midnight Mass in a stately church, to the men and women who had gathered with Chaplain Miller it would have a richness and beauty all its own. Miller especially remembered a tiny field organ that "squealed and struggled" as the congregation sang. During the signing of "Silent Night," an incident occurred that he found both deeply heartbreaking and profoundly moving.

> The hymn came to an end. For a moment there was silence. In the midst of the silence there came a sob, heavy and unrestrained. No man moved. No man turned around to see. It was one of the nurses, undoubtedly one who had seen almost all that war had to offer, who knew the meaning of bodies torn beyond all recognition. [Soon] her pain moved on to those about her. Strong men bowed their heads, and tears streamed down their cheeks . . . they were close to home and to Him who makes home what it is.[14]

As winter in the Apennines deepened, William O'Brien found that the weather was fully as menacing an enemy as the Germans. "Raining, blowing and cold," he wrote in his diary one day. "Supper was bitter—biting wind and slashing rain. Feet freezing. I wondered if Italy could ever get warm and pretty again," he asked himself as he gazed in dismay at the sea of mud around his pup tent.[15]

Finally, the Italian campaign claimed its first priest-victim. Arthur Lenaghan of Fall River, Massachusetts, died only a few days after the New Year had begun. He had already seen combat in North Africa, where he had served with the 6th Infantry Regiment and had received the Legion of Merit for his heroic efforts to rescue wounded men during an intense series of clashes in Tunisia. Ever a gentle, quiet-spoken man, he seemed a most unlikely rescuer of casualties from the field of battle, but his retiring personality proved no obstacle as he scoured the battlefields of Morocco and Tunisia for the dead and the wounded. Now in the mountains of central Italy he did the same, sparing no effort to meet the needs of the men around him. Working with a medical battalion close to the Gustav Line's stoutest fortifications, he seemed never to stop working. The clock ceased to have any meaning for him, nor did danger or distance.

On January 6, 1944, the last day of his life (and only his fourth day of combat in Italy), Lenaghan seemed busier than ever. At the aid station at the base of Mount Porchia, he worked frantically all day, trying to keep up with the constant flow of wounded men. The Germans had stiffened their defense of the peak and were repulsing repeated, often heroic, attacks by the Americans. Litter bearers kept carrying in an unending stream of bloodied, mutilated men, but Lenaghan insisted on seeing each as soon as they arrived. When evening came, most of the corpsmen and litter carriers left the battlefield, since the hazards of night searches posed too high a risk. But Lenaghan, knowing that many more injured men lay waiting for rescue, volunteered to enter the area to pick up the remaining dead and wounded.

He walked slowly into the almost-invisible scene of the day's conflict. Then came a sudden flash of light, a wrenching explosion, and he collapsed on the ground, gravely wounded in the head. A German 88-millimeter artillery piece had seized another victim. He was taken first to the aid station he had just left, then to an evacuation hospital several miles to the rear. A chaplain-friend read the prayers for the dying over his quiet, deeply comatose body. An operation revealed massive damage to the frontal lobe of the brain, with no chance at all of recovery. On Friday, January 7, 1944, he departed the Chaplain Corps, his beloved 6th Infantry Regiment, and his friends in Fall River, Massachusetts, forever. Hardly anyone in his regiment would have disagreed with a colleague's final assessment of him: "He was beloved by the men. . . . He is going to be difficult to replace." Another chaplain, also from Fall River, agreed. On every possible occasion, he said, Lenaghan "had shown a profound sense of devotion to the men under his care which was not to be stopped no matter what the danger involved."[16]

As the winter campaign progressed, disaster seemed to follow disaster for the beleaguered Allies. Everywhere they struck, the American Fifth and the British Eighth armies suffered heavy casualties while gaining little ground. By the middle of January, they had progressed only seventy miles beyond Salerno and were still eighty miles from Rome. So many men had given their lives, and so little had been gained. Knowing that they had to make a decisive move of some kind, the Allied generals prepared an imaginative scenario to achieve a breakthrough. It would depend, however, on an adroit use of surprise tactics and a simultaneous launching of two new offensives, precisely the complicated kind of warfare in which the Allies had failed to distinguish themselves so far.

The plan called for an amphibious invasion of Anzio, thirty miles south of
Rome and sixty miles north of the Gustav Line, and a massive attack on the
Gustav defenses at Monte Cassino at the same time. Would the Allied forces,
at long last, be able to seize the moment? No one knew.

The scheme called for the bulk of Allied strength to make an all-out attack on
Monte Cassino. The mountain loomed like Gibraltar to the men in the valleys
below it, not only blocking their drive to Rome but menacing them with its
height and bulk. With an elevation of 1,700 feet, it dominated the plains below
and gave the Germans who held its flanks an excellent view of the Allies' camps
and trenches. Worse still, the massive monastery on top stood another 150 feet
high, had a width of 660 feet, and boasted walls nearly 10 feet thick. The Allies
had hoped that they would never have to scale the terrible peak or fight in the
vast precincts of the abbey, since it was not only the oldest Christian monastery
in the Western world but a much-treasured edifice as well. Unfortunately the
building (formally known as the Archabbey of Monte Cassino) overlooked the
best available pass through the Apennines, and gaining it would give the Allies
entry to the broad valleys beyond that led directly north to Rome. The mountain range had proved impregnable at every other place they had tried to pierce.
They would cross the range at Cassino or nowhere.

After almost a week of bloody fighting, with repeated hand-to-hand skirmishes, it became clear that the mountain would fall only after infantrymen
demonstrating remarkable courage had rooted out the enemy yard by yard. It
would be like the Volturno campaign all over again, only this time the stakes
were far higher, the defenses were much more formidable, and the eventual casualty lists would be far longer. As the Fifth Army approached the mountain,
the monastery seemed to loom ever higher and more menacing, and it had a
profoundly melancholy effect on the soldiers far below. Because it stood so
high and occupied so perfect a position for an artillery observation post, it was
easy for the men to convince themselves that the Germans had already entered
the abbey and were using it for that precise purpose.[17]

The monastery's sinister appearance had a profoundly disheartening effect
on chaplains, too. Karl Wuest gazed up at the abbey and concluded that "our
every act before it was exposed to the eyes of the enemy." To another, it resembled a "Cyclopean eye" relentlessly searching the valley below for ever
more victims. Whenever the Germans bombed his camp, he felt certain that
their "directing power came from the Monastery." Every day for the past
three months he had felt the ominous gaze of the abbey, and as the weeks
dragged by, he and his men had become ever more convinced that they were
dealing with some kind of "Frankenstein monster."[18]

Whether the Germans were making use of the building or not, the Allies knew they first had to take the mountain underneath it. The attack began on January 24, 1944. William O'Brien, serving with his tank battalion only a few miles south of the front lines, lay in his tent in the early morning hours when the sudden pounding of artillery awakened him. He looked through his tent flap at the northern sky and saw it flashing brilliantly with shell bursts. He thought to himself: "Out there boys on both sides are dying. . . . Poles who can't help themselves; Germans who all their lives have known nothing but trouble; Americans who have never known privation like this. Fighting and killing." He wondered how anyone could possibly survive such a hurricane of fire and steel. He wondered about his own survival.[19]

Several chaplains experienced frighteningly close calls with German shelling, leaving them shattered in spirit and asking themselves, too, why they were still alive. One priest from Ohio reported that only a few moments after he had left his tent a shell exploded some twenty feet away, reducing his tent to shreds. But even though the concussion had hurled him to the ground, he was otherwise unscratched. Had he stayed in his shelter a minute longer, he would have joined Arthur Lenaghan on the list of chaplains killed. Another time, a bomb hit the road no more than ten yards in front of his jeep. "The jeep received a flat tire and I a sore ear drum," he reported laconically. Reflecting on the two encounters, he could only say, "God has been with me."[20]

It became clear that progress on the mountain had been far too slow and at too great a price in lives lost. By mid-February, nearly everyone had come to the conclusion that the baleful-looking structure was the cause of all their woes. The Germans were in it—the Allies *knew* they were inside it and using it both for observation and for artillery. Eventually, even the priests in the Fifth Army came to the same conclusion. Although familiar with the abbey's ancient history and its role in the development of the Western world, they too came to see the structure as an ogre casting its gloomy eyes on the Allied troops located far below. No one liked the idea of blitzing one of religion's most fabled monuments, and probably all of the priests would have agreed with one chaplain who, when he saw it for the first time through his binoculars from far away on a dazzlingly clear December morning, exclaimed to himself, "It looked so beautiful."[21] But if the enemy had seized it—and everyone seemed quite certain that they had—then the choice seemed clear.

Thus it happened that the Archabbey of Monte Cassino was annihilated. Allied policy ruled out the destruction of religious, cultural, and historic monuments, but it did allow such actions if "military necessity" demanded it, and Allied military and political leaders decided that such action was necessary in this case. After the decision had been reached at the highest levels, planning for the destruction of the monastery began, and on Tuesday, February 16, 1944, 250 Allied bombers flew over the monastery and dropped almost 600 bombs, while American artillery in the valley below hurled 190,000 shells at both the abbey and the settlement of Monte Cassino at the base of the peak. At the end of the attack, the "Cyclopean eye" of Cassino had become a shrunken socket—dull, lifeless, unblinking. For the fourth time in human history, the abbey had fallen. For the first time ever, however, nothing remained. The Allies had succeeded where their less well-armed predecessors had failed: They had achieved the obliteration of the archabbey.

A Jesuit from Chicago took a fatalistic view of the bombing: "I watched the ancient Abbey go down in a heap of ruins. I suppose things will be knocked down from time [to time]." His belief that "terrible things have to be done in war, because that's what happens in war" was hardly unique. Unquestionably it represented the majority opinion among the Catholic chaplains serving in Italy, and one was positively enthusiastic about the blitzing. Cyprian Zeitz, a Franciscan who had also watched the building fall, reflected later that he felt a sense of profound "relief" that the Allies had finally razed the monastery. It had come as no surprise to him when he heard that the Germans had been using it, since he had long believed that both sides in the war used churches for war purposes. (Allied authorities vigorously denied any such practice.) He wondered whether it was "any more immoral to destroy a church than to destroy a house full of people." Nor did he think he had the right, as an ordained minister of his church, to assess the morality of the bombing. "I don't think I would be a fit judge to make a decision." Nor was anyone else a fit judge, either, in his view, and he would grow sharply critical of what he called "armchair theologians" back in the United States who condemned the attack when they were "not directly concerned with it," as he was.[22]

The bombing of the monastery, however, only served to intensify the struggle for the mountain, and the mauling the two sides continued to give each other wore down both chaplains and infantrymen. After fifty-nine straight days of battle at Cassino, without relief by another chaplain or even a day of rest, Denis Moore began to feel a depth of exhaustion that he had never experienced before. He had begun his career in combat by landing in North Africa with the invasion troops, and he had seen almost all of the fighting in Sicily. By the end of February, he had depleted all of his remaining reserves of strength, but he would have to continue because there was no one to take his place. Every night he would take mules into the battlefields and search for wounded and dying soldiers. When he found a man, he would drape him over a mule and continue his mournful trek. In addition to his nightly forays, he cared for the men of his company as if they were part of his own life. One GI said of him later that he was "a friend and buddy who always stayed up there with us."[23]

After 126 days of siege, Monte Cassino at last fell on May 18, 1944, to the valiant troops of the 2d Polish Corps, whose men had not forgotten the ruthless German subjugation of their homeland. The battle for Monte Cassino had ended, giving the Allies an incomparable moral and strategic victory, but the cost in lives lost on both sides was staggering.

As the Allied forces tried to crash through the German barrier at Cassino, the other part of the plan, the invasion of Anzio, stalled completely. The Americans and British had hoped that Anzio would act as a diversionary tactic, distracting the Germans from Monte Cassino and pulling some of their troops away from it. Unfortunately, it failed to do anything of the sort. The Germans quickly took the Alban Hills lying behind the city of Anzio and pinned down the Allied troops in their trenches, tunnels, and caves. With all movement severely limited, the troops in the perimeter (less than ten miles deep) literally had nowhere to go and no possible escape route except the Mediterranean itself. Such a departure, as at Salerno, would have meant a calamity almost beyond imagination.

Denis Moore, who would later endure the horrors of Cassino, made his fourth amphibious landing of the war at Anzio, and as he moved about the beaches in the days that followed, searching for casualties, he learned how to ignore the shells and bombs exploding nearby. Eventually, however, his luck ran out. One day, while walking to a medical post, a piece of flying shrapnel sliced across his skull, knocking him down. With blood pouring from his head, he reported to the station, rested briefly, and then returned to combat, soon receiving a Purple Heart for his gallantry. He was one of many chaplains, representing several denominations, who received decorations for their work in the first days of the campaign for Anzio.[24]

The battle turned into a full-scale siege, its grim, day-by-day sameness unchanging: nightly attacks by the Luftwaffe; men cowering in their trenches and caves, fearing instant death from the high explosives; a brief return to a semblance of normal life after the enemy bombers had completed their mission. By day, long-range German cannon and low-flying, strafing fighter planes replaced the high-flying bombers. The furious combat took an appalling toll of American troops. Chaplain Francis McCarthy received a call at 3 A.M. one foggy morning asking him to take communion to a group of new recruits stationed at the front lines. He took along twenty-two of the "hosts" (the Catholic word for communion wafer) and by sheer coincidence, found twenty-two Catholics in the dugout ready to receive the sacrament. He first heard each man's confession, then gave each communion. The next day, a German shell hit them directly, and he buried all twenty-two.[25]

Karl Wuest quickly learned what to expect in an air attack. First came brilliant flares from enemy planes, which lit up the beaches like the Great White Way (as Americans then called New York City's Broadway). Next came "the crunching whoomp of the bombs, the roar of planes, the spitting of anti-aircraft fire, deafening noises all." The sounds would repeat themselves in his mind years after he had left Anzio, giving him what he called his "ghastly nightmares." William O'Brien suffered a severe earache from three close-falling shells. It could have been far worse, however. Late one night, while he was away from his tent during an air raid, a piece of shrapnel tore a hole through sixty-four folds of his blanket. Had he chosen to stay in his tent, he, too, would have ended up on Anzio's casualty lists.[26]

A few of the more fortunate chaplains fared better during the siege. The three ranking clergymen at Anzio (a Protestant, a Catholic, and a Jew) found excellent accommodations for themselves in a wine cellar fifty feet underground in the city of Anzio. A typical evening in the chaplains' quarters would find the Catholic engaged in his newly acquired hobby of painting, the Protestant writing poetry, and the Jewish man playing casino or writing to his family. Even though the nature of their work demanded that they go above ground to observe the work of the chaplains under their authority, they still had their comfortable "apartment" fifty feet below to which they could retire.[27]

The fighting had one positive, if unintended effect: It helped bring uniformed chaplains of differing denominations closer together. Michael English, a Jesuit from Chicago, spoke often and warmly of his "good friend," Protestant Chaplain Joseph Walker. Despite his age (Walker was over forty at the time) and his continuing exhaustion, he managed to hold out through the worst of the fighting. English thought that forty was "not the ideal age at which to begin sleeping in mud puddles," and he wondered how his colleague managed to endure. An emotional climax for both men came when army authorities ordered Walker back to the United States to regain his strength. On his return to America, he went far out of his way to visit English's elderly and frail mother in Chicago. When he returned to Italy near the end of the campaign, English embraced him enthusiastically and welcomed him back to the regiment.[28]

Though sporadic flare-ups between Catholic and Protestant chaplains continued to break out, they seemed fewer in number and diminished in intensity. On one occasion, a Catholic chaplain received orders to hold services for a group of Jewish soldiers who had not seen a rabbi for a long time. Chaplain Raymond Copeland, a Jesuit from California, visited the men, but instead of giving them a full liturgy with scriptural readings, songs, prayers, and a sermon—all of which non-Jewish chaplains routinely provided when they took the place of a rabbi—he simply rounded them up, "gave them a talk" (his own words), and left. No great advocate of interfaith cooperation either during the war or after, he had carelessly thrown away an opportunity to bring much-needed consolation to men who could have perished the same day.[29]

After four months of stalemate, the Allies at last seemed ready to break out from the beaches of Anzio. On May 30, after the usual clamorous artillery bombardment, they aimed their tanks at the enemy and advanced past the old city of Anzio into the Alban Hills beyond. The Germans began falling back slowly, but they showed none of the signs of cracking that Allied infantrymen, frustrated after their long imprisonment on the beach, so devoutly desired.

The smash through the German lines not only exhausted the Fifth Army's chaplains, it also took the life of one of them. Joseph Gilmore from upstate New York first saw combat when his troops, the men of the 88th Infantry Division, began a fierce struggle for the city of Giulianello just twenty-five miles southeast of Rome. During the night of June 1, 1944, German airplanes made three runs directly over the aid station near the front where Gilmore was working. The first came at 11:45 P.M, and bullets tore up several tents. A few minutes later, a bomb landed about twenty feet away from the main tent, killing several men but leaving the medical personnel and Gilmore untouched. At 1:30 A.M. on June 2, a 500-pound bomb plowed directly into the receiving tent where Gilmore was working. Nine men perished immediately in the huge blast, eight of them soldiers lying on stretchers waiting for treatment; the ninth was Gilmore, who died instantly from the blast's concussion. His body bore no wound marks of any kind, save for a slight bruise on his cheek.

Because the night's repeated attacks had caused so much havoc, none of the priests in the vicinity could leave their posts to administer the Last Rites to Gilmore. During the long period of waiting, Gilmore's friends in the division (both Protestant and Catholic) formed a close circle around his body and recited the church's Act of Contrition and similar prayers to him on the slight chance that some kind of life might remain. Their actions also gave a quiet but deeply moving testimonial of their affection for him. Three hours after the blast, Chaplain Gregory Kennedy arrived. He first blessed Gilmore's body,

Chaplain Gregory R. Kennedy gives out communion on Easter Sunday, 1944, during a pause in enemy shelling in the fighting south of Rome. (Source: National Archives)

then opened his friend's hand and found that he was still holding a piece of cotton dipped in oil, which he had used during the night while administering the Last Rites to the soldiers in the medical tent. He had died ready, as one Protestant chaplain said, "to carry on his earthly work even until the God he served called him home." The next day his chaplain friends placed him to rest in a nearby cemetery.

Frederick G. Lamb, a Protestant chaplain who knew Gilmore well, was nearly beside himself with grief at Gilmore's passing: "I am truly lost for words to express [my] intense grief in the loss of this splendid young priest," he wrote a friend. "To me his death has been a particularly hard blow." Though Gilmore had not served at the aid station very long, "within a few days he had completely won the hearts of his associates and [had acquired] a reputation for tireless devotion to duty." The affection of the enlisted men for Gilmore became even more clear at his funeral Mass, where a non-Catholic chaplain noticed that "most of those attending the Mass were Protestant," and he found their presence there that morning "a splendid tribute to Father Gilmore's popularity among the men."[30]

On the day that Gilmore died, the Fifth Army captured the cities of Velletri and Valmontone, and despite the fury of the German resistance, the Allied capture of Rome was no longer in doubt. The coming triumph had nevertheless exacted a fearful price. The bloody drive from Monte Cassino and Anzio to Rome would cost the Allies perhaps as many as 40,000 casualties, a number equal to the population of Pasadena or Stockton, California, in that same year.[31]

"First among cities, the home of the gods, is golden Rome." So wrote the fourth-century Roman poet Ausonius when he sang the glories of the capital of the ancient Mediterranean world. Though near exhaustion as a result of the long drive on the city, the men of the American Fifth Army who marched into Rome on June 4 and 5, 1944, would still find strength to wonder at its golden glories during their days there. Which unit first entered Rome early in the morning of June 4, 1944, remains a matter of conjecture; equally disputed is the name of the first Catholic chaplain to do the same. Two chaplains claimed the honor for themselves, while two others had the distinction attributed to them but said nothing about the matter.[32]

What most Catholic chaplains thought about as they came into the city was not which one of them had arrived first, but something like, "Thank God that Rome is still intact." The great churches of the city had not fallen, and the Colosseum still stood with the traffic swirling around it. Most reassuring of all, only one bomb had fallen on the historic Basilica of St. Peter, doing little damage and leaving the pontiff, Pius XII, unharmed. Many had forgotten what an unravaged city looked like. "How refreshing it was to see a city that was not in ruins," remarked one.[33]

The chaplains would participate in the thunderous welcome that the people of Rome accorded the victorious Allies. "Cheering crowds lined the streets and children tossed flowers into our vehicles as we passed," said one priest from Colorado. "We had [our] pictures taken by newsreel cameramen!" he exclaimed. In the few days they would spend in Rome, a few priests went to Vatican City, where they offered Mass at St. Peter's tomb, saw the pope, and enjoyed the artistic treasures of the Vatican Museum and the Sistine Chapel. Most, however, acted as tour guides for the men in their units, showing them the fabled monuments, churches, and public squares of the city. One Jesuit chaplain said afterward that he had spent all day, every day, leading his young charges through the city's labyrinthine streets and "all night talking with

them about it." Few chaplains had a chance to catch up on the rest that they
so badly needed while in Rome; for most, recuperation would have to wait
until the end of the war.[34]

Pope Pius XII was the star attraction for the Catholic troops and their chaplains. Hour after hour, America's young Catholic soldiers streamed into St.
Peter's, sometimes accompanied by their priest-chaplains, sometimes led by
Vatican officials in formal diplomatic garb who ushered them into the massive
audience rooms where they would see the pope. Many GIs unthinkingly carried their weapons along with them, a practice that enraged the Swiss Guards
who were in charge of the personal safety of the pope. The pontiff himself,
however, soon let it be known that he had no objection to the Americans
bringing their weapons with them if doing so would make their visit to him
easier. Later, when told that the American soldiers had taken to washing themselves and their filthy clothes in the resplendent fountains of St. Peter's
Square, scandalizing many of the Vatican's residents, he decided that was all
right, too—they could wash there as much as they wanted.[35]

If the pope enjoyed the spontaneity of the American soldiers, he seemed
even more deeply moved by the priest-chaplains who accompanied them. A
man of profound circumspection and measured response, the pope changed
style completely when he talked to the chaplains and openly proclaimed his
admiration for these Catholic men of God who had become, in a time of
emergency, men of God at war. On June 30, 1944, he spoke to a gathering of
sixty-four Catholic chaplains from the Fifth Army, and his unqualified praise
of their work was truly the high-water mark in the story of the American
Catholic chaplaincy in World War II. The leader of worldwide Catholicism deliberately cast aside his usual guarded manner of speaking and called them,
quite simply, "the best."

The scene of the audience would remain imprinted on the minds of the
chaplains for the rest of their lives. As protocol dictated, all sixty-four waited
in silence until the pope entered the room; then they rose and remained
standing until he sat. In the fifteen minutes that followed, he gave them what
they later called "a pep talk," the likes of which they would never hear from
anyone again.

"We bless and commend" your work, he told them, work that has brought to
so many suffering people "consolation amid the sorrows caused by war." He had
granted many "most gratifying audiences" to the Americans since their coming
to Rome, he said, but this particular meeting filled his heart "in a very special
way." Reading from his prepared text with great emphasis, he declared, "You are
Our Joy and Our Crown." Even more, "You have hurried with eager, unselfish

zeal in pursuit of souls that have been caught up in the maelstrom of war and thrown into the perils of battle." No "ordinary" priests could ever have risen to such challenges, he said. In giving you to the armed forces, "your bishops and religious superiors . . . gave nothing but their best" for this awesome and unparalleled work. The chaplain-priests sat stunned as he handed his papers to an assistant and then indicated that he wanted to meet as many of them as possible. Many noticed that as he passed among them, he seemed unusually warm and spontaneous as he asked where they had come from and what they thought of their work in the American military. The meeting finished, he disappeared silently down a nearby corridor, and they left the chamber knowing they had just received the highest possible approbation from the highest possible source in their church. If they had ever entertained doubts about the intrinsic value of their work, those were gone forever.[36]

When the pope met later with smaller groups of chaplains in his daily audiences, he often went out of his way to speak with them. Sometimes he would ask them about their part of the country, which often gave him a chance to recall his own memories of the same place. Or at least he had a stock answer he could use in all such situations: He invariably said that the place was quite "beautiful." Thus, when a priest from the Holy Cross Fathers told him that he lived at the University of Notre Dame, the pope smiled and said, "It is very beautiful: I was there, you know." Indeed he had been there on a visit to the United States while papal Secretary of State, just before his election to the papacy in late 1939. He recalled, however, that Indiana had shown him its dark, sad face on the day of his visit, since the summer rains had poured without stop the whole time. All of this Father Joseph Barry from Notre Dame recalled all too well, since he had been there at the time of the visit. Nevertheless, he appreciated Pius's attempt at bonhomie. On the same day, three chaplains from San Francisco attended yet another papal reception. This time, when the pope's assistant introduced them and told him the name of their home city, the pope smiled and said, "Ah, California! A most beautiful country!" By now, some of the chaplains had begun to catch on to the pope's routine and were not surprised when he turned to the next chaplain and, told that he came from Chicago, said, "Chicago is beautiful too!"[37]

Pius also showed that he could respond with a most exquisite compassion to a chaplain who had suffered too much or seen too much of the war. One morning, he met a young Benedictine priest and said to him, "You must be very happy to represent the Benedictine Order on the front lines." When the man began to weep, the pope replied: "I know that many of your young men are no longer living and that is why you are crying, but you . . . are doing

Archbishop Spellman, Military Vicar of the U.S. Army, talks with Catholic chaplains in Rosignano, Italy, in 1944. (Source: National Archives)

more for your Order than you could ever do in a lifetime in the monastery." The pope then took the man's hands and silently, gravely, made a sign of the cross on the back of each one. With a single, powerful gesture, he had demonstrated his solidarity with his brother-priests around the world who had answered the call to military service.[38]

The priest-chaplains of the American Fifth Army would do well to enjoy their sojourn in Rome, since they would have little to look forward to in the coming months except more battles, as the Allies renewed their drive up the length of the peninsula to the Alps far to the north. Casualty lists would continue to lengthen as the campaign wore on, and again the troops would meet stout German resistance at every turn. The worst aspect of the war in Italy, however, was its newly diminished role in the larger European conflict. Just two days after the first American column marched into Rome, the Allies landed in Normandy, and the Italian campaign soon took a backseat in the news. The war in Italy would grind on, with more Allied thrusts against fiercely resisting German lines and more fighting in the same kind of snow, mud, and devastating cold that had bedeviled the troops earlier in the war, but the world's attention had turned elsewhere. Not even a visit from Archbishop Spellman could cheer up the Catholic chaplains on the Italian front. Karl Wuest gave vent to the frustrations of all of the men of the Fifth Army when he wrote that they had become "the men of the 'forgotten front.' "[39]

7

NORMANDY AND FRANCE

No pair of knees ever shook more than my own, nor any heart ever beat
faster in time of danger.
—Chaplain Francis Sampson, on D-Day

Everything was ready. The Allied invasion fleet, the largest single collection of
ships ever brought together in the war, was positioned for attack. Nearly
5,300 ships and 175,000 troops stood fully assembled in battle formation. A
steely gray line stretched from the North Sea to the Isle of Wight just off the
south coast of England, and seen from the cliffs of Dover, the silhouettes of
the fleet covered the entire ocean. Hundreds of warships seemed to crowd
against the horizon while troop transports, a few miles off the coast, rocked
up and down in the heavy swells. It was Monday, June 5, 1944, the day before the invasion of Normandy, D-Day.

The men of the five Allied divisions who would lead the attack the next day
sat in their rolling transports. Many were seasick or frightened. By now, they
knew the invasion plan: At a precise moment the next morning, before their
landing ships began heading for the shore, the warships of the massive convoy
would hurl tens of thousands of artillery shells at the beaches, hoping to shock
the enemy into paralysis. A few minutes later, the same ships would begin flail-
ing the low hills lying behind the coast. Then the first waves of infantrymen
would take their places in the landing crafts and begin moving toward the
coast of France. By the time the invasion had come to an end, the pebble-
strewn shores would be known to every American as Utah Beach and Omaha
Beach, two of the most famous place-names in American history. No one
could have guessed the horrors that Omaha, especially, would bring to the
American soldiers who would land there.

The troops who formed the first wave of the attack, however, would not come from the sea but from the sky. They were the paratroopers of the British 6th Airborne Division and the American 82d and 101st Airborne Divisions. If all went well, they would first establish themselves securely behind the beaches and then secure the flanks of the area in which the infantrymen would soon land. A few hours later, just as dawn was beginning to break, Allied infantrymen would attempt to rush all five landing beaches (three for the British and Canadians, two for the Americans). Their mission? Nothing less than sweeping the Germans off the shoreline. Absolutely critical to the success of the Allies on D-Day was the establishment of a defensive perimeter so powerful that it could repel even a massive German counteroffensive.

What of the chaplains who would accompany the troops on every step of the invasion? Like their fellow clergymen who had gone into battle earlier in the war, they knew full well that they would share the same fate as the men to whom they ministered. Landing with the airborne divisions would be the "paratrooper padres," who would jump into the flooded fields and streams that covered much of the Normandy landscape behind the beaches. They knew that some of their men would drown even before they could fire a shot. Five hours later, the infantry chaplains would struggle up Utah and Omaha beaches with the foot soldiers. Every minister, rabbi, and priest who went with them shared a single, heartfelt desire: the hope that no American would die in Normandy untended by a chaplain. Five of the chaplains who accompanied the infantry on D-Day were Catholic. Four would survive the war without a scratch, and the fifth—perhaps the most loved of all the Catholic chaplains in the European theater—would perish five months later in Germany. Meanwhile, as the final hours before D-Day crept by, they supported the men as best they could, with counseling for all and confessions and Mass for the Catholics.[1]

American and British intelligence experts had made no attempt to underplay the obstacles that the airborne troops would face and had estimated that casualties might run as high as 80 percent. The men in the flying transports would face an appalling collection of obstacles: deadly German artillery fire on the ground, anti-aircraft bursts in the air, and unpredictable head winds. All of these problems would make the flight across the Channel and into occupied France a journey of almost unparalleled danger. Before leaving England just after midnight on June 6, most of the airborne troops spent their final hours checking their packs one last time, talking quietly to each other, and writing letters to their folks back home.

They also went to church. Every camp offered religious services to the men

Marine Chaplain Joseph Mannion at Camp LeJeune, North Carolina, is shown here just after making his first successful jump from an airplane. Mannion was the first navy chaplain to become a paratrooper; army paratroop-chaplains went through the same kind of training as other paratroopers. (Source: U.S. Navy)

who wanted them, and not surprisingly, most did. Chaplain John Maloney of New York spent a grueling afternoon hearing the confessions of nearly all of his regiment's Catholics, but time soon ran out, and he found himself giving a general absolution to the paratroopers he had not been able to see. Soon he would fall through the blackened night into German-occupied France, taking the same appalling chances as they. He would be a paratrooper with a difference, however: He would carry his Mass kit so that any soldier who landed nearby and wished to receive Holy Communion on the spot could do so. Seeing a kind of humor in the image of a Catholic priest with the host falling toward the earth, his men had given him a unique nickname: For the rest of the war, they would call him "the Bread from Heaven."[2]

Another Catholic chaplain with far too much to do in too few hours was a priest who would soon become the most celebrated of the "paratrooper padres," Francis L. Sampson of the 101st Airborne Division. Possessed of a store of energy that amazed the men of the division, most of them far younger than he, Sampson found that he needed all the strength he could summon that day because he had received orders to cover two airfields 100 miles apart. He could only reach them by flying back and forth—rushing to conduct services and see as many men as he could in one place before running back to his waiting plane. Hearing the confessions of all of the Catholic men at the two fields, as well as tending to the personal needs of the non-Catholics, left him exhausted.[3]

An hour before midnight, the airborne troops shouldered their packs and parachutes and headed for the transport planes that lined the airfields in long, precise rows. Few spoke, except for the men who held last-minute, muttered conversations with the chaplains. As his men boarded their planes, Sampson shook the hand of each, then climbed aboard himself. At the same time John Maloney was doing exactly the same with his men. A few minutes later, the planes began climbing into the sky, flying smoothly over England, then hitting a few bumps over the English Channel. When they began crossing over France, violent head winds began buffeting them, while German anti-aircraft slashed holes in some of the transports and gliders, causing other planes to fly wildly off course.

At 1:14 A.M., Maloney's transport (a DC-3) began unloading its men out of the side door, dropping them into the inky skies over the Normandy countryside. Just as Maloney leaped out the door, the plane lurched violently, apparently hit by a burst of enemy anti-aircraft fire. He made a safe jump, however, and would later describe his leap into the night as his "most exciting experience of the war." As he tumbled through the air, it looked to him as if German fire had created a Fourth of July fireworks over France. He hit the earth with a sound smack but managed to stand up slowly, dazed but unhurt. All around him he could see nothing but hedgerows, thick fences made of dirt, brush, and trees. In the darkness of the night, they looked menacing and unsafe. Like all the men of the division he had received a toy cricket that he was supposed to crack to catch the attention of other paratroopers landing nearby. He snapped it vigorously, but nothing happened. He snapped it again; no result. The device refused to work. He could hear nothing and see nothing—no sound, no movement, and no other paratroopers. For fifteen minutes, Chaplain John S. Maloney of Rochester, New York, was alone in Normandy, thousands of miles away from home, and certain that he faced the greatest possible peril. He would say years later that those yawning fifteen minutes seemed more like a year and a half.[4]

Chaplain Ignatius Maternowski, a priest of Polish extraction from Maryland, landed at almost the same time as Maloney. It was his atrocious luck to drop straight into the heavily defended confluence of the Merderet and Douve rivers, which flowed into the ocean between Utah and Omaha beaches. To cross the flooded delta, Maternowski and his men had to walk along a causeway carrying a railroad that linked the transportation centers of Carentan and Cherbourg. Murderous German gunfire covered every foot of the embankment. A German shell killed Maternowski only minutes after he had started walking down the tracks. While bending down to help a wounded soldier lying on the causeway, he was shot from behind. The German troops later apologized, saying that they would have held their fire had they known that Maternowski was a chaplain and insisting that they had been unable to see his chaplain's identification in the darkness. An angry chief of army chaplains rejected their explanation, saying that no excuse sufficed for the shooting of an unarmed man in the back. Maternowski's remains were later taken to the nearest cemetery (probably the huge American facility near the village of Ste. Mère-Eglise just a few miles away), and a Mass of Requiem was celebrated over his grave. Sadly, nothing more is known about Maternowski or his final hours with the infantrymen he served.[5]

As waves of airborne troops continued to land in Normandy and fan out across the sodden countryside, the five divisions of infantry prepared to assault the beaches only a couple of miles away. Men of every religious persuasion (and of none at all) tried to ready themselves emotionally for the unknown dangers that lay ahead. Not surprisingly, a large number of Catholics also went to confession, just as the paratroopers of the same faith had done earlier. The infantrymen who were about to land at the beach code-named Omaha would face formidable defenses that would cause them even more grief than the obstacles the airborne troops had faced. Attacking Omaha would be exactly the same as assaulting a heavily protected fort head-on with no possibility of a flanking movement around the sides. The heart of the enemy's defense system lay behind the four-mile beach on which the Americans would set foot: Three lines of fortifications, each more formidable than the previous one, awaited the invaders. Long-range German weapons, 128 in all, covered every inch of the beach and each of its four exits. No one in the European theater had yet faced such a monumental rank of defensive lines; no one would face its like again.

The first battalions to land on Omaha ran straight into withering enemy fire. Men fell in the water everywhere, their lifeless forms bobbing up and down in the surf, their blood turning the six-foot waves into deep crimson froth. In terms of casualties per minute, Omaha Beach was the most costly

Chaplain Peter McPartland blesses a tank crew at a port in southern England four days before the invasion of Normandy. (Source: National Archives)

amphibious effort undertaken by any of the Allied nations in the battle for the Continent. It was the Tarawa of Europe.[6]

One Catholic chaplain crawling up the beach saw disaster all around him. Fabian Flynn, a priest from New Jersey, landed only minutes behind the first wave of troops, and as his landing craft approached the shore, he could hear what he described as the "thundering roar of shore batteries vomiting destruction," the terrible crack of the dreaded German 88-millimeter cannon, and the sickening sound of direct hits on nearby vessels. He wondered how he would ever survive such a maelstrom of fire and carnage. Dozens of men lying on the beach tried pathetically to make their bodies look as small as they possibly could, but German fire snuffed out their lives even as they clung to the shore. All around Flynn, soldiers stumbled under their packs, many of them bleeding from wounds, while waves of incoming troops pushed at them relentlessly from behind, forcing the first ranks ever further into the deadly fire now raking the beach. It looked to him, as he squinted through the haze and smoke, as if the attack had fallen completely to pieces. Everywhere on the

Army Air Corps Chaplain Michael S. Ragan blesses the crew of a B-17 Flying Fortress at a base in England before they left on a raid of German-held Europe. Chaplains were always careful to insist that they blessed a plane's crew, not the bomber or the bombs it carried. (Source: National Archives)

beach, he heard frantic cries of "medic!" as badly injured men cried for help. German machine guns and mortars ripped into small groups of men trying to form around aid stations or looking for safety near a concrete seawall that separated the beach from the hills behind it.[7]

Forty minutes after the beginning of the battle, Chaplain John Kelly of Hartford set foot on Omaha. He was fortunate enough to land on a part of the beach that seemed marginally safer than the rest of the shore, although nearby bursts of enemy machine-gun fire still forced him to move with great care. An accomplished swimmer, he had managed to flail his way through the heavy surf without losing either his life or his Mass equipment, and at the end of the day he would be able to write his parents, "I have not even a scratch on my body."[8]

While Kelly was working frantically to save the lives of the men around him, a priest-friend from Hartford, Joseph Lacy, was carrying out the same work not far down the beach. He spent the whole day in one spot, administering the Last Rites to the Catholics and "whatever spiritual consolation I could" to the non-Catholic infantrymen. When he found a dying Catholic soldier, he would kneel next to him and say, "I am a priest. Let's say the Act of Contrition." Many times that day he watched the men as their panic "gave way to peace."[9] Said Lacy's commanding officer after the battle, "Every time we caught it really bad it was the padre who was in there when the stuff was worst." Short, plump, and generally unimpressive looking (one friend described him affectionately as "no streamlined figure"), Lacy had a physical endurance and a personal devotion to the wounded that deeply moved the men who saw him work.[10] As the injured piled up in ever-swelling numbers, he directed crews of litter bearers, often standing up while bullets whizzed past his head. His courage inspired many of the terrified men to move about more freely, and the army later awarded him the Distinguished Service Cross for his heroism.

Among the many images that Lacy would carry away with him from Omaha Beach, one remained fresh in his memory over forty years later. Through the haze of battle, he could see a group of senior officers standing fully erect about a mile down the beach, discussing the battle and pointing to various parts of the shoreline and the hills beyond. None made any attempt to avoid enemy fire. "They were thorough professionals, and paid no attention to the bursts of fire landing no more than three or four feet away. They had taken it upon themselves to rescue the operation."[11]

Meanwhile, on Utah Beach, the 4th Infantry Division was finding the going much easier. Thanks to the success of the airborne troops the night before, the division found it had little fighting to do. The paratroopers had seized so many bridges and blown up so many German strongholds in this area that its 14,000 men poured ashore almost without opposition. By the end of the day, they had pushed six miles inland and had joined forces with the 101st Airborne Division. The Americans now held an unchallenged toehold on the northern coast of France.[12]

The airborne troops, however, had run into such intense opposition that many of the men of the 82d and 101st were still battling for their lives. Francis Sampson spent the day at the regimental aid station located in a large French farmhouse, which also housed the unit's command post. As casualties poured into the old Norman building, he assisted the doctors and helped the dying as best he could. He would work without stopping for all of D-Day, the night that followed, and well into the next day. Late in the afternoon of June 6, the fighting around the house became so intense that the regiment moved its headquarters away from the town, leaving the medics undefended. Sampson volunteered to stay behind to take care of the fourteen most seriously injured men, none of whom could be moved.

Since German troops were moving about in the woods surrounding the house, Sampson decided the best course was to put himself and his men at their mercy: "I made a white flag from a sheet and hung it out the door. Every fifteen minutes I would go out and wave the white flag, because I was afraid the Germans, suspecting a trap, would fire hand grenades and mortars into the house before approaching it." He spent all of that night and the rest of the following day running back and forth between the flag and the wounded. Although he took a frightening risk in assuming that the Germans would respect the white flag, he succeeded in saving both himself and his men from direct attack. Years later, his principal memory of those two days would be the aching fear that he felt the whole time. "No pair of knees ever shook more than my own, nor any heart ever beat faster in time of danger." Nevertheless, he felt at the time that it would have been "unthinkable" to allow fear to control his actions while in the presence of "those fine boys who fought and died so bravely." Nor did he ever doubt that any other chaplain, facing the same circumstances, would have done precisely the same.

A crisis came in the late hours of the afternoon when a band of enemy troops spotted the flag and immediately seized the house. After a tense interrogation and the leveling of many threats at Sampson, they left the chaplain and his troops under heavy guard, but unharmed. For the rest of the day, that night, and the next day as well, he worked furiously, trying to keep his injured men alive. After the battle, the army took special note both of his ingenuity in dealing with the Germans and his devotion to the wounded by giving him the Distinguished Service Cross and praising his perseverance "in the face of the most hazardous and difficult conditions to keep the men alive."[13]

Meanwhile, John Maloney, still with the men of the 506th Airborne Regiment, spent most of D-Day carrying out the same work as Sampson and under similar harrowing conditions. "I thought that day would never end," he remarked candidly forty-two years later.[14] Early in the afternoon, litter bearers brought in a lieutenant who was gravely wounded and growing cold from shock. He desperately needed blood plasma, but none of the doctors or corpsmen were free to administer it. Maloney decided to do it himself. He grabbed a bottle of plasma and a syringe and watched with relief as life ebbed back into the lieutenant's body. After the war, the officer stayed in the army and eventually rose to the rank of general. Not surprisingly, the two men became lifelong friends.[15]

Despite the heavy losses on Omaha and the continuing difficulties of the paratroopers to the rear, it was clear that the Allies had come to stay. Nearly 155,000 British, Canadian, and American troops had landed on the five beaches in the Normandy sector, far too many for the Germans ever to dislodge. Furthermore, the Allies had chalked up a list of remarkable accomplishments: They had breached Hitler's vaunted Atlantic Wall, they had shorn his Fortress Europa (as he called it) of its outer defenses, and nearly sixty square miles of France now lay in their hands. The cost for the Americans, however, had been horrendous: Out of 55,000 participating in the battle, approximately 5,000 had died, suffered injury, or remained missing. The worst losses, not surprisingly, came at Omaha, which cost at least 2,000 casualties.[16]

When the struggle for the five beaches finally ended, the Allies faced a new and at times baffling problem: impenetrable rows of tall, deep hedges that cut across the countryside like the infamous tank traps of World War I. The hedgerow sector began immediately behind the beaches and rolled away in a ragged arc across Normandy nearly twenty-five miles wide and sixty miles long. The Allies knew that they would get nowhere in France while the Germans could still use these splendid natural fortifications against them. The seemingly endless rows of hedges formed the best defensive bulwark that the Germans would have until they retreated beyond the Rhine River early the following year, and to their credit, their marksmen and antitank teams quickly learned to use them to excellent advantage.[17]

Probably no chaplain, Catholic or otherwise, saw more of the horrors of the hedgerow campaign than Francis Sampson. On the second day of the struggle, he was still with his group of wounded men in the aid station, although a doctor did finally arrive, giving Sampson a much-needed respite from the medical responsibilities that the circumstances of the battle had thrust upon him. He continued to wave the white flag every fifteen minutes from the front door of the house, but unfortunately the area had been taken over by a unit of SS troops (the Waffen SS was the military arm of the Nazi party). Early in the morning, Sampson suddenly heard a wild commotion outside. Grabbing his white flag, he ran out the front door, waving the pennant frantically. An SS soldier suddenly "jumped at me and stuck a gun in my stomach." At the same time, two German paratroopers who were walking up the road caught sight of Sampson. Asking no questions, they proceeded to march him down the road, plainly intending to shoot him on the spot. Sampson had never prayed so hard as he did then. So frightened was he, however, that instead of reciting the Act of Contrition (the usual Catholic prayer for forgiveness of sins), he repeated the Catholic blessing before meals: "Bless us, O Lord, and these Thy gifts, which we are about to receive through Thy bounty through Christ Our Lord. Amen."[18]

After lining him up against a wall, the Germans had just raised their weapons when a German officer fired over their heads. He began running up the road and did not stop until he reached the soldiers and the priest. "I told him I was a Catholic priest and showed him my credentials," Sampson said later. To his amazement, the officer "snapped to attention, saluted, made a slight bow," then showed him a Catholic medal pinned inside his uniform. The officer also insisted that Sampson view, and admire, the pictures of his baby that he kept next to the religious medal. Sampson did—and fairly exploded with admiration at the photographs of the officer's progeny. Smiling with pleasure, the officer dismissed the soldiers and led Sampson down the road to a German intelligence post. After a cursory interrogation, the intelligence experts released him, having found him neither menacing nor interesting. The German officer, who had clearly saved his life, promised him that a German doctor would come by in a day or two to tend to the wounds of the American soldiers.

Shortly after Sampson returned to the medical post, German artillery began smashing into the area, missing the house by only a few yards and shaking it for nearly four hours. Finally, an especially fierce blast knocked down a roof protecting two of the most seriously wounded men. One of them called to Sampson for help. He knelt down and held the boy in his arms, until he felt the soldier's final heartbeat. The explosion had crushed the body of the other soldier, killing him instantly. More close calls would come before help finally arrived. Near midnight, American troops began to move into the countryside around the building. Soon they found Sampson's house, and thinking that

Germans were hiding in it, they riddled it with machine-gun and rifle fire. Sampson remembers that a tracer bullet ricocheted off the ceiling, "grazed my leg and set my pants on fire." Out of the corner of his eye he could see an American rifleman sneaking up on the building holding a grenade in each hand. Sampson dashed outside the building, shouting as loudly as he could that wounded Americans lay inside. The soldier, startled to hear English, put down his weapons; he then told Sampson that the building he was inhabiting was the only one still standing in the area.

During the remainder of the night, both the Germans and the Americans brought their wounded into the makeshift hospital. Once, when the litter bearers brought in a young paratrooper in desperate need of blood, Sampson rolled up his sleeve, gave his own blood to the man, and then, without bothering to stop for a rest, spent the rest of the night and the following day working without stop in the hospital. The army cited his remarkable act of generosity to the paratrooper in its citation for the Distinguished Service Cross.

At times the Germans showed their own generosity toward others. Late in the day, Sampson saw an injured German soldier whose stomach wound was so severe that it shocked him every time he looked at it. Despite the soldier's condition, however, the man still found strength to come to the aid of a wounded American who lay next to him. After a doctor had put a blanket under the head of the GI, the German saw that his head had slipped off it and was lying on the cold stone floor. Sampson watched in amazement as the young German "crawled off his litter and along the floor on his back to the side of the American, fixed the folded blanket under his head again, and crawled back to his own litter." The Good Samaritan from Germany, far more grievously injured than the American, died only a short time later.[19]

Despite all the danger, Sampson somehow escaped the hand of death, but other priests in Normandy were not so fortunate. Besides Ignatius Maternowski, who died in the first hours of the invasion, Chaplain Philip Edelen of Raleigh, North Carolina, suffered the same fate during the hedgerow campaign. At 11:00 P.M. on June 9, Edelen was with his unit in the city of Trévières when an artillery shell exploded on top of him, blowing off most of his left leg. He soon suffered a cerebral hemorrhage as well, and at three in the morning on the next day, June 10, he passed away quietly. When the doctor at the aid station sent out an emergency request for a Catholic chaplain, two responded immediately. They blessed his body, then offered up a Mass for the slain priest in the aid station's kitchen. The next day, another chaplain buried Edelen quietly in the nearest cemetery, a hastily built affair with crude, temporary grave sites.

When a French countess who lived near the cemetery learned of his death, she wrote a letter to his mother assuring her that her family would put flowers on his grave every day and that they would photograph it for her as soon as they could. Some time later, she invited the elderly Mrs. Edelen to stay at her home after the war, remaining with them as long as she wished, so that she could visit her son's grave as often as she desired. "We'll be happy to welcome you," she said.[20]

Dominic Ternan, a Franciscan, perished on June 19 at the end of the second week of the Normandy campaign when his battalion, part of the 315th Infantry Regiment, encountered heavy enemy machine-gun fire. Almost everyone was hit except Ternan who, thinking that the firing had stopped, ran to a wounded sergeant lying in a ditch by the side of a road. A German sniper saw Ternan, fired, and hit him. The wounded sergeant would survive, but Ternan expired immediately. Once again, a German infantryman expressed his deep regret that he had slain a chaplain, but he insisted that the raincoat Ternan was wearing had hidden his chaplain's insignia and his Red Cross arm band. Both the army and the chief of chaplains treated his apology with contempt, condemning it as an exercise in arrogance and self-service and unworthy of a serious response.

No one questioned the quality of the slain chaplain's work or the gravity of his loss to the 315th. The warmest praise for Ternan came from a leading Protestant churchman, Dr. Daniel A. Poling, the father of an army chaplain who had perished on a troopship in the North Atlantic two years earlier. Poling had visited Ternan only a few days before he passed away, and a deep mutual respect had quickly formed between the two men. When told of the priest's passing, Poling said that Ternan had given "the perfect picture of Christlike devotion to his high calling," one that he proved by his courage in kneeling next to a wounded soldier while in open battle. The army concurred with Poling's assessment and accorded Ternan the Silver Star.[21]

The battle for Normandy entered a decisive phase on July 5, 1944, when the drive on St. Lô began. The Allied plan was to capture this key transportation center and then use it as a staging point to aim a knockout blow against the enemy. If all went well, they hoped to chase the enemy across France and into Germany itself. The Germans, however, chose to follow another scenario. Although they were hopelessly outmanned, outbombed, and outgunned, they continued to maintain a precarious hold on the city, putting up the kind of stiff resistance that the Allied forces had seen earlier in North Africa, Sicily, and Italy. Even so, it was too late for the Germans to maintain a protracted defense, since by mid-July the Allies had landed over 900,000 troops in Europe.

The horrors of the hedgerow campaign ended with the liberation of St. Lô on July 18, 1944, but the Americans had been forced to annihilate the city in order to take it. As one GI put it, "We sure liberated the hell out of this place."[22] Several chaplains who saw the city after the Americans seized it were shocked and saddened at what had been done to a superb medieval city. John Bradstreet, a Jesuit from California, remembered the fires—and the waves of acrid smoke—that had broken out each time the American bombers flew over the city. The ground on which he stood, just outside St. Lô, shook for hours on end, and he would remember the experience as the most vivid of his nearly two years in northern Europe. Others found a greater tragedy in the suffering of the city's helpless civilians. A priest assigned to a general hospital in the city found horror everywhere: "Children, young people, old people," all drifting up and down the highways like "lost souls." Tragically, "no one knows where they come from, where they are going, or what they eat." The older ones "stare with haunting eyes" while "the filthy, gaunt bodies of children are covered with sores. Poor people!" he exclaimed.[23]

Nor did the plight of St. Lô elicit the best behavior from its American liberators. Several chaplains watched in shock as bands of American soldiers roamed freely about the deserted streets machine-gunning German soldiers even as they tried to surrender. Sometimes the GIs forced the Germans to stand in front of a wall, then mowed them down. Bradstreet saw an American private gun down a German sergeant standing all by himself, unarmed, and in the act of raising his arms in surrender. When the private looked in the German's pouch, he found a letter that the man had just written to his wife and baby. The GI admitted to the priest that the German was "a handsome young fellow" but argued that "if I hadn't killed him, he would have killed me." The chaplain angrily pointed out that such was hardly the case since the German bore no arms. Another time, a group of American infantrymen carrying machine guns saw an American soldier marching three captive Germans back to his command post. The machine gunners told the American to fall to the ground, then promptly shot the three prisoners with their weapons. A dismayed Bradstreet heard one say to the others, "Well, that's the easiest guard duty I've had yet."[24]

After the fall of St. Lô, the Allied forces began to ready themselves for a massive breakout from Normandy, the Americans led by what they trusted would be the winning leadership of Lt. Gen. George Smith Patton, Jr. First, however, the American chaplains faced a daunting and profoundly heart-rending task, the burial of both the Germans and the Americans who had fallen during the protracted campaign for Normandy. Francis Sampson had a series

of experiences at the huge American cemetery near the city of Ste. Mère-Eglise
that typified the sorrowful work he and his fellow chaplains had to undertake.
On his first trip to the place, dismay and grief overwhelmed him when he saw
the bodies of the hundreds of men in his division who had perished during
the battle for northern France. They lay side by side now, placed in long rows,
each wrapped in his own parachute.

> I was shocked to find so many of my faithful boys among the dead. It
> didn't seem possible that these young men who had been so confident a
> week before, and whose hands I had shaken before we boarded the planes
> . . . were in eternity now. . . . I read the burial ritual for all, and re-
> mained most of the afternoon for the actual burial.[25]

While Sampson was still at the cemetery, a young GI recognized him and
ran up to him. He told Sampson that enemy fire had killed his brother, William Nyland, and he asked Sampson to see if he had been buried at Ste. Mère-
Eglise. A careful search of the cemetery's records revealed no record of him,
but it so happened that a soldier named *Roland* Nyland had just been interred
there. "Oh gosh, Father, that's my brother too." The soldier tried to choke
back his grief but soon broke down in heavy sobs. The two men said a few
prayers over young Nyland's grave, then went to another cemetery about a
mile away. Sampson remembers that they soon found the grave of the other
brother, *William* Nyland. To add to the tragedy, a few days later Sampson had
to tell the stricken young man that he had just lost a third brother in the Pacific. Using his influence as an administrative chaplain, Sampson arranged for
the immediate departure of the young man to his mother's home. "His
Mother, therefore, still has one son to comfort her," Sampson wrote sadly to a
friend.[26]

By the end of the Normandy struggle, the fighting had begun to exact an
awesome toll on Catholic chaplains, but when one priest's health broke
down, no replacement could be found for him, and the remaining chaplains
had to carry the extra burden as best they could. The shortage of Catholic
chaplains in the battle for France had become a crisis, with chaplains now
working until they fell asleep while on duty or had to be evacuated because of
exhaustion. The situation never got much better—in either theater of combat.
The Catholic church's hierarchy in America simply would not send its quota
of chaplains, arguing that the needs of the home front took first priority. As a
result, the priests at the front had to do the work of two men and sometimes
even three or four.[27]

Soon, however, the breakout from St. Lô turned into the rout of the enemy that the Allies had hoped for, and by the end of July, it had become clear to the generals that their armies were achieving the destruction of the German forces in France. With enemy opposition seeming to weaken almost every day, Gen. Omar Bradley, in charge of American ground operations, exultantly told Eisenhower that "things on our front really look good." The Normandy campaign clearly marked the beginning of an entirely new phase of the war in Europe, and the long dark night of the people of France was about to come to an end.[28]

When George Patton's Third Army burst loose at St. Lô and began racing across central France and slicing through the reeling German armies, it seemed an almost miraculous turn of events. The more the war changed, however, the more it seemed to remain the same; whether moving only yards or miles a day, men continued to die or suffer wounds. Between the beginning of operations on the Normandy coast and the capture of St. Lô, nearly a quarter of a million soldiers from both sides became casualties. Included among these was a Catholic priest from Philadelphia, young Peter Bonner, who perished, as did so many of his fellow chaplains, while attempting to reach a wounded soldier. Said a colleague after Bonner's burial, "He was every man's friend." The statement could well have served as his epitaph.[29]

Two days after he had been laid to rest, twelve American armored and infantry divisions cracked through the German lines like freight trains, one drive bolting toward the strategic harbor of Brest on the Brittany peninsula to the west, the other plunging east toward the Seine River—with Paris and the German border itself not far beyond. As Americans at home watched the newsreels of the victorious Allied armies, it looked as if the end of the war in Europe was only a short time away. From St. Lô eastward, so many dead Germans lay in the fields that it often took four or five days to bury all of them. "The condition some of the bodies were in!" said one chaplain serving with the field artillery. "This is where we really saw the results of war." For the next several weeks, Chaplain Adolph Thillman and the 119th Field Artillery Group moved so rapidly that he could neither keep track of where they were nor say what towns they had passed through. "We did little firing and just kept after the Jerries," he reported happily.[30]

The chaplains with the American forces watched in awe as the scene unfolded. "The Germans are fleeing us," exulted Chaplain Donald Murphy of the 90th Infantry Division, which led the charge to the east.[31] Everywhere the Allies went, ecstatic French citizens flocked to greet them, throwing flowers, cake, wine, and champagne as they rode past in triumph. At an intersection of two main highways, Murphy saw General Patton himself standing imperiously on a jeep, dramatically exhorting the passing troops to "keep moving."[32] These were heady days indeed for the Allies, and above all for the Americans. At precisely the same time that the Anglo-American juggernaut was rolling across France, American forces in the Pacific were earning hard-won victories in the Mariana Islands (Guam, Tinian, and Saipan) and putting their long-range bombers within reach of Japan. "The war will be over by early fall, at the latest," many Americans were saying to each other, a view that the troops on the European front and their chaplains also shared.

They seemed, at the time, to have sound reasons for their optimism: Patton's Third Army, a brilliantly disciplined force of 250,000 men, first stormed across the plains of central France and then began threatening the border of Germany itself. In one of the most spectacular drives of modern times, Patton's army covered 350 miles in forty-five days. To the north and south, other American and British forces also streamed across the French countryside, rolling up the demoralized and disorganized Germans as if they were children at play.[33]

The enemy, however, had not yet given up. One day as the battle lines rolled eastward, a unit of German troops suddenly counterattacked and seized a medical aid station where Chaplain William Hayes of New Jersey was working. The SS 2d Panzer Division suddenly swarmed over the complex, capturing Hayes, the doctors, nurses, and even some wounded prisoners. Since many injured soldiers were far too ill to be moved, Hayes and the doctors protested vehemently, but the SS commandant took them along anyway. In the short time that he was a captive of the Germans, Hayes had a unique opportunity to observe at close hand some of the SS troops (Hitler's "own favorite sons," as the chaplain sarcastically dubbed them).[34]

When Hayes entered the prison compound, he told the officer in charge that he was a Catholic priest. Although the priesthood meant nothing to the officer, Hayes's insignia showing that he was an American officer inspired immediate respect, and he was treated correctly, if formally. Some of the SS enlisted men, however, took an entirely different attitude toward the captured chaplain. When two of them heard that he was a priest, they immediately went up to him, shook his hand, and told him that they, too, were Catholics. Complaining angrily, they told him how much they missed Mass, communion, and confession. "One of them held my hand," Hayes reported, "and said he was so happy to see a priest again." Hayes gave each man a medal, blessed them, and was about to talk with them some more, when German

guards suddenly bundled him off to the camp's headquarters for questioning.[35]

After interrogating him for nearly four hours, the Germans released him
and returned him under a safe-conduct pass to the American lines with orders
to arrange for an exchange of prisoners. When Hayes reached the American
command post, he had to submit to another siege of questioning. As he
talked, he could think of little except the radiant faces of the young Catholic
SS soldiers who had seized so eagerly at the chance to speak about their religion to a Catholic priest.[36]

The race across France continued, even accelerating. Leading the pack, Patton's relentless Third Army at one point covered 140 miles in five days for an astonishing average of 28 miles per day. As the troops rolled across the provinces of
France, the local inhabitants poured their gifts and affections on their Americans
liberators. They opened up their churches, too, when the troops camped outside
their towns. Adolf Thillman, assigned to a field artillery group, remembers the
hospitality of both the people and the local cure at the village of Heudreville,
which happily had suffered little damage in the fighting. Thillman first helped his
men pitch their tents, then walked into the town. When the people of the village
saw him and his group heading toward them, they gave them a stomping, cheering welcome—one enthusiastic enough to warm the hearts of even the most exhausted GIs. A High Mass in the local church, attended by both soldiers and
townspeople, completed the celebration.[37]

As the American drive against the Germans picked up momentum, it
brought its chaplains a host of problems. They found first that they had a distressing lack of time for the orderly interment of the enemy's dead. Another
difficulty was the profound weariness that so many of them now felt, a difficulty caused, ironically, by the sheer velocity of the American charge. Chaplain John T. O'Brien wrote his superior that he had just endured his "60th
consecutive day of combat"; the long drive had left him drained beyond his
considerable powers of description.[38] The continuing and ever-worsening
shortage of chaplains at the front meant that fewer chaplains had to do ever
more work, wearing themselves out in the process. It also meant that they
sometimes neglected not only the burial of fallen Germans, but also the needs
of many Americans still alive. "We have no priest, no Mass, no nothing," a
Catholic infantryman complained.[39] Despite the increasingly desperate need,
the Catholic church in America did not supply the number of priests necessary for the troops in combat. The result was a chronically fatigued band of
priest-chaplains who grew progressively more worn-out as the war went on.

As the Allies thrust toward the German border in the north, the Germans also found themselves threatened on a new front. On August 15, 1944, at 8:00 A.M., a combined force of Americans and Free French troops hit the beaches of the French Riviera, encountering only light opposition. Few amphibious assaults have been carried out so perfectly, or ended with so few casualties for the invaders, as the attack on southern France. Fewer still have succeeded in taking so much territory from the enemy with such speed.

The force that bore down on the coast of France between Toulon and Cannes consisted of 94,000 troops in 880 ships, protected by more than 2,000 bombers and fighters. None of the American and French commanders expected an easy landing; all of them would be wrong. Before the day ended, three American divisions had advanced ten miles inland against opposition that surprised everyone by its feebleness. The invasion itself went so unexpectedly well that it looked, in retrospect, like a practice landing that had gone off exactly the way the army's manuals said it should. Maj. Gen. Lucian Truscott, Jr., the man in charge of the operation, pronounced the invasion an "astounding success."[40]

A most enthusiastic observer of the scene was none other than the Roman Catholic Archbishop of New York himself, Francis J. Spellman. On hand to visit the invading troops, he had made an astonishing request of General Truscott just before the day of the invasion: He wanted to accompany the men in a landing craft and remain with them on the beach as long as they needed him. The request must have stunned Truscott, who knew full well that under no circumstances could he allow any visitor, and especially one as well known as Spellman, to enter the battle. Truscott thus made a counteroffer: Would the Archbishop instead like to fly over the landing scene in an army aircraft? Spellman assented and had the privilege of a panoramic view of the invasion.[41]

As the French and American armies raced north up the Rhône River valley, they crushed German units unable to get out of the way, while bypassing an occasional pocket of resistance that other forces could deal with later. The Allied roller coaster seemed almost unstoppable. American casualties remained small compared to Normandy, while over 50,000 Germans became prisoners of war. So many German soldiers had lost their bearings that on one occasion a Catholic chaplain succeeded in nabbing two of them himself. Jordan Brown had just finished pitching his tent one evening when he noticed two German bodies lying nearby. Thinking they were dead, he decided he would carry them to the nearest cemetery and bury them. To his amazement, he discovered when he walked up to them that they were not only quite alive but fully armed as well. Thinking quickly, he commanded them to lay down their arms and walk ahead of him. When they complied meekly, he led them off in triumph to an American command post located not too far away. Despite his audacity, Brown did not receive a medal, quite possibly because as a noncombatant, he had no business taking prisoners. Nor did the army give an award to an American officer who turned away several more prospective prisoners the same day, explaining that he was simply too tired to take them into custody. He volunteered the possibility that perhaps they could present themselves for capture the next day, if they would be so kind as to come around at a convenient time.[42]

As the Americans continued to roll northward, their air force, now in virtual command of the air, smashed the German ranks at will. "Trucks of all description are lying by the roadside wrecked, ditched and burned," wrote Chaplain James Martin from Maryland. "In places whole convoys seemed to have been caught," he observed, while rows of tanks lay crushed along the roadside. Nor did French civilians escape serious harm. One small town he passed through had been bombed and detonated into extinction. No matter how much they suffered from the fighting, however, the French people still welcomed liberation. "All along the way they stand and wave," Martin wrote. He found the French children especially delightful. Although they were too polite to yell at the Americans for candy, like young people everywhere they found ways to make it "quite evident they would like to have some."[43]

Just forty-one days after the landing on the southern coast of France, advance units of the Free French Army under Gen. Jean Tassigny de Lattre met up with a patrol from Patton's Third Army at the village of Saulieu, 150 miles southeast of Paris. The joining of the northern and southern Allied forces marked the end of Operation Dragoon, the campaign in the south of France. In that drive, the French and American armies had seized a third of occupied France from the German occupiers, while taking over 80,000 prisoners and killing or wounding tens of thousands of others. By mid-September, over 900,000 Americans had landed at Marseilles, Toulon, and other southern ports, all of them destined to swell the armies bearing down on the eastern border of France and Hitler's famed Siegfried Line defenses lying just beyond.[44]

As the Allies raced up from the south, other armies streamed across central and northern France, with cities falling like dominoes on an unsteady table: Brest, Rennes, Le Mans, Chartres, and Orleans all capitulated quickly before the Anglo-American juggernaut. On August 19, during a torrential rainstorm, an advance patrol of the American 79th Division crossed the Seine just north of Paris. After two days of bitter fighting, the forward elements of Maj. Gen. Jacques Leclerc's 2d Armored Division entered Paris, followed closely by the American 4th Infantry Division. At 9:22 P.M. on August 24, a column of tanks led by Leclerc rolled up to the Hôtel de Ville (Paris's historic city hall), giving an unmistakable signal that the French had taken back their capital from the hated Nazis.[45]

The next day, for the first time in four years, the bells of the churches of Paris rang again, thus beginning one of the greatest of all wartime celebrations—one that boggled the imagination of even the jaded American veterans, who by now had seen dozens of such occasions. It began with the marching of the French soldiers through the Arc de Triomphe and down the Champs Elysees, followed by what seemed like endless miles of American troops. The delirious Parisians broke through police barricades to offer the GIs bread, wine, flowers, and (it being Paris) kisses without end. They gave their liberators bottles of their best, driest French champagne (one American officer, riding in a jeep, managed to collect sixty-seven bottles). Another American soldier said later that August 25 was "the day the war should have ended," so delirious was the welcome that the Parisians bestowed upon the Americans and their own French Army.[46]

Chaplains riding with the 4th and 28th Infantry Divisions also found themselves caught up in the frenzied momentum of the day. Leo Picher of Hartford, Connecticut, who claimed to be the first American chaplain inside the city, described the people as "madly enthusiastic."[47] A few days later, Picher had the pleasure of delivering the sermon at a Mass of Thanksgiving held in the Cathedral of Notre Dame. Over a thousand American soldiers who crowded into the church heard Picher speak fluently in both French and English and saw the Archbishop of Paris, Emmanuel Cardinal Suhard, presiding regally over the elaborate proceedings. At the end of the liturgy, the cardinal first addressed the American visitors, then bestowed a solemn blessing on the entire congregation. The American troops in attendance, non-Catholic as well as Catholic, seemed deeply moved by the experience, and many seemed unable to talk about much else in the days that followed.[48]

Like all visitors to Paris, the chaplains toured the sights of the city, fortunately still intact because a courageous German general had refused to carry out Adolf Hitler's orders to destroy the city. One priest told his family that "the delirious joy" of the people that he saw far "overshadows" any account they would ever read in the newspapers.[49] As the Americans walked and taxied from place to place, they found themselves surrounded by "chattering, handshaking, cheek-kissing Frenchmen" who first thanked them for their deliverance from the Germans, then explained at great length "what they have suffered during the four years of German domination." Their hearts went out to these emaciated-looking Parisians, many of whom looked close to starvation. They needed food above all, but "thank God and America," one priest said, food had finally begun trickling into the city. Even the reclusive Gertrude Stein joined in the victory celebration. An American chaplain who met her walking one evening with her white poodle recounted, "We stopped and had an interesting talk for over half an hour," Chaplain John Strmiska reported. He also claimed that at the end of the conversation she expressed, in an elliptical Steinian way, her joy that the war was over.[50]

Even as the Americans triumphantly passed through the still-resplendent City of Light, intelligence sources saw trouble looming ahead. The Germans had started to reassemble and reinforce their shaken forces, and the Allies' precious stocks of fuel were dwindling. Would Patton and his fellow commanders have enough oil to drive all the way into Germany? No one could say for sure, but worries about the future of the Allied march grew daily, and with good reason: On August 31, just as Patton crossed the Moselle River, his Third Army ran out of fuel. Within hours, the other two American armies had also stopped in their tracks. Meanwhile, the Germans had reorganized their divisions, brought in fresh reserves, and prepared for a protracted engagement. What the Allies had long feared most, a winter stalemate, now loomed in front of them.

In the prolonged stall that lasted from mid-September to mid-December, over 100,000 Americans became casualties of the campaign for the Siegfried Line, or the West Wall as it was sometimes called. Slowly the Allies edged forward, encountering stiffening resistance and taking only feet and yards instead of the many miles they had seized earlier. The weather brightened a little as summer faded into autumn, and small French towns continued to fall, but the long-term prospects seemed dim indeed. The momentum of the drive had clearly dissipated. Moreover, the troops had to live now in the open fields, unprotected from the cold of the night or surprise attacks by the enemy. With the continued fighting leaving everyone in a state of chronic weariness, morale plummeted, even among the clergy in the military.[51]

Nor did the slowing of the Allied drive mean less fighting or fewer casualties. American enlisted men and officers still perished in German artillery attacks and from nighttime air raids. Chaplain Clarence Ford had to bury one of his most inspiring young men, an infantry captain whom he eulogized as "a grand boy and one of the best captains. Never a Sunday did that boy miss

Mass." When told of his death, Ford rushed to the medical post where the captain's body rested and read the Catholic church's prayers for the dead over him. "I've lost a few boys like this lad, and it sure does hurt me away inside," he said later. "When you lose the good ones it just makes things a little more [tough]."[52]

The halt in the Allied campaign resulted in a ceaseless but inconclusive struggle against a well-entrenched and resilient enemy, and the mounting toll of casualties made increasing demands on fewer and fewer priests and other chaplains. A series of violent battles took place all along the near-static front, of which the most intense were probably the struggles for the cities of Aachen and Metz. It was precisely at this perilous time that Archbishop Spellman chose to make a third trip to the American troops in France, this time as a guest of General Patton. Spellman joined Patton at his command post east of the city of Aachen, where the Third Army was in the middle of an energetic but largely unsuccessful drive on the Siegfried Line. Patton's magnetism, self-assurance, and driving force nearly swept Spellman off his feet. Though the archbishop nurtured a respect bordering on idolatry for all American fighting men, he came to regard Patton as an almost superhuman being, possessed above all with an indomitable strength of character. The general impressed him as a magnificently "striking figure" who "strides along, straight and as supple as a sapling." He also found the general "frank and outspoken," something that Spellman found "a most engaging quality."[53]

Patton could, if he chose, play the role of the gracious host with consummate virtuosity. He arranged for Spellman to visit the troops near the front line, including a visit to one unit that had just made a historic crossing of the Moselle River the day before. He also provided a room for Spellman next to his own quarters, which gave the two an opportunity to stay up late and talk, something both men vastly enjoyed. Later, Spellman reported that in the conversational department, "I did as well as he." Spellman found Patton a reasonable and sensible man and "extremely well informed in many fields other than the military." The bishop left Patton's headquarters convinced that he had just met not only one of the greatest generals in American history, but a giant of a man who carried out his numerous assignments with zeal, intelligence, and a good soldier's desire to win at any cost.[54]

Patton, on the other hand, found Spellman a "very clever little Irishman" and a "most interesting" one to boot. In Patton's view, however, the archbishop was not without certain limitations of character: He had come across unmistakably as "anti-Roosevelt, anti-CIO, anti-Negro, anti-Jew and [anti-] English."[55] Patton's statement was quite an indictment—and it did not seem to occur to the general that he shared most of the same prejudices himself, perhaps in an even more virulent fashion than the archbishop.

The assault on the Siegfried Line had thus far resulted in a ghastly series of campaigns, but little Allied movement had resulted. Worst of all, the lengthy battles had given the Germans time to prepare for a great winter offensive, a massive counterthrust that would send the Allies reeling 52 miles back toward the English Channel and would bring the Americans their darkest hour in the war in Europe.

8

THE BATTLE OF THE BULGE

Father, this is Christmas Eve. You will have to say a good prayer with us
tonight.
—American soldier to Catholic chaplain

They called it the Forest of the Ardennes: a gentle timberland of open mead-
ows, meandering streams, and tree-shaded country lanes. Long acclaimed for
its mineral baths and charming resorts, it drew enormous crowds of visitors every year. It offered rejuvenation of body and spirit as well as some of the loveli-
est scenery in northern Europe. The Ardennes, however, has also been a battlefield.

In the middle of December 1944, the area suddenly exploded with the
sound of warfare when the Germany Army staged a massive counterstrike
against the Allies. The six-week struggle that followed would turn the woods
and marshes of the Ardennes into a forested hell, a wintry purgatory where
death came in many forms: by cold, by hunger, or by an unseen shot in the
dark from an enemy rifle. Seldom in World War II did the shadow of Golgo-
tha hang so heavily over a battlefield, exacting so fierce a price from both vic-
tors and vanquished. Although historians have often called the campaign the
Ardennes Offensive, the far more common name for it is the Battle of the
Bulge.

Hitler knew that in order to reverse his fortunes he needed to achieve a surprise attack such as the one he had staged in the spring of 1940, when his
troops stormed across the Low Countries and then into France, shocking
western Europe with the speed and daring of his invasion. He had convinced
himself that he could succeed once again and could stun the Allies with a massive and unexpected assault. The Führer, it seemed, knew the Forest of the Ar-

dennes all too well; the Allies, all too little. Hitler's initial success in the operation would stem in part from shrewd planning and in part from the belief of the Americans that the Germans were now so weak they were incapable of fighting effectively. Most ominous of all, the Americans completely ignored the advance warnings of an impending attack that they received for at least two weeks before it started. They had no one but themselves to blame for the disaster that swept over them on December 16, 1944.

A month before the invasion, Hitler started quietly assembling forces behind the Siegfried Line. His plan was to make one gigantic thrust through the thin American lines and drive them all the way back to Antwerp, the principal entry point for most of the supplies the Allies were using in northern Europe. Once Antwerp lay in German hands, he thought, the Americans and the British would wither on the vine, their offensive would be stopped for good, and their lines would fall to pieces against the renewed German onslaughts.[1]

December 16 fell on a Saturday that year, and at 5:30 A.M., on a calm, bitterly cold morning, a barrage of German artillery shattered the deep silence of the front. All along an eighty-five-mile line, screaming shells jarred the men of the 28th, 99th, and 106th Infantry Divisions out of their sleep. What was going on, they asked each other as they flung on their clothes and raced for their posts. Branches of trees and pieces of shrapnel flew past them like flying scythes. A few minutes later, huge searchlights began bouncing light off the low cloud cover, casting an eerie glow over the forest. Soon German infantry wearing camouflaged white clothing began moving quietly through the trees toward the forward posts: American soldiers in the front lines who saw the enemy filtering through the slim lanes of trees froze in terror at the sight.

Behind the rows of ghostlike figures moving stealthily through the Ardennes stretched the last great force that Adolf Hitler would hurl against his enemies in the west. Thirty divisions, numbering 200,000 men, would oppose an American force of only 83,000. By 8:30 in the morning, the Germans had already begun to encircle two regiments of the 106th Infantry Division. That unit, with its 15,000 men and officers, would soon meet disaster along a ridge on the western edge of the Ardennes known as the Schnee Eifel. As Gen. Freiherr von Manteuffel's Fifth Panzer Army charged down on the untested unit, resistance simply melted away. By 8:30 A.M. on the next day, the Germans had succeeded in surrounding the entire 106th, and in the next two days, they would take 7,000 of its men prisoner. With the destruction of the 106th, the Americans lost all hope for a quick halt to the German drive.[2]

On the second day of the battle, a Catholic chaplain offered Sunday Mass in a tiny village for a small band of infantrymen from the 106th who had managed thus far to elude the rampaging Germans. After Mass, as he was walking down the main street of the town with a young man who wanted to talk to him, a German artillery shell "exploded right behind the house I was headed for." When another bomb came screeching by a few seconds later, the two men executed what the chaplain called a "perfectly synchronized swan dive" into the basement of the house.[3]

As Hitler's troops rolled over the collapsing American lines, they quickly gathered up the men with nowhere to hide. Most of them soon became unwilling guests of the German government for the remainder of the war. Although most would survive their captivity, almost all would suffer severely from it, and none would emerge from the experience unscathed. At least seven Catholic chaplains fell into German hands, three of them from the 106th. Chaplain Paul Cavanaugh, a Jesuit from the Midwest, and several thousand men from the 106th had managed to elude the Germans for the first four days of the battle, hiding out in isolated farms and villages in the forest. On the fourth day, however, the officers leading the group committed a major error: They decided the time had come to stop running from the enemy. Instead, they would attempt to slip unnoticed through the German lines and try to reach the American positions further to the west.

Cavanaugh remembers that the morning of December 19 began exactly as the previous four days had: up early, no Mass because no time for it, no breakfast because no food, only a quick dash to the line of trucks waiting to move the convoy to the next location. He could see clearly that their situation was rapidly becoming hopeless. An hour later, when the caravan stopped so that the officers could decide where to go next, the Germans made their decision for them. The sharp snap of a German rifle shattered the quiet of the woods. When machine-gun fire began to rake the rows of trucks, Cavanaugh realized the enemy had surrounded them, and he threw himself into a furrow along the edge of the road. Soon he could see four German tanks rolling over the top of a nearby hill, moving implacably in his direction. "I tried to make myself as flat and as small as possible," he said, but to little avail. Bullets thudded into the ground all around him. It seemed strange to him that despite the peril of his situation, he could hear a voice deep inside himself saying insistently, "I am not afraid to die."[4]

Later that day, German guards loaded Cavanaugh and the other prisoners into a row of railroad cars, part of a long train bound for a prisoner-of-war camp near Limburg, due north of the Ardennes. For two days, the train failed to move at all, and the men suffered from the brutal cold and continued privation. They saw no one, heard nothing but the lookouts (who ignored their cries for food and water), and resigned themselves to a grim fate. On the fourth day of their imprisonment, the Germans moved the train to Bad Orb, a prisoner-of-war camp seventy-five miles east of Limburg. There, the men of the 106th shuffled into squalid makeshift barracks. Although not as shameful as the Japanese prison camps, Bad Orb would acquire a fearsome notoriety all its own for its total lack of heat in an intensely cold winter, its wretched food served in minuscule portions, and its brutal guards, whom the Americans soon dubbed "the goon squad." When asked after the war about his experiences at Bad Ord, Cavanaugh refused to discuss them, saying only that he had "suffered extreme cold and hunger."

In this camp (officially called Stalag IXB by the meticulous Germans), Cavanaugh and his men from the 106th observed that most moving night of the Christian year, Christmas Eve. Their wretched surroundings brought them closer to the poverty and lowliness of the nativity scene than anything they had ever experienced before. As they huddled close together that evening, trying to ward off the intense cold, one of them suddenly said to Cavanaugh: "Father, this is Christmas Eve. You will have to say a good prayer with us tonight." Cavanaugh obliged as best he could, talking about the first Christmas Eve in Bethlehem and how it demonstrated God's continuing love for each of them. He told them that His love was somehow present even on that winter night when their hopes lay frozen on the barracks floor.

Soon he approached the end of what he sensed might well be the best Christmas sermon he would ever give. He prayed to the God of Christmas (the God, he realized, of both the Germans and the Americans): "Lord, grant peace to the world. . . . Grant that the peace which Christ, who is called the Prince of Peace, came to bring us may be established all over the world. Amen." Then, without pause, he led the men in the singing of a Christmas carol, and afterward, the men sang all the other old, familiar hymns that they could remember. Then came a great, deep silence that lasted the rest of the night. Cavanaugh turned to the young man slumping against him. "Paul, are you awake?" he whispered. No answer. In a louder voice he asked, "Is everybody satisfied?" Still no answer. At long last, all was "still and calm and peaceful, and I was very happy."[5]

Word of the disaster developing in the eastern sector of the Ardennes slowly filtered back to the areas behind the American lines until it finally reached the Versailles headquarters of Gen. Dwight Eisenhower, the Supreme Commander of the Allied Expeditionary Force. By the time he heard the news, the German breakthrough was almost half a day old. The position of the American forces in the Ardennes deteriorated so badly during the night that Eisenhower met early the next morning with his field generals. When Patton offered to lead an immediate relief expedition, Eisenhower accepted. Help for the beleaguered Americans would soon be on the way, it seemed, but would it arrive soon enough to prevent a total collapse? No one, not even Eisenhower, could answer with certainty.

Soon word began to circulate among the men in the front of a frightening new development: The dreaded SS troops had appeared and were committing atrocities against both American troops and Belgian civilians. It was well known that the SS respected no one and considered themselves bound by none of the basic laws of decency. Before their rampage would end, at least 350 American soldiers and 100 unarmed Belgian civilians would die at the hands of the SS. One of the worst atrocities occurred at a small crossroads town called Malmedy. Early one afternoon, SS troops discovered an American field artillery battalion, which quickly surrendered. At a signal from an officer, the Germans opened fire on the prisoners with machine guns and pistols. At least eighty-six unarmed, defenseless American soldiers perished. When SS troops saw that some of the men still showed signs of life, they smashed them in the head with rifle butts or shot them again. A few Americans managed to escape, and they immediately reported what had happened. Word of the event spread like wildfire through the American ranks, stiffening the resolve of the troops to deflect the enemy attack.[6]

When the chaplains heard about the atrocities, they, too, seethed with anger. "From the SS, deliver us, O Lord," said one priest, assigned to the post of chaplain at an Allied prisoner-of-war camp filled with SS troops. He would be only too happy, he said, when the army finally moved all of them to the rear as he found them a thoroughly abominable bunch. He was especially shocked by the behavior of one man who had just been taken prisoner and put into the camp hospital. The German sat up in his bed and "in haughty Hitlerite fashion and language broke into an insulting tirade against the Americans for my benefit, until I rapped him across the teeth." Almost without exception, he reported, they acted in a "sullen" and "quarrelsome" manner, and provided a constant irritant to the people who attempted to work with them. Chaplain Leo Weigel came to the conclusion that the SS was "a menace that should be exterminated now because it will not be checked any other way."[7]

By the third day of the counterattack, it became clear that the climax of the struggle for the Ardennes would come at the town of Bastogne. Why Bastogne? Because it was the most important crossroads in the whole region, the meeting place of seven major highways and many smaller roads. To the German command, Bastogne meant only one thing: an essential point on the path between Germany and Antwerp, their ultimate goal. The side that held Bastogne held the most direct route to the Belgian port city, and Hitler knew that if he failed to take the town, his entire campaign would collapse. The struggle for Bastogne thus became the turning point of the Ardennes campaign. One of the most perilous chapters in the European war for the American forces, it marked both the longest and the most violently fought contest in the entire Battle of the Bulge. By the time the nine-day struggle for control of Bastogne had ended, it was plain that the Germans had exhausted themselves in their attempts to take the town.[8]

Eisenhower ordered the 82d and 101st Airborne Divisions to Bastogne, telling them to set out immediately. The command came as something of a shock to the paratroopers in the two divisions, since they badly needed a period of rest after recent heavy fighting in Holland. No matter, they would have to leave by early morning the next day. The 101st received word of the new orders while camped in a small French town just outside Paris. Francis Sampson and his roommate, a Protestant chaplain, both had much work ahead of them, writing letters of condolence to the families of the men in the division who had perished in Holland. After several hours, they both decided to sleep the rest of the night.

Sleep, however, would have to wait. At two in the morning, a messenger aroused them and told them that the Germans had broken through in the Ardennes and that they would have to leave without delay. With no time to hold religious services, the two chaplains began visiting as many paratroopers as they could. Sampson called the Catholics of each unit together for communion and a general absolution and then met with as many non-Catholics as possible. His Protestant colleague carried out his usual tasks for the companies that he was able to visit. Both men thought it especially important to contact the several hundred new men who had just arrived in the division and were facing the prospect of going into battle for the first time. Finally, the troops of the 101st Division climbed into trucks and jeeps and began a frigid, twenty-four hour journey to a village near Bastogne, where they would regroup and then prepare to move into the embattled city.[9]

Sampson's fellow paratrooper-priest, John Maloney of the 82d Airborne Division, received word of the Ardennes incursion at the same time as Sampson. He was told that the Germans were "chopping great holes" in the American lines and that the division would have to move to the Ardennes early the next day. He, too, visited as many companies as he could reach, then grabbed his backpack, put on his helmet, and ran off in the darkness to the waiting convoy. Like everyone else in the two divisions, he had little idea of what he would soon meet—a hurricane of warfare that would put him in constant peril of his life.[10]

On Tuesday, December 19, the airborne troops and the Germans arrived in Bastogne at virtually the same time. Having succeeded in surrounding the city, the Germans chose to "greet" the Americans by probing their lines at several points, then hurling a massive assault at them from two directions at once. The newly arrived paratroopers halted the drive, but not before the Germans came frighteningly close to blasting a gaping hole in the American perimeter. By the narrowest possible margin, the Allies at Bastogne had survived their first test. Many more would follow in the days that lay ahead.

Soon after the struggle for the town began, Francis L. Sampson of the 101st Airborne Division fell into the hands of the Germans for the third and final time. Now he would have no possibility of escape, for the Germans would send him far to the east and he would spend the rest of the war as a German captive at a camp near the city of Neubrandenburg, north of Berlin. As before, he had fallen into a German trap, doing so while trying to do a good deed. When he heard that the Germans had ambushed a group of paratroopers in a wild skirmish near the perimeter, Sampson and a soldier raced to the scene of the fighting. As they drove up the side of a hill, several hundred German soldiers suddenly appeared, jumping out from behind trees and rocks and shouting at them in German. At the same time, several machine guns mounted on large trucks swiveled in their direction. Sampson, knowing now that he would fall into the hands of the Germans yet again, told the trooper that he was "sorry to have gotten him into this mess."[11]

John Maloney, meanwhile, managed to avoid capture, but not trouble of another kind. He suffered injuries two days in a row, the first in his arm, the second in his shoulder. The first came while he was visiting troopers crouching in their foxholes near the edge of the American defensive lines surrounding Bastogne. Suddenly he heard the clatter of a German artillery shell flying toward him, and as he ran for cover, a piece of shrapnel put what he called "a neat hole" in his right forearm. The next day, while tending the wounded at a field hospital, another round of explosives landed nearby, this time giving him a mere "flesh wound," as he called it, in his right forearm. After the war, he would insist that none of his injuries had been at all "serious" and that he needed almost no care, rest, or hospitalization. His only real wounds, he said, were "a decided tendency to duck at squeaking doors and low-flying jeeps," not to mention "967 gray hairs." The army, having its own views about the gravity of Maloney's injuries, awarded him a Purple Heart, later adding an Oak Leaf Cluster to the same medal.[12]

By the third day of the battle for Bastogne, the American situation appeared so grim that the Germans sent a message to the American commander, Brig. Gen. Anthony C. McAuliffe, demanding the immediate surrender of all his forces. Soon the whole world, it seemed, had heard his singularly terse reply, "Nuts!"–probably the most famous one-word quotation to issue from the war. The next day, the weather turned fair for the first time in several weeks, and the fog that had covered the ground like a shroud burned away entirely, allowing American planes to make a desperately needed supply drop on Bastogne. The Allied forces were still short of food, ammunition, and medicine, but their overall strength had improved enough so that they now had a fair chance of surviving a prolonged encirclement.

On Christmas Eve, religious services helped raise the spirits of the city's defenders. Conditions for worship could hardly have been more primitive. The only light in the temporary chapel came from dim-burning candles, carefully shielded so that the enemy would not be able to see them. There were no Christmas decorations and no choir or field organ to lead the singing. It little mattered. The men brightened perceptibly as they worshiped together and sang the Christmas carols they had learned at home and could never forget. At a Christmas Eve Mass held in the early evening, the priest told his paratroopers: "Do not plan, for God's plan will prevail."[13] Apparently God's plan included the survival of the Americans at Bastogne. A savage enemy assault early the next morning nearly tore a hole in the defenses, but at the last moment they held. Late in the afternoon of the following day, forward elements of Patton's relief force at last arrived on the scene. The imprisonment of Bastogne had ended.

Christmas in the Ardennes also produced the most famous prayer to come out of the war, Patton's celebrated "Prayer for Fair Weather." Earlier, in December 1944, before the Germans had begun the Ardennes offensive, his Third Army had come to a sudden halt outside the Saar basin, the heartland of Germany's mining industry. Not only had German opposition tightened, but weeks of chilling rains and snowstorms had left Patton's armored divisions thrashing hopelessly in mud and ice. The general finally decided it was time to call on the Almighty. Patton summoned his supervising chaplain, James H. O'Neill, and told the priest: "I want you to publish a prayer for good weather. I'm tired of these soldiers having to fight mud and floods as well as Germans. See if we can't get God to work on our side." When O'Neill objected that it would take "a pretty thick rug for that kind of praying," Patton retorted, "I don't care if it takes the flying carpet. I want the praying done." "May I say, General," O'Neill suggested tentatively, "it usually isn't a customary thing among men of my profession to pray for clear weather to kill [one's] fellow men." Patton replied brusquely that if he wanted a lesson in theology, he would ask for one. He then demanded: "Are you Chaplain of the Third Army? I want a prayer."[14]

O'Neill returned to his office planning to use a Catholic prayer for good weather as the basis of his own. To his astonishment, he found that none of the Catholic prayer books he used had a prayer for fair weather, though one did have a perfectly stunning plea for victory over one's enemies. Since the chaplain had just gone on record with Patton as opposed to such warlike entreaties, he asked his deputy, young Chaplain George Metcalf (an Anglican), to see if he could find a formulary for fine weather in his own texts. Metcalf quickly located one, and the two men sat down together and composed the final prayer, one combining Catholicism's resounding prayer for victory with the Anglican plea for favorable weather.[15]

When Patton saw the finished product, he approved it without comment, even accepting O'Neill's suggestion that the general put his personal Christmas greetings to the men of the Third Army on the leaflet's other side. The prayer combines sentiments of petition with a ringing plea for triumph in arms:

> Almighty and most merciful Father, we humbly beseech Thee, of Thy great goodness, to restrain these immoderate rains with which we have had to contend. Grant us fair weather for Battle. Graciously hearken to us as soldiers who call upon Thee that armed with Thy power, we may advance from victory to victory, and crush the oppression and wickedness of our enemies, and establish Thy justice among men and nations. Amen.[16]

The prayer begins innocently enough on a note of supplication but ends in a fury of bellicosity, clearly designed to bring God to the American side. After "humbly" beseeching the Lord, it asks for fair weather but for one purpose only, for "Battle" (using what seems to be intentional capitalization), a "Battle," that is, against the German enemy. It asks that "armed" with divine "power," the Third Army advance from "victory to victory" so that it can "crush" the "oppression and wickedness" of the enemy. Finally, it prays for the establishment of "justice," though the kind of justice remains unspecified (possibly the type that one achieves over one's adversaries by using what the

Old Testament chillingly calls a "terrible swift sword"). The prayer seems, at first glance, to aim at a balance between humble supplication (the first part) and warlike petitions for success (the second part), but it acts far more as a call to arms than as a suppliant's request for divine assistance. The verbs and nouns it used would bring joy to the heart of even the most pugnacious of warriors, as they resonate with the sounds of victory in combat—"battle," "armed," "power," "advance," "crush," "oppression," "wickedness," "enemies," and "victory" (twice).

When the campaign in the Ardennes began, Patton's staff shelved the prayer temporarily. After a few days, however, it became clear to Patton that foul weather had again become a major deterrent to success, and he ordered the printing of 250,000 copies of the prayer, one for every officer and enlisted man in the Third Army. The fog did indeed lift over the Ardennes, the snow stopped, and Patton's Third Army was at last able to lead the rout of the German forces. If Patton's deputy is to be believed, when the general saw the clearing skies, he exclaimed: "God damn! look at the weather. That O'Neill sure did some potent praying. Get him up here. I want to pin a medal on him." A few minutes later, Patton pinned a Bronze Star on the startled O'Neill, telling him: "Well, Padre, our prayers worked. I knew they would." Then he gave him his highest sign of approval: "He cracked me on the side of my steel helmet with his riding crop." It was Patton's unique way of saying, "Well done." At last, the commanding general of the Third Army could rest easily—no one could seriously deny that he had a supervising chaplain "with powerful influence in heaven," as the general himself later announced emphatically.[17]

Whatever it was that an often inscrutable deity wanted for the Ardennes, a German victory no longer seemed a possibility, for with the end of the battle for Bastogne, the German attack quickly lost its momentum. Early in the morning of December 27, an American armored division routed the 2d Panzer Division, led by a general of the panzer troops, Heinrich Freiherr von Luttwitz. At the town of Celles, four miles east of the Meuse River and fifty miles short of Antwerp, American armored forces stopped the forward march of the German Army for good.

The fighting left behind thousands of civilian and military casualties, and the chaplains in the Ardennes now faced an almost insurmountable challenge: They had to take care of far more victims of the German drive than they could possibly assist, in far too little time, and while in a state of near-exhaustion themselves. Nor were their lives any safer than earlier in the fighting when the

Americans were on the defensive. One chaplain nearly had his head blown off in the battle for a crossroads town at the southern edge of the Ardennes. While visiting the local priest in his rectory, a mortar shell smashed through the wall behind him, missed him by less than a yard, then shot through the wall on the other side of the house and fell harmlessly to the ground outside. Despite flying through two thick walls, it had failed to explode. The chaplain, thoroughly shaken up, wondered how he had escaped. "The Lord must have saved me for something important," he thought to himself. "I wonder what?"[18]

Despite all the dangers they faced, the religious fervor of the men continued to make the chaplains' work worthwhile. A priest from Vermont marveled at the goodness and generosity of his infantrymen. He saw them repeatedly make great sacrifices for each other, especially their wounded comrades. The supervising chaplain of one division reported that his "pride and consolation" were the troops and officers of his unit. "The religious life of these men will go down in history as something as outstanding as the great deeds they are accomplishing in battle." The men of the division would continue to be an inspiration to him, as they had been to most of the chaplains in the Ardennes struggle, both Catholic and non-Catholic.[19]

If the German surge had stopped, the fighting and the casualties had not, and two Catholic priests, the only chaplains to die in the Ardennes engagement, perished in the final days of the campaign. John J. Verret was killed on January 8, 1945, the same day Adolf Hitler decided to begin withdrawing his troops from the Belgian front. A member of a small religious order called the Society of St. Edmund, Verret had entered the army after a short but successful assignment to a parish in Burlington, Vermont. He had accompanied his men to England in August 1943 and was still with them when the whole 17th Airborne Division received orders to move to the Ardennes. Shortly before departure two days before Christmas 1944, Verret wrote a letter to his family and friends in Burlington. Although he could not have known that it would be his final letter home, a sense of foreboding overshadowed it. "We envisage a sure victory," he told them, "but the speed is all too slow." Despite the maelstrom of war all around him, he thought every day about his people back home, and it only increased his longing to return to them for good once hostilities had ceased. He trusted that they would continue to pray for his fellow servicemen, who were ready to sacrifice "their lives, if necessary," for peace in the world. As he and his men trained for their coming departure to the Continent, "our thoughts turn to home." Without realizing it, he had bidden them farewell.[20]

Monday, January 8, 1945, marked the twenty-fourth day of the Battle of the Bulge, the eighth month of the war in northern Europe, and the beginning of the fourth year of American participation in World War II. On that day, Chaplain John J. Verret walked into a medical station near the city of Laval, bringing in several wounded men he had just rescued from a field covered by enemy fire. He was helping a corpsman lift an injured paratrooper into an ambulance when a German artillery shell knocked both of them to the ground, killing them instantly. When the men of the 507th Airborne Regiment to which he belonged heard the news, they were deeply shocked. Verret had been with them from their first days together in the United States, then in England, and finally in the Ardennes. He had gone wherever they went, and nothing had ever seemed to discourage him. The army agreed, awarding him the Silver Star posthumously.[21]

Just two weeks later, the Battle of the Bulge took the life of a second Catholic chaplain, Anthony Czubak of Rhode Island. The precise circumstances of his death remain unknown, though it appears that a German shell exploded near the spot where Czubak was helping the wounded. He was the only man hit, and like Verret, he died immediately. A nearby priest anointed him and accompanied his body to the closest medical facility, where the doctors declared him dead on arrival.[22]

The struggle in the Ardennes left not only the troops but all of the chaplains in a profoundly depleted state. One reported that until the fighting began, he had enjoyed "excellent" health. Now he felt "fatigued habitually with recurrent headaches" and seemed constantly "on edge." Another said "the pace is a killer" and that he felt "all foggy" most of the time. He wondered how he would fare after the war: Would he still be able to teach, to preach, to take part in retreats, and to hear confessions "if and when I get back"? He reported that he ended every day so thoroughly drained that his whole body cried out for a good night's sleep, but even at night he had to work—writing letters of condolence to the families of the men who would not return home.[23]

With the ferocity of the battle leaving so many thousands of American soldiers dead and injured, the chaplains could barely keep up with the demands made on them. Worse than the long hours of work, however, was the sight of the injured men. One chaplain at an army hospital in the Belgian city of Liège described the human carnage that met his eye every time he made the rounds of the wards:

Men with gaping chest wounds gushing blood, men with intestines chopped apart by shrapnel, men with nose, lips, and teeth missing, men with bloody oozing caverns where eyes had been, men with [a] leg or arm dangling from some stringy finger that looked like chewed muscle, men through whose bodies bullets had gone exploring like ground-moles, men who had virtually burned to death in tanks but were alive and lay like mummies wrapped in a three-inch thickness of gauze, men with steel lodged in the brain, the heart or the spine causing total paralysis.[24]

Naturally they had to take care of the enemy as well as their own men. When a German soldier filled with machine-gun bullets was brought into a hospital one day, a chaplain anointed him and heard his confession in German. When the priest had finished, the man said softly, *Gott ist gut* ["God is good"]. He fell into a coma, but unlike so many of his comrades, this particular soldier survived his injuries.[25]

One priest in the Third Army expressed the grief that all the chaplains felt when they saw young men dying and knew that neither their own valiant efforts nor the best that modern medicine could do would save them. "It is a heart-breaking experience," he wrote, to stand helpless next to a bed and watch life ebb away from a "strong young man who has so much to look forward to in this life." What saved most chaplains from outright despair was the knowledge that through their ministry, they could bring a few moments of peace to a man who had nothing to look forward to in his life except the end of it. Another priest, who made many visits every day to a nearby field hospital, expressed the thoughts of all when he said: "I was privileged to assist many at their last moment. It was a consoling thought for me to be able to help these men who were giving so much for us all." When asked what was the most satisfying moment he experienced during the war, another chaplain said that it was "the day the war ended." Yet in some ways, that was also a most depressing moment. "When I think of all the men left behind . . . I still have tears in my eyes." Forty years after the war, the memory of the men he had seen for the last time in the Ardennes continued to haunt him.[26]

Victory over the Germans in the Battle of the Bulge finally came to the Americans. The reason for their ultimate success, however, was less the brilliance of the Allied generals than the stubbornness and bravery of the men at the front. Once again, they had shown their leaders that if tragedies were to turn into triumphs, they alone would achieve them. Their chaplains knew this

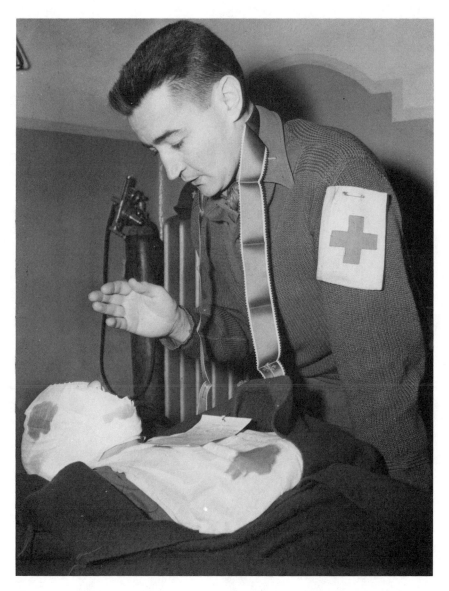

Chaplain Harold O. Prudell administers the Last Rites to a seriously wounded infantryman in Luxembourg during the Battle of the Bulge. (Source: National Archives)

as well as anyone, since they had stood next to them as the Germans surged inexorably toward their lines, then swarmed all around them. And if the men and their chaplains had lived to see the vanquishing of the Germans, they had also lived to see the brutal cost that the battle had exacted in terms of human life.

9

THE FALL OF GERMANY

Our chaplains are simply playing out. They are not quitting. They are
not giving up; they are simply exhausted and unable to go farther.
—Chief of Army Chaplains

William Arnold did not exaggerate when he described the exhaustion of his
Catholic chaplains in Europe. By the time the Allies had defeated the Germans in the Ardennes campaign, an alarming number of the priests serving in
Europe had approached the breaking point, and when the final push against
the Germans began in February 1945, some of them had already fallen apart
and had had to leave the front. The cause was easy to find: Neither the bishops nor the superiors of religious orders at home would send enough priests to
fill the ranks of the military clergy, arguing that the need for priests at home
was greater than it was overseas. In the last six months of the war on the Continent, so many combat chaplains became casualties themselves that the resulting shortage caused even more pressure on the remaining priest-chaplains.
A crisis had come, and there was no relief in sight.[1]

Some priests became so exhausted they could no longer function in combat. One supervising chaplain, for instance, reported that a man in his division, even though of "very rugged spirit," had been so "beaten down" by
the long string of battles that he had taken as much punishment "as he could
physically stand." Although he knew that he had no one to take John T.
O'Brien's place, he concluded that he had no choice but to send him back to
England for rehabilitation and eventual reassignment to a noncombat position.[2] But where would the army find his replacement? The Chaplain Corps
had begun taking much older priests, even some who were considered "marginally handicapped," and putting them into combat positions at the front.

Army Chaplain Edward T. Boyle blesses a group of infantrymen just before they enter the fighting along the Rhine River in late March 1945. (Source: National Archives)

Most of these men, however, soon found their new assignments far beyond their capacities, though they gave heroically of their limited resources. How long would they last? Not long, many feared. An ominous number began to weaken, then snap, under the strain of what Arnold called the "grueling and hazardous" task of supporting combat infantry. "Of course they won't last long and then what?"[3] Would they break under the pressure, or would they manage, somehow, to stumble across the finish line? Arnold and his colleagues in the corps could only pray and hope for the best.

By early March, British and American troops had reached the Rhine in three places and immediately began to search for suitable crossing sites. Thanks to a combination of luck and daring, they found such a place at the medieval city of Remagen, where, almost miraculously, a bridge still spanned the river. On the morning of March 8, American forces seized the span. In the next twenty-four hours, 8,000 troops would cross it—and thus put, as Gen. Omar Bradley phrased it, "an open wound" into the side of the Germans.[4]

Enemy resistance soon intensified, however, and in the first two weeks of fighting east of the Rhine, 800 Americans died, among them a Catholic priest from Oakland, Clarence A. Vincent of the Redemptorist order. While serving as a widely admired professor in the Redemptorist seminary, he had demonstrated a natural instinct for dealing with the soldiers in nearby army camps, where he assisted in services on weekends. Officers quickly noticed his success with the troops. "The common soldiers" are "wild about him," said a general who observed his weekend service with the troops—and who lobbied (without success) to have Vincent assigned to his division.[5] Vincent could speak the soldiers' language, yet never seemed to demean himself; he won their confidence with his open manner and impressed them with his approach to their problems.

After entering the service and attending the army's Chaplain School, he served for six months at a series of large army posts at home, distinguishing himself with his energetic attention to the enlisted men and earning high praise from all his commanding officers. After what he thought was too long a wait, the army fulfilled his long-cherished desire to serve in a combat zone. Assigned to the 7th Armored Division, he left New York on June 7, 1944, for France. The division received its first taste of combat in mid-August during the drive from Paris to the provincial capital of Chartres, a hundred miles to the south of the capital. Weeks of hard fighting followed in eastern France, Belgium, Holland, and finally Germany itself.[6]

During Vincent's final month of service in February 1945, the division struggled past the Siegfried Line and slowly forged a path across the plains and cities located on the west side of the Rhine. He offered Mass in bombed-out churches, tents, empty buildings, even outside in the cold. During those final weeks, he became something like a big brother to many of the soldiers in the division. In addition to dealing with the long lines of men waiting outside his tent to see him, he heard the confessions of nearly 500 men (possibly a record in the European theater) and visited tank columns, artillery batteries, and medical aid stations. The end of his life came without warning: Shortly after the Americans seized the bridge at Remagen, Vincent's battalion received orders to patrol the river north of the town. On March 13, 1945, almost a week after the capture of the bridge, a lone enemy bomber slipped across the Rhine and attacked Vincent's unit in the riverside village of Mehlem, just north of Remagen. One of the bombs killed Vincent and three other men instantly. A group of chaplains in the area took care of his burial in a cemetery in western Belgium, and the 7th Armored Division awarded him the Purple Heart. He is remembered, a half-century later, by his Redemptorist friends as a "little fight-

Protestant Chaplain Yoder P. Leith gets a light from Catholic Chaplain Alvin J.
Jasinski during a brief lull in the fighting in Germany east of the Rhine in late March
1945. (Source: National Archives)

ing man" and an animated extrovert filled with a "restless energy for action"
and a powerful drive to "get things done."[7]

Vincent did not live to see Germany's final, convulsive struggles in the last
weeks of the war. Within days of his passing, the Allies succeeded in putting
nearly all of their frontline troops across the Rhine, and the Germans offered
so little resistance in some places that at times the fighting almost seemed to
stop. By the end of March, Eisenhower was ready to throw a gigantic ring of
steel around the remaining pockets of enemy resistance, hoping to aim a final
knockout blow against the Germans. His armies would first encircle the enemy completely, then cut off every escape route, leaving them trapped from

every side. If the strategy worked, it might well end the war in early April; if it failed, then no one could safely predict the end.

Once again, the Germans proved harder to defeat than the Americans had expected. In some places they fought fiercely, with mounting casualties on both sides. Chaplains on the scene filed dismaying reports about the number of American soldiers they had to bury, one priest saying he had interred nearly 300 men from his own regiment. In the same period, a priest with the 415th Infantry Regiment, which endured much of the hardest fighting, wrote 168 letters of condolence to families at home.[8]

Despite the carnage, a few of the chaplains found nothing but triumph and glory in the sweep of the Allied troops across Germany. A Franciscan from the Midwest, for instance, reported exultantly how his division (whose nickname, "the Timberwolves," he greatly relished) had "raced out into the plains" past Cologne, then "behind the excellent blocking" of an armored division had "dashed in to take Cologne." That done, he and the men of the 104th Infantry Division found that they had so little to do that they simply "loafed and licked our wounds and waited for the Third Army and the rest of the war to catch up with us."[9] Most of the chaplains, however, viewed the situation in Germany in a far harsher light, finding nothing but desolation everywhere they looked. Prewar Germany's magnificent and prosperous cities and its sprawling industrial plants had all melted away. "What we've seen of this country is a sorry looking mess of rubble," exclaimed one chaplain. Another found that a once-beautiful Germany had turned into a land of "wrecked and burned vehicles, dead horses along the way, and demolished towns." Saddened, "there was nothing to do but continue moving slowly along."[10]

The German people themselves seemed to present different faces at different times. One chaplain heard them complaining bitterly that they had lost their cities and their families because of the Allied assault; nevertheless, they kept on repeating, "What is there to do but fight on until the last?" He came to the reluctant conclusion that the Allies would "have to destroy every town that is ahead of us." To another chaplain, they seemed a terribly "sullen lot," much given to "protesting every restriction" put on them and taking every opportunity "to excuse themselves from obeying military laws." Try to be considerate of them, he said, and they quickly take advantage of you; try to be firm, and "they accused you of being worse than the Nazis."[11]

At other times, the German citizens seemed the most exhausted, depressed, and deeply anxious of people. German refugees heading back toward what had once been their homes, "trudged down the highways with a sad and weary step," Chaplain John Hamme reported. "They had seen too much suffering'' and wanted only to rebuild their lives and their homes. He could not forget, however (as most American soldiers could not), that these were the same people who had ''cheered their armies as they swept through Poland, Holland, Belgium and France.''[12]

As the Allies marched ever deeper into the crumbling Reich, they liberated the camps in which the Germans had held their American and British prisoners of war. One of those freed was Francis L. Sampson of the 101st Airborne Division, who had first fallen into German hands twice during the Normandy invasion, escaped, and then was captured a third time in the early days of the Battle of the Bulge. He later described his five months in a German camp as his most difficult time during the war—more traumatic even than the Normandy invasion or the parachute drop into Belgium. After six days on a German prisoner-of-war train, living without food or water, he and 2,000 others arrived at their destination, a compound outside the city of Neubrandenburg north of Berlin.[13]

When the train arrived at Neubrandenburg, the prisoners stumbled out of the cars only to find the city enveloped in a blizzard, a chill portent of the winter days in the Baltics that lay ahead. German guards shouted at them, ordering them to walk the remaining four miles to the camp, located on the outskirts of the city. Suffering from the long trip on the train, the men staggered along the road, many of them scooping up handfuls of snow to slake their thirst. Sampson did the same: ''Ice cream never tasted half so good,'' he could recall vividly many years later. When they finally reached the barbedwire enclosure, the prison authorities dispatched them to the showers, and the men were shocked to see how much weight they had lost during the sixday ordeal on the prison train. ''Looking at my own body I could scarcely believe that it was mine. Normally heavy men looked skinny and thin men looked like skeletons.''[14]

The food served at the camp (designated Stalag IIA) barely kept the prisoners alive. A steady diet of cabbage soup (with worms), rotten turnip soup (with worms), and a tenth of a loaf of bread (both with and without worms) made up the daily fare. The inmates received so little sustenance that many of them grew violently ill, and many perished. Sampson and the camp's doctors could do little but watch in dismay as the men of Stalag IIA faded away. Eventually Red Cross food parcels began to arrive, but they came too late to save large numbers of prisoners. Sampson's daily visits to the prisoners' hospital became an increasingly difficult ordeal as the health of the men in the camp deteriorated visibly. One afternoon he watched helplessly as a Polish doctor amputated both legs of a young American soldier, then applied compresses made of toilet paper and bandages cut from newspapers. Gangrene had set in after the soldier's feet had frozen, and the doctor had no choice but to amputate them in order to save the young man's life. As tears streamed down his cheeks, he told Sampson that this was the fifth American to lose both legs so far, while eighteen others had lost one apiece.

Life at Stalag IIA might have become totally unendurable for Sampson and the other prisoners had the men not built a chapel. Sampson immediately set up a series of religious programs, one for the Protestants in the camp, one for his fellow Catholics, and one for the Jewish soldiers. The men flocked to the services, and the rude, homemade chapel soon became what Sampson called "a spiritual oasis" for the men of the camp, a place where they could find a sense of temporary sanctuary and renew their spirits for another day at Neubrandenburg.

Sampson held daily Mass in the early morning hours and offered nondenominational services twice weekly. At other times, he assisted the Jewish prisoners in their own ceremonies. He quickly learned that they were the neediest in the compound. Quite simply, the Jewish men stood in daily peril of their lives because of the virulent anti-Semitism of the guards and the camp's administration. On the first day of their imprisonment, the German soldiers had herded all of the Jews into their own barracks. Sampson and the American officers had vehemently protested this treatment, but to no avail. The authorities would not relent. The Jewish men stayed where they were, separate from the rest of the camp and most of its life. They went out every day to work with the rest of the prisoners, and though they generally received the same treatment as everyone else, Sampson worried constantly about reprisals against them, especially as the war began to wind down in late March and early April. Nor were his fears for the safety of the Jewish prisoners entirely groundless: For instance, when guards found a collection of phonograph records in one barracks, they smashed to bits any record that had a Jewish name on it (for composer, orchestra, or producer), even—to Sampson's consternation—Irving Berlin's "White Christmas."[15]

In mid-April, after nearly four months of bitter wintertime imprisonment, the men in the camp suddenly began to hear the muffled pounding of Russian artillery in the distance. Marshall Konstantin Rokossovsky's Second Belorussian Front was approaching Neubrandenburg from the east, remorselessly grinding up everything in its path. Soon, the Russians would be at the outskirts of Neubrandenburg, then at the gates of the camp itself. What would happen when they finally appeared? At midnight on April 28, 1945, Russian tanks roared into the encampment, converging on it from all sides at once.

They smashed through the barbed-wire fence, flattened the guard towers, then wandered aimlessly around the prison compound, turrets pointed recklessly at the barracks and at groups of prisoners scurrying for cover. The Russian troops were enough to throw terror into the hearts of even the most hardened of men. They ran around the camp acting like "wild men," recalled Sampson, reeling drunkenly from vodka and stolen German beer and firing their rifles and submachine guns aimlessly into the air. They were the ferocious, thoroughly barbarian Mongols and Siberians, whose reputation for unwonted ferocity and mindless mayhem had long preceded them.

Acting more like new commandants of the camp than its liberators, they first stripped Sampson and the other officers of their wrist watches (which they greatly prized), then forced them to dig latrines for the Russians' exclusive use. Most of the "liberators" were drunk when they arrived, and most remained besotted until they finally left the camp several days later. Disgusted at their behavior, Sampson tried to report his grievances to the Russian commander but found to his shock that he, too, was drunk. Soon the prisoners of Stalag IIA began to ask themselves what they could do to free themselves from their Russian Allies, who clearly posed a far more serious threat to their security than the Germans ever had. The Russians gave them every reason to be fearful: One day, Sampson watched in horror as the frenzied Russian troops first raped, then beat up, then finally murdered a group of captured women and girls in the nearby city of Neubrandenburg.

His worst experience in the whole war came when he visited the nearby home of a German priest who had repeatedly given much-needed assistance to the chaplains in the camp. Sampson worried that perhaps the Russians would molest the priest's mother and two sisters who lived with him. When he knocked on the door of the rectory, he learned to his astonishment that a band of marauding soldiers had just raped the priest's elderly mother, his two sisters (one a German nun), and forced the priest and his aged father to watch the entire spectacle from beginning to end. The three women sat huddled together on a couch, vacant stares glazing over their eyes. "I judged that they were on the verge of losing their minds; they were certainly beyond tears, and beyond receiving any expressions of sympathy." A rosary dangled from the fingers of the priest's mother. "As she sat there with her eyes closed I couldn't be sure that she was alive." What Sampson called "Genghis Khan warfare" had just destroyed a Catholic priest and his family.[16]

A few days later, an American colonel arrived at the camp and took over official control of the compound. The condition of the American prisoners shocked him, and to facilitate their quick removal to American lines, he ordered another officer to take Sampson to argue the case with American military authorities. (Under orders from General Eisenhower, all troops were to remain in camp, with Sampson being the only exception.)

On May 2, the two drove out of the camp north across the German lowlands toward the American lines to the west. Several days later they arrived at the city of Ludwigslust, which marked the border between the American and Russian areas of occupation. When they reached the checkpoint between the two zones, a suspicious Russian guard ran out of his post, stopped the jeep, and demanded that the driver produce a special pass authorizing him to cross to the other side. An alert American guard on the other side of the line saw their predicament, ran up to the Russian soldier, and engaged him in an animated conversation. As the two men shouted and argued vociferously with each other, the American officer slammed the gas pedal to the floor and sped to safety. A few minutes later, Sampson was receiving a hero's welcome from the 82d Airborne Division, which had heard of his exploits as the 101st Airborne's legendary Paratrooper Padre. The two also were told that it was V-E (Victory in Europe) Day. The war in Europe was over at last.[17]

Paul Cavanaugh, who had also fallen into German hands during the Battle of the Bulge, experienced an even more frightening end to his time as a prisoner of war. Uprooted from his first camp at Bad Orb, he and his men now found themselves incarcerated near the city of Hammelburg, almost in the center of the German heartland. Their new camp bore the official designation of Oflag XIIIB. Upon arrival, they first underwent the usual showering and delousing (the Germans always seemed far more concerned with the cleanliness of their prisoners than with their health). Then each man stood in front of a guard for an inspection of personal belongings. When a guard found a pair of dice in Cavanaugh's pockets, he sneered, "You are some priest," in fluent English, and walked away haughtily. Cavanaugh, however, cared little about the guard's contemptuous attitude. He still had his precious dice, which he knew would help some of the men to pass the time.[18]

Like all Allied chaplains in German camps, Cavanaugh and his colleagues in the ministry insisted on their right to hold religious services as often as they deemed necessary. The camp's lower-level bureaucrats, however, put up a fierce resistance to the request, insisting on their right to censor all sermons ahead of delivery. Cavanaugh was furious and appealed immediately to the commandant of the prison, a captain named Stammler. In his conversation with the captain, Cavanaugh found him, surprisingly, to be the soul of courtesy. Seizing his opportunity, Cavanaugh proceeded to cite the Geneva Convention, the inherent right of all men to freedom of worship, and other arguments that happened to occur to him as he presented his case to the commandant. When he had finished, Stammler astonished Cavanaugh by first eliminating the censorship requirement and then granting his request that all the clergy in the camp be free to hold services whenever they wished.

Before the commandant would allow the priest to leave, however, he treated him to an imperious disquisition on the place of Catholicism in world history, pontificating at length on the role of the Catholic church in Germany, the development of the liturgy in German Catholicism, and above all the superiority of German cathedrals to those of every other country, especially those in France. Swallowing hard, Cavanaugh saluted smartly, then left. The next day he conducted the first religious services ever held in the camp, first a Mass for the Catholics, then a nondenominational service for the other prisoners. During the remainder of his imprisonment, Cavanaugh offered Mass every day and was often surprised to see Stammler himself in attendance. Neither Cavanaugh nor anyone else had known that the commandant was a Catholic, but after the Mass, he would invariably come up to Cavanaugh and tell him, in polished High German and with an icy smile, that he had a brother in Bavaria who was a priest. Cavanaugh would act suitably impressed.[19]

In March, the Germans shocked their prisoners by telling them they would all leave the camp and be moved east—toward the Russian front. The reason was obvious enough. The British and Americans were now less than sixty miles away, and there was a real danger that the western Allies might overrun the camp. The prisoners were told to be ready to leave in fifteen minutes and that they could take with them only what they could carry. Their route would take them into the eastern provinces of Germany, and for their food they would have to make out as best they could off the land and the largesse of the German people. They left at 2 A.M. on March 28, 1945. A day or two later, most of the Germans guards simply drifted away, leaving the Americans to their own devices. The first problem now was whether they should continue to go east, which would mean running straight into the Russians, whose reputation for indiscriminate ferocity had preceded them. On the other hand, going west could land them in the middle of the fighting between the Germans and the western Allies. After brief discussion, they decided to avoid both and head south into Bavaria.[20]

For the next five weeks, the tattered group would fight a daily battle for survival as the men stumbled through Bavaria's valleys and low-lying hills. Their hardest days came when Allied bombers hit German targets close by. They took every possible precaution to avoid the raids, walking at night and avoiding industrial complexes whenever possible, but despite their best efforts, they ran into trouble on April 5, the ninth day of the march. Twenty-five prisoners lost their lives, and forty more suffered serious wounds. The disaster came in the early afternoon as the group was walking along a railroad track next to a cluster of factories on the outskirts of Nuremberg. A swarm of B-17s suddenly appeared in the distance, clearly heading in their direction. "My God, we're on the target!" a man screamed as he spotted the silvery bombs falling directly down on them. Cavanaugh looked up and saw the "thin white trails" of the shells falling "almost perpendicularly upon us."[21]

Where to hide? He looked quickly around and saw nothing that offered even the slightest safety: no boulders, no shelters, not even an open hole large enough to hold a man lying on his stomach. Not knowing what to do, he jumped up and shouted at the men standing around him, "Make an act of contrition!" Seconds later, bombs began falling on the factories located on the other side of the tracks. "I fell prone and pulled my blanket over my face and began to pray," Cavanaugh remembered. As more bombs fell, he could feel the ground toss and heave underneath him. The terrible explosions continued a few seconds more, then stopped abruptly. He glanced up, but all he could see were towering columns of flame and smoke billowing out of the factories. Finally he spotted a group of soldiers running at full speed away from the field. "Keep down!" someone shouted at them. Suddenly another wave of B-17s appeared overhead. This time German anti-aircraft batteries opened up. A minute later came a third wave of bombers, then a fourth, and finally a fifth. "This must be the end," Cavanaugh said to himself. He looked around and saw bands of men standing bolt upright, open-mouthed in terror. Many others lay on the ground, apparently dead, while still others seemed alive but were clinging to the ground and trembling.

Near the end of the fifth attack, a cluster of five bombs landed in the middle of the field where most of the men were lying, killing two dozen of them at once. The concussion from the blast was so powerful that Cavanaugh estimated the bombs had slammed to the ground only fifty or sixty feet away from him. Somehow he had survived, and he began running across the field, trying to anoint the dead and wounded men before still another wave of planes arrived. "Beginning with the nearest mangled body I anointed every dead and prostrate form I could find. I ran from one to another. . . . I paid slight attention to the identity of those whom I anointed. Few were recognizable where they lay. The farther I went the more dense the dead and dying became."

At one point, a soldier found the body of one of the four Protestant chaplains who had accompanied the group. The remaining three clergymen were kneeling around him when Cavanaugh reached the spot, and as he looked at the dead man, he realized with a shock that he had already anointed him, not even realizing who he was—a brother chaplain. Grief suddenly overwhelmed him, because the two men had entered the military service at the same time, attended Chaplain School together, and joined the 106th Infantry Division on almost the same day. Paul Cavanaugh had just lost one of the best friends he would ever have. Later that afternoon, German trucks rolled into the field and picked up the most seriously wounded. Then Cavanaugh and the other chaplains combed the area one final time, looking for remaining victims of the raid. While they worked, other men walked around the grisly area, filling two huge boxes with the human remains of the raid on Nuremberg. It was a ghastly collection, Cavanaugh recalled: legs, feet, arms and chunks of flesh.''[22]

As the remaining men moved further south, their fortunes seemed to improve a little. Sometimes farmers would allow them to sleep in their barns, and a few even shared what little food they had with the emaciated Americans. The Catholic priests in Bavaria were especially generous, offering the men whatever small stores of food, clothing, or medicine they had in their rectories. Cavanaugh had only one serious complaint: A voracious horde of lice had taken up residence on his body, causing him torment both day and night. "I was literally a lousy chaplain," he recalls ruefully.[23]

After thirty-seven days of marching across Bavaria, the group arrived finally at the end of its walk to freedom. On May 3, 1945, the men stumbled wearily into the village of Gars-am-Inn, a small city on the German side of the Inn River across from Austria, and at 4:30 that afternoon, a small convoy of American tanks, part of the 14th Armored Division, lumbered into the town square and announced that Gars-am-Inn now belonged to the Allies. Not a shot was fired. Instead, wild shouts of joy went up from the whole village, with both Americans and Germans rejoicing. A new life was about to begin for the Germans, for Cavanaugh, and for the remnants of the American 106th Infantry Division.[24]

As badly as Cavanaugh and his fellow prisoners had fared at the hands of the Germans, others suffered far worse misfortunes. While the survivors of the 106th were heading south, rapidly advancing American and British armies began freeing the victims of the notorious Nazi concentration camps—and uncovering a series of horrors that would constitute perhaps the most dismaying chapter in the history of the war on the Continent. In the first week of April, a column of American tanks battered its way into Ohrdruf, 200 hundred miles southwest of Berlin, and liberated the first of the camps to fall to the western Allies. A chaplain who visited the compound several days later saw rows of "naked bodies . . . piled up like wood." It looked to him as if some of the inmates had tried to escape but had been shot and left on the side of the road to fester and rot away. In a nearby barracks he found another stack of corpses, legs and arms twisted into grotesque shapes by rigor mortis. "If there ever was an organization which seemed diabolical, it was the SS," he said.[25]

Chaplain Guy Moews, whose group stumbled upon the horrors of the camp at Illesheim, told his family that they should discount any rumors they might have heard that Allied propaganda was manufacturing grisly details in order to stiffen Allied morale for the final weeks of the war. Propaganda? "Take it from me, none of it is." Moews did admit, however, that until he had seen the horrors of Illesheim, he was one who had refused to believe what he had heard and had dismissed the tales as just another example of wartime hysteria. When he finally saw the unmistakable evidence himself, he realized that no one had invented anything. It was all too appallingly true.[26]

Near the end of April came news of the most appalling discovery of all, the infamous Dachau, soon to become a synonym around the world for heartless brutality. An armored column from Patton's Third Army liberated the camp, finding over 30,000 inmates still alive, but huge piles of grotesque cadavers as well, in addition to the crematoria the camp's leaders had used to incinerate the bodies of those who had perished. Of special interest to the chaplains who accompanied the relief force were the Catholic priests in the camp, whose numbers had fallen from an original count of 2,000 to fewer than 700. So enraged was Andrew Pollack, who saw the emaciated survivors just after their liberation, that he decided "the notion of unconditional surrender" did not "sound so extreme" after all. The Germans, he believed, merited nothing less.[27]

Soon stories about the fate of the Catholic clergy in the camp began to emerge, horrifying Catholics around the globe. Dachau's priests (most of them Polish) had been forced to endure every possible trial that their captors could invent. One day a savage guard had trampled one of them to death for no reason at all. When another asked for treatment for his legs, which had become swollen "to the thickness of wooden posts," the camp authorities refused. Since his pain had driven him into a frenzy, another prisoner choked him to death so that he would not suffer any longer. Guards had worked still another priest to exhaustion in the local quarries, and when he could no longer stand up, had sent him to the gas chamber. Catholic chaplains who interviewed the priests who had survived became bitter and determined to see that the perpetrators of such deeds received justice.[28]

Despite liberation, the health of the priests in the camp continued to deteriorate alarmingly. Deeply concerned about their welfare, the Chaplain Corps assigned one of its men to work full time with them. His orders were to see that their total rehabilitation (of body, mind, and spirit) proceeded as rapidly as possible. One of his first acts was to make it possible for the Polish priests to celebrate Mass every day, something the Germans had relentlessly denied them—which meant they had had to hold Mass in secret, often at great danger to themselves. He also arranged for them to have a festive Mass of Thanksgiving on May 3, the traditional day on which Polish Catholics commemorate their devotion to the Blessed Virgin Mary. The oldest priest at Dachau acted as principal celebrant, assisted by 200 others, and nearly 10,000 former prisoners participated in the first public Mass in the camp's twelve-year history.[29]

As American and British troops liberated the last of the prisoners of war, one last Catholic chaplain lost his life. Ralph Antonucci of Buffalo died just two days before the war in Europe ended when the small observation plane he was flying in exploded in midair. Possibly the target of German fire (though some blamed the Russians), the craft burst into flames when it crashed to the ground.[30]

Germany surrendered on May 7, 1945, but the symbolic end of Adolf Hitler's Reich came on May 3 when American and French forces entered Berchtesgaden, the Führer's mountain villa where he had spent his happiest days with his mistress, Eva Braun, his devoted secretaries, and assorted aides, generals, and other Nazi leaders. The name of the first chaplain to enter the huge installation remains unknown, but probably the best-known claimant was Raymond F. Copeland, a Jesuit from California.[31]

The end of the conflict in Europe meant not only a series of frenzied celebrations in Europe and America, but also the final counting of the dead and wounded. More than 500,000 Americans had died or suffered injury in the European Theater of Operations, with over 130,000 of them offering the ultimate sacrifice. Among the dead were twenty-three army chaplains, a third of them Roman Catholic.[32]

The remaining chaplains waited impatiently for their turn to go back to the United States for a much-needed restoration of body and spirit. Fortunately, none would have to go to the Pacific, where the fighting would continue for another three months. Few could have served there effectively, so deeply had their exhaustion overwhelmed them by the time V-E Day arrived. They had suffered too much, worked too hard, and seen too much war and bloodshed to be able to tolerate any more. For the men of God who had joined the men of war in Europe, combat had finally come to an end.

10

THE MARIANAS:
SAIPAN, TINIAN, GUAM

This I will always remember, that they had a deep and simple faith.
—Chaplain Joseph Tschantz

Before Pearl Harbor and the ensuing war in the Pacific, probably fewer than one out of every hundred Americans had ever heard of the Mariana Islands. That situation would change overnight when marine and army forces landed first on Saipan and then on Tinian and Guam in the summer of 1944. The ferocity of the struggle for Saipan, especially, quickly made that name a synonym for the savagery of war. The neighboring island of Tinian, though more easily subdued, would also become celebrated, for it would later serve as the base from which a B-29 Superfortress, the *Enola Gay*, would take off to drop the first atomic bomb on Japan. A few weeks after seizing Tinian, the Americans conquered Guam, the first former American territory to be wrested back from the Japanese. Most important of all, the American victories on all three islands marked a turning point in the war with Japan, since the islands were only 1,000 miles away from Tokyo, which put Japan's cities and sprawling industrial complexes within reach of the B-29s.

The first order of business, however, was to seize the Marianas—no easy task, for they lay nearly 3,200 miles from Hawaii, the invasion's principal staging point. Moving a convoy of over 500 ships, with a quarter million men in five divisions, presented challenges of logistics and navigation that American war planners had never dealt with before. The fact that the journey was accomplished without major incident is a tribute to the foresight and skill of admirals Richmond Kelly Turner, Raymond Spruance, and Marc Mitscher who guided the flotilla across the Pacific.

Saipan, the most heavily defended of the group, was the first target. American intelligence erred by gravely underestimating enemy strength on the island: Waiting for the invading forces (the 2d and 4th Marine Divisions and the army's 27th Division) were 32,000 seasoned Japanese troops, among the best that Japan had. Strengthening the Americans, however, was the continued interdiction of Japanese supply lines, which had kept the island's defenders from constructing the kind of stout defensive fortifications that the marines had been forced to face at Tarawa. If the campaign for Saipan was to prove less bloody than that earlier battle, the invaders could thank the navy's submarines and the bombers of both the army and the navy, which had smashed whole convoys of Japanese ships long before they could arrive at the island.[1]

Many of the marines and their chaplains had to make the voyage in unwieldy LSTs, which many of them insisted stood for "long slow trip" rather than Landing Ship, Tank, the official designation. In addition to the constant heaving of the ship, the hot and tightly confined compartments, and the massive outbreaks of seasickness, the chaplains also had to deal with the overwhelming tension that gripped many of the men as the unwieldy craft floundered across the ocean. "That's when you had a lot of men to talk to," remembered Joseph Gallagher of the 5th Marine Regiment. "They got more tense by the day." And so did Gallagher. As always before an attack, he caught influenza and quickly became so ill that he had to spend much of the final four days of the voyage sleeping in his bunk instead of tending to the needs of the men, as he would much have preferred. The night before the assault, however, he suddenly felt better, and he went to the sick bay to tell the doctors he felt in good shape for action the next day. While there, he spotted a strapping young lieutenant named Wiseman lying on a cot receiving an intravenous infusion of glucose. "He is burned out from nervous exhaustion," explained the doctor, who doubted the young officer would make it out of bed in time for the invasion. (The lieutenant, however, had other ideas. The next day he dragged himself out of bed and landed with his regiment in the early hours of the attack; a few minutes later, a Japanese mortar blast killed him.)[2]

Late in the evening on the day before the invasion, a Catholic chaplain spoke over the ship's loudspeaker and delivered what may well have been the most inappropriate announcement made by a chaplain in the war: "Most of you will return," he said, "but some of you will meet the God who made you. . . . Repent of your sins . . . those of the Jewish faith repeat after me . . . now the Christian men, Protestants and Catholics, repeat after me." If he had set out deliberately to panic the men, he could hardly have done a better job. Officers aboard the ship complained angrily, and forty years later, they were still protesting to Gallagher about the foolishness of Chaplain Peter Scully.[3]

Gallagher landed with the second wave, touching the shore at 8 A.M. He came close to death even before he reached the island. During the whole trip, he could see a blazing arc of fire vaulting over his head as Japanese batteries on shore exchanged salvos with American ships and fighter planes. Enemy fire blew up one plane, and to his horror, Gallagher could see it "coming right over our heads, just missing our amtrac [amphibious tractor] and crashing into the water only a short distance away." Waves from the explosion sent the craft bouncing so violently that he feared it might tip over.[4]

Marines crouching low in the landing boats shuddered as they heard Japanese shells exploding in the water around them. Enemy artillery and mortar pieces scored a series of harrowing near-misses, sending gigantic plumes of water rocketing skyward. Japanese fire proved more intense than accurate, however, and in the first twenty minutes of the invasion, 700 landing craft brought 8,000 troops ashore, and most of the little ships reached the landing beaches intact. Gallagher's was one of them. He jumped into the water, clambered up the sand, then threw himself flat on his stomach. "We lay on our bellies because we were being laced by mortar fire. The Japanese had zeroed in on everything—they had it all measured off." As he looked around to see where the other men were, he spotted a marine with a bad head wound. He crawled up to the man and shouted, "Are you all right?" "I'm OK, father," the marine said. "It's that guy over there—he was next to me on the amtrac, but he just got hit by mortar." A Marine Corps combat photographer standing nearby snapped a picture of Gallagher as he wiped the blood off the marine's helmet and back. A few minutes later, the photographer himself, a young man named Bernie Siegel, lay dead on the sands of Saipan.[5]

About the same time, Chaplain John Whalen made it safely to the beach as well, but no more than three minutes later, a heavy burst of mortar fire hit the sand dunes where his battalion had taken cover. Three shells landed almost at once and so close that he could feel what he called the "hot breath" of the explosions on his face. A Jewish corpsman lying next to him suddenly shouted, "Father, I've been hit." He had a look of "great surprise" on his face, Whalen remembered, as if he had expected to survive the onslaught without receiving a scratch. Just before leaving the troopship, the corpsman had asked Whalen if a priest could assist an injured marine who was not a Catholic. Whalen had assured him there was no problem at all. Less than an hour later, the man perished:

I turned around and saw two men holding the Jewish corpsman. They had a patch on his face. He was bleeding badly. It looked as if an artery had been severed. One of the men told him not to worry. "How can I help worrying?" he replied. Then he became unconscious. I think those were his last words. . . . He was failing fast. I went over to the boy, knelt beside him. I had a prayer book in my pocket which had prayers for the dying for Catholics, Jews, and Protestants. I read the Jewish prayer. Shells were still bursting around us. Men were cringing around the boy when he died.

That night, Whalen wrote the young man's parents to tell them of their son's death. On that same day, 532 other marines and army soldiers perished on the beaches of Saipan, while over 1,000 more suffered wounds, most serious enough to take them out of the rest of the war.[6]

Minutes after the corpsman died, a piece of shrapnel hit Whalen. What chaplains often called "luck and Divine Providence," however, seemed to be on his side: The shard embedded itself in his backpack, which was large enough to absorb most of the impact. His wound was thus small enough that he could return to the beach after a short stop at a nearby aid station. He was one of seven marine and army chaplains, all of them Catholic, who would suffer injury in the twenty-four day campaign for the island. All would recover in a day or two, and all would see further combat against the Japanese.[7]

Gallagher believes that he, too, would have ended up a casualty had it not been for the battlefield experience his assistant (a veteran of the Guadalcanal and Tarawa campaigns) brought with him to Saipan. By scrupulously following the younger marine's directions, Gallagher managed to stay alive. He was wise to do as he was told. Early in the first hours of the attack, the assistant pointed to a vehicle and told him, "That amtrac's going to blow up. We have to get away from here." They scampered away from the spot, and true to the assistant's prediction, a few minutes later it exploded with a thundering eruption, lifting the two men off the ground and throwing them down again. "I'm sure he saved my life just by being there," Gallagher readily admits. A second close call came just an hour or two later when Gallagher, taking a brief rest, was sitting against a stump. A marine kneeling next to him was carefully scanning the tops of the palm trees in the area, looking for Japanese snipers. "At one point, he turned around and started looking at me, then suddenly jumped up and began shooting into a hole right in back of me. There was a Jap down there. He could have reached up and cut my throat, but since there were several of us standing around, he just played 'doggo' [dead]."[8]

By nightfall, 20,000 marines guarded a beachhead that stretched 10,000 yards along the coast, though in most places it was perilously thin, less than 1,000 yards in depth. The situation was profoundly precarious, and the marine commanders knew that it was one the Japanese were sure to exploit. Officers issued strict instructions for the coming night: absolute silence, all weapons loaded and ready to fire, no movement of any kind, all bayonets fixed. Since Japanese infiltrators would certainly shout "corpsman" or "chaplain" in English, hoping that someone would move to give assistance to a wounded man and thus expose himself, all corpsmen and chaplains received instructions not to move, even if they thought they recognized the man's voice. The final instructions were curt and to the point—if a Japanese soldier leaped into a trench, stab him with your knife or bayonet to kill him silently and swiftly.

The minute the tropical sun had set and darkness enfolded the island, the Japanese began to fire star shells high into the sky in an effort to locate the Americans' foxholes. Other Japanese walked upright through the lines to try to unnerve the jittery men lying in the trenches. The marines, disciplined as always, held their fire. Then, at 2:30 in the morning of June 16, the Japanese flung a succession of suicidal charges at the American lines, shrewdly exploiting a gap between the 2d and 4th Marine Divisions. In a series of furious skirmishes, the marines used bayonets, clubs, stones, hand grenades, and anything else they could grasp to stop the screaming enemy troops.

Caught in the middle of the maelstrom was Chaplain Ronald Dinn, a Franciscan from Indianapolis. Shrapnel fell all around him, and enemy artillery shells exploded so close that he felt the earth shudder under him and saw clouds of dirt and debris hurled high into the sky. "You lay there expecting any minute to be your last, thoroughly convinced there is no possibility of ever coming out alive, only praying that the end will come quickly without too much pain." The sheer "helplessness of the situation" was enough to "unnerve" him, he said later. During a lull in the attack, a brilliant flare suddenly illuminated a band of Japanese walking calmly down a road no more than four or five feet away from where Dinn lay trembling in his foxhole. They sported a nonchalant air, daring the Americans to shoot at them but knowing that they probably would not. "The sight of those glistening bayonets, however, so close to you—burns itself indelibly into your memory." Years later, he could still remember every second of that longest night in his life.[9]

A Presbyterian chaplain also felt the brunt of the fanatical Japanese attack. Ignoring strict orders to stay put, he crawled to the aid of several critically wounded marines lying nearby, gave them what assistance he could, and then helped them prepare for their final hours of life. After the battle for the island had ended, the army awarded Charles Brubaker the Bronze Star, acclaiming the risks that he had taken on that worst of all nights for the Americans in the Marianas.[10]

For two weeks, the marines slowly pushed the Japanese away from the beaches on the western side of Saipan toward the island's northern and southeastern corners. The enemy resisted with its usual fanaticism, fighting bitterly for every yard of territory. Some of the hardest combat in the campaign came at the end of the first two weeks when the 4th Marine Division and the 27th Infantry Division pushed the Japanese onto a rocky promontory called Nofutan Point, which jutted out from one corner of the island. During that frenzied struggle, two chaplains were injured, Ronald Dinn and Paul Brunet.

While anointing a sergeant who had been shot in two different places, Dinn suddenly felt a series of sharp stabs all over his body. An enemy mortar shell had exploded only a few feet over his head, sending pieces of shrapnel into six different places, with the most serious wounds on his left arm, right leg, and the left side of his chest. Had he not been wearing his identification tags at the time, the shard that hit his chest would almost certainly have pierced his lungs. "It stopped just at the rib over my heart," he wrote afterward.[11] Dinn was taken to a hospital ship for treatment; he had seen his last both of Saipan and the war in the Pacific. On the following day, Brunet was climbing a hill not far from where Dinn had been injured, searching for wounded men unable to make their way to an aid station. A Japanese sniper fired from nearby, and a bullet grazed Brunet's right ankle. Although the shot knocked him down, it had missed the critical parts of his foot, and after receiving first aid, Brunet was able to return to combat.[12]

Joseph Gallagher also came perilously close to losing his life on Saipan. One day, while standing in a group of twelve men discussing the course of the battle, a mortar shell exploded nearby. "I remember it just taking out one or two officers standing right next to me, and several others also. I was only ten feet away from the shell. It got some, missed others." Asked why it missed him, he says, "I was so very, very lucky. It's just the hand of God." Gallagher also recalls a young trooper who came to him one day saying that he thought he had just desecrated a church. It seems that while patrolling the perimeter around his command post, he had walked into a chapel that the Japanese had used as a storage dump. As he looked around the ruined edifice, he spotted a Japanese soldier lying underneath the altar. He looked as if he were dead, but "just after I went past the altar," the soldier told Gallagher, "he suddenly opened his eyes, and reached for a hand grenade. I laced him with my carbine, giving him a couple of rounds, and killed him. Have I committed a sacrilege?"

Gallagher assured him that he had not, since the Japanese had long since destroyed the building's sacral character by removing its pictures and statues and by using it to store supplies.[13]

Despite the hazards, the island's priests and ministers held religious services on Saipan whenever the commanding officers deemed it safe enough to do so, though everyone understood that no place on the island was truly secure. Joseph Gallagher found that when he offered Mass he had to contend not only with the enemy but with the elements as well. The worst problem was the island's clouds of voracious flies. They were so fierce that Gallagher had to make sure he kept the chalice covered at all times and that he elevated the host as quickly as possible, otherwise swarms of flies would have landed on it. The flies proved especially nettlesome during burials. Since the Japanese took no interest in burying their own dead and the Americans took care of their own first, the enemy's bodies bloated and festered in the sweltering tropical heat. When it came time to bury them, the worst cases attracted thick clouds of flies, and their burial became a test of will for both the marines involved and for their chaplains.

The hardest aspect of the interment process, however, was always the shocked response of many young marines when they saw their buddies waiting to be buried. One day a youthful marine from Georgia looked suspiciously at a body, then shouted to Gallagher, "Oh my God, Father, that's my best friend." It seemed that the two had met one afternoon several years earlier at a soda fountain in the small Georgia town where they both lived and had vowed that they would enter the marines together the next day. They had taken their physical examinations in the same place, then gone their separate ways, and the young marine had not seen his friend again until that moment in Saipan. Gallagher had all he could do to help the young man regain his composure.[14]

After burying the bodies of the Americans and the Japanese, Gallagher would sometimes ask if any of the men wanted to go to confession. Dozens of Catholic men would usually respond to the invitation, doubtless moved by the sight of their fallen comrades. Occasionally, however, a response would take him by surprise. One day, for example, after he had made the usual invitation, a southern voice drawled out, "Well, I ain't no Catholic, but when this is over, I'm sure gonna be!"[15]

One Catholic priest left Saipan before the battle ended, not because of enemy action, but because of a deep-seated stubbornness and refusal to submit to military regulations. The tragedy in his case was that few marine chaplains of any denomination had shown more courage or cared for their men with greater generosity than Charles C. Riedel of the 2d Marine Division.

Chaplain Charles Riedel of Chicago stands in front of the remains of a Japanese tank on Saipan. The holstered pistol he is wearing was a violation of both army and navy regulations, since the services strictly forbade chaplains from carrying or using firearms. (Source: U.S. Marine Corps)

During the invasion of Tarawa the year before, he had buried over 300 men under heavy enemy fire, risking his life every time. The red-bearded, pipe-smoking young priest had also visited hundreds of men in the island's medical posts, going virtually without sleep for the whole four days of the campaign. When it finally ended, he wrote nearly 500 letters to families who had lost their sons in the grisly struggle. On Saipan, he distinguished himself again, of-

fering Mass under the most hazardous of conditions, ignoring shrapnel and
flying debris to help men stricken by enemy fire, and often carrying the bodies
of the fallen by himself to the nearest burial ground. At other times he could
be seen helping carry wounded men on stretchers or standing next to the doctors as they performed surgery on the injured, many of whom would not survive.[16]

Riedel, however, was a vehemently outspoken man and not one who was
given to unquestioning obedience. Shortly after the invasion of Saipan had
begun, he thought it might be interesting to get a bird's-eye view of the unfolding conflict, and without securing permission from his commanding officer, he asked a pilot friend to take him for a short flight over the island. Three
days later, when Riedel's commanding officer heard about the unauthorized
flight, he issued a stinging rebuke, confined Riedel to headquarters for the
next five days, imposed further restrictions, and told him that a copy of his
punishment would be placed in his official record in Washington.[17]

The priest wrote a furious reply to the officer, saying his punishment was
"asinine," and warning that if the order were not rescinded, he would appeal
directly to Archbishop Spellman in New York. He was confident the archbishop would take his side in the affair, since the restrictions imposed on him
would keep him from administering the Last Rites to the Catholic men
wounded in the fighting. If anyone were to be "reprimanded," he said, it
should be the commanding officer himself, though Riedel admitted he would
have to carry out such proceedings through the "proper military channels."
The proper military channels acted on Riedel's inflammatory reply in the way
it doubtless deserved: He was relieved of his duties as a chaplain in the U.S.
Marine Corps, and it was determined that he would be kept in confinement
until authorities in Washington could decide what to do with him. The
priest's reaction was to fire off a second, even more vehement, protest to his
commanding officer, accusing him of excessive "vanity," acting in a "Pat-
tonesque" manner, and guilty of a "damnable bit of vicious stupidity."[18]

The Marine Corps wasted little time: Two days later, a cable ordered him
home and he was instructed to say nothing about the incident to anyone, especially newspaper reporters and radio broadcasters. After Riedel had reported
to a new assignment in Washington, D.C., he continued to defend his cause
and did succeed in enlisting the help of several officer-friends in the corps. The
Navy Department, however, ignored his efforts to get himself back in its good
graces and issued him a discharge without the usual "certificate of satisfactory
service." It did, however, award him the Bronze Star for his work at Tarawa
and Saipan.[19]

Several months later, the Navy Department quietly let him back into the Marine Corps. The reason for this seemingly inconsistent behavior? Both the navy and the army were desperately short of qualified battlefield chaplains, and Riedel unquestionably fit the need. It seems almost certain that he would have been sent back to the Pacific, where he probably would have seen action in the battles for Iwo Jima, Okinawa, and the Philippines, but, true to form, he got himself in more trouble. This time, he lost his temper at another Catholic chaplain, knocking him down and quite thoroughly out. Asked by Archbishop Spellman to explain himself, Riedel said he had never struck a brother priest before and would most assuredly refrain from doing so in the future. He added that all the violence he had seen in the Pacific had, unfortunately, left him a little violent, too. Spellman remained unconvinced and withdrew his endorsement, while the navy, giving Riedel the benefit of the doubt, gave him an honorable discharge. Thus did one of the Marine Corps' most productive, yet thoroughly irascible, chaplains retire from the scene.[20]

Had Riedel remained on Saipan only a few days more, he would have witnessed one of the most famous bayonet charges of World War II, the massive Japanese banzai (suicide) attack of July 7, 1944. Shortly after midnight, some 4,000 Japanese soldiers charged out of the northern tip of the island, their last remaining stronghold. Running at top speed toward the American lines, they screamed at the top of their lungs, tossed hand grenades into trenches, and threw themselves into guns pits and command posts. Wave after wave of seemingly endless Japanese dashed toward the Americans, acting as if they were totally bereft of fear. One soldier who survived the onslaught thought the scene was like "one of those old cattle stampedes in the movies": They "just kept coming and coming. I didn't think they would ever stop."[21] Joseph Gallagher, who watched the melee from a nearby hill, could see the Japanese "running around crazed, running with pen knives lashed to spears." He wondered if the whole world had returned to the era of the cave man.[22]

The Japanese took the risky gambit because they had discovered a weak link in the chain that made up the American defenses, and, indeed, they came close to dividing the American forces. No more than four or five minutes into the battle, the Japanese managed to surround two battalions, and had it not been for heroic assistance from nearby amtracs, the Japanese might well have annihilated them completely. Casualties in the action were heavy for the Americans (1,045) but far worse for the Japanese, who lost over 4,000 men. Told to slay ten of the enemy for every one lost of their own, the Japanese suffered over four times as many casualties as the Americans, the largest number the Japanese had yet sustained in any single battle of the war.[23]

By the time American command declared the island secured, enough Japanese and Americans had perished (44,000 in all) to equal the population of San Bernardino, California, in the same year. For Joseph Gallagher of New York City, however, the struggle held a meaning far beyond the terrible number of casualties. First, he had discovered that no matter what crises or disappointments he would have to endure in later years, nothing would ever be as bad as Saipan. No matter what nasty twists his life would take, no matter how many disappointments he would have to suffer, none would be worthy of comparison to what he had seen, to what he had experienced in the struggle for the Marianas. Nothing.

Second, he would always feel a strange sense of uneasiness whenever he thought about the battle. He developed what psychologists would later call "survivor guilt," as he asked himself why so many others, most of them far younger than he and with their lives and their careers ahead of them, had perished in the struggle while he had been spared. And if God had protected him to use him afterward for the work of the priesthood, was he really living up to the challenges posed by his calling? He would often ask himself in later years if he were giving of himself to the people in his congregation as generously as the army troops who fell at Saipan had given of themselves to the Marine Corps and the nation.[24]

As the marines battled their way up the length of Saipan, a smaller group attacked its neighbor, Tinian. Though a shorter campaign than Saipan, it was hardly a bloodless one. Of slight consequence economically or politically, the island's historical significance goes far beyond its tiny size and scruffy outward appearance. One year and one month after the island's seizure by the Americans, the *Enola Gay* took off from one of its vast runways and dropped an atomic bomb on Hiroshima; three days later, it did the same to Nagasaki. Neither the world nor Tinian would ever be the same again.[25]

The final chapter in the struggle for the Marianas would take place on the largest of its fifteen islands, a banana-shaped piece of sand and coral called Guam. An American victory there would mean the use of the finest harbor and airfield in the chain for the remainder of the war in the Pacific; the victory also marked the first recapture of American territory taken by the Japanese in 1941 and 1942.

The island's stout defenses tested the courage of both the 77th Infantry Division and the 3d Marine Division. Chaplains in the convoy approaching

Chaplain Joseph Gallagher reads the burial service over the body of a marine killed at
Tarawa. (Source: U.S. Marine Corps)

Guam found that, as usually happened when combat neared, the minds of
many men turned to thoughts of sudden annihilation and the hereafter. Joseph Tschantz of Brooklyn discovered that the marines in his care needed no
urging from him to attend Mass and go to confession—they kept him and another priest on the same ship busy most of the day and sometimes far into the
night as well. The seriousness with which they took their religion impressed
him deeply. "This I will always remember, that they had a deep and simple
faith," he wrote later.[26]

One army chaplain, Thomas Donnelly of New York, had a somewhat different experience in the days before the invasion. For over two years he had tried
to put some religion into the lives of his men in the 77th Infantry Division but
with little success. The Catholics, it seemed to him, were the worst of all, for
nothing he tried worked. Now it occurred to him that the looming prospect
of the invasion might bestir them when every other stratagem had failed, and
shortly before the assault, he secured permission from the regiment's commanding officer to address each of the units on board ship. "I really let go at

Chaplain Joseph Gallagher presides at deckside obsequies for marines of the 4th Marine Division killed at Tinian in July 1944. (Source: U.S. Marine Corps)

them," he said afterward. He reminded them bluntly that combat lay just a few days away and warned them that "some would not come back." The stern message seemed to hit home, and the response was excellent. The six Catholic chaplains on board the transport had all they could do in the next few days to listen to the long lines of serious young men who wanted to see them, and near the end of the trip, Donnelly felt the men were ready for battle both "militarily and spiritually."[27]

Early on the morning of the invasion, some of the priests held Mass for the men who were able to attend, though they had to use their ingenuity to find a place to do so. Joseph Tschantz found that the only place he could use was his tiny cabin, which would only hold four marines. Dozens of others jammed the hallway outside, quietly participating in a ceremony they could neither hear nor see. Later, he and most of the other priests distributed communion— Holy Viaticum, communion given to Catholics in danger of death—to the large numbers of men who could not attend Mass.[28]

The invasion that followed the navy's crushing bombardment of the coast

was technically well executed, and nearly 15,000 troops landed in the first
hour alone. Unfortunately, the Japanese held the high ground behind the
beaches, and many of their largest artillery pieces, all of them well-concealed,
had survived the shelling. A blitzkrieg of fire and steel raked the Americans
huddling on the coastal strips below and kept them pinned down most of the
day. In addition, the Japanese counterattacked on both the northern and the
southern beaches of the American perimeter, and although the counterattacks
were repulsed, they left the ranks of the invaders bloodied and shaken.

The Japanese defense proved stoutest on the northern end of the island,
and marines on those beaches seemed to fall everywhere. Paul Redmond, a
Dominican, watched in horror as a navy medic amputated the leg of a
wounded man without anesthetic because none was available. A short time
later, he helped a young corpsman who had lost an eye get to a medical facility
for treatment. To his astonishment, he saw the same man four or five hours
later, administering blood plasma to another injured marine. Horror, it
seemed, went hand in hand with raw courage on that terrible Friday morning
on the island of Guam.[29]

The marines also lost a Catholic chaplain that day, young Anthony Conway
of the Archdiocese of Philadelphia. Enormously popular with both officers
and troops, the men remembered him not only for his youthful appearance (a
friend recalls him as red-headed, freckled, and "boyish" looking) but also for
his intense interest in them and his quiet, solid attitude toward his work. On
the afternoon before the attack, Conway had written his family what he suspected might well be his last letter to anyone:

Dear Pop and Mom and Everyone:
    It isn't too often I have to write a letter like this one. This is a pre-inva-
sion letter. We go into Guam tomorrow. I am not so much afraid now.
But tomorrow morning, no doubt, I will be plenty scared. But I love the
adventure. And then, the good I am doing makes fear take a back seat.
    If the worst should happen to me, know that it is God's will, and I
gave my life for the Church and the God who rules it. I took the vow at
ordination to obey. My work here is obedience at its best.
    Yes, no doubt, I will be doubly scared on this major operation. Christ
was scared when He was going to His death, for He cried out "Father, if
it be possible, let this chalice pass from me." He did it for me, I must do
it for Him. I'd go in if it were even to save one soul.
    All the good I am going to do in there makes me courageous for

"Courage is fear that has said its prayers." And there's no greater prayer than squaring souls away for God.

This afternoon, in sight of Guam, I will be offering the Holy Sacrifice on topside for all our men entering this combat, in the presence of all on board, that we might come through successfully whether dead or alive. That's why I joined the war . . . If I am a victim I know God will give me time to give [Holy] Viaticum to myself so that I will go into Eternity as I went into Guam.

Many blessings and peace. Let this be my farewell to Tom and Elmer. I haven't time to write more. Treat Tom and Elmer as you would me; they actually are your sons.

With a happy ending from your priestly son, Tony.[30]

Early the next morning, a Japanese shell blew his landing craft apart just as it touched the shore, instantly killing every man on board. When a rescue team reached the spot a few minutes later, they found Conway's body lying in the wreckage with his arms still wrapped tightly around his Mass kit. At a Solemn Requiem Mass held two months later in Philadelphia, the eulogist exhorted the congregation to live as Conway had died: "We, too, must hold on to the things of Christ, right to the end."[31]

In the three weeks of battle that followed the invasion and Anthony Conway's death, chaplains found that offering services on Guam was fully as perilous as in earlier campaigns in the Pacific. Thomas Donnelly learned at first hand what it meant to be in the front lines guarding against nighttime Japanese infiltrators. Told to stand watch just like everyone else, he sat scrunched into the bottom of his trench "with a pistol in one hand, extra clips of ammunition by my side and a knife close to my other hand, the latter to be used in close combat."[32] Happily, he never had to use any of his weapons—unhappily, he should never have had them in the first place, since they patently violated his status as a noncombatant.

Even though one may well question Donnelly's lack of judgment, no one could accuse him of a lack of courage. During one particularly severe episode of fighting on a Sunday morning, a sudden burst of mortar and artillery shells began pounding the area where he was working. He leaped instinctively into the nearest ditch and "prayed like I never did before. I was really scared." Then a shout came that enemy fire had hit someone, and without hesitating a second, he began running from foxhole to foxhole trying to locate the wounded man. "Hey Padre, get down, take cover," someone shouted at him, but he ignored the warning in his anxiety to find the stricken soldier. Later the same afternoon, however, his fear of death returned: When a power generator behind him suddenly turned on with a loud noise, he nearly fell apart with shock. "I almost dove through the earth," he said later.[33]

The battles for the Marianas proved extremely costly to both sides, consuming the lives of almost 20,000 Americans and Japanese and resulting in a total casualty count of over 50,000 dead, wounded, and missing.[34] As difficult as the struggle had been for the Americans, however, victory meant they could now prepare to invade the place where the Pacific war had started nearly three years before, and where American troops had fallen ingloriously to the Japanese. They were about to return to the Philippines.

11

THE LIBERATION OF THE PHILIPPINES

Enclosed is ten dollars. Please buy a flower and put it on my boy's grave.
Also please take a snapshot of his grave and send it to me.
—Parents of a slain soldier to a chaplain

"I shall return," Gen. Douglas MacArthur said in 1942. Ordered by President Roosevelt to leave the Philippines immediately, the general had left Manila for the safety of Australia. Now, two years later, he returned in glory. Wearing what one writer has called his best "man of destiny expression," MacArthur waded through knee-deep surf onto Leyte's Red Beach and marched purposefully up the sloping shore. A few minutes later, he gave the forces on the beach a cursory inspection, then strode with characteristic self-confidence toward a waiting radio microphone. "People of the Philippines," he intoned, "I have returned. By the grace of Almighty God, our forces stand again on Philippine soil. The hour of your redemption is here." It was vintage Douglas MacArthur. It was also Friday, October 20, 1944, the first day of the first battle in the American campaign to retake the Philippines.[1]

Enemy opposition to the invasion had proved gratifyingly light, and by late in the day, American forces had established themselves securely on Leyte's eastern shore. They seemed within easy grasp of their first targets, the port cities of Tacloban and Dulag, which they would need to supply the rest of their operations on the island. Japanese resistance began to stiffen, however, when the Americans entered the verdant Leyte Valley lying just beyond the coast and running the length of the island. With its airfields, cities, and road systems, the valley was clearly one of the keys to the campaign. Japanese artillery batteries, though not as powerful as the American firepower, nevertheless in-

191

flicted considerable damage, and Japanese infiltrators added to the misery of the Americans.

While the army was slogging its way across Leyte Valley, the navy was engaging in the largest naval action in world history, the Battle of Leyte Gulf. The action, which took place only thirty miles south of Red Beach, would mark the beginning of the end for the Japanese navy and the ultimate triumph of American ocean forces. It would also cost the Americans six ships and perhaps as many as 3,000 men.[2]

Near the end of the engagement, the Japanese resorted to suicide tactics, sending their famous kamikaze ("divine wind") planes against the vastly superior American fleet. Their small planes, each carrying a 550-pound bomb, began diving into the ships in an effort to destroy them or at least to take them out of further action. No other enemy tactic so severely tested the mettle and the endurance of the American fleet as the kamikaze campaign. By the end of the battle, Japanese planes had sunk one carrier and one destroyer and had damaged ten other ships. Worse would follow in the months ahead in the campaigns for Luzon and Okinawa.[3]

The escort carrier *Suwanee* was one of the most severely damaged of the American ships. At 7:51 on the morning of Wednesday, October 25, a kamikaze plane plowed into the ship's stern and set off explosions both on its flight deck and on lower levels. By the time the crew had put out the fires, 85 sailors had perished and another 160 were wounded or missing. Edmund Walsh, a chaplain on the carrier, received the Silver Star (given to only 5 of the 2,900 navy chaplains) for his service to the men of the *Suwanee*. The citation praised him for "constantly risking his life in his efforts to reach the dying and wounded" all during the bombing, and it added that his "courage, enduring cheerfulness and the dignity and simplicity with which he invested the burial of officers and men" had contributed greatly to the morale of the sailors and ensured that "his actions will never be forgotten by the injured and uninjured alike."[4]

While the navy was grappling with the kamikazes and the army was attempting to consolidate its gains on the eastern side of Leyte, prisoners of the Japanese in camps on the island of Luzon, south of Leyte, faced a peril of their own. The Japanese had decided to begin evacuating large numbers of their captives, including thirty-three army chaplains (twenty-one of them Catholic), and were planning to load them onto prison ships bound for Formosa and Japan. Few would survive the journey, which cost twelve Catholic priests their lives.

The magnitude of the suffering these prisoners endured on the journey staggers the imagination. Crowded into the foul, noisome holds of cargo ships, they received almost no food, water, or medicine and had almost nothing in the way of sanitation facilities. They sweated unmercifully on hot days and shivered violently during the cold winter nights. Virtually every hour of the day and night one or more prisoners perished, and the others could only watch helplessly as their bodies moldered and festered before them. The Japanese refused to bother throwing enemy corpses over the side, and the prisoners were too weak from malnutrition and disease to carry the bodies up the ladder from the hold to the deck far above. One study indicates that at least 4,000 Allied prisoners died on the prison ships.[5]

The Japanese even refused to paint the customary red cross on the side of the ships to indicate they were not ships of war, which might well have given them protection against attack by the Americans, but the Japanese seemed to care as little about their own safety as they did about the welfare of their prisoners of war. Consequently, American submarines and planes repeatedly attacked the unmarked ships, believing they were Japanese merchantmen, and since the Americans now controlled the ocean completely, any Japanese prison ship in the Pacific was almost certain to be attacked. Most of the prisoners understood the peril of their position, and the thought that they might die at the hands of their own countrymen only added to their anxiety. The story of just one of the chaplains on these ships illustrates the remarkably selfless service that was probably characteristic of all of them.

A talented, energetic young priest from Lafayette, Louisiana, Joseph V. LaFleur, had been taken prisoner by the Japanese while serving at Clark Field on Luzon. During the next two years, he wrote home several times and always gave an optimistic picture of himself as he tried to hide his real condition. Instead of enjoying good health, as he wrote his mother, one officer who escaped from the same camp reported that LaFleur was a "bed patient" in the camp's hospital and in only "fair" condition. Despite his ill health, however, he often replaced other men who had become too weak to work in the rice fields and still managed to attend to his regular duties of caring for the sick, attending the dying, and burying the prisoners who perished as a result of the loathsome conditions in the camp. Other escaped prisoners reported that he had sold his own eyeglasses and watch to buy much-needed food and medicine from the local Filipinos and that he had given most of his food to others.[6]

His greatest challenge came just a few months before he left the Philippines on a prison ship. The camp authorities announced one day that construction would begin immediately on an airfield the Japanese air force planned to use in the event of an American invasion. They selected 750 men (mostly the youngest and the strongest) for a task that promised to be so brutally demanding that it would amount to a death sentence for many. Since the Japanese would allow no chaplains to accompany the work details, LaFleur volunteered to go as an ordinary worker. Just before the project began, he wrote a letter to his mother on the back of a label taken from a can of evaporated milk and gave it to a fellow chaplain with instructions that it be sent to her if he failed to return. Perhaps he sensed that it would to be his last letter home, since he took pains to describe how he felt about his career in the military:

> Mamma, ever since I've heard about this detail I've had a feeling that something would happen and that a Chaplain should go. . . . I do not have to go, but if I didn't and something did happen I would never go back to the States, as I could never face any of you again.[7]

Almost miraculously, he somehow survived the work detail. A while later, when word reached the camp that a group of prisoners would soon leave for Formosa and that chaplains were needed to accompany them, LaFleur was among the first to volunteer.

He and the other prisoners sailed on a rusty, unwieldy Japanese scow called the *Shinyo Maru,* part of a five-ship convoy, which came to grief early in the voyage. At 4:15 in the afternoon of September 7, 1944, the American submarine USS *Paddle* struck the prison ship with two torpedoes, and of the 750 prisoners aboard, only 80 escaped the rapidly sinking vessel. LaFleur refused to leave the ship, preferring instead to remain on it so that he could help the others get off. Men swimming in the water last saw him standing on the merchant's steeply listing deck, helping the panic-stricken prisoners leave. Said one young lieutenant who witnessed the scene: "The last I saw of our friend Chaplain LaFleur he was helping wounded men get out of that hell hole onto the deck. The Japs were still shooting at them and I think only two or three of them survived. I never saw Father LaFleur again."[8] He had acquitted himself outstandingly well, though probably no more so than many of his fellow chaplains, both Protestant and Catholic, who died in the Pacific in the remaining year and a day of the war with Japan.

In the weeks following the invasion of Leyte, American forces pushed steadily inland; but after a full month of strenuous fighting, they had advanced only two miles and had suffered over a thousand dead and wounded. The last pitched battle on Leyte came at the city of Ormoc, a key port on the western side of the island. In a grueling five-week operation, the Americans battled furiously against bitter resistance, with the worst of the fighting coming on the principal road to the city. The Americans failed to gain the upper hand until the 77th Division landed on December 7, 1944 (by chance, the third anniversary of Pearl Harbor). A Japanese defeat at Ormoc was now inevitable, but not before they had bloodied the American assault forces and thrown a fright into both troops and chaplains.

The ferocity of the struggle shocked Chaplain Thomas Donnelly, who only three months earlier had witnessed the terrible mauling the Japanese had given his division on Guam. He thought that he had seen all of the horrors that the Pacific war could produce, but he was wrong. Early in the fighting for control of the main road, he was following a tank as it rattled down the highway, when a Japanese mortar slammed into its side. The vehicle exploded in flames, forcing him to stay at a safe distance. When the inferno had subsided and the tank had cooled off enough for him to approach it, he went up to the smoldering hulk and lowered himself into the turret. He must have gagged at what he saw: a heap of charred corpses lying in the bottom of the tank. Unsure of how to get them out, he finally found a rope and was able to direct a rescue crew in the removal of the incinerated remains.[9]

As gruesome as that particular task had been, Donnelly experienced an equally nauseating incident a few days later. As he stood one evening on the porch of an abandoned house, he saw in the distance a native carrying something on a stick. When the man drew closer, he could see that the "stick" was in reality a human head. Shocked at the sight, he asked the man what he thought he was doing. The Filipino replied that he was carrying the head of a Japanese soldier whom he had just dispatched to the land of his ancestors. Quick interrogation revealed that for the past several days, the Filipino had been making a nuisance of himself at a local army headquarters, and a colonel at the post, in order to get rid of him, had told him to "go out and get the heads of some Japs." Apparently it had not occurred to the officer that the would-be warrior might take him literally. Threatening dire punishment in this life as well as eternal suffering in the next, Donnelly finally got the youth to agree to bury the head, and the macabre incident came to an end.[10]

The horrible struggle for Ormoc pushed the men of the 77th Division to their limits. The closer they drew to their goal, the more relentlessly the enemy fought back. One day, when the Japanese counterattacked with unusual vehemence, Donnelly threw himself down on the ground and listened, trembling, as bullets "snapped and whined overhead." The barrage frightened him so much that at one point he began feeling a terrible hatred for the buttons on his shirt because "they kept me from getting closer to the ground."[11]

The ferocity of the enemy's artillery stunned everyone, and nothing, not even the crack of a sniper's rifle, so terrified the men on Leyte as the explosion of a close-falling shell. "A single sniper or two can make you hit the side of the road mud or no mud, water or no water, but they don't make your heart pound or your throat dry up as does the whine of a shell coming close," said Joseph Pohl of Baltimore. Once, he and a general jumped into the same muddy trench when they heard the ominous whistle of a Japanese shell. After the bombardment had stopped, Pohl realized that during the barrage the general had snatched Pohl's helmet off his head and clamped it solidly on his own. The general's helmet was still hanging on a nail 100 feet away, where he had inadvertently left it when the shelling started. "Since one doesn't argue with Generals about helmets," Pohl mused, "I let him keep mine."[12]

As the division approached Ormoc, weary chaplains wondered how much the situation would worsen before the struggle to take the city finally ended. One chaplain wrote that as the incessant tropical rain pelted down "in the darkness of the night," he lay in his trench "alert for the wily enemy who stalks in the darkness," and as the ground shook and heaved under him with the smash of artillery, he found that "God begins to enter the picture of life." It puzzled him that he had managed to survive, when so many others had fallen. Why had he been so fortunate? "I am certain the prayers of my loved ones and friends warded off the shell fragments," he said. "Others were not so lucky." The army awarded him the Bronze Star in recognition of the many times he had put the needs of his men ahead of his own. The citation noted that he had repeatedly gone "without hesitation" into areas under heavy artillery attack to assist men who were injured or had been killed by enemy fire. His "courageous action," it concluded, had won for him the "respect and admiration of the entire combat team" that he had accompanied into battle.[13]

That this priest, whom I shall call Chaplain X, was present in the Philippines at all was a tribute to the integrity, compassion, and uncommon good sense of the army's leadership in the Chaplain Corps. Earlier, he had committed an indiscretion that nearly resulted in his expulsion from the service. He had begun his career in the chaplaincy as something of a self-appointed avenging angel, and while on duty in England, he had more than once created a cause célèbre by opposing the army's practices of selling what he deemed "pornographic magazines" in its stores and of issuing condoms to the men when they left camp for an evening on the town. Unfortunately, his opposition to sexual license failed to reflect itself in his own personal life, and he had contracted venereal disease as a result of a liaison with a woman. Prompt hospitalization quickly checked his illness, but news of his lapse had spread quickly through the whole regiment, and the question now facing his superiors in the chaplaincy service was what to do with him.[14]

His supervising chaplain, Maurice Reynolds (a Protestant), took the man's measure carefully and decided that he liked what he saw. Chaplain X could hardly have had a more contrite attitude about his misdeed and did not attempt to "palliate it or excuse it." Not only had he done formal penance for his mistake, but he had "suffered bitterly" from it, said Reynolds, who argued that the man ought to be given a second chance. "He is more valuable to the service than he has ever been before," and "if he is sent to a combat zone, which he would welcome I know, we will receive valuable rewards from his service." Chief of Chaplains William Arnold agreed, and Chaplain X was sent first to a post in the United States, then to Leyte. There he distinguished himself in precisely the way that Reynolds had predicted and won the Bronze Star for repeatedly and "without hesitation" bringing "comfort and spiritual aid to the wounded and Last Rites to the dying."[15]

Few men in the chaplaincy force more deserved compassion, or gave more freely of the same, than he. A deeply caring man, he has never lost his passion for serving his fellow men, especially the neediest among them. After the war he said that his most valuable experience during that time was "being with the men when they really needed you the most, especially under fire with the wounded, the dying, and [the] dead all around you. . . . The men appreciate[d] the chaplain. It is like knowing your mother is around, when you were a kid."[16] His deep sense of moral responsibility toward all the peoples of the world also led him to condemn the Allied bombing of civilian populations, whose safety seemed to him "less and less taken into consideration" the further the war progressed. Not many chaplains took such an adamant stand against the bombing campaign so ruthlessly pursued by the British and the Americans as he.[17]

He also condemned the dropping of the atomic bomb on Japan, arguing that it was an act of "mass murder" and saying that he almost quit the army when he heard about Hiroshima and Nagasaki. After much soul-searching, he stayed in the service for the duration of war so that he could continue to assist the men in uniform. Nor did he blame the GIs he knew for thinking, almost universally, that the use of so dreadful a weapon was justifiable. They had been "misled by their government," he thought, and did not know any better. Of the Catholic priests who served in uniform, he stands out as one of the most admirable. He had made a mistake in his personal life, he had received a second chance, and he ended up giving himself totally to his men, his country, and his God in a manner that was exemplary in every way.[18]

When Ormoc finally fell, on December 10, Chaplain X, who saw the city immediately after its liberation, thought the city looked like the old paintings he had seen in his youth depicting the burning of Rome. Nothing stood in the mass of smoldering ruins except a solitary chimney or two. When he glanced into a hut and saw the remains of a Japanese soldier who had just hanged himself, he continued to wonder about the stubborn preference of the Japanese for death over surrender. With the capture of Ormoc, the most important fighting in the campaign for Leyte had concluded, though the Japanese would continue to hold out in isolated pockets in the hills east of the city until the end of December.[19]

Christmas brought the men on Leyte the best possible present, an announcement from MacArthur that the campaign for the island had ended. Concluded the general, "This closes a campaign that has had few counterparts in the utter destruction of the enemy's forces with a maximum conservation of our own,"[20] even though the number of American casualties had exceeded those of Guadalcanal, Tarawa, New Guinea, New Georgia, and Bougainville combined. In the battle for Leyte, over 4,000 American soldiers and sailors lost their lives, and another 13,000 were injured.[21]

As always, the chaplains took a deeply personal view of the cost of the campaign, one far transcending the numbers on the casualty lists. One of them remembered that his division alone had left three cemeteries behind on Leyte. Another spoke movingly of the many "harrowing days" he had spent accompanying the dead of his regiment to the graveyard. The cost to him, as their friend, mentor, and chaplain, had been enormous. "These were men with whom I had served for three years; they were fine lads," simply "the best" he had ever known. No less wrenching were the letters he received from brokenhearted families at home. Wrote one mother: "Enclosed is ten dollars. Please buy a flower and put it on my boy's grave. Also please take a snapshot of his grave and send it to me."[22] For sensitive men such as Chaplain Thomas Donnelly, high-sounding statements from MacArthur about the "maximum conservation" of American forces sounded cruel and hollow. A piece of his heart, and a piece of the hearts of all his fellow chaplains on the island, would remain buried forever on the island of Leyte.

Despite the heavy cost of the fighting, the American cause in the Pacific had taken a major leap forward. As the Japanese leaders in Tokyo realized all too well, only 1,200 miles of ocean now separated them from the onrushing Americans. From this point on, they could expect nothing except a continuance of the merciless American bombing of their cities and a further tightening of the Allies' naval blockade. The Americans, however, faced a challenge of their own. When they invaded Luzon, they would have to seize a much larger and more mountainous area. They would also have to battle an enemy force that, though greatly weakened, was more determined than ever not to retreat again. Only the foolish predicted an easy victory; the combat-wise made no predictions at all but waited to see what would happen when the final, climactic battle for the Philippines began.

Luzon is the largest of the more than 9,000 islands in the Philippine archipelago, and the battle for it would be the bloodiest thus far in the Pacific. By the time it ended and the last gun had fallen silent, the casualty count would number over 40,000 Americans and at least 160,000 Japanese. In terms of the magnitude of human slaughter, it would be surpassed only by the struggle for Okinawa, which would begin only a few months later. Why so expensive an operation against an enemy weakened by a lack of supplies and a string of previous defeats? Quite simply, the Japanese refused to give up. The Allied drive on Manila succeeded only after the Americans and the Filipinos had blasted the Japanese out of their prepared positions, with victory coming only after a protracted struggle in the rubble-strewn city. In the end, the Americans achieved victory in the rugged mountains in the northern part of the island only after many long months of prolonged and bitter fighting.

Even before the Americans set foot on Luzon, they had to endure more Japanese kamikaze attacks. No one suspected that after a somewhat tentative use of their new weapon in the earlier campaign for Leyte, the Japanese would suddenly unleash unprecedented numbers of the deadly little planes in the battle for the larger island. By the time the seaborne struggle for Luzon had ended, suicide planes had sunk or damaged twenty-five American and Australian ships, taken the lives of 900 American sailors, and injured nearly 1,500 more—one of the worst disasters the navy sustained in World War II.[23]

The Luzon Attack Force, as the navy called its armada, included a powerful collection of carriers, battleships, cruisers, and destroyers whose assignment was the destruction of both the Japanese forces on the landing beaches and the airfields and strong points in back of them. As the American troopships headed toward the shore in a huge bay on the western side of the island called Lingayen Gulf, the Japanese aimed their kamikazes at the attack force. One of the most heavily damaged ships was the carrier *Ticonderoga,* which was hit twice on Sunday, January 21.

Chaplain Cornelius O'Brien of New York had just finished his noontime radio broadcast to the crew, giving the war news for the day and announcing the day's religious services. He had started to walk back to his cabin when the ship's loudspeaker barked out a peremptory order: "All hands, man your battle stations. On the double!" O'Brien had just started running to his assigned position when a Japanese plane smashed through the ship's flight deck, its 550-pound bomb exploding between two lower decks. Sheets of fire and clouds of smoke soon began spreading the length of the ship, enveloping it from stem to stern. "I started out, and *whang,* we got hit. The whole ship shook. We were trapped below the hanger deck."[24] Running down the corridor, he had gone only a few yards when he came across a body lying facedown in the hallway, the first of many bodies of young men that he would see that day. This particular victim was a pleasant young Catholic sailor who had served at O'Brien's Mass only that morning. "His whole goal" had been "to get out of the service and get himself a jeep. A real nice kid," O'Brien remembers, "about nineteen."[25]

Twenty minutes later, a second kamikaze rammed into the stricken carrier, "spattering everybody," as O'Brien puts it, with shrapnel and more fire. "I got wounded—burned a little, but not bad. I was lucky. Everybody around me got it pretty badly. I went around, anointing people, and trying to get order out of chaos. I was scared to death, but I just did what I had to do." Asked years later if he considered himself a hero, in view of the risks that he took that day for the men on the ship, he replied vehemently: "Nobody can tell you that they're a hero. That's a lot of bull. Everybody's scared to death. Everything happens so fast. Either you get hit, or you don't get hit."[26] Many men on the *Ticonderoga* had been hit, however, and O'Brien would have many burials to conduct and many letters to write to the next of kin at home during the weeks that lay ahead.

Amazing as it might have seemed to those on board the *Ticonderoga,* the worst of the kamikaze attacks had ended by this time because so many of the young Japanese pilots who flew them had perished. By the middle of January, the Japanese had only twelve kamikazes left out of their original pool of over two hundred, and the suicide attacks would cease for four months. During that period, the Japanese would increase the number of kamikaze pilots sufficiently to launch a final onslaught, the worst of the war, on the American navy at Okinawa.

The first American troops landed on the wet, sandy shores of Lingayen Gulf at 9:30 A.M. on January 9, following heavy naval and air force attacks on the Japanese-held shoreline. Less than a week later, 175,000 American troops had reached the beachhead and were ready to move into the interior of the island. Japanese opposition proved light at first, a mere "walkover" in the estimate of the campaign's historian, but Japanese resistance soon stiffened, with so many

men falling in the first week of the drive that the army had to set up a temporary cemetery only a mile or two beyond the beaches. Assigned to burial duty,
Jesuit Chaplain William Leonard of Boston drove his jeep to the cemetery one
morning, and his heart fell as his eyes took in the scene before him. What
struck him first was the sheer magnitude of the place—3,500 new white
crosses lined up row after dismal row. Later he noticed an odor of a "disgust-
ing, sweet" character, one that he could not identify. He asked a young soldier standing nearby what it was. "Bodies, Father," he said. "Those are our
guys' bodies. We can't dig graves fast enough."

As Leonard walked among the rows of crosses, he began to notice how
young those buried there had been when they died. Here and there an older
man lay buried, but most of the dead were youngsters only eighteen or nineteen years of age. The scene put a chain of thoughts into motion that changed
the rest of his life. "For this, some poor woman labored for nine months,
brought the child into the world, took care of every need, watched him grow
up, proud, and this is the way it ends? There's got to be a better way." The
magnitude of the catastrophe overwhelmed him and changed his views about
the justice of warfare. "I became a pacifist, and still am," he says. No war was
worth such a price.[27]

As the Americans began their assault on Luzon, Catholic and Protestant
chaplains, as well as hundreds of other prisoners, continued to perish in ships
taking them from Manila to Formosa and Japan. Three more chaplains would
die at sea, and the same number would fall in the campaign for Luzon itself.
Finally, at the end of January, the last priest-chaplain to die in the sea gave
gave up his life. He was William P. Cummings, to whom history has attributed authorship of the phrase, "There are no atheists in foxholes." Like all
the other chaplains whom the Japanese had captured, he had endured a seemingly endless ordeal, first at Bilibid in Manila, then Cabanatuan to the south
of the city, and finally the agony of the trip across the ocean. His ship, however, was attacked more than once by the Americans. The first assault came in
Manila Bay, the second at a harbor in Formosa. The same ship would later undergo a third bombing at the hands of American forces, but by that time
Cummings was dead. The few prisoners on his ship who managed to last until
the end of the war told an astonishing tale of Cummings's nightly talks to the
men deep in the confines of the ship. One night as they squirmed for space in
their fetid quarters, fought for air, screamed for food and water, and stumbled
over the bodies of the dead, the sound of their cries rose higher and higher.

Just when it seemed that they might turn into a hysterical mob, a voice rang out over the clamor. As one officer recalled:

> Father Cummings began to speak. The sound was clear and resonant and made me feel he was talking to me alone. The men became quiet.
>
> "Our Father who art in heaven, hallowed be Thy name. Thy kingdom come. Thy will be done on earth as it is in heaven.". . . The voice went on. Strength came to me as I listened to the prayer, and a certain calmness of spirit.
>
> "Have faith," he continued. "Believe in yourselves and in the goodness of one another. Know that in yourselves and in those that stand near you, you see the image of God. For mankind is in the image of God."
>
> For a while sanity returned to the faces around me. Then slowly the wails and cries began to rise again. But some of us continued to be held by the strength in that voice, the voice of a man who believed and who wanted us to believe.[28]

Over the course of the ship's month-long passage to Formosa, Cummings so spent himself in the service of the men on board the vessel that it seemed to some as if he never slept or ate. He gave of himself totally to his fellow victims, until finally he had nothing more to give, and his life simply withered away. As the ships in the Japanese convoy crashed through the heavy winter seas, snow fell through the open hatches, and ice rimmed the sides of the ship and the cargo compartment in which those still living struggled to stay alive. One day, two prisoners found Cummings lying silently next to the icy wall of the ship. He looked dead. They rubbed his arms, hands, and face, and life slowly returned; first his eyelids flickered, then he opened them wide and said, "I'll be all right." But illness and malnutrition had taken their toll. That evening, he gathered what little strength he had left to lead his men in prayer one last time. In the middle of the prayer, his body sagged, and his companions knew that he had passed from their midst. Ropes tumbled down into the hold, and winches lifted the body out of the darkness. As the Japanese guards unceremoniously threw his body on the top of a pile of other cadavers, "I closed my ears against the sound of the bodies as they went down into the water," a man said afterward.[29]

The loss of over twenty army priests and ministers in the Philippines was a disaster for the Chaplain Corps, but hope for some of those still imprisoned in the Philippines began to rise as American forces advanced down Luzon. Three weeks after the landings at Lingayen, a 300-man force of Rangers rescued the Allied prisoners of war still incarcerated at Cabanatuan in an operation that has few equals in terms of bravado, courage, and sheer derring-do. One morning in late January, as a heavy storm lashed Cabanatuan and the nearby city of Los Banos, the prisoners inside the camp abruptly heard the snap of small-arms fire coming from the rear of the enclosure. Then they heard firing on another side, and finally on all four sides. Everyone quickly hit the ground. Jesuit Chaplain Eugene O'Keefe was so anxious to dig himself as far into the ground as possible that when he realized his arm was lying awkwardly outside his trench, he wondered how he could possibly get it under cover without exposing his whole body. Suddenly he heard someone say, "The Yanks are here," and he looked up. A lanky Ranger officer stood over him.

"Boy, I'm sure glad to see you," O'Keefe said.
"Glad to see you, too."
"Where are you from, soldier?"
"Oklahoma."
"That's good enough for me. Oklahoma is a state I'll never forget."[30]

A task force of American Rangers and Filipino troops immediately launched an attack on the barracks of the Japanese soldiers, and after twenty minutes of violent skirmishing, the shooting stopped, leaving one American soldier dead and the Japanese garrison annihilated. The Rangers had freed the prisoners of Cabanatuan, though all of them still had a long and perilous journey to make through Japanese-held territory before they reached the American lines many miles away. By the end of the day, they had finally reached the safety of the American-held town of Guimba, where a riotous welcome awaited them.

"It was like a triumphal march," said one Catholic chaplain, describing the trip past lines of cheering American troops who offered them cigarettes, chocolates, and candy. Even the Supreme Commander of the Southwest Pacific Area, General MacArthur himself, paid them a visit. Wearing his accustomed informal garb, he delivered a speech of welcome, then passed out cigars to everyone. He quite overwhelmed the chaplains. "We were really back home now," John Dugan of Boston said to himself, "with our old chief, our beloved leader." Ended were the long years of what another priest called a "barbaric, cruel and often bestial existence." Ahead lay an entirely new life, one with lengthy hospitalization for some but new assignments for others. All looked forward to the conclusion of the war with the Japanese and the trip home. "God was with us," Dugan said to a reporter from Boston. No one would disagree.[31]

They would live to see both the liberation of the Philippines and the most awesome chapter in the history of the retaking of those islands, the battle for the city of Manila. Before the Americans could enter the capital, however, they first had to run a fierce gauntlet of obstacles that the Japanese had thrown in their way. The drive from the north, though less than fifty miles in length, would be a furiously contested assault that would take nearly three weeks, cost thousands of casualties to both sides, and leave much of the northern part of the island a wasteland.

The drive to reach Manila began less than two weeks after the initial landings in the Lingayen Gulf. MacArthur gave unmistakable orders to his field commanders: "Go to Manila, Go around the Nips, bounce off the Nips, but go to Manila."[32] To spur his forces on, he divided them into two groups ("flying columns," he called them), hoping that rivalry between the two forces would accelerate the capture of the city. The Japanese tried mightily to slow the 100,000-man American mastodon, and with the help of heroic efforts by their frontline troops, they managed to make the campaign much more difficult and longer than a frustrated MacArthur had hoped. At last, on Saturday, February 3, at eight in the evening, the 8th Cavalry Flying Column entered the city's suburbs, although it would be a month before the Allies had secured the city.[33]

As darkness fell on February 3, tanks of the 44th Tank Battalion broke through the outer walls of San Tomas University, which the Japanese had turned into a prison, and freed the 4,000 emaciated prisoners garrisoned inside. Their condition shocked the Americans who saw them. William Leonard found a priest-friend from Boston who had been "huge" when Leonard had last seen him ten years earlier. "He must have weighed 257 pounds," Leonard recalls. Now, "here was this specter, who weighed about 90 pounds. He had to tell me who he was."[34] The city itself had fared no better. The magnificent district called Intramuros (walled city), the pride of the nation, had virtually disappeared. "I felt like a ghost in a dead city," lamented Filipino political leader Carlos P. Romulo as he walked slowly through the capital of his native country.[35] Leonard thought it looked as if some "mad giant" had marched across the city "swinging a bloody, flaming scythe." The principal buildings, many of them architectural marvels, had become "mere walls about eight feet high, filled with rubble." Everywhere Leonard and his companions walked, a "sickening stench filled the nostrils, and we saw dead and decaying bodies of Japs and Filipinos lying in grotesque postures—some half burned, with clouds of flies rising above them."[36]

Army Chaplain Raymond Ponda offers Mass in front of the Church of Saint Augustin located inside the Intramuros (walled city) sector of Manila. The liturgy, the first in the sector since the Japanese captured the city in January 1942, took place two days after Manila had been regained by the Allies. Artillery-shell marks are clearly visible in the church's walls, columns, and statues. (Source: National Archives)

When the American troops reached the notorious Bilibid Prison, a priest from Rochester, New York, became a virtual one-man ambulance force in his attempts to rescue wounded soldiers during a savage battle around the camp's observation tower. Elmer Heindl had earlier seen combat on Bougainville, where he had earned medals and honors, but the battle at Bilibid would push his resources and his courage to new limits.

After a fierce struggle, the Americans had finally succeeded in wresting the tower from the Japanese and had put three observers on top to follow the enemy's movements in the rest of the compound. Late on the night of February 6, however, the Japanese decided to try to take the tower back and began pouring a devastating rain of machine-gun fire onto it. When a bullet smashed into one observer (a young private), he shouted for help, and Heindl and an army corpsman quickly ran out into the yard and began climbing the narrow wooden stairs to the post on top. Streams of bullets followed them all the way. Just as they reached the platform, a bullet hit another observer. The medic turned on his flashlight for an instant in an attempt to locate the wound of the first injured man, but his light gave the Japanese an excellent target, and they fired again. Somehow they missed all of the Americans huddling on the bottom of the platform.

Heindl, meanwhile, had knelt next to one of the soldiers and was offering prayers for his soul. When he had finished, he and the medic began handing down the wounded men to a rescue party standing at the bottom of the stairs, who in turn carried them across the prison yard to safety. When another soldier tried to occupy the post later that night, the Japanese shot him, too, and again Heindl went up the stairs and helped to carry him out. Two days later, Heindl crawled across the prison compound while under heavy fire to rescue a wounded officer and succeeded in moving him, too, back to an aid station.

For his magnificent efforts during the fighting for Bilibid Prison, Elmer Heindl received the Distinguished Service Cross. When asked, many years later, what it was like to be a war hero, he insisted that heroism had nothing to do with it. The award "doesn't add one bit to my stature," he said. "I went down there to do my duty as a chaplain," and that was all there was to it. He insists that in a lifetime of serving the military, he has failed to meet even a single veteran of combat who said that he had received anything but "pain" out of what he had to do. "We hate the Rambo image," he added.[37]

On March 3, Douglas MacArthur could at last announce the end of Japanese resistance in Manila—but the Allies had paid a fearful cost. At least 100,000 Filipino citizens lay dead, over 1,000 American soldiers had perished, and another 5,000 had been wounded. The carnage had annihilated at least 16,000 Japanese as well, many of them young sailors commanded by a maniacal Japanese admiral in charge of the city's defense, who most earnestly desired to have all of his men perish in flames rather than surrender either themselves or a livable city.[38]

Although the Allies had gained control of Manila, the Japanese still held parts of Luzon, and early on the morning of April 9, 1945, Chaplain Robert Hearn of the 1st Infantry Regiment found himself caught in the middle of a brief but sharp skirmish near the coastal hamlet of Darago. His battalion soon stormed into the town, quickly took control of it, then set up headquarters in a large building adjoining the town's tiny church. All went well until nightfall when the Japanese abruptly staged a well-timed counterattack, forcing the Americans outside to retreat into the building, shooting as they went. Anxious to get a better view of what was happening, Hearn went up to the second story. While watching the fighting below, the sounds of the battle began to quiet down, though he failed to notice the change. What he did not know was that the Americans had run out of ammunition and had abandoned the village. Hearn had his first hint of a bad time to come when, after a long silence, he heard the chattering of Japanese voices below.

He managed to hide in a closet just seconds before the Japanese smashed into the building, bounded up the stairs, and began shooting stray bullets into all the rooms. One hit Hearn in his right shoulder, another his left side, but somehow he kept from screaming out in pain. Then the soldiers ran into the room in which he had hidden himself and began opening the closets. There were three of them, all in a row. They opened the first, found nothing, then opened the second. Hearn's throat was so dry he thought he would choke, but he dared not make a sound. He wondered if they could hear the ticking of his watch, and he had a sudden urge to give himself up, but the thought of decapitation, instantly administered on the spot, deterred him. Just as a hand began turning the doorknob on the third closet door, his closet, an American artillery shell landed on the roof of the building, showering the room with plaster and paint and distracting the Japanese from the third closet. He stood, riveted, behind the unopened door.

For the rest of the night, he waited in rigid silence, making not even the slightest noise, because he knew that any sound at all would betray his presence. He wanted to recite his rosary but feared that the clicking of the beads would give him away, so he repeated "Our Fathers" and "Hail Marys" as fast as he could say them, fully convinced that each one would be his last prayer on earth. Sometime around 2 A.M., the Japanese began using the room as an emergency aid station and carried in the worst of their wounded men. Without ceremony or anesthesia, Japanese doctors proceeded to amputate limbs and core out injuries; Hearn thought that he would vomit and once again wondered if perhaps he should give himself up just to end the agony. Just before daylight, a Japanese officer appeared in the room, smiled, then bowed ceremoniously to each patient. He spoke in a crisp professional manner to the physicians, then examined each casualty carefully to see if he was still battle worthy. Those he judged unfit, he promptly dispatched with a swift slice across the throat. Hearn looked at the scene and froze with horror. By now he was wondering how much more shock he could possibly take.

Unbelievably, relief arrived. With the first rays of dawn, shots rang out, and Hearn heard American voices. When the firing stopped, he wondered whether the Japanese had fled or were simply staying quiet so that they could ambush the Americans when they entered the building. What to do? His heart smashing against his throat, he decided he would open the closet door. No one there. Where were the Japanese? He stepped quietly into the corridor and looked both ways. Still clear. He walked to the top of the staircase and saw twenty American soldiers standing at the bottom, all with their machine guns pointing straight up at him. Nonchalantly he walked down the stairs, saluted briskly, said, "Hi guys, it's me," and proceeded to walk jauntily out the door. They looked at him with stupefaction; they had thought the Japanese had caught and killed him the night before.[39]

When Hearn returned home to Baltimore later that year, he too arrived as a bona fide war hero—bemedaled, wounded in two places, and the subject of one of the most harrowing war stories experienced by any chaplain in the conflict. Like Elmer Heindl, he took a skeptical view of battlefield heroics. "When you're caught in artillery fire you want to be any place but in a hero's niche," he insisted. "But then something happens, and though your teeth are chattering, you say, 'Well, here I go. Stand by, Guardian Angel,' and there you are. And they give you a medal."[40]

Another chaplain rendered fervent appreciation for the awarding of—what shall I call it—a less-spiritual favor. The Almighty, in His infinite bounty, had blessed him at long last with a good stiff drink of whiskey. A third chaplain, assigned to the same area, had also endured three piteously long years in the Pacific theater deprived of what he dubbed "the old creature" (alcohol). When he searched, of an evening, for the solace that only such a drink could provide, all he could find was what he called the wretched "native liquor" dispensed by the local purveyors, which he judged terrible in every way. "Its stench is enough to break a chronic alcoholic," he lamented. When the fighting in the area finally ended, it seemed to him as if the heavens themselves truly smiled down upon him, for the Quartermaster Corps managed to find him a quart of the most exquisite vintage. The pleasures of victory had never seemed so sweet.[41]

Another priest-chaplain perished in the struggle for the second-largest and most southerly of the islands, Mindanao. Aquinas T. Colgan, a Carmelite priest from Chicago, seemed an unlikely candidate for the military chaplaincy. He was short, thin, and heavily bespectacled. Gifted, however, with boundless energy, a natural wit, and a deep concern for his men, he soon won the affection of the overwhelmingly Protestant 31st Infantry Division, called the "Dixie" Division because of its entirely southern origins.

Although loved for his humor, no chaplain ever took his ministry more seriously, and when the division moved to New Guinea and entered combat, he seldom left the front—a fact his men would later recall with the deepest admiration. Colgan's devotion to the foot soldier came to the notice of his regimental commander, who described him as both a "cheerful and intelligent chaplain" and "a decided asset to the morale of any regiment."[42] By the time the 124th Regimental Combat Team landed on Mindanao, its officers and enlisted men had come to the conclusion that he was easily the most popular chaplain in this least Catholic of regiments (indeed, many of the men in the regiment had never even seen a priest before the war). As happened so often in the war, religious differences had become irrelevant.[43]

Colgan and 3,700 other American soldiers would suffer grievously in the campaign to subdue Mindanao. Most of the operations on the island went quickly, but the battle took an ugly turn in the north, where 100,000 ill-supplied but determined Japanese troops made the Americans pay bitterly for any success. Fighting in atrocious terrain, three American divisions found themselves battling not only Japanese snipers and machine guns but a tropical climate of almost unparalleled horror as well. The Americans had found hell in Mindinao: It rained nearly forty inches a month, a so-called highway turned out to be nothing more than a jungle trail, swarms of locusts gravely weakened many men, and treacherous native tribesmen called "Moros" turned out to be totally unreliable.[44]

In this relentlessly hostile atmosphere, the 124th received an assignment to drive north on the gloriously named but almost impassable Sayre Highway. Ministering to the men while often slipping and sliding in the mud, trying to survive violent tropical drenchings, fighting temperatures hovering between 90 and 100 degrees, and often going with little food or rest for three or four days at a time left Colgan worn out and discouraged. Still, he carried on. His last day of service was in a now-idyllic glen in the mountains of northern Mindanao called Colgan Woods. The place is still difficult to reach, but once there one finds a virgin stand of rain forest, swarms of brilliantly colored butterflies, and trees hanging heavy with tropical fruit. One might even be fortunate enough to catch a glimpse of the magnificent and rarely seen Philippine Eagle. Today, the glen looks much like a scene from a National Geographic documentary on tropical rain forests.

In this tranquil setting raged a furious struggle between forward elements of the 124th Regimental Combat Team and a heavily armed Japanese battalion. The skirmish reached a frenzied climax shortly after noon on Sunday, May 6, 1945. Colgan had just finished offering Mass a few yards from the forest, when he heard the sound of gunfire and men shouting for help. The Japanese had quickly detected what the Americans had hoped would be a surprise attack and had poured heavy mortar fire into their ranks. The Americans withdrew, fired their own mortars, then sent their infantry back into the thicket a second time. This time the Japanese hurled all the ammunition they had at the troops now caught in the heavy undergrowth. Those who survived scrambled back to safety; the rest lay dead or bleeding in the dank jungle.

The cry of "medics" went out, but when several corpsmen ventured into the area, they too fell victim to withering enemy fire. When Colgan reached the area, he told the officer in charge that he intended to go into the brambles immediately. "Those are my boys in there," he said. "They need me. I should be with them." The officer argued vehemently, insisting that he should stay out of the area because snipers were everywhere. Colgan ignored his protests and began running, a corpsman accompanying him. "He must have known that he had little hope of coming out alive," the same officer said later.[45] At the edge of the woods, the two men threw themselves to the ground and inched their way forward on their stomachs. They had scarcely made it to the side of a wounded soldier when volleys of enemy fire killed each of them instantly. It was six days before rescue crews could safely go into the thicket, but when they did so, they found Colgan still clinging to the legs of the soldier he had tried to drag to safety. That is why the men of the 124th Regimental Combat Team named the place after their fallen chaplain. That is why they called it Colgan Woods. And that is why it still bears his name today.[46]

It can be said of Aquinas T. Colgan that the Army Chaplain Corps had none more loved, nor any more greatly missed. The supervising chaplain of the 31st Infantry Division, a Protestant, told of visiting a field hospital a few days after Colgan's death. Many of the men he talked to remembered a day, only a week earlier, when Colgan had talked to them at Mass and had told them how much they had all inspired him and how their bravery had moved him to the depths of his soul. Now he was gone. Both officers and men, the chaplain reported, "had tears in their eyes as they spoke of him."[47] For most of the men, he had been the "little padre," the happy-go-lucky fellow with the cross on his lapel who had crawled up slippery gorges and slogged his way through knee-deep mud just as they had. To the officers who watched his work from a higher plane, he was even more. Gen. Robert Eichelberger, who led the campaign in Mindanao, paid written tribute to him years later when he wrote, "Father Colgan repeatedly risked his life to bring in wounded men who lay exposed and helpless." The "GIs idolized him," he noted, and so, apparently, did Eichelberger himself.[48]

Three months later, Gen. Isoroku Yamashita, the officer in charge of Japanese forces in the Philippines, surrendered himself and his command of 50,000 troops on Luzon. But even while the army remained locked in combat with the Japanese in the Philippines, an even more fearsome battle was unfolding 1,500 miles northeast of Manila, one that would become the most storied battle of the Pacific war and would be called, by common agreement, the Marine Corps' finest hour. The battle took place on a tiny, unknown island called Iwo Jima.

12

IWO JIMA

It was a flash, a concussion. . . . When I came down my feet and the
lower part of my body were buried about six feet under the ground; my
head was about one and [one-half] feet under.
—Chaplain James J. Deasy

Iwo Jima: the bloodiest battle of World War II in the Pacific, the Marine
Corps' finest hour, and a turning point in the war against Japan. The struggle
has become the stuff of legend, epitomized above all by the celebrated photograph of the raising of the American flag on top of Mount Suribachi.

If the campaign for Iwo Jima has emerged over time as the greatest accom-
plishment in the 200-year history of the Marines, it was also its costliest victory, with 30 percent of the invading force either perishing in the volcanic
sands of the island or wounded. The men of the Marine Corps garnered
twenty-seven Medals of Honor in recognition of their heroism, but they also
lost whole companies and battalions in the slaughter that preceded their triumph over the Japanese.

At the time, many Americans wondered why a major engagement had to be
fought over the island: Iwo Jima, it seemed, was utterly worthless, without
any discernible intrinsic value. Nature had failed to endow it with a single
growing thing—no plants, no trees, no grass—not even a water supply of its
own. On the other hand, nature had made it a perfect bastion for defense,
with its slick gray volcanic ash, a 550-foot peak, and deep, easily fortified
ridges and gorges. Then why Iwo Jima, especially in view of the enormous
number of casualties, over 45,000 for both sides?

In the space of only a few months, the island had assumed a military importance far beyond its small size and despicable appearance. After the fall of the

Mariana Islands in the summer of 1944, the Army Air Force began sending its huge, long-range B-29 Superfortresses against the Japanese home islands, and only one problem stood in the way of the continued success of the bombing campaign—the island of Iwo Jima. Unhappily for the Americans, it lay almost exactly halfway between the Marianas and Japan and afforded the Japanese an opportunity to sabotage the bombing effort. From airfields on the island the Japanese sent up swarms of fighter planes to harass the largely unprotected B-29s and severely interdict the navy's air-sea rescue efforts. Most ominous of all, the Japanese had spiked the island with radar antennas that picked up the massive bombers as they sped north to Japan, giving ample warning to the Japanese at home that an attack from the air was imminent. As a result, a hot reception often awaited the planes when they approached the enemy's shores. The next move seemed obvious: Iwo Jima had to fall.[1]

The Iwo Jima task force left the Marianas just four days before the scheduled beginning of the invasion. The navy had assembled the largest convoy yet seen in the Pacific war, a vast, rolling armada of nearly 500 ships lined up in pencil-straight columns 70 miles long. The target lay almost 600 miles away in a due northerly direction, and as the convoy swept northward through heavy, white-capped seas, the temperature dropped steadily every day. The long journey to Iwo Jima would be no South Seas adventure for the marines aboard the transports.[2]

The 70,647 men of the 3d, 4th, and 5th Marine Divisions would carry out the attack, and as always, their chaplains accompanied them. Fifty-eight chaplains, representing every major denomination in the United States would either land with the troops on the island or serve the support groups waiting offshore. Nineteen were Roman Catholics, and of those, two were Jesuits: Charles F. Suver from Oregon and James J. Deasy of California.[3] I will focus principally on them because their work on the island is by far the best documented. The experiences of the other chaplains on Iwo Jima differed little from their own. Both Suver and Deasy came within inches and seconds of losing their lives, not just once but several times, and both remain haunted by their memories of the struggle. They also recall the unparalleled heroism of the marines who took the island yard by bloody yard and sometimes even foot by foot. Most important, both found that the Iwo Jima experience gave them a deepened appreciation of their vocation as Roman Catholic priests, just as it did for their non-Jesuit and non-Catholic colleagues.

The daily schedule on the way to Iwo Jima provided for periods of exercise and entertainment in the morning and afternoon, followed by lectures about the island in the evening. During the day, the men played football, smoked, wrote letters home, and, of course, saw their chaplains. After dinner, intelligence officers aboard each ship briefed the men on what to expect. They would face a set of truly daunting obstacles: stiff Japanese defenses, the certainty that the Japanese knew exactly where they would land because the island offered only one set of beaches suitable for an invasion, the expertise and courage of the 23,000 Japanese Imperial Marines who held the island, and their suicidal determination to keep it for the glory of the emperor. The marines knew that they could expect an extraordinarily high number of casualties.

The maps and models of the island were sobering, and the marines examined them silently, many stupefied at what they saw. Some went away quietly shaking their heads, wondering what would happen when they finally landed, and James Deasy remembers that two or three men on his transport jumped overboard and drowned themselves rather than face the prospect of landing on Iwo Jima.[4] As the convoy closed in on its target, all of the clergymen experienced increasing demands on their time from the young men on board, as they prepared to face what would certainly be a fight for their lives. Charles Suver noted a rising tension, with most of the conversation centering on Iwo Jima instead of the usual subjects of women, beer, and professional sports. Deasy and the other chaplains saw the same anxieties. The men knew that they were heading toward the toughest marine operation thus far in the Pacific, and the strain showed in everything they said. "Believe me there is a grand rush to the Sacraments," Deasy noted. As far as his own feelings went, he felt secure even in the face of the battle. "God will be with us," he wrote his superior in California.[5]

On the day before the assault began, the navy served the traditional preinvasion fare, the best food that could be provided. Deasy remembers the "large Turkey dinner at noon, juicy steak at night, and steak again the next morning" at 4 A.M. "They tell me that San Quentin acts this way—[it] feeds their men well the day before execution."[6] Deasy was not the only man in the 5th Marine Division to have the uneasy feeling that death lay only hours away.

After supper, Suver and some friends in his battalion gathered in his cabin for a chat. Little did they realize that their casual, offhand remarks would lead to one of the most famous events of the battle, making Father Charles F. Suver an overnight celebrity. One young officer in the group said that if he could take an American flag from the landing craft, perhaps someone could hoist it on top of the volcano on the island, Mount Suribachi. Challenged a young lieutenant, "Okay, you get it and I'll get it up there!" Not to be outdone, Suver added, "You get it up there and I'll say Mass under it."[7] Six days later he would keep his promise.

The day of the landing, February 19, dawned bright and clear, with the sea a glassy calm. Despite the favorable weather, the first day of the battle was a near-disaster, a collective catastrophe that might well have destroyed any other military force less disciplined and less meticulously trained than the three marine divisions that carried the battle that day. The wonder is that in a day of unmitigated carnage, they managed to land 30,000 men on the beaches to the north and west of Mount Suribachi. Casualties for the day totaled 2,500, or 12 percent of the landing force. By the time the struggle ended, the marines' casualty rate would reach almost 30 percent, the highest in their entire history. Part of the reason for the high number of casualties was the fact that under the leadership of one of Japan's most brilliant soldiers, Lt. Gen. Tadamichi Kuribayashi, the Japanese had fortified the island's hundreds of natural caves with their heaviest and most accurate weapons. From their vantage point high over the landing beaches, they could detect every move the Americans made.[8]

At 5 A.M., Charles Suver offered Mass in his cabin for the men in his unit. Marines pressed tightly around him and watched in deep silence as he said a Mass that he knew might well be the last one for him or for the men attending it. The ceremony finished, he joined his marine congregation for a quick breakfast of sandwiches and hot coffee. Not only would it be their last hot food, it would be their last food of almost any kind for the next five days. At 7:30, an order rang out for the marines to enter the landing vessels floating next to the transports. Suver and the men of his company clambered over the side of the ship to a waiting LVT (Landing Vehicle, Tracked), which then moved slowly, laboriously, to the "line of departure," as it was called, to wait. A dead calm had settled over the sea.[9]

Suver squeezed himself into the rear of the craft, next to the two officers in charge of his unit, called Fox Company. His landing craft reached the line, and as it headed for the landing beaches, a Japanese mortar shell hit the water a few yards away. The marines ducked instinctively, but they had crowded into the craft so tightly they had almost no space to move. Suver noticed how the faces of the men now showed their anxiety—their jaws tensed, their eyebrows furrowed, all of them clutching their equipment as tightly as possible. "There was no cursing, no joking," he noted. Everywhere he looked he saw "a tension you could almost chin yourself on."[10] Soon the bouncing vessel reached its goal, a strip of steeply sloping shore called Green Beach. It was the closest of all seven landing beaches to Mount Suribachi, only 500 yards from its massively protected base. In all likelihood, there was no more dangerous spot on the island. Japanese gunfire grew heavier and more accurate the closer the ship came to the shore.[11]

Suver arrived in the ninth wave of landing craft, hitting Green Beach at 9:40 A.M., which he thought was "far too early for a priest." He had often heard that strange thoughts go through the mind of a man when he faces extraordinary danger, and now he found how true that was: "My big worry was keeping my feet dry." How could he get out of the LVT while carrying his Mass kit without letting the sea drench his shoes and socks? Happily for him, he spotted a huge ammunition box on the beach, close to his ship. He jumped on top of it, then had his chaplain's assistant, Jim Fisk, pass him the kit. The gambit worked, but keeping his feet dry was the only pleasant experience he would have that day.[12]

Once on the beach, they crawled past wrecked landing craft and huge mounds of supplies, all blown apart by Japanese artillery. Soon it became clear to Suver that he and Fisk would have to crawl over the first sand dune, having no idea at all what lay on the other side, then dash across an open space and clamber up the next hill. Every dash made them a perfect target for Japanese small-arms fire, which grew more intense as the morning progressed. Soon the Mass kit posed a problem. Not only was it too heavy to carry, but Suver's chances of holding Mass in such a hazardous area seemed almost nonexistent. He decided to bury it, then come back later for it when it was safer. Fisk objected strenuously to burying it, arguing that if he left it out in the open, someone might well pick it up later and return it to him, since it had his name plainly written on it. Suver reluctantly agreed, and the idea worked. The next day a Catholic marine on a half-track spotted the box and brought it to him.

At first, Suver was unable to find the aid station belonging to Fox Company because of the chaos that prevailed on the shore. At one point, as he and Fisk were wandering around looking for it, a burst from a Japanese light machine gun kicked up the ash around them, forcing them to throw themselves to the ground. The uproar caused by bombers and heavy artillery made it impossible for them to locate the source of the Japanese fire, and it was not until much later that they learned they had somehow wandered behind Japanese lines and had stumbled into the middle of a nest of five Japanese machine guns. The two men at last found the aid station on a strip of beach nearby, where corpsmen were carrying an endless stream of wounded marines into the makeshift hospital. It would be Suver's residence for the next three days, but one that was more hell than home. "The days that followed were a jumble of misery and torture and suffering," he remembered years later.[13]

James Deasy had even more harrowing experiences that day. He and the artillery unit he served had to wait on their transport until late afternoon because so many landing craft had piled up on the beach (most of them smashed to pieces by Japanese fire). As the boat plowed through the breakers, he could hardly believe what he saw: bloated bodies of marines and severed heads, legs, and arms, all floating grotesquely on top of the waves. In some places, the waves that smashed against the beach and the sides of the vessel had begun to turn crimson.[14]

Dead, dying, and wounded men lay everywhere. Deasy walked carefully among them as they lay on the beach, giving communion to the men whose dog tags indicated they were Catholic. To the many who would not live, he gave absolution, administered the Last Rites, and prayed quietly with them. "Men were dying right on the water's edge. What a horrible sight! . . . trucks of ammunition blown up, bodies burning alive, the groans, the cries, the agony." It was almost more than he could endure. Iwo Jima had suddenly become the world's largest emergency room, and Deasy had the overwhelming feeling that he was the only chaplain available for duty.[15]

Finally, at 5 P.M., marine commanders on the beach declared a halt to offensive operations for the day. Everyone dug foxholes as deep as possible, with two men to a foxhole, ate their K-rations, and kept a constant watch for the enemy. Night finally descended on Iwo Jima. Officers had told their men to expect suicidal counterattacks, but the Japanese decided not to charge against the Americans, choosing instead to use their artillery to pound the marines' positions all night. Most marines were so exhausted, however, that in most foxholes one man slept profoundly while the other maintained a vigil against the enemy. Suver and Fisk both fell into a fathomless sleep, content that "the others around us were standing their watches."[16]

Deasy, however, experienced a terrible night. Since so many men in neighboring dugouts were wounded and desperately needed his attention, he spent most of the night crawling from foxhole to foxhole. He took an enormous risk, since what he called "trigger-happy marines" were likely to give him "the works" even though a password system had been devised to identify men who approached during the night. The next four nights would offer more of the same for Deasy. When not attending the wounded, the dying, or the men who had become hysterical from combat stress, he shivered in the bitter evening cold and listened to the incessant crashing of Japanese artillery shells. He has no hesitation in admitting that he felt "scared out of his wits" the whole time. Would the next artillery shell, mortar blast, or sniper's bullet "have his name on it?" as the marines liked to say. He kept his "eyes and heart lifted up to heaven" while he asked repeatedly, "Is it my turn, O Lord, is it my turn[?]" For five days, he had almost no sleep and received no hot food or water. A thick layer of dirt now covered his body. Never had he felt so terrified, so filthy, or so hopeless. He survived "on nerves alone."[17]

When daylight returned, he would try to bury the bodies of marines who had fallen, but the overwhelming danger made it impossible to do so for the first four days. Everyone was fighting for their lives, and the burial of the battle's victims would have to wait. The stench from decomposing bodies quickly turned Deasy's stomach. Even worse was his sense of loss at the death of his fellow marines, some of whom he numbered among the best friends he had ever made. A quiet, sensitive man (known to his fellow marines as Gentleman Jim), Deasy grieved deeply as he looked at the bodies of the men he had once known so well and with whom he had shared so much.

Suver learned from hard experience the dangers that awaited anyone attempting premature burial of the dead, or even looking at them too closely. On the second day of the campaign, he spotted several Japanese bodies lying in an open space about 100 yards away from where he was standing and decided to examine them more closely to see if any were still alive. He looked at the first man and saw that he was dead. He had started walking toward the second body when machine-gun fire "kicked up the dirt at my toes." He dashed for the nearest foxhole. "I freely admit I was pretty scared," he said later. Later the same day, while working at an aid station, he was holding a cigarette for an injured marine when "suddenly we both cried 'ouch' simultaneously. A sniper's bullet had creased my leg just above the knee, just barely enough to draw blood; the same bullet went into the side of the wounded lad. I called for a corpsman to dress the new wound. As I remember the lad went on smoking and I went on holding the cigarette."[18]

On the same day, Deasy lost two friends. The first was a young college student he had known even before the war while working as the dean of students at Santa Clara University near San Francisco. By an extraordinary stroke of luck, Deasy had seen the young man, Al Garcia, late on the day of the invasion and had been delighted to learn that he seemed as congenial and friendly on Iwo Jima as he had been in college. "I saw him with his old familiar smile; before he took over a section of the front lines I heard his confession." Less than twenty-four hours later, a sniper killed him. The second was a Catholic officer, the father of four young children. Universally respected by his comrades for his stamina, leadership qualities, and exceptional intelligence, a bond of friendship had developed between the two men. Tragically, "his life was snuffed out by a direct hit" from a Japanese mortar shell.[19]

On February 21, nature provided the embattled marines with a diversion of an entirely unwanted kind: a cold, wind-driven, drenching rainstorm. The lashing torrent lasted all day, turning the slippery volcanic ash into sucking, unyielding mud. The rain posed no problem of visibility for the Japanese in their caves and tunnels, however, and they continued to blast every marine position through the driving rain. For the Americans, the deluge deeply compounded an already intolerable situation. "What use to put a blanket on the wounded," Suver complained in frustration, when "their stretchers were soaked, their clothes saturated." The rain brought him not only personal discomfort but a minor defeat of sorts. "It rained so steadily that the water began trickling down into my shoes," making "that nice squashy sensation when I walked." All too soon he had lost his heroic battle to keep his feet dry.[20]

During the third night on the island, Deasy came perilously close to losing his life. The artillery unit to which he belonged had been ordered to stand fast for the night in a largely unprotected area about 700 yards from the foot of Mount Suribachi. Everyone, including Deasy, had dug the deepest foxholes they could make, then shored up the sides with heavy boards to give themselves a measure of extra protection. Every marine knew, of course, that no amount of construction would help in case of a direct hit, but they all hoped that the night would pass without such a disaster. Wrung out from the day's exertions, Deasy fell into a deep sleep as soon as he had finished digging his trench. Sleep was not to last, however, as around midnight the Japanese commenced an all-out artillery attack on Deasy's unit. On this occasion, as during the whole time of the battle, he was carrying the Eucharist in a small container, and he told the men of his battalion that if he were killed, they should consume the host or take the container to the nearest priest. Around four in the morning, a 700-pound Japanese mortar shell smashed into the ground just a few feet away from where he was lying. "It was a flash, a concussion. I was lifted with my foxhole about six feet into the air. . . . When I came down my feet and the lower part of my body were buried about six feet under the ground; my head was about one and [one-]half feet under."[21]

This, he thought, was surely the end. The boards he had put into his foxhole for protection now squeezed painfully against his chest and stomach. He could barely expand his chest. Two completely fortuitous events probably saved his life. First, as he fell back to the ground, with tons of volcanic ash cascading on top of him, his helmet somehow fell over his face, its open part stuck to his nose. A tiny amount of air thus remained trapped inside his helmet, and in the end, it would prove enough to save his life. Second, as he fell in the sand, he managed to keep his right arm above his body, and his fingers remained just barely sticking out of the ground. He knew that he had to keep wiggling his fingers until someone saw them and organized a rescue party.[22]

In the midst of battle, two brothers from Detroit (one a marine officer, the other a navy ensign) receive communion from Chaplain Lawrence Calkins of Chicago. Moments before, they had met for the first time since entering their respective services early in the war. (Source: U.S. Marine Corps)

For three and a half hours, Chaplain James J. Deasy was trapped underground. At some point in the furious Japanese bombardment—he cannot remember when—two men in the foxhole next to his called out asking if he were safe. With characteristic unconcern for himself, he shouted back that he was "buried, but safe" and asked them not to come to his aid until the firing had stopped. Around 7:30 in the morning the shelling stopped, and the two marines dashed to his rescue. It took over half an hour of frantic digging to extricate him from the ash. Deasy is candid today about his experience. "It is funny how convinced I was that it was all over" and yet "hope was always there." Was he frightened? "Of course I was petrified. Who would not be in such circumstances?" If nothing else, however, he had learned a valuable lesson about how to behave in combat. Previously, the men in his battalion had worried because he had not been careful about taking the necessary precautions when in combat. Now, it would be different: "From then on I hit the deck at the least sound of fire."[23]

On the fifth day of the battle Suver kept his promise to offer Mass on the top of Mount Suribachi provided that someone could put up a flag there. His presence at precisely the right moment was a result of his own personal courage, correct advice from the marines around him, and simple luck. He and his assistant were working with the wounded at a battalion aid station near the bottom of the hill when he noticed a patrol of four men carefully edging their way toward the top. He watched them for a minute, then told his assistant to fetch his Mass kit and carry it along. The two began crawling, then running, toward the peak. As Suver and Fisk approached, an American flag suddenly appeared at the top. Cheers rang out all around, and some of the men on the plains below wept as the flag snapped in the stiff breeze. Remembers Suver: "All of us experienced a thrill that none of us will ever be able to describe."[24] Once on top himself, Suver approached the officer in command and asked his permission to celebrate the Mass. The officer approved, but warned Suver not to "congregate the men." Precisely how it was that he held a Mass without having a congregation in attendance is something that Suver himself has never explained—nor did the Marine Corps ever ask.

He could see that the bowl of the volcano was not safe for Mass, because several Japanese soldiers stuck their heads out of a cave just a few feet below where he and Fisk stood and it was clear that other caves were filled with Japanese as well. The marines were doing their best to clear the caverns, but the bowl of the volcano remained manifestly unsafe, which is why the photographs of Suver celebrating the Mass show the marines in the congregation holding their rifles at the ready in case hidden Japanese should attack during

Marine Chaplain Charles Suver celebrating Mass for the men of the 5th Marine Division only minutes after they took the summit of Mount Suribachi on Iwo Jima. (Source: U.S. Marine Corps)

the service. As Suver conducted the liturgy—in Latin, as was then the universal practice—he could clearly hear Japanese soldiers chattering in nearby caves. For the celebration of Mass, Suver wore khaki vestments made by a Protestant friend, while two marines held up a poncho behind him to protect him from the wind, which he said was "blowing like a blizzard." A board perched on top of two empty gas drums served as an altar. At precisely high noon Suver began the liturgy, with some twenty exhausted marines gathered around him.[25] The event was a historic one. Not only was it the first Mass ever offered on the top of Mount Suribachi, in all likelihood it was the first Mass ever offered anywhere on Iwo Jima. A short time later, Alvo O. Martin, a Presbyterian chaplain, conducted Easter services for the men of the 3d Marine Division. Unlike Suver, he had the help of a makeshift choir and a small field organ, and neither a steady drizzle nor the sounds of battle in the background could dampen the spirits of Martin and his men.[26]

News reports of the capture of the mountain gave the world the distinct impression that with Suribachi conquered, the worst of the fighting on Iwo Jima had ended, and even some of the marines on the island, thrilled by the sight of the flag whipping in the wind, had deluded themselves into thinking that the worst was over. They were wrong. After the capture of the peak, twenty-nine more days of battle remained, much of it even more intense than the fighting that had preceded the taking of the mountain. In the days following the flag raising and his Mass, Suver saw that the peak's importance as a military victory "paled into insignificance." So many of the men he had seen on top of Suribachi were to "remain behind on Iwo." One of the severely injured was the brash young lieutenant who had boasted that he would put the flag on top. Tragically, he had been shot in the back before the flag raising and remained paralyzed for the rest of his life. Another marine had carried the flag to the top.[27]

What followed the capture of the peak was a bloody, twenty-nine day battle up the center of the island, and it was in this period that the marines incurred most of their casualties in the campaign. As they turned north and fought their way over the rest of Iwo Jima, they found that the Japanese had fortified every crag, every crevice, every ridge, and every hill with sets of interconnecting caves, all of them packed with Japanese marksmen and heavy weapons. The length and the ferocity of the struggle has few parallels in American military history, and the names of the individual battles tell the story: Turkey Knob, the Meat Grinder, Death Valley, and the Quarry, to list only a few. The determination of the Japanese to contest every square yard never faltered, making each step forward a possible leap into what many marines ironically called their "permanent address."

For the marine chaplains, combat meant brutally punishing days and endless nights of nonstop work attending casualties, assisting the medics in the aid stations and hospitals, and burying the dead. Photographs of the marines on Iwo Jima show gaunt men with blank stares—victims of physical exhaustion, anxiety, and prolonged emotional stress. The chaplains suffered fully as much as everyone else, though all of the clergy, almost miraculously, escaped death and serious injury.

A continuing problem was to find some way to give decent interment to the dead in the absence of the bulldozers needed for large-scale burials. All were desperately needed for battle. Deasy remembers that when the corps finally selected a graveyard, burials began immediately, but in a manner that at first shocked him: "No coffins, no box, just a shroud" (nothing else was yet available on the island). When bulldozers finally became available, four of them working constantly could not keep up with the flood of corpses carried into the cemetery by burial parties. The huge machines first gouged out trenches four feet deep, then teams of men scooped out individual graves two feet deeper still. "The burial detail did a fine job," Deasy insists, but the magnitude of the task was simply overwhelming.[28]

As the battle progressed, Suver became upset at what he came to believe were ruthlessly devious tactics on the part of the Japanese. One day, he noticed a group of four or five Japanese bodies lying in a row; someone had thrown a piece of canvas over them to protect them until they could be buried. Shortly afterward, a mortar shell exploded in the middle of a group of marines standing nearby, then a second mortar, then a third. A thorough search of the area revealed no Japanese snipers or infiltrators anywhere. Finally someone happened to pull back the canvas from the row of Japanese corpses, and there, alive and quite well, was the culprit—a Japanese soldier who had crawled into the area under cover of darkness and hidden himself next to his deceased comrades. He had a portable weapon called a "knee-mortar" next to him, and he had been using it to fire on the marines. He would slowly, carefully, stick the opening of the weapon out of the canvas, fire it, then pull it back under the canvas. Commented Suver bitterly, "You could never guess where they were or what trick they would use next." Suver's anger at the Japanese continued to grow as load after load of American wounded was brought into the hospital. "I often found myself cursing (under my breath) the Japs and coming pretty close to hating them. Had any of them walked into the hospital tent I would have been among the first to shoot. . . . I doubt very much if I was alone in feeling that way."[29]

James Deasy, meanwhile, found his personal situation beginning to get a little better as the battle lengthened. The increasing number of American airplanes in the skies over the island made him feel more secure than earlier, and there were small improvements in his personal situation. At the end of the first week on the island, "I had the luxury of a pint of water to wash my face and hands. By that time the Iwo dust was caked on the face and instead of washing our face[s] we just peeled off the dirt." On the twelfth day of the campaign, he enjoyed his first shave. "I never realized that I had so many gray hairs on my face," he remarked ruefully. Still, his exhaustion deepened as the fighting ground on, and he found himself living in a continuing fog of weariness, grief, and near-despair. Iwo Jima was, he said, something "I never want to recall if God wills I get thru [sic] this operation," he wrote his superior in California. He also remembered that he had long wanted to enter the military for the invaluable "experience" it would give him, "but I never bargained for all this."[30]

Nor had anyone else. The marines had estimated that the battle would last about fifteen days; it took thirty-six, and casualties also far exceeded what had been estimated. It must have struck the thirteen out of nineteen Catholic priests on Iwo Jima who had Irish names as exquisitely ironic that the navy declared the island "secured" on the eve of Saint Patrick's Day. Unfortunately, the Irish-American chaplains would enjoy neither the pleasures of the day nor the actual end of the campaign, since it would take the 5th Marine Division until March 25 (nine more days) to wipe out the remaining pockets of Japanese resistance in a ravine ominously called Death Valley. When the fighting finally ended, James Deasy's first reaction was the sudden realization that for the first time in 34 days he felt safe. "Never once during our thirty-four day sojourn at the gateway to hell were we secure. We lived from breath to breath never knowing when we would be snuffed out of this earthly existence. Everybody was afraid. If they were not there was something radically wrong with them."[31]

Nearly 6,000 marines perished and 17,000 more suffered wounds during the campaign—a full third of the total landing force—and only at the end of it could the chaplains finally give the dead a decent interment. Burial parties removed remains from temporary, makeshift burial grounds and placed them in permanent, vastly more dignified cemeteries. One sad day, Deasy looked out over the seemingly endless rows of crosses for the 5th Marine Division, his 5th Marine Division, the unit that had incurred the highest losses of the three divisions, with 2,265 dead and 1,640 wounded. The cemetery took the form of a crucifix, he noted, and had a large American flag and a cross in the center. "What a sight to see those crosses row after row almost as far as the eye could see." He noted an occasional Star of David among the rest. For the remainder of his life, he would remember that field of the dead on Iwo Jima. The hulking presence of Mt. Suribachi in the background only seemed to make it all the more solemn and funereal.[32]

As he gazed at the long, neat rows of his fallen comrades for one last time, he had two contradictory thoughts. One was simple gratitude: "I'm mighty happy to be still alive." Yet he also felt guilty that so many fine young men had died while he had escaped Iwo Jima without even a scratch. "At times I wish I was worthy to have died with so many on Iwo Jima." He still finds it impossible to reconcile these two seemingly contradictory feelings, and he wonders if perhaps these aspects of his wartime experience are problems for which only God has an answer.[33]

Even after the dead had been buried, with the final, dignified services they vastly deserved, the work of the chaplains still continued. Now they had to write letters of condolence to the families of the dead, perhaps the saddest task of all. Deasy found that as difficult as it was to write to the families back home, it was even harder to read some of the replies that he received. Many parents rose heroically to the occasion, generously thanking him for his kind words and bravely trying to deal with a devastating loss that no one could ever undo. One family wrote thanking him for his "kindness and good deeds which you have extended not only to our boy, but to all Catholic boys." Another, to whom he had written that their son had died with his rosary in his hands, replied: "This has indeed been a great comfort and blessing to us. It indicates the great Faith and good which your mission has accomplished and will never be forgotten by us." They also asked that he "accept our tender and heartfelt gratitude for the spiritual help with which you have prepared our boy."[34] Others wrote bitter, despairing letters. The parents of an only son who had perished on the island asked harshly:

> Did he die quick, with a rifle bullet or was he blown all to hell with a mortar or torn up by shrapnel. Did he last long enough to see the flag go up on Seribachi? . . . We spent eighteen years raising this boy and it took eighteen months for the Marines to finish the job, and we have an engraved certificate to show that he died for liberty. You will have to admit that it is a damn sorry swap.[35]

The battle for Iwo Jima ended, as all great battles do, with a mixture of triumph and tragedy, but for the chaplains on Iwo Jima, the battle signified not just a major victory against the enemy, but the prevailing of the Almighty over the forces of darkness. One Protestant chaplain may well have put it best:

> This has been an awful experience. My two closest buddies are now dead, as well as other close friends among the officers and men. But despite the loathsomeness and tragedy of it all, I can see how God has already begun to use even this battle for his glory.[36]

None of the marines or their chaplains who took part in the worst bloodbath of the Pacific war would ever be the same again. The struggle had left its mark on their souls as well as on their bodies, scarring them with the most violent month of fighting in American history. None could ever forget Iwo Jima. None would ever have anything good to say about it. They had all passed through the gates of hell and seen what lay beyond.

13

JOSEPH O'CALLAHAN, THE *FRANKLIN,* AND OKINAWA

With the ship rocked by incessant explosions, with debris and fragments raining down and fires raging in ever increasing fury, he ministered to the wounded and dying, comforting and encouraging men of all faiths.
—Medal of Honor Citation, Chaplain Joseph O'Callahan

The largest and bloodiest campaign of the war in the Pacific began on a day that was at once profane and sacred. For strictly military reasons, however, the Americans invaded Okinawa, the last and most powerful of Japan's island strongholds, on April 1, 1945. It happened to be April Fools' Day; by chance, it was also Easter Sunday. The Americans made the decision to invade Okinawa because, quite simply, they had no other choice. The island posed far too large a threat from the rear to any force that might attempt to bypass it. Further, in order to carry out the assault on the Japanese home islands that they were planning, Okinawa would be the logical staging ground, not only because of its air bases and excellent anchorages, but also because it lay only 350 miles from Kyushu, the southernmost of the Japanese islands. The Americans had managed to bypass a few of the Japanese-held islands in the Pacific, but clearly they could not avoid Okinawa. Nearly 60 miles long, it bristled with well-developed airfields, the largest concentration of enemy artillery in the Pacific, and 100,000 troops ready to defend the island at any cost.[1]

Before the Americans could launch a seaborne assault on Okinawa they first had to neutralize the Japanese air bases on Kyushu, as the planes located there posed a serious threat to any incursion on Okinawa. The navy therefore ordered Task Force 58 to attack the numerous fighter and bomber fields on Kyushu, and its four fast-carrier groups moved out on March 10. The assault against the bases around the city of Kobe proved effective, but the Japanese managed to damage four of the sixteen carriers in the process and so desperately mauled another that few people expected it to survive. Against overwhelming odds, however, the ship's crew fought a veritable hurricane of explosions and succeeded in saving the ship. A key figure in the story, and the rescuer of more than 300 men trapped below decks, was the ship's Catholic chaplain. A Jesuit priest from Boston, he was the only clergyman in either Chaplain Corps to receive the Medal of Honor during World War II. His ship, the most heavily damaged American vessel of the war to survive, was a storied one. It was the USS *Franklin,* and the chaplain was Joseph Timothy O'Callahan.

Born in an Irish section of Boston, he had attended Catholic schools in Boston and then continued his formal education at Boston College. He displayed talent both in athletics, excelling in track and tennis, and in his studies, especially mathematics. After a period of teaching at the College of the Holy Cross in Worcester, he began graduate work in mathematics at Georgetown University, but he soon came to the conclusion that the men in the navy needed his services more than the world of mathematics did. After brief consultation with his Jesuit superiors, he joined the navy's chaplaincy service the year before Pearl Harbor.[2]

No chaplain ever loved the navy more, or the Japanese less. When asked one day why the Japanese bombers that raided the U.S. fleet never illuminated the ships with flares in order to see them better, his answer would have made sense to any patriotic American at the time: "Only those who understand the working of the Jap mind can explain why their search planes did not drop flares." Although he did not define what he meant by "the Jap mind," it is clear that he, like many Americans, thought of the Japanese as a race of people who had become irredeemably mindless and corrupt.[3]

After brief stays at navy posts on the West Coast and Hawaii, he reported for duty on board the carrier USS *Ranger,* which saw action in the invasion of North Africa. The *Ranger* would always remain his favorite ship, despite the honors that would come to him a year and a half later while serving on the *Franklin.* While on the *Ranger,* he began a custom he would maintain for the rest of his wartime career: He made it a point to eat one meal a day in the enlisted men's mess hall. By doing this he not only heard about their personal problems, but he also assimilated their language (minus the vulgarities, for which he relentlessly charged fifty cents a violation). Sailors on both ships came to feel so much at ease with him that they often teased him about his daily appearances in the mess hall, charging that he conspired with the cook ahead of time to make sure he ate with them only when they received their best meals. Underneath their joshing, however, lay a deep fondness for the chaplain. "He only believes in two things," one man said. "He believes in God and the enlisted man."[4]

The men of the *Franklin* would meet their greatest challenge early in the morning hours of Sunday, March 19, 1945, when their ship participated in the assault on Kobe. Although they expected danger, they had no idea that by the time the day had ended, the carrier would look like a "half-eaten shredded wheat biscuit," in the words of one survivor.[5] When O'Callahan awoke that morning, his first thought was that the day was the Catholic feast of St. Joseph, the patron saint of a happy death. The possibility of soon facing his own end seems not to have occurred to him, though a deep exhaustion in his "weary old bones," as he put it (the result of the previous day's intense fighting), weighed heavily on his mind.[6]

His first duty that day was to pronounce a general absolution on the ship's crew over the public address system. Then he visited the pilots in their briefing rooms as they readied themselves for their early morning bombing runs over Kyushu. He repeated the formula of pardon for sins ("This absolution is for the Catholic boys but we'll let you non-Catholics in on it—guaranteed not to hurt!" he joked), then led each group in the Lord's Prayer. These early tasks finished, he walked next to the officers' wardroom for breakfast. The time was 6:05 A.M. At that moment, the ship was 95 miles southeast of the tip of Kyushu. A report from the bridge announced the approach of enemy planes, and a squadron of American fighters immediately left the *Franklin* in pursuit. The carrier's crew soon began congratulating itself that its planes had chased the enemy away, but they had failed to see that one plane had eluded them. As O'Callahan hunched over his plate eating his French toast, he heard first a loud *bang,* then the sound of shattering glass. Diving quickly under the table, as did the other officers in the room, he felt overwhelmed by what he called a "mad clutch for life." "This is it," he said to himself. He had always wondered what it would be like when an attack came. Now he knew.[7]

He quickly gave a second general absolution to the ship's crew and then groped his way down a darkened passageway as clouds of smoke billowed around him. Deep inside the ship, where the enemy plane's 550-pound bomb had exploded, chaos reigned. A second after the blast, the carrier's watertight doors had slammed shut, trapping hundreds of men in deep compartments. Explosion followed explosion, walls of flame incinerated men standing at their posts, and clouds of suffocating smoke raced through the decks. Nearly 1,000 officers and enlisted men perished in the conflagration, making it one of the worst disasters to beset an American vessel in World War II.

As O'Callahan and his companions from the wardroom made their way down the passageway, an explosion sent them reeling. "The whole ship quivered in a mighty blast," he remembered, and he grew increasingly anxious as he thought about the hundreds of men trapped below. O'Callahan and a Protestant chaplain, his Methodist friend Grimes W. Gatlin, battled their way down a blackened passageway to the junior aviators' bunk room, responding to reports that some wounded pilots had been brought there a short time before. They spent a minute or two with each pilot while medics applied sulfa powder, burn jelly, and morphine. Several of the more severely burned young men died in O'Callahan's arms, and he would never forget the look of peace that stole over their faces after he had prayed with them. "When I die, I hope to go to Heaven, and I expect to meet these boys," he said later without embarrassment.[8]

Looking up through the wreckage of the ship, he caught a glimpse of a small twin-engine plane. Before he could ask himself if it were friend or enemy, he saw it drop two slim, silvery bombs. He prayed that somehow they would miss the ship, but the stricken carrier had lost most of its power and lay wallowing in the ocean, a target almost too large to miss. It was 9:52 when a second bomb slammed into the *Franklin* and exploded on the hangar deck, one level below the flight deck. The blast that followed was so violent that men on the carrier *Bunker Hill*, well over the horizon, heard it clearly. "The ship felt like a rat being shaken by an angry cat," said O'Callahan. Parts of airplanes and human bodies shot into the air, then rattled down on the deck over his head, clattering like oversized hail. The blast hurled him and a nearby doctor onto the floor, and both felt an irresistible urge to crawl into their helmets as they looked frantically for whatever safety they could find. Meanwhile, panic-stricken men crowded against the bottom of the only ladder leading to the upper deck, making it impossible for anyone to move. "Here boys," O'Callahan shouted, "single file," as he directed them through the hatch. Somehow he managed to restore enough order so that eventually all of them got out.[9]

When he reached the flight deck, he saw that fire engulfed almost all of it and towering pillars of flame snapped angrily in every direction. Clearly, the firestorm on board the *Franklin* had burst out of control. He saw "burned bodies, mangled, bleeding bodies; everywhere the stench of burned flesh, the sound of deep groans, the clammy feel of men already dead. This was our flight deck." Suddenly he spotted an ominous sight on the top deck. Stacked next to a forward gun turret, a pile of five-inch shells was growing hotter by the minute and in grave danger of exploding. He knew that if they went off,

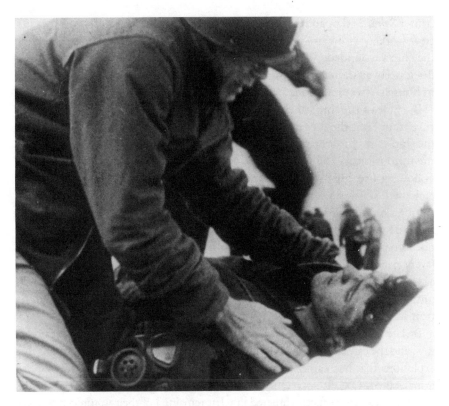

Navy Chaplain Joseph T. O'Callahan bends over a stricken sailor during the attack on the carrier *Franklin* on March 19, 1945. The sailor, a native of Perth Amboy, New Jersey, survived his wounds. (Source: U.S. Navy)

the shock might well sink the carrier. He quickly organized a crew of men and directed them to dump the bombs over the side of the ship. Only a short distance away, he discovered six 1,000-pound bombs that were also growing perilously hot, and he swiftly gathered another group of men and directed them in the careful hosing down of the shells. He insisted above all that they bounce the water off the deck instead of hitting the bombs square with the full stream, since the force of the water might blow them up. "That's right, Father," piped up one sailor. "Let's not take any unnecessary chances!"[10]

By late morning, the carrier had lost all power and lay dead in the water. American planes hovered protectively overhead, and several other ships steamed close by, but they were reluctant to come too close lest a final, cataclysmic eruption destroy the *Franklin* and themselves as well. Finally the cruiser *Santa Fe* slipped bravely alongside the carrier, and for thirty minutes, its crew worked with extraordinary efficiency and daring to evacuate over 800 of the ship's wounded. When it moved away, the men left on the *Franklin* felt desperately abandoned and helpless. "For better or worse," O'Callahan said to himself, "we were alone."[11]

But at least the ship still floated. To keep it from sinking, its crew would first have to put out the fires that still surged through its decks. O'Callahan helped the ship's fire chief organize bands of fire fighters to attack the flames, above all the furious blazes still raging out of control deep in the interior of the vessel. Following the chief's lead, the men walked single file down a long series of darkened stairways and along the flaming decks, probing a careful path through broken girders that looked strangely like stalagmites and stalactites in an underground cavern. At some point in the morning—O'Callahan could not remember precisely when—a bomb fragment sailed between his legs and "very nearly split me in twain." Although it left an ugly gash on his left leg, causing him to lose a considerable amount of blood, he continued to work until much later in the day when a doctor-friend stopped him long enough to treat him.[12]

By late in the day, a heavy cruiser, the *Pittsburgh,* had taken the *Franklin* under tow, and the carrier's crew had established a measure of control over the flames and explosions that had earlier imperiled the ship. Its survival, however, was still far from assured. O'Callahan recalls that at 10 P.M., wrung out from the day's work, the ship's surviving officers gathered in what remained of their wardroom to relax for a few minutes. O'Callahan whispered something to the ship's doctor, then tiptoed out of the room to fetch some useful items from his box of what he called "religious books." A minute later he paraded triumphantly back into the room, a quart of whiskey in hand, and invited the navy's officer corps to imbibe at will. "Pass that bottle!" the fire chief shouted. "I want to be able to tell my grandchildren that aboard ship, where Navy Regs [regulations] forbid it, the Padre passed me a quart of whiskey and offered me a drink."[13]

The chief had quoted "the Regs" correctly: The navy explicitly forbade (and still prohibits) the use of alcohol on ships at sea, both in war and in peacetime. Precisely how O'Callahan carried out so spectacular a violation of navy law with total impunity remains unclear. As commanding officer on the *Franklin,* Capt. Leslie Gehres held ultimate responsibility for the misdeed, but neither he nor anyone else ever took action on it, perhaps because the ongoing crisis had created its own regulations. Pangs of conscience never afflicted O'Callahan, who proudly recounted the deed ten years later in his autobiography, *I Was Chaplain on the Franklin.*

The next two days brought new challenges to the crew of the *Franklin*. First came the grim search through the length of the vessel for bodies, then the difficult and often heart-breaking task of extricating them from the wreckage, followed by brief but reverent services at the railing of the ship. A quiet splash in the ocean marked the end of the ceremony for each man.[14]

Two months later, on May 17, 1945, the *Franklin* finished its 11,000-mile voyage home when it sailed quietly into New York harbor. Since wartime security forbade a formal welcome, its journey up the East River went almost unnoticed, as did an awards ceremony that was held on board several days later. As a ship's officer read the long list of men recommended for medals—a few still alive, but most of them dead—Chaplain Joseph Timothy O'Callahan found that he had a difficult time getting a clear view of the proceedings. He blamed it on the sun, which was shining directly into his face. The glare must have been exceptionally strong that day, however, because he had to "blink against it quite often." A part of his life, a piece of his heart, had passed away forever.[15]

The ship's skipper, Captain Gehres, enthusiastically recommended O'Callahan for the Medal of Honor. In a statement quoted by almost every newspaper in the country, he said that O'Callahan was "the bravest man I've ever seen in my life."[16] After a delay of several months, which gave many Catholics grave doubts that O'Callahan would not receive the honor, President Harry Truman awarded the Medal of Honor to O'Callahan and four other officers in a ceremony at the White House on January 23, 1946. The citation that accompanied the medal bestowed the highest praise on O'Callahan:

A valiant and forceful leader, calmly braving the perilous barriers of flame and twisted metal to aid his men and his ship. . . . With the ship rocked by incessant explosions, with debris and fragments raining down and fires raging in ever increasing fury, he ministered to the wounded and dying, comforting and encouraging men of all faiths. . . . Serving with courage, fortitude and deep spiritual strength, Lieutenant Commander O'Callahan inspired the gallant officers and men of the *Franklin* to fight heroically and with profound faith in the face of almost certain death and return their stricken ship to port.[17]

His autobiography adds some telling insights into his character. His worst moments, he said, came when his lifelong problem with claustrophobia nearly overwhelmed him. At one point he had to slip into a darkened gun turret to help with the removal of live shells from inside. "I did not so much mind the thought of being blown up," he readily admitted, but "did very much mind being hemmed in." Making a supreme effort to control his fears, he emptied the last bomb from the turret, then rushed through the tiny door into the cool air outside.[18] Ever a modest man, he repeatedly tried to steer reporters' questions away from himself and toward the crew, whom he credited with saving the ship. Visibly nervous during meetings with the press, he seemed especially tense when asked to describe his own exploits. "Any priest in like circumstances, should do and would do what I did," he insisted.[19]

As the *Franklin* began its long trip home, American forces were preparing to sweep down on Okinawa. No one expected the battle to go easily, but few guessed that it would become the greatest bloodbath of the war against Japan and exhaust five American divisions, three army and two marine. Nature seemed not to have destined the island for such a titanic struggle. One Redemptorist chaplain described it as "a lovely island" with "terraced hills, rocky sea coast," and "small, well-cultivated fields." The weather seemed almost ideal, noted another chaplain who had served earlier in the Philippines and had detested the climate there. It had none of the steamy tropical heat of Manila, he noted, but boasted a most beguiling environment.[20]

The Japanese Imperial High Command had determined that if Okinawa should fall, the invaders would have to pay a bitter price for it. Knowing that halting the Americans on the beaches was impossible, Lt. Gen. Mitsuru Ushijima, the commander of the huge force defending the island, decided to concede the initial landing. He resolved, instead, to husband his resources for a furious defense of the mountainous southern third of the island. The fortifications that he had constructed there were a triumph of Japanese military engineering, comprising three concentric defense lines anchored by deep natural caves and a set of tunnels running the length of the island's rocky spine.

The greatest resource the Japanese had on Okinawa was their artillery, since they had taken every possible measure to make the island their most heavily defended outpost in the Pacific. They had placed their artillery pieces on the cliffs overlooking the plains that they knew the invaders would inevitably have to cross. The Americans would soon realize an indisputable fact about the war on Okinawa: Before they could take it, they would have to blast the Japanese defenders out of the caves and tunnels that ran the length of the island's rocky spine. For their part, the Japanese were convinced that nothing less than the survival of the whole Japanese empire was at stake in Okinawa, as indeed it was.[21]

The fleet the Americans assembled to invade Okinawa dwarfed all previous invasion fleets in the Pacific. An awesome convoy of 1,200 ships, built around four carriers and eighteen battleships, it carried 180,000 men to Okinawa. As the force approached the island, chaplains noticed that the men became increasingly tense. They had heard terrible stories about the fighting on New Guinea, Tarawa, and Guadalcanal. Would Okinawa be as difficult? Or would it be worse? Chaplain John Byrne of New York noticed that the men seemed especially anxious during the evenings, when they had little to do before going to bed. A gregarious man, he organized songfests, leading the men in a hoarse but bellowing baritone. Despite his best efforts, he could not be sure that he had done much to lighten the mood aboard ship.[22]

On the day the invasion began, the Japanese held their fire in their underground labyrinths and allowed the Tenth Army to walk onto the island virtually unopposed. By evening, 50,000 troops occupied a seven-mile front along the southwest side of the island. Said one soldier, "I've already lived longer than I thought I would."[23] So easily did the invasion proceed in the first four days that the combined army and marine forces succeeded in capturing an area that the operation's planners had thought might take as long as three weeks to occupy. The Japanese, however, were watching and waiting.

On the fifth day, kamikazes suddenly attacked the fleet anchored just off the island, and the American troops on the island experienced their first taste of Japanese defensive tactics, Okinawa-style. The horror of kamikaze attacks reached a grim climax on Okinawa. What the Americans had seen earlier at Leyte and Luzon hardly compared to the massive waves of suicide planes that now descended on them. Before the assault ended, over 3,000 American sailors had died and 6,000 more had been wounded; sixty-six vessels were damaged, and twenty-one more lay at the bottom of the East China Sea. The damage that the kamikazes inflicted deeply shocked the chaplains who ministered to the dead and wounded. "I have never seen such burns," wrote Brian Mahedy from the hospital ship *Hope*. Some sailors had turned "as red as lobsters" from their burns, and when navy physicians saw the remains of the victims, they found that "even the lungs had been cooked by the inhaled steam." As Mahedy wrote his superior, "You really see the hell of war on a ship like this."[24] Chaplain Samuel H. Ray of the submarine tender *Hamlin* made at least one trip a day, and sometimes more, to the nearby island of Zamami where he and his fellow chaplains interred the victims of the kamikaze attacks. Day after day, he watched silently as trucks loaded with bodies rolled into the cemetery. He found it a "ghastly sight" that he would never forget.[25]

On April 28, a Japanese plane deliberately bombed the hospital ship *Comfort* and took the lives of twenty-three men, one of them Chaplain Fidelis

Wieland, a Catholic. One attempts in vain to make adequate excuses for the
Japanese. The *Comfort* had observed all of the regulations of the Geneva Convention for the identification of hospital ships, and any pilot could easily have
recognized its status as a noncombatant. Tragically, Wieland was only the first
of three chaplains to die in the struggle for Okinawa before the island was
taken by the Americans in late June 1945.[26]

Now the Americans' advance slowed to a desperate crawl, with the Japanese
making them pay dearly for every yard of territory gained. The first of a series
of furious clashes came when the Americans approached a long, low escarpment, called the Kakazu Ridge, running sinuously across the middle of the island. Nothing seemed to dislodge the enemy. Tanks rumbled across the plains
in front of the ridge, their muzzles belching chemical flames and hundreds of
tons of high explosives, all to little effect. One division gained only 6,000
yards in one week and had to be replaced because of heavy losses and exhaustion. Another division, ordered to seize four knobs on the top of the ridge,
failed to take any. The American honeymoon on Okinawa was over.[27]

Determined to root out the Japanese, the Americans unleashed the heaviest
artillery barrage of the war against the Kakazu Ridge. Eighteen of the navy's
largest warships, more than 600 airplanes, and over 300 pieces of artillery
pounded the linchpin of the line, an ancient fortress called Shuri Castle, which
also was the site of General Ushijima's near-impregnable headquarters. At first
nothing seemed to happen, and it looked as if the Japanese had decided to
stay inside the castle until the last man perished. That night, however, they
quietly evacuated the castle under cover of darkness and moved to their next
line of defense. There they would fight again, and later they would give battle
in their third and final line.[28]

Among the many thousands of casualties resulting from the struggle for the
Kakazu Ridge was Lawrence Lynch, the second Catholic chaplain to perish on
Okinawa (he was also the twenty-first to die in the war with Japan and the
thirty-sixth to fall since the war had started a little over three years earlier).
Lynch, a Redemptorist priest from Brooklyn, was without question the most
flamboyant and successful of all the Catholic chaplains who served in the Pacific. Had it not been for Joseph O'Callahan's greater fame, Lynch would have
emerged from the war as the best-known and perhaps the most-loved of the
nearly 3,000 Catholic priests who had worn the military uniform. The success
that he enjoyed with his men and the depth of the impact that he had on their
lives can scarcely be described adequately, much less measured with precision.

Few chaplains possessed such an array of talents as Lynch. An accomplished
orator, poet, counselor, athlete, painter, and radio speaker, he was above all an

organizer of religious enterprises such as missions and retreats. A whirlwind of activity who seemed never to rest or sleep, his biographer dubbed him, not imprecisely, "Father Cyclone."[29] He had his limitations. He could be fiercely dogmatic in his religious views, he often used high-pressure methods to herd Catholic soldiers into confession and Mass, he affected a swaggering manner and gait, and he was not above boasting of his own accomplishments. Nor did anyone who knew him well ever accuse him of excessive modesty. Yet both officers and enlisted men, non-Catholics and Catholics, readily acknowledged his deep personal piety and, above all, his unflinching commitment to the welfare of all the men he served. When he died while attempting to rescue a group of men severely injured by enemy artillery, many said that the manner of his death had been fully in keeping with his life, one of total self-sacrifice.[30]

Protestant chaplains assigned to the same posts as Lynch found in him a strong ally. When one of Lynch's assistants upbraided him for planning a special picnic for the Protestant clergymen on the post, he retorted, "They're good guys. . . . Just because a man wasn't born a Catholic is no sign that he's going to hell; a man who goes regularly to his own church, lives up to its rules, obeys the letter and sense of the law—he's got a fair chance of heaven too."[31] His benevolent attitude toward Protestants not only separated Lynch from many other Catholic chaplains, it also put him well ahead of his time. Not until the Second Vatican Council in the early 1960s would such an open-minded attitude toward Protestants come from the official leadership of the Catholic church.

One incident that occurred while his regiment was training on the island of New Caledonia for the invasion of Okinawa illustrated both his determination to succeed and his refusal to put up with unreasonable opposition, no matter what the source. At lunchtime one day, he sent his assistant to the regimental mess hall to tell the men that during the meal he would be hearing confessions in the nearby chapel. After the assistant made the announcement, the officer in charge of the hall, a tough major named Herman Lutz (known to the troops as "Herman the German"), said in a loud voice, "Yeah, you guys who think you're going to have your sins forgiven, go over to the chapel." Lutz stood about six feet four inches, boasted a spectacular musculature, and had earned a fearsome reputation as the bully of the regiment.

Lynch's assistant slipped out of the hall, went to Lynch's office, and reported what the major had said. The stocky chaplain stormed into the hall and asked Lutz if he had really made such a statement. Lutz looked down at him defiantly and said, "Yeah, so what if I did?" Lynch promptly flattened him with a single punch. The troops jumped to their feet and gave Lynch a cheering ovation as he stalked out of the room. From that time forth, he had little trouble convincing the Catholics in the regiment that they should go to Mass or show up periodically for confession.[32]

Lynch possessed an instinct for the dramatic that may well have been without equal in either of the military chaplaincies. Where other priests merely offered up Mass, he turned it into an opportunity both for instruction and for a triumphant celebration. He would begin by putting on his vestments in front of the men, explaining the meaning of each garment as he put it on. Then, while giving his sermon, he would walk up and down the aisle, looking the men in the eye, telling stories in their own colloquial kind of speech, and often slipping in jokes to keep their attention. He held them spellbound. No soldier snickered, slept, or even stirred, and few forgot afterward what Lynch had said. Somehow, he also managed to let them know—without saying so in as many words—that their personal welfare, especially their safety in combat, was always his first concern.[33]

When Lynch's 165th Infantry Regiment arrived on Okinawa, it swung immediately into action, joining units already fighting on the Kakazu Ridge. On days when he held Mass, he urged his men to "pray to the Blessed Virgin Mary hard so that she will put a curve on those artillery shells of the Japs, making them miss us." He also suggested that in their prayers they call Mary their "Old Lady in Heaven" and God their "Old Man in Heaven." He was especially active around the front lines in the evenings, and the men would see him visiting foxholes and gun emplacements in various parts of the battlefield. They noticed that he would first make the sign of the cross over the men, then reach into his huge overcoat and pull out the chocolates, candy, and cigarettes that he had "liberated" from the army's supplies during the day. If time remained before he had to dash off to the next spot, he would chat with the men for a few minutes or would hear a confession if a Catholic asked him to do so.[34]

On the evening of Wednesday, April 24, the Japanese began to shell the regiment with a fearsome number of 150-millimeter rounds. Casualties poured into the regimental aid station, located in a cave a short distance away. Lynch and the medics worked frantically to save as many lives as they could. Suddenly a shell exploded nearby, and a wounded man screamed. Lynch recognized the voice and knew that it belonged to a Catholic soldier named Peter Sheridan, a friend. When he announced he was going to go help Sheridan, the colonel in charge ordered him to stay in the cave, arguing that he would almost certainly be killed if he left the safety of the shelter. When an urgent call distracted the colonel, Lynch took the opportunity to run out into the night.

He knew from previous observations that the Japanese took exactly two minutes to reload their artillery pieces and fire them again. He reached Sheridan and two other wounded men and was in the act of giving communion to Sheridan when a shell burst nearby. He was killed instantly when a piece of shrapnel pierced his heart. Seeing Lynch fall to the ground, the colonel ran out of the shelter, and when he reached the group, he took the host out of Lynch's clenched fist and quickly consumed it, as Catholic custom dictates. Inside Lynch's pocket, he found a crumpled picture of the Virgin Mary, to whom Lynch had dedicated his life as a youthful seminarian some eighteen years before.[35]

Some of Lynch's men had known him as "Holy Hurricane" or "Father Cyclone"; to others he had been "Butch" or "Champ," the same names he used for them. To all of them, knowing Chaplain Lawrence Lynch had been an unforgettable experience. Memories of his dynamism, electrifying oratory, unfailing sense of humor, and kindly personal touch would remain with all of them. The next day, his fellow chaplains interred his remains in the 27th Infantry Division cemetery on Okinawa. One of them noticed that his grave lay in the corner of the graveyard, and he found that fact symbolic of Lynch's entire military career. "I thought that in death, as in life, he stood as a spiritual sentry, on the perimeter of the men whom he had come to serve."[36]

Few chaplains in either theater of war received so warm and impressive a memorial service as Lynch. Three months later, after hostilities with Japan had ceased, forty-five Catholic chaplains simultaneously offered up a Solemn High Mass of Requiem in the presence of 4,000 people. At the memorial service, several officers shared their recollections of Lynch, offering their highest possible praise. Many of the men at the service had wept when they had first heard the news of his passing and now they wept again. He had earned not only the respect and confidence of his fellow officers, but the affection of foot-soldiers as well. Probably no one would have taken more delight in their approval than Lawrence Edward Lynch himself. When his mother heard of her son's death, she said slowly: "He was so happy. . . . His work must be finished and God called him home. We mourn and rejoice at the same time. He did his best and gave all for his brothers in combat."[37]

Sadly, Lynch did not live to see the withdrawal of the Japanese from Kakazu Ridge. On the night that he died, General Ushijima reluctantly concluded that his position on the ridge had become untenable and decided to move his remaining troops northward to their next prepared position, a long, rocky outcrop fully as daunting as Kakazu Ridge. It would take until the last week of

April for the infantry and marines to rout the Japanese out of their caverns, tunnels, and hilltop bastions. Only at the end of May did the Americans begin moving forward on all fronts, slicing the Japanese positions into ever-smaller pockets.

Even in their final desperate days, however, the Japanese continued to fight with courage and ferocity, which meant that much of the island was still unsafe. Chaplain James McNeil quickly learned that caves, especially, could be dangerous, no matter how quiet or empty they appeared. "You'd never know when a cave was inhabited," he said, "until all of a sudden a hand grenade came flying out of it in your direction. Then you knew." Chaplain Marion Budny of Brooklyn tried to offer Mass on an Okinawan hilltop during the same period and nearly perished in the process. As he was saying Mass for a group of Seabees, a Japanese plane appeared overhead and dived straight down toward him. Instinctively, he threw himself on top of the altar in an attempt to protect the wine and the bread that he had just consecrated. Fortunately anti-aircraft guns in the area quickly brought the plane down. After the campaign, the Seabees took the aluminum propeller and melted it down, fashioning it into three large, handsome crucifixes. They gave one to Budny, who still has it in his Brooklyn rectory.[38]

By the middle of June, it had become inescapably clear to General Ushijima that the Japanese cause on the island was lost. On the evening of June 20, therefore, after carefully observing all the prescribed rubrics for the proper carrying out of *seppuku,* the ancient Japanese ritual of suicide by disembowelment, he took his own life. His chief of staff soon did the same, and with these two acts, the Japanese empire on Okinawa ceased to exist. On June 22, 1945, Maj. Gen. Roy S. Geiger raised the American flag over his headquarters. The island was now said to be "secure," that is to say, it was as secure as it could be, given the fact that large numbers of Japanese soldiers still hid out in the island's hills.[39]

The campaign for Okinawa had cost one American life for every ten Japanese: 7,000 Americans and 70,000 Japanese died. Not only had Okinawa been the scene of the greatest number of deaths in any battle for the Pacific, it took the greatest psychological toll as well. A record number of the men who had participated in the campaign suffered breakdowns or combat-induced insanity. Even chaplains fell victim to the endless days of counterattacks, kamikaze strikes, and clashes with the enemy's fearsome artillery. One priest from Buffalo, physically exhausted from the battle and totally spent emotionally, had to leave the service before the war had ended because of his shattered nerves. Although he lived for twenty more years, his psychological problems tortured him to the end of his days. He and others like him were as much casualties of the Okinawa campaign as the men who perished there.[40]

What had the Americans gained by their spectacular but deeply costly victory? The answer hinged on whether the Japanese would decide that the time had come to surrender or whether they would steel their resolve to continue the struggle, even if that meant taking the fighting to their homeland. Gen. George C. Marshall, the army's chief of staff, estimated that an invasion of Japan would cost at least one million American casualties. Would the victory on Okinawa lead only to that? In many ways, the Americans had achieved a matchless triumph. But if the Japanese chose to pursue their hopeless cause, their achievement could also lead to a holocaust, one far more destructive than anything they had yet seen.

14

THE END OF THE WAR—THE BOMB

A bomb is a bomb is a bomb.
The dropping of the weapons was an act of heartless and diabolical revenge.
—Two Catholic chaplains on the use of the atomic bomb

The American role in World War II ended the way it had begun at Pearl Harbor: not with a whimper, but with a mighty bang. The first and only atomic bombs ever used in human history were the two the Americans dropped on Hiroshima and Nagasaki in the first two weeks of August 1945. The debate over the effect of the bombs on Japan's decision to surrender still goes on, and much recent research suggests that the Japanese were ready to capitulate even before they were dropped. Whatever the reason, the Japanese signed the surrender document on board the USS *Missouri* at 9 A.M. on Sunday, September 8, 1945. The ceremony came a month and two days after the dropping of the first atomic bomb and 1,364 days after the attack on Pearl Harbor.

Before the Japanese surrendered, however, they inflicted one final blow, giving the Americans a profound shock and making them wonder if the war would ever end. Only a few weeks before the Japanese decided to ask for terms, they sank a large and historic American warship; by chance, it happened to be the same vessel that had transported the atomic bomb to Tinian that the *Enola Gay* dropped on Hiroshima. The ship, a 9,000-ton cruiser named the *Indianapolis,* first ran into bad luck at Okinawa, where it suffered severe damage from a direct hit by a kamikaze. It had returned to California for extensive repairs, and after a thorough refitting at Mare Island, California, it had sailed to Tinian, where it deposited the nuclear device, then stopped briefly at Apra Harbor in Guam. On the morning of July 28, it departed

Guam for Leyte with a full complement of 1,200 men. It had orders to take the standard route between the two islands, zigzagging for protection from submarines only at the discretion of the skipper, Capt. Charles B. McVay.

The ship's chaplain was Thomas Conway of Buffalo, a popular and generous young priest who had the misfortune to receive assignment to the last American warship sunk by enemy fire in World War II. He would also be the last Catholic chaplain to die in that war. While the *Indianapolis* was undergoing repairs at Mare Island, he had taken a long tour around the country, visiting the families of the nine men who had been killed at Okinawa. The ship's crew would later remark on his magnanimity in undertaking such an exhausting trip, with its midnight flights, daylong bus rides, and wrenching visits to grieving parents. No one seemed surprised, however, at what he had done, since his devotion to the men of the ship had become almost legendary. When it concerned the welfare of his men, no problem ever seemed too slight to call for his undivided attention.[1]

During the previous year, while serving on the ship, Conway had earned the support and affection of the enlisted men, the officers, and Captain McVay himself. His weekly general services for the non-Catholic men soon became so crowded that two mess halls had to be cleared for their use. The ship's doctor, Lewis Haynes, led the singing, usually choosing the traditional Protestant hymns he remembered from his New England boyhood, while Conway read the prayers and gave the weekly sermon, in which he often showed a rare talent for touching the hearts of the men. He had also worked hard, and with great success, to improve the cruiser's recreational programs. Captain McVay felt compelled to say later that "he had done so very much to lighten the burdens of my crew that I consider the reputation of the *Indianapolis* as a happy ship was in a great measure due to his fine spirit and his extraordinary ability to impart it to those about him."[2]

Before the *Indianapolis* left Guam, it received two warnings of enemy submarine activity along the route it would follow. No one, however—not McVay, the experts on his staff, or even the higher command in the navy itself—gave much credence to the reports. Everyone knew that the end of the war was near and that most of the Japanese Navy now lay on the bottom of the sea. The sense of unassailable security that had settled over the navy would cost it a major ship of the line and 800 lives. The fact that the sinking occurred only seventeen days before the Japanese sued for peace made it all the more tragic.[3]

At eleven o'clock on the night of Sunday, July 29, one day out of Guam and 300 miles west of the same island, the *Indianapolis* was steaming at a leisurely sixteen knots in a perfectly straight line. McVay apparently thought that the cloud cover overhead would give him ample protection from submarines. Unfortunately, he failed to take into account the full moon that kept breaking through the clouds. The Japanese submarine I-58 (whose captain, Lt. Comdr. Mochitsura Hashimoto, had witnessed the attack on Pearl Harbor from a midget submarine) spotted the *Indianapolis* during a brief period when moonlight broke through the clouds. Hashimoto could scarcely believe his good fortune. The cruiser was traveling across his path like a slow-moving bull's-eye in a huge target range. He took careful aim and fired a spread of six torpedoes, three of which smashed into the starboard side of the cruiser. Two explosions tore up the ship's communications system, thus preventing anyone from sending out a distress call, and also shattering the water mains, which would have made an effective battle against the ensuing fires at least possible. Minutes later (some said in less than fifteen minutes) the stricken vessel plunged into 7,200 feet of ocean, carrying over 300 men trapped inside to their deaths.[4]

For the next three days, the survivors floated helplessly in the ocean, bobbing up and down in the swells and often under attack from sharks. In their haste to leave the ship before it went under, the men had launched only twelve lifeboats and six floating nets. The few who survived the disaster told not only about their battles with sharks and the lack of food and medicine but also about the atrocious torment they endured from the tropical sun. It was high summer, and they were less than 1,000 miles north of the equator. Many also described Conway's heroic attempts to ease their sufferings, as well as his ceaseless work with the dying. For three days and nights he moved among them, administering the Last Rites to the weakest, praying with others, and attempting to comfort those who had become overwhelmed by panic and the total absence of rescue craft in the vicinity.[5]

After seventy hours of working without sustenance, water, or rest, Conway himself lapsed into a comatose state and began thrashing furiously about in the water, shouting incoherently. A husky sailor from Texas tried to calm him by holding him out of the water, but he was near exhaustion himself and soon had to let Conway go. By chance, he floated by his friend Dr. Haynes, who swam to his side, put his arm through the priest's life jacket, and held him up. In only a few minutes the priest breathed his last, and Haynes despairingly let him go and watched him float away into the distance. He was gone. For the rest of his life, the doctor would think often of Chaplain Thomas Conway and remember "this man who had served all men" but was now "beyond the reach" of all.[6]

Eighty-four hours after the ship went down help arrived, and navy rescue crews began pulling the exhausted, near-hysterical survivors out of the water. The penalty for the navy's lack of alertness? A later tally revealed that 883 men had lost their lives and only 316 had survived. Conway and his fellow victims now rest in 1,200 fathoms of water, uncomplaining victims of one of the worst (but least necessary) disasters to beset the United States Navy in the war.[7]

By now, Japan's industry was flattened, its navy was wrecked, and its armies had suffered defeat everywhere. The country had nothing left to continue the battle except the forces that it had always kept at home. Despite their desperate state, the Japanese refused to reveal their next move. Seeing that their cause was lost, would they finally capitulate? Even in late July, no one could say, since the Japanese government seemed paralyzed and incapable of responding coherently to the peace feelers coming to it from both Allied and neutral powers. To hasten Japan's surrender, the Americans prepared to use a new and shockingly destructive weapon, one they hoped would bring the Japanese to their senses and make an invasion of the Japanese homeland unnecessary.[8]

In order to prepare for the day when orders might come to drop an atomic bomb on a Japanese city, the Army Air Force stationed a unit on Tinian, the 509th Composite Group, which was made up of the best B-29 pilots and crews then available. After considerable discussion, American command finally chose the city of Hiroshima as the first target of the massive bomb. Shortly after the unit arrived on Tinian, Catholic chaplain George Zabelka of Michigan joined it as its chaplain. In the course of his assignment, his views on the bomb would move from total ignorance about the device, to enthusiastic approval after it had been dropped, to growing horror at its devastating effects. Finally, at a later time in his life, he would condemn its use completely.

As the combination priest-minister-rabbi for the 509th, he carried out all the usual duties, and like almost all of the men on the island, he had no idea that the group was training to drop a radically new bomb, called an "atomic bomb," on a Japanese city. He and the others assisting the 509th had heard the new weapon referred to as a "gimmick bomb" and presumed that it differed from the usual explosives only in size and power. Early in the morning of August 6, 1945, Zabelka blessed the crew of the *Enola Gay* (but *not* the plane or the bomb, he is quick to insist), just minutes before they took off for Hiroshima. Then he watched as the plane pounded down the runway, heavily loaded with its 9,000-pound bomb, and finally lifted off just before it reached the end of the tarmac. By the time the bomber returned home several hours later, Zabelka and everyone else on Tinian had heard about the bombing of Hiroshima, and had also learned that the bomb had a magnitude equal to 20,000 tons of TNT. Three days later, a second and more powerful atomic bomb was dropped on the Japanese city of Nagasaki.[9]

In the weeks that followed, most (but not all) of the Catholic chaplains formed a positive opinion about the use of an atomic weapon. When 200 surviving chaplains responded to a 1983 questionnaire about their wartime experiences, they were asked whether they thought *at the time* that the country was right in dropping the bomb, and 65 percent said that they had supported its use. The reasons for this widespread view are not hard to find. A spirit of revenge against the Japanese was rampant in the United States, a view held by chaplains as well as the general populace. Some chaplains also argued that "a bomb is a bomb is a bomb," and if military necessity had already dictated the saturation bombing of Japan, then it was surely no different to drop a larger explosive. Finally, the fact that the Japanese sued for surrender only nine days after the bombing of Hiroshima, and six days after the destruction of Nagasaki, seemed to prove that the two bombs had brought the Japanese to their knees and thus ended the war.[10]

The intensity of the feelings of those who supported using the bomb may perhaps occasion some surprise today, when so much of public opinion has turned decisively against it. However, when one considers the virulence of the hatred that most Americans, including chaplains, felt toward the Japanese at the time, their views seem less extreme. One especially angry priest thought that dropping the bomb on Japan was a good way to get even with the enemy for attacking Pearl Harbor. "We didn't start the war, remember?" Another chaplain argued that the bomb had achieved what nothing else had up to then: It had made the Japanese "say uncle." In the view of one chaplain, whatever worked was morally acceptable, whether the weapons used were "chemicals, nuclear, artillery, or from the air. Wars are for the purpose of subduing the enemy by any means possible," he asserted bluntly. Some priest-chaplains seemed angered most of all by their fellow priests who condemned the use of the bomb as immoral. Thus, one chaplain, an Italian-American from Chicago, charged that all the priests who opposed the bomb were nothing but "fruits" and "liturgists."[11]

The vehemence of the majority notwithstanding, a significant minority of the Catholic chaplains responding to the questionnaire, 15.5 percent, saw fit to condemn the use of the bomb. With the government, the military, and a huge majority of the American people all determined to punish the Japanese in any way possible, it seems remarkable that so sizable a group of Catholic priests chose to take an entirely different path, and to do so in the absence of leadership of any kind from the church's hierarchy. Moreover, they expressed their condemnation of the bomb fully as passionately as did the bomb's most enthusiastic chaplain-supporters. One priest spoke for many others when he described the dropping of the two weapons as an act of "heartless and diabolical revenge," while a number of others thought its use an act of outright "murder" and the wanton slaughter of "countless noncombatants." One called it an act so "horribly complete" that he feared it would take generations for the Japanese to recover, both as individuals and as a society.[12]

Some of the respondents admitted that they felt confusion when they first heard about the bombing of Hiroshima. They complained that the earliest news reports gave them little idea of how massive the destruction was or of the huge number of people destroyed in the firestorm that followed. With the appearance of the first photographs of Hiroshima, however, some quickly changed their minds. Said one: "When I finally learned the horrors of Hiroshima and Nagasaki, I was furious." Others withheld judgment until the postwar period of occupation when they had a chance to see the two cities. Most needed only a few minutes of walking around the devastated areas to conclude that the Americans had inflicted a moral monstrosity on the Japanese people.[13]

Even after the two bombs had fallen the question still remained, would the Japanese surrender? The deadlock in the government appeared unbroken, and mounting intelligence pointed at one factor as the overwhelming cause of the Japanese delay—the doctrine of unconditional surrender. Most Japanese seemed to fear that it would mean losing the emperor, whom they revered with an intensity totally unfathomable to the Allies. They had good reason for so thinking since American public opinion had become inflamed against all the Japanese, and above all Hirohito. The key, therefore, would be to find some way to let the Japanese know that no harm would come to the emperor without antagonizing the American people, who vehemently opposed any kind of compromise with Japan. Under the direction of President Truman, Secretary of State James F. Byrnes crafted a document that said nothing at all about the emperor but did state emphatically that the future government of Japan would be subject to the Supreme Commander, Allied Powers in Japan, Gen. Douglas MacArthur.[14]

On August 15, the Japanese accepted Byrnes's terms, largely because of the direct intervention of the emperor himself. When the news of surrender was made public, some of the American troops in the Pacific quickly got out of hand. On Guam, for instance, troops grabbed their rifles and began shooting them with reckless and highly dangerous abandon. It looked in many ways like a typical American fireworks celebration, except that the fireworks had a lethal component.

A chaplain watching the dizzying celebration from a safe distance noticed that some of the men, after watching the display for a few minutes, quietly walked to the post chapel. There he saw them kneeling silently as they offered their prayers of thanks that their wartime ordeal had ended. Both he and his division had much for which to render thanks: For the past month they had been practicing intensively every day for the invasion of Japan, and only the day before they had learned that they would spearhead the assault. For a full month they had slept with their bags packed, ready to move toward Japan on only six hours' notice. Now it was all over. After gazing at the fireworks a bit more, he, too, went to the chapel and made his own prayer of thanksgiving.[15]

Another priest-chaplain, one who had served in both the Mediterranean and Pacific theaters, rang the bell on his ship for thirty-five minutes without stop, until finally the rope snapped in two. Jerome Kircher of Wisconsin ended the war with two blisters on his hand, but he thought it a small price to pay compared to what some of his shipmates and fellow navy chaplains had endured.[16]

The actual signing of the surrender document took place on September 2, 1945, in a properly dramatic setting. The representatives of the Allied nations met the Japanese emissaries on the vastly imposing USS *Missouri,* the last battleship the United States commissioned in World War II. With its nine sixteen-inch guns and 887-foot length of steel from stem to stern, the 45,000-ton behemoth seemed ideally suited for the occasion. The day dawned with scattered clouds over Tokyo Bay, but before long they burned away, providing a splendid scene for the day's historic ceremony. With an unerring sense of the dramatic, MacArthur had specifically chosen Tokyo's splendid harbor as the site for the final dissolution of the Japanese empire in Asia and the Pacific.

The Japanese representatives came aboard clad in stiff diplomatic attire, looking pale but expressionless. By now, a throng of dignitaries and newsmen had gathered on the deck of the ship under the same American flag that had flown over the Capitol in Washington on December 7, 1941. MacArthur took his place behind a simple mess table with a green felt cover. ''We are gathered here,'' he intoned sonorously, ''to conclude a solemn agreement whereby peace may be restored.'' Chaplain Paul O'Connor, one of three clergymen on the ship, looked down on the scene from the signal bridge high

over the dignitaries and saw that the gravity of the occasion was having a physical effect on MacArthur. No fan of the new Supreme Commander, he admitted that "it gave me no end of consolation to see that M[a]cArthur's hand
and knees shook quite visibly all during his speech."[17]

O'Connor and his Jesuit friend, Chaplain Charles Robinson, who stood
next to him, would both be grateful for the rest of their lives that they had
been given the opportunity to watch the ceremonies at such extraordinarily
close range. But even as they watched, they were preoccupied with rumors
that their brother-Jesuits at Sophia University in Tokyo were in dire straits,
suffering from sickness and severe malnutrition, and they feared that unless
they received help soon, some of them might not survive.

Two days after the surrender ceremony, the two of them and a third Jesuit
from the navy chaplaincy, Samuel Hill Ray from New Orleans, loaded as
much food and clothing as they could stuff into their jeep and set off from the
naval base at Yokohama for downtown Tokyo, sixty miles away. The most
challenging part of the trip, it turned out, was getting past the guards protecting the entrance to the road connecting Yokohama to Tokyo. Security had become so tight that even high-ranking officials without the necessary papers
had been turned back, without even an apology, by the soldiers at the checkpoint. Knowing the obstacles they faced, Ray had used his influence with an
officer-friend to secure a pass with a suitably impressive appearance, but his
collaborator could give him no guarantee that the document would work.
The military authorities, it seemed, had become almost obsessively worried
that some unstable American might get into Tokyo, upset the Japanese, and
start the war all over again.

As they approached the barrier, they saw a formidable-looking military po-
liceman looking their way. Acting on a sudden impulse, Ray handed the pass
to Robinson, who with his wavy gray hair, overseas cap, and foul-weather
jacket looked for all the world like some distinguished (but otherwise unknown) American admiral. "Do your stuff, Robbie," he hissed at him. Assuming an insouciant air implying both the dignity of high rank as well as a
certain careless disregard of the same, Robinson saluted the soldier and announced briskly, "I am Chaplain Robinson on Admiral Badger's staff, carrying food to refugees in Tokyo." With a snappy salute, the soldier barked "Advance!" and the three were off through the gate. The guard had not even
glanced at the pass that Robinson was holding.[18]

After a long and difficult drive, they finally arrived at Sophia University,
where the twenty-one Jesuit fathers and brothers still living there greeted
them joyously. Their clothes and shoes had worn out, and they all had what

O'Connor called "that deep-eyed look" he recognized as malnutrition. They were surviving on minuscule portions of soybeans, rice, and an occasional tiny scrap of meat. So far no one had starved to death or perished in the daily bombing raids, but death was surely not far away for any of them now. Nor did they have any money, though they insisted that they needed none, since Tokyo offered nothing for purchase. Both Robinson and Ray, however, insisted they take some of their own anyway.

After brief introductions, the visitors unloaded the jeep and carried in bundles of beef, butter, sugar, coffee, canned soups, and canned milk. Fearful that they still had not provided enough food, they left their K-rations as well. To the men of the Jesuit community at Sophia University, it seemed as if a "band of angels" had dropped down from the heavens. The three chaplains, however, enjoyed sharing their bounty as much as their friends delighted in receiving it. At the end of the brief visit, the three sadly left the university and drove along the ruined streets of Tokyo, knowing, at least, that the survival of their brother-Jesuits now seemed assured. It had been a landmark meeting in the history of the order, whose work in Japan goes back nearly four hundred years.[19]

Quite possibly the happiest people in Japan after the surrender were the former prisoners of war, who were now freed from their captors and safely in the hands of the military. After their arrival at the army's rehabilitation centers, they first underwent examination by American doctors, and unless they had to report to a military hospital for immediate treatment, they went next to hastily constructed rest camps where the army treated them to the best food, clothing, and medical care it could provide. When Chaplain John Wilson arrived in Tokyo aboard a rescue train filled with fellow ex-prisoners from Osaka, he saw to his astonishment that General MacArthur, flanked by General Eichelberger, was there to greet them. He shook hands vigorously with each of the 400 men as they left the train and wished everyone well. "We needed it," said Wilson.[20]

Wilson had endured the Bataan Death March, imprisonment at both Camp O'Donnell and Cabanatuan, three months on a prison ship, and six months more in a camp not far from the ancient capital of Osaka (happily spared the ravages of the American bombing campaign). On September 2, he and the other prisoners had sat next to a jury-rigged radio set and listened to the surrender ceremonies aboard the *Missouri*. Immediately afterward, he had led the men in a thanksgiving Mass, using the same tattered, threadbare vestments he had carried all the way from Bataan. He covered the altar with one of the parachutes the Americans had used to drop emergency food supplies a few days before, and above it he placed a small American flag.

Wilson first realized that help was truly on the way when on August 14 (the day before the Japanese announced their acceptance of the surrender terms) American planes flew over the camp near Osaka. Instead of dropping bombs, however, they released thousands of leaflets with a single, heart-stopping message, *DO NOT OVEREAT!* A few minutes later, packages of food, medicine, and clothing were parachuted into the camp. "We knew the war for us was over," Wilson recalls. Two weeks later, rescue vehicles pulled up to the front of the camp, loaded the men onto a special train, and carried them away to freedom. Less than a week later, Wilson boarded a ship for home and wrote his superiors in far-off Carthagena, Ohio, "Gradually I am getting over the first reactions: good food, seeing our first live, free Yanks." Looking back on his three and a half year ordeal, he could only think of his "guardian angel," who clearly had been "working overtime, especially during the last year. If I have learned nothing else, I have learned to pray."[21]

As the ship slowly made its way across the Pacific, Wilson confessed he had only one remaining desire—"to bury myself in a monastery for a few months." His superiors and friends in the Precious Blood Fathers would see to it that, in time, he received every wish he entertained. First, however, he had to have a proper welcome home from the fathers and brothers of the order in Carthagena. He proved to be a modest guest of honor during a weekend of thanksgiving services and parties. His superiors insisted that he first describe his adventures to everyone (a task that took over two hours), and then everyone was given an opportunity to enjoy his company, and he theirs. Asked later by a reporter how he felt about the whole wartime and prison experience, he replied unhesitatingly, "If given the chance, I'd do everything the same as before."[22]

As Wilson was rediscovering life at home in Ohio, the American Army was beginning its occupation of Japan, giving both the troops and their chaplains a chance to see what the policy of "total war" had meant for the Japanese. When Chaplain John Foley reached Tokyo, he found it a "hollow shell" of its former self, with "building after building" blitzed far beyond repair. One structure particularly struck him. Once a beautiful twelve-story office building clad in white brick with red stone trim, it now looked absolutely "ghastly, almost like a human being whose face had been horribly burned." Fires had torn away its interior, then destroyed its outside. The debris, however, had been carefully cleared away and put into neat piles, evidence of the unstoppable industriousness of the Japanese people.[23]

As Foley walked down streets lined with rubble on both sides, he felt deeply self-conscious, as did the groups of American sailors he saw walking around the same area. He was not surprised. After all, their own American bombers, not the Japanese government (which they had grown to hate), had caused the destruction of the city. Meanwhile, the enlisted men, he noted happily to himself, maintained excellent behavior as they moved around the blackened metropolis. They would continue (with few exceptions) to conduct themselves the same way throughout the occupation period.[24]

A few days later, another chaplain sadly toured the remains of nearby Yokohama. After walking for several hours and seeing where the fires and bombs had destroyed the center of the city, he suddenly spotted a white steeple with a cross on top of a hill overlooking the ruined city. Somehow, it had survived the repeated firestorms. He walked to the crest of the hill and entered the church, which turned out to be Catholic. Chaplain Clarence Duhart sat and rested there for a few minutes, charmed by the neatness and cleanliness of the edifice and reflecting on what a welcome contrast it made to the devastation outside.[25]

Everywhere they went around the country, the chaplains found the Japanese people always the same: polite, civil, and almost unfailingly friendly. Although dressed in rags and wearing shocked expressions on their faces, they smiled when addressed and willingly answered any questions the Americans might ask. "War had visited these people in its more horrible forms," Foley noted, as he watched them moving slowly through the battered streets of both Yokohama and Tokyo. But though their country had been reduced to "impotency," they had refused to give up and had started to pick up the shattered threads of their lives. In places, the odor of decay hung heavily over the ruined cities, and the only sound to be heard was the clattering of an occasional streetcar rumbling along rusted trolley tracks. Still, he saw "no evidence of hostility at all."[26]

Moreover, they all found the Japanese extremely hardworking. One priest, assigned to a hospital in the city of Sasebo, not far from Nagasaki, thought their remarkable industriousness "beyond compare." Early every morning, he watched as groups of men, women, girls, and boys marched into the hospital's compound, always with one of their number in command. Once they had received their orders, they set about cleaning up the area. They took no mid-morning break but worked diligently until midday, when they ate a spartan lunch they had brought with them. They worked, without further respite, until six o'clock in the evening. It looked to him, as he wandered around the city, as if everyone else acted in the same way. All the people he saw, "from six to sixty," were working diligently at one task or another. The nation had been beaten, but its tradition of earnest application to work had survived.[27]

At least one chaplain, however, took a relentlessly dim view of the former enemy. Samuel Hill Ray thought that the Japanese people he saw looked the way "an animal looks when he just emerges from a stupefied sleep," and he thought them, without exception, "a short, underfed, ugly people." Still, he believed that there was some hope for them: With MacArthur at the helm, the Americans might be able to bring the benefits of the Western world to the Japanese, turning them into what he termed "a civilized people."[28]

After what seemed like an interminable period of waiting in both Japan and Europe, the chaplains who wanted to leave the service and return home (over 90 percent said they wanted no more of the chaplaincy) were able to start leaving. Karl Wuest, still with the 88th Infantry Division in Italy, moved first to Trieste, then to Naples, then to a port in North Africa, where he boarded a ship heading for Hampton Roads, Virginia. As the troopship approached the pier after the long voyage back to the United States, a band was playing the popular hit "Sentimental Journey." Wuest and others spent the night at a camp near the city and were told that for dinner they could have anything they wanted and as much of it as they pleased. Without the slightest hesitation, Wuest drank two quarts of milk and ate a huge bowl of fresh salad, explaining that these two foods had become complete "strangers" to him while he had been away in Italy and were the ones he had missed the most. After dinner, long lines formed at the telephones as each soldier phoned his family to tell them he had just returned from overseas and was "safe if not sane," as Wuest put it.[29]

The next day, the whole group took a train for their last army post, Fort Knox, Kentucky. The railroad cars were ancient by any measurement, but the ride would be their last with the military, and the men took it good-naturedly. At Fort Knox, Wuest underwent a final deprocessing, including the army's last attempt to get him to sign up for another tour of duty, which he laughingly declined. Soon he was off for home. Hitching a ride with a fellow officer who lived in the same town, he slept soundly as the America he had not seen for three years quietly slipped by his window. There, after waving goodbye to his driver, he walked down a familiar street toward his family home, where the first thing he noticed was that the house was "unscarred," unlike so many that he had seen in Italy. "Without question, I knew that my loved ones would be inside." He was home, he was alive, and he was free.[30]

NOTES

A&MDB	Archives and Museum, Diocese of Buffalo
AABAL	Archives of the Archdiocese of Baltimore
AADET	Archives of the Archdiocese of Detroit
AADUB	Archives of the Archdiocese of Dubuque
AAH	Archives of the Archdiocese of Hartford
AALA	Archives of the Archdiocese of Los Angeles
AAMS	Archives of the Archdiocese of the Military Services
AANY	Archives of the Archdiocese of New York
ACAPSJ	Archives of the California Province, Society of Jesus
ACFMCP	Archives of the Carmelite Fathers, Midwest Commissary Provincial
ACFPSA	Archives of the Capuchin Fathers, Province of St. Augustine
ACFPSJ	Archives of the Carmelite Fathers, Province of St. Joseph
ACHCIP	Archives of the Congregation of the Holy Cross, Indiana Province
ACHGB	Archives of the Congregation of the Holy Ghost, Bethel Park, Pennsylvania
ACHPSJ	Archives of the Chicago Province, Society of Jesus
ACHS	Archives of the Congregation of the Holy Spirit
ACMP	Archives of the Congregation of the Mission, Philadelphia
ACPPC	Archives of the Congregation of the Passion, Province of Chicago
ACPPSP	Archives of the Congregation of the Passion, Philadelphia
ACPPSR	Archives of the Congregation of the Passion, Province of South River
ACSCIP	Archives of the Congregation of the Holy Cross, Indiana Province
ACSV	Archives of the Clerics of Saint Viator
ADB	Archives of the Diocese of Brooklyn
ADCL	Archives of the Diocese of Cleveland
ADCR	Archives of the Diocese of Crookston
ADL	Archives of the Diocese of Lafayette, Louisiana
ADP	Archives of the Diocese of Providence
ADPSJ	Archives of the Detroit Province of the Society of Jesus
ADR	Archives of the Diocese of Raleigh
ADROCH	Archives of the Diocese of Rochester
ADS	Archives of the Diocese of Springfield in Illinois
AFFPSB	Archives of the Franciscan Fathers, Province of Santa Barbara
AFFPSH	Archives of the Franciscan Fathers, Province of the Sacred Heart

AFFPSJ	Archives of the Franciscan Fathers, Province of Saint Joseph
AFFPSJB	Archives of the Franciscan Fathers, Province of Saint John the Baptist
AHCA	Archives of Holy Cross Abbey
AMOMIEP	Archives of the Missionary Oblates of Mary Immaculate, Eastern Province
AMOMIS	Archives of the Missionary Oblates of Mary Immaculate, Southern United States Province
AMPSJ	Archives of the Maryland Province, Society of Jesus
ANEPSJ	Archives of the New England Province, Society of Jesus
ANYPSJ	Archives of the New York Province, Society of Jesus
AOFMPSH	Archives of the Order of Friars Minor, Province of the Sacred Heart
AOFMPSJB	Archives of the Order of Friars Minor, Province of St. John Baptist
AOPWDP	Archives of the Order of Preachers, Western Dominican Province
APFPCH	Archives of the Passionist Fathers, Province of Chicago
APFPNJ	Archives of the Passionist Fathers, Province New Jersey
ASPB	Archives of the Society of the Precious Blood
ASSE	Archives of the Society of St. Edmund
ASTIG	Archives of the Stigmatine Fathers and Brothers
AUND	Archives of the University of Notre Dame
AUSF	Archives of the University of San Francisco
CAASF	Chancery Archives, Archdiocese of San Francisco
DCR	*Denver Catholic Register*
GCMRL	George C. Marshall Research Library
HADP	Historical Archives, Diocese of Pittsburgh
JMPA	Jesuit Missouri Province Archives
NA	National Archives
OSV	*Our Sunday Visitor*
PHA	Passionist Historical Archives
PP	Primary Program Records and Personal Files for Navy Chaplains, 1775–1972
RG 247, NA	Record Group 247, National Archives
RPABP	Redemptorist Provincial Archives, Baltimore Province
RPASLP	Redemptorist Provincial Archives, St. Louis Province
TPC	*The Provincial Chronicle*
WLTOC	*Weekly Letter to Our Chaplains*

INTRODUCTION

1. "Pilot Gives Absolution," *Army and Navy Chaplain* 14 (January–February 1944): 31.

2. Robert L. Gushwa, *The Best and Worst of Times: The United States Army Chaplaincy, 1920–1945* (Washington, D.C.: Office of the Chief of Chaplains, Department of the Army, 1977), pp. 16–17, 108; Clifford M. Drury, *The History of the Chaplain Corps, United States Navy, 1939–1945* (Washington, D.C.: Bureau of Naval Personnel, 1950), pp. 58–59.

3. Drury, *History of the Chaplain Corps,* p. 312; Gushwa, *Best and Worst of Times,* pp. 208–209. Although neither service ever announced a formal "quota" for any denomination, it was widely understood that each should contribute about 8.5 percent of its membership. Catholicism never gave its full share, and since Catholics of the time had

been schooled to believe that the presence of a priest, administering the church's sacraments, was a great help to their salvation, the shortage created severe hardships for Catholic men and women in the services—and for the chaplains themselves, who had to make up for their small numbers as best they could. The worst offenders were the Archdiocese of Philadelphia and the church's largest order, the Jesuits.

4. On the tank chaplain, see Patrick Flaherty Papers, ACSV.

5. For the total number of Catholic chaplains, see William McCarty, Report of the Military Ordinariate, November 2, 1945, "Circular Letters to Bishops and Religious Superiors" folder, box 12, O'Hara Papers, AUND. On the army, see Gushwa, *Best and Worst of Times,* p. 192. On the navy, see Drury, *History of the Chaplain Corps,* pp. 298, 305; William Arnold to R. E. Hoyle, November 28, 1941, box 209, RG 247, NA. See also Arnold to John F. O'Hara, November 10, 1942, box 77, vol. 5, ibid.; O'Hara, Circular Letter No. 8, May 26, 1941, "Circular Letters to Bishops and Religious Superiors" folder, box 12, O'Hara Papers, AUND; Daniel A. Poling, "Strong Men of God," *Sign* 24 (May 1945): 547.

In the middle of the war, when General Arnold told George C. Marshall, the army chief of staff, that only 23 of the 5,200 chaplains had to be separated from the service, Marshall told an aide that it "created a doubt in my mind as to whether we were being sufficiently exacting in requiring a high degree of effectiveness on the part of chaplains" (George C. Marshall to A[ssistant] C[hief] of S[taff], G-1, April 15, 1943, reel 306, item 4661, George C. Marshall Research Library).

6. Drury, *History of the Chaplain Corps,* pp. 155, 159, 207; Luther D. Miller to A[ssistant] C[hief] of S[taff], War Department, December 5, 1945, box 45, "Army Statistics," RG 247, NA. See also Christopher Cross, *Soldiers of God* (New York: E. P. Dutton and Company, 1945), pp. 189–230; Gushwa, *Best and Worst of Times,* p. 141; *Brooklyn Tablet,* November 3, 1945; *Catholic News,* August 5, 1944; Roy Honeywell, *The Chaplains of the United States Army* (Washington, D.C.: Office of the Chief of Chaplains, Department of the Army, 1958), p. 249; William McCarty, Report of the Military Ordinariate, November 2, 1945, "Circular Letters to Bishops and Religious Superiors" folder, box 12, John F. O'Hara Papers, AUND; George A. Rosso to [James H. Griffiths], November 5, 1946, and Patrick J. Ryan to [Griffiths], November 8, 1946, in Robert I. Gannon, *The Cardinal Spellman Story* (Garden City, N.Y.: Doubleday and Company, 1962), pp. 233, 428.

7. The only other country participating in the conflict that so far has produced a detailed study of its wartime chaplains is Germany (see Georg May, *Interkonfessionalismus in der deutschen Militärseelsorge von 1933 bis 1945* [Amsterdam: B. R. Gruner, 1978]). The absence of such works makes comparative examination of national chaplaincies impossible. On the Catholic chaplains in Great Britain, see Martin Dempsey, *The Priest among the Soldiers* (London: Burns, Oates, 1947), which is an interesting collection of stories but not a systematic study.

CHAPTER 1. PEARL HARBOR

1. William A. Maguire, *Rig for Church* (New York: Macmillan, 1942), pp. 241–242.

2. Ibid.

3. Throughout this book, I use the term "Last Rites" rather than "Extreme Unction" (the Latin term sometimes then in use) or "Anointing of the Sick" (the current phrase), since "Last Rites" was the one most widely in use during the war.

4. William A. Maguire, *The Captain Wears a Cross* (New York: Macmillan, 1943), pp. 1–2, 9–10, 12, 15; Maguire, "Fleet Chaplain's Report," *Catholic Digest* 6 (August

1942): 26; Maguire, *Rig for Church*, pp. 243–244; Clifford Drury, *History of the Chaplain Corps, United States Navy, 1939–1949* (Washington, D.C.: Bureau of Naval Personnel, 1950), pp. 21, 24–25.

5. Maguire, *Rig for Church*, p. 245; Maguire, *The Captain Wears a Cross*, pp. 13–15.

6. Maguire, *The Captain Wears a Cross*, pp. 12, 15.

7. Daniel B. Jorgensen, *The Service of Chaplains to Army Air Units, 1917–1946* (Washington, D.C.: Office of the Chief of Air Force Chaplains, 1961), p. 84; Christopher Cross, *Soldiers of God* (New York: E. P. Dutton and Company, 1945), pp. 23–26.

8. Cross, *Soldiers of God*, pp. 24–26; Roy Honeywell, *The Chaplains of the United States Army* (Washington, D.C.: Office of the Chief of Chaplains, Department of the Army, 1958), pp. 276–277; Robert L. Gushwa, *The Best and Worst of Times: The United States Army Chaplaincy, 1920–1945* (Washington, D.C.: Office of the Chief of Chaplains, Department of the Army, 1977), pp. 84, 102–103.

9. *Boston Pilot*, December 27, 1941, November 14, 1942, October 30, 1943; Shelby Stanton, *Order of Battle: The U.S. Army in World War II* (Novato, Calif.: Presidio Press, 1984), pp. 59–66; Barrett McGurn, "Soldier-Priests," *Sign* 21 (June 1942): 666; Maguire, *The Captain Wears a Cross*, pp. 111–112.

10. Clifford M. Drury, *The History of the Chaplain Corps, United States Navy, 1939–1949* (Washington, D.C.: Bureau of Naval Personnel, 1950), p. 22.

11. Maguire, *The Captain Wears a Cross*, p. 114; Barrett McGurn, "Soldier-Priests," *Sign* 21 (June 1942): 666; John P. Kelly, "The First Was Last," *Catholic Digest* 6 (May 1942): 47; Stephen Bower Young, *Trapped at Pearl Harbor: Escape from Battleship Oklahoma* (Annapolis, Md.: Naval Institute Press, 1991), pp. 18, 24, 70.

12. *Boston Pilot*, December 27, 1941, November 14, 1942, October 30, 1943; Drury, *History of the Chaplain Corps*, pp. 22, 124–125; Young, *Trapped at Pearl Harbor*, pp. 18, 24, 70.

13. Drury, *History of the Chaplain Corps*, pp. 22, 124–125; *Boston Pilot*, December 27, 1941, November 14, 1942, October 30, 1943. Recent evidence suggests that Schmitt's battle station was the ship's sick bay. It is unclear, however, whether he was in that particular room when he began helping men leave the ship. The historian of the *Oklahoma* has recently asked why the navy failed to give Schmitt "a much higher award, for he gave his life so that others might live, the highest sacrifice an individual can make" (Young, *Trapped at Pearl Harbor*, p. 157).

14. Cross, *Soldiers of God*, p. 21.

15. Padre [Karl Wuest], *They Told It to the Chaplain* (New York: Vintage Press, 1953), p. 4.

16. Maguire, *The Captain Wears a Cross*, p. 18.

17. Ibid., p. 34; Jorgensen, *Service of Chaplains to Army Air Units*, pp. 84–85; Cross, *Soldiers of God*, pp. 33–34; Drury, *History of the Chaplain Corps*, pp. 25–26.

18. For a critique of the myths stemming from the attack, see Gordon W. Prange, *At Dawn We Slept: The Untold Story of Pearl Harbor* (New York: Penguin Books, 1981), pp. 839–850.

19. "New U.S. War Songs," *Life* 13 (November 2, 1942): 43; David Ewen, *Panorama of American Popular Music* (Englewood Cliffs, N.J.: Prentice-Hall, 1957), p. 35; David Ewen, *American Popular Songs: From the Revolutionary War to the Present* (New York: Random House, 1966), p. 317; Paul F. Boller, Jr., and Joan George, *They Never Said It* (New York: Oxford University Press, 1989), p. 94.

20. Maguire, *The Captain Wears a Cross*, p. 166.

21. Ibid., pp. 166–167, 184–186; Frank Scully, "The Padre and the Song," *Catholic Digest* 8 (June 1944): 2; *Life* 13 (November 2, 1942): 43. No copy of the official de-

nial, or even a version of it, has ever come to light. Maguire remains the only source for the demurral.

22. *Los Angeles Times,* October 23, 1944; "Praise Be, a War Song," *Newsweek* 20 (October 5, 1942): 77; "War Songs," *Time* 40 (October 20, 1942): 50. For the subsequent story, see "Mr. Bill Lewis, Office of War Information, You Asked for It, Here It Is," *Variety* 148 (September 16, 1942): 45; Richard Lingeman, *Don't You Know There's a War On? The American Home Front, 1941–1945* (New York: G. P. Putnam's Sons, 1970), p. 212; O'Hara to Arnold, October 12, 1942, box 77, vol. 5, RG 247, NA; William R. Arnold to John F. O'Hara, October 23, 1942, box 77, vol. 5, ibid.

The most recent version of Maguire's alleged exploits has Maguire putting a machine gun on the altar, firing it at the Japanese planes, and shouting "Praise the Lord and pass the ammunition" (Arthur Zich, *The Rising Sun* [Chicago: Time-Life Books, 1977], p. 56).

23. Maguire, *The Captain Wears a Cross,* pp. 40–41.

CHAPTER 2. THE FALL OF THE PHILIPPINES

1. B. H. Liddell Hart, *History of the Second World War* (New York: G. P. Putnam's Sons, 1970), pp. 199–211.

2. Louis Morton, *The Fall of the Philippines* (Washington, D.C.: Office of the Chief of Military History, Department of the Army, 1954), pp. 85–86; John A. Wilson, supplementary questionnaire, April 1986.

3. Wilson, supplementary questionnaire, April 1986.

4. Wilson to Donald F. Crosby, February 20, 1986; *Catholic Telegraph,* August 15, 1980; Wilson, supplementary questionnaire, April 1986.

5. Daniel B. Jorgensen, *The Service of Chaplains to Army Air Units, 1917–1946* (Washington, D.C.: Office of the Chief of Air Force Chaplains, 1961), pp. 85–86; *Brooklyn Tablet,* June 6, 1942; "Distinguished Service Cross," May 2, 1942, John L. Curran, box 120, vol. 1, RG 247, NA; John Way, "The Soldier Priest," *Dominicana* 28 (Summer 1943): 92; *Brooklyn Tablet,* February 14, 1942.

6. "Hatred for None," *America* 66 (January 10, 1942): 379.

7. William T. Cummings, Monthly Report, December 18–31, 1941, Cummings Papers, RG 247, NA; Sidney Stewart, *Give Us This Day* (New York: W. W. Norton and Company, 1956), pp. 38–41.

8. Liddell-Hart, *History of the Second World War,* pp. 221–223.

9. Clifford Drury, *History of the Chaplain Corps* (Washington, D.C.: Bureau of Naval Personnel, 1950), p. 35; *Boston Pilot,* October 30, 1943.

10. Ronald H. Spector, *Eagle against the Sun: The American War against Japan* (New York: Vintage Books, 1985), pp. 110–119, 134–135.

11. William R. Arnold to Charles C. Rutson, January 26, 1942, box 2, folder 5, Arnold Papers, GCMRL.

12. Ellwood Nance, ed., *Faith of Our Fighters* (St. Louis, Mo.: Bethany Press, 1944), pp. 102–103; *Brooklyn Tablet,* May 2, 1942; Distinguished Service Cross, May 2, 1942, John L. Curran, box 120, vol. 1, RG 247, NA; John Way, "The Soldier Priest," *Dominicana* 28 (Summer 1943): 92.

13. "Army and Navy Chaplains Report," *Gasparian* 5 (September 15, 1945): 1; "Father Wilson," *Gasparian* 5 (June 1942): 1; *Catholic Telegraph,* August 15, 1980; John A. Wilson, supplementary questionnaire, April 1986.

14. Allen Raymond, "Nurses of Bataan," *Catholic Digest* 6 (August 1942): 63–64;

Christopher Cross, *Soldiers of God* (New York: E. P. Dutton and Company, 1945), pp. 37–38; Daniel A. Poling, "Strong Men of God," *Sign* 24 (May 1945): 548.

15. On examples of the use of the phrase, "No atheists in foxholes," see Donald I. Rogers, *Since You Went Away* (New Rochelle, N.Y.: Arlington House, 1973), p. 194, and Mary Dilts, *Army Code for Women* (New York: Longmans, Green and Company, 1942), p. 71. On the fragility of foxhole religion, see questionnaires of Clement Buckley and John A. Griffin, December 1983; Henry D. Buchanan to [William R. Arnold], n.d., box 180, vol. 5, RG 247, NA; Jorgensen, *Service of Chaplains to Army Air Units*, p. 279, and Elisha Atkins, "Second Thoughts," in Willard Sperry, ed., *Religion of Soldier and Sailor* (Cambridge, Mass.: Harvard University Press, 1945), p. 101.

16. Sidney Stewart, *Give Us This Day* (New York: W. W. Norton and Company, 1957), pp. 85–87, 89.

17. Arthur Zich, *The Rising Sun* (Chicago: Time-Life Books, 1977), pp. 97, 100; William R. Arnold, "We Are Strong in Spirit," *Country Gentleman* 112 (October 1942): 89; Nance, *Faith of Our Fighters*, p. 102; Louis Morton, *The Fall of the Philippines* (Washington, D.C.: Office of the Chief of Military History, Department of the Army, 1953), p. 467; Wilson to Donald F. Crosby, February 20, 1986; Wilson, supplementary questionnaire; *Catholic Telegraph*, August 15, 1980.

18. Arnold, "We Are Strong in Spirit," p. 89.

19. Spector, *Eagle against the Sun*, pp. 396–398.

20. *Catholic Telegraph*, August 15, 1980; Wilson, supplementary questionnaire, April 1986.

21. Wilson, supplementary questionnaire, April 1986.

22. Ibid. and John F. Hurley, "Wartime Superior in the Philippines" (manuscript, n.d.), p. 12, Hurley Papers, ANYPSJ. Though Gaerlan never held a commission in the army's Chaplain Corps, he served many of the Americans who fought in the islands.

23. Zich, *The Rising Sun*, p. 97; Morton, *The Fall of the Philippines*, p. 573; Wilson to Donald F. Crosby, February 20, 1986.

24. Morton, *The Fall of the Philippines*, p. 573; John K. Borneman, "From Bataan through Cabanatuan," *Army and Navy Chaplain* 16 (April–May 1946): 23.

25. John J. Dugan, "Life under the Japs," *Boston Globe*, April 2, 5, 11, 1945.

26. Ibid., April 2, 1945.

27. Ibid.

28. John K. Borneman, "From Bataan through Cabanatuan," *Army and Navy Chaplain* 16 (April–May 1946): 23.

CHAPTER 3. GUADALCANAL

1. B. H. Liddell Hart, *History of the Second World War* (G. P. Putnam's Sons, 1970), pp. 356–360. Rafael Steinberg, *Island Fighting* (Chicago: Time-Life Books, 1978), pp. 18, 24, 32; T. Grady Gallant, *On Valor's Side* (Garden City, N.Y.: Doubleday and Company, 1963), p. 212. Guadalcanal's size is almost exactly double that of Long Island, New York.

2. Samuel E. Morison, *The Two-Ocean War: A Short History of the United States Navy in the Second World War* (Boston: Little, Brown and Company, 1963), pp. 141, 177.

3. Steinberg, *Island Fighting*, p. 32; John Toland, *The Rising Sun: The Decline and Fall of the Japanese Empire, 1936–1945* (New York: Random House, 1970), pp. 338–339.

4. Gallant, *On Valor's Side*, p. 212.

5. John Foley, "Haec Olim Meminisse Juvabit" (Manuscript, n.d.), p. 187; James E. Dunford to Richard J. Cushing, June 7, 1943, box 13, "Solomon Islands" folder, John F. O'Hara Papers, AUND.

6. Steinberg, *Island Fighting*, p. 18.

7. Reports differ over the origin of Kelly's nickname. Thomas Reardon, a fellow chaplain, insists that he was known as "Nose" Kelly because of his prominent proboscis, but a marine officer recalls that he was called "Foxhole Kelly" then and in later years (Thomas M. Reardon, interview, January 8, 1987; Leo A. Dulacki to Donald F. Crosby [ca. January 1, 1989]; Richard Tregaskis, *Guadalcanal Diary* [New York: Random House, 1943], p. 3).

8. Elizabeth McFadden, "The Beachhead Was His Parish," *Sign* 23 (March 1944): 462; Tregaskis, *Guadalcanal Diary*, pp. 3, 21–22.

9. Liddell Hart, *History of the Second World War*, pp. 135–138; Reardon interview, January 8, 1987.

10. Tregaskis, *Guadalcanal Diary*, pp. 21–22.

11. Morison, *Two-Ocean War*, p. 139.

12. McFadden, "The Beachhead Was His Parish," p. 462; Reardon interview, January 8, 1987.

13. McFadden, "The Beachhead Was His Parish," p. 463; *Brooklyn Tablet*, August 21, 1943; Dorothy F. Grant, *War Is My Parish: Anecdote and Comment Collected by Dorothy Fremont Grant* (Milwaukee, Wis.: Bruce Publishing Company, 1944), p. 73.

14. Gallant, *On Valor's Side*, p. 347; McFadden, "The Beachhead Was His Parish," p. 463. None of the marines on Guadalcanal was buried in a wooden casket because wood was so scarce on the island.

15. McFadden, "The Beachhead Was His Parish," p. 463.

16. Ibid.; *Brooklyn Tablet*, August 21, 1943; Reardon interview, January 8, 1987.

17. McFadden, "The Beachhead Was His Parish," p. 463; Reardon interview, January 8, 1987.

18. Reardon interview, January 8, 1987.

19. Frederic Gehring, *A Child of Miracles* (Philadelphia: Jefferies and Manz, 1962), pp. 26–27.

20. Gehring interview, June 28, 1983.

21. Gehring, *A Child of Miracles*, pp. 9–12.

22. Gehring interview, June 28, 1983.

23. Gehring, *A Child of Miracles*, pp. 5–6.

24. Gehring interview, June 28, 1983; Gehring, *A Child of Miracles*, p. 131.

25. Drury, *History of the Chaplain Corps*, pp. 175, 177, 193; W[arren] Wyeth Willard, *The Leathernecks Come Through* (New York: Fleming H. Revell Company, 1944), p. 139; Reardon interview, January 8, 1987.

26. Gehring interview, June 28, 1983.

27. O'Neill interview, June 22, 1983.

28. Ibid.

29. James P. Daly, interview, June 24, 1983.

30. Ibid.

31. James P. Daly to Donald F. Crosby, ca. June 1, 1993; Daly interview, June 24, 1983.

32. O'Neill interview, June 22, 1983; Reardon interview, January 8, 1987.

33. Said O'Neill: "Fred was a great guy . . . [but he] loved publicity. He got it. It was no place for me to get publicity after he left there. He locked it all up." Gehring's chaplain-critics also note that Richard Tregaskis' *Guadalcanal Diary* describes the work of the marine chaplains on the island at some length, but fails to mention him. Tre-

gaskis left Gehring out of his story precisely because he was not, in fact, a chaplain specifically assigned to the corps (O'Neill interview, June 22, 1983; Reardon interview, January 8, 1987).

34. *Brooklyn Tablet,* March 13, 1943.

35. Ibid., March 20, 1943; Barney Ross, "A Second Note," *Catholic Digest* 7 (May 1943): 19; Gehring interview, June 28, 1983; Gehring, *Child of Our Time,* pp. 158–159; Paul McNamara, "Father Gehring," *Catholic Digest* 9 (January 1945): 47–48; McFadden, "The Beachhead Was His Parish," p. 464.

36. O'Neill interview, June 22, 1983; Reardon interview, January 8, 1987; *Denver Catholic Register,* June 24, 1943.

37. Reardon interview, January 8, 1987.

38. Ibid.; John Foley, "Haec Olim Meminisse Juvabit" (Manuscript, n.d.), p. 221.

39. Daniel B. Jorgensen, *The Service of Chaplains to Army Air Units, 1917–1946* (Washington, D.C.: Office of the Chief of Air Force Chaplains, 1961), p. 163.

40. Robert Leckie, *A Helmet for My Pillow* (New York: Random House, 1957), p. 95.

CHAPTER 4. FORWARD IN THE PACIFIC

1. *Catholic Universe Bulletin,* November 2, 1947; Fidelis [Wieland] to Father [Gregory], October 19, 1944, Wieland Papers, AFFPSB; William D. Savage to Father Pauley, September 7, 1945, Savage Papers, HADP; Roman J. Nuwer to William R. Arnold, June 19, [1944,] box 4, folder 22, Arnold Papers, GCMRL; Raphael Steinberg, *Island Fighting* (Chicago: Time-Life Books, 1978), p. 54.

2. Robert L. Eichelberger and Milton MacKaye, *Our Jungle Road to Tokyo* (New York: Viking Press, 1950), p. 21.

3. Edward Connolly to John F. O'Hara, March 10, 1943, box 11, Connolly folder, O'Hara Papers, AUND.

4. Steinberg, *Island Fighting,* p. 54; John Milner, Jr., *Cartwheel: The Reduction of Rabaul* (Washington, D.C.: Office of the Chief of Military History, Department of the Army, 1959), pp. 147, 216, 234–254, 316–319; B. H. Liddell Hart, *History of the Second World War* (G. P. Putnam's Sons, 1970), p. 613; Ronald H. Spector, *Eagle against the Sun: The American War against Japan* (New York: Vintage Books, 1985), p. 294.

5. Shelby Stanton, *Order of Battle: The U.S. Army in World War II* (Novato, Calif.: Presidio Press, 1984), p. 168; Ulysses Lee, *The Employment of Negro Troops* (Washington, D.C.: Office of the Chief of Military History, Department of the Army, 1966), pp. 529, 531–533.

6. *Brooklyn Tablet,* August 8, 1942; *Boston Pilot,* August 15, 1942; Albert S. Foley, *God's Men of Color: The Colored Catholic Priests of the United States* (New York: Farrar, Straus, 1955), pp. 187–190; John W. Bowman (Manuscript, ca. July 1987); John W. Bowman, questionnaire, July 1987; "First of His Race," *Interracial Review* 16 (June 1943): 90; Richard F. Eggers, Indorsements, March 10, 1944, Bowman, Monthly Report, February 1944, Bowman Papers, RG 247, NA; Efficiency Reports, December 31, 1944, and June 30, 1945, Bowman Papers, RG 247, NA; Ernest W. Meissel, Efficiency Reports, Bowman, December 31, 1944, and August 6, 1945, ibid.; Oscar E. Holder, "Chaplain Evaluation Record," Bowman, August 7, 1945, ibid.; Bowman [July, 1987], ibid.; Bowman to William R. Arnold, April 21, 1945, ibid.

7. John W. Bowman to William R. Arnold, April 21, 1945, Bowman Papers, RG 247, NA.

8. Steinberg, *Island Fighting*, p. 146.

9. Spector, *Eagle against the Sun*, pp. 292.

10. Killian Dreiling to Joseph M. Marling [ca. April 14, 1945], *WLTOC* 78 (April 14, 1945): 78-2; Dreiling to Marling, July 22, 1944, *WLTOC* 44 (August 19, 1944): 44-2.

11. Roman J. Nuwer to William R. Arnold, June 19 [1944], box 4, folder 22, Arnold Papers, GCMRL.

12. *Catholic Universe Bulletin*, November 17, 1944.

13. Fidelis [Wieland] to Father [Gregory], October 14 and 19, 1944, Wieland Papers, AFFPSB; Michael J. MacInnes to Father Paul, February 11, 1945, MacInnes Papers, AFFRSB.

14. JN 1: 23; Edith V. Knowles, ed., *Ever, Your Ben* (West Point, Ga.: Crossroads Productions and Publications, 1981), pp. 106-107, 147, 161-162, 168-169.

15. Watt M. Cooper, *With the Seabees in the South Pacific* (Graham, N.C.: W. M. Cooper, 1981), pp. 81, 91, 173.

16. John B. Young to William Arnold, October 8, 1943, box 45, "Battles and Battle Reports," RG 247, NA.

17. Steinberg, *Island Fighting*, pp. 135, 140-141, 144-146, 148.

18. Samuel E. Morison, *Aleutians, Gilberts, and Marshalls: June 1942 to April 1944* (Boston: Little, Brown and Company, 1951), pp. 69-70, 148, 185.

19. Dorothy Grant, *War Is My Parish* (Milwaukee, Wis.: Bruce Publishing Company, 1944), pp. 147-148.

20. Henry I. Shaw, Jr., Bernard C. Nalty, and Edwin T. Turnbladh, *Central Pacific Drive* ([Washington, D.C.]: U.S. Marine Corps, 1966), p. 636; John Toland, *The Rising Sun: The Decline and Fall of the Japanese Empire, 1936-1945* (New York: Random House, 1970), p. 469; Spector, *Eagle against the Sun*, pp. 259-261.

21. Steinberg, *Island Fighting*, p. 106.

22. Shaw, *Central Pacific Drive*, pp. 30-31; Eric Hammel and John E. Lane, *76 Hours: The Invasion of Tarawa* ([Pacifica, Calif.]: Pacifica Press, 1985), pp. 20-22.

23. Robert Sherrod, *Tarawa: The Story of a Battle* (New York: Duell, Sloan, and Pearce, 1944), pp. 54-55.

24. Sherrod, *Tarawa*, p. 45.

25. *Catholic Courier*, January 6, 1944; Hammel and Lane, *76 Hours*, pp. 30, 33.

26. Morison, *Aleutians*, pp. 155, 161-162; Spector, *Eagle against the Sun*, pp. 262, 264-265; Steinberg, *Island Fighting*, p. 110.

27. Clifford Drury, *History of the Chaplain Corps* (Washington, D.C.: Bureau of Naval Personnel, 1950), p. 168; Dorothy Grant, *War Is My Parish* (Milwaukee, Wis.: Bruce Publishing Company, 1944), pp. 147-148. Willard's denomination was Northern Baptist (Drury, *History of the Chaplain Corps*, p. 186).

28. *Catholic Courier*, February 22, 1945; Citation, Legion of Merit, John V. E. Loughlin, n.d., "Navy Department Honors Chaplains," *Navy Chaplain's News Letter* 2 (May-June 1944): 3; Citation, "Legion of Merit," March 1, 1944, Chaplain File, ADR; *OSV*, December 31, 1944; Drury, *History of the Chaplain Corps*, p. 186.

29. Hammel and Lane, *76 Hours*, pp. 98, 102.

30. Drury, *History of the Chaplain Corps*, p. 186; Citation for Legion of Merit, Frank W. Kelly, n.d., "Navy Department Honors Chaplains," *Navy Chaplain's News Letter* 2 (May-June 1944): 3; Citation for Legion of Merit, John V. E. Loughlin, n.d., ibid.; Sherrod, *Tarawa*, p. 46; *OSV*, December 19, 1943, October 29, 1944, December 31, 1944; Earl J. Wilson, *Betio Beachhead: The U.S. Marines' Own Story of the Battle for*

Tarawa (New York: G. P. Putnam's Sons, 1945), p. 94; *Catholic Standard and Times,* December 17, 1943.

31. Morison, *Aleutians,* p. 168; Steinberg, *Island Fighting,* p. 129.

32. Morison, *Aleutians,* pp. 172–178; Steinberg, *Island Fighting,* pp. 116–118; Spector, *Eagle against the Sun,* p. 266.

33. Wilson, *Betio Beachhead,* p. 148.

34. *Brooklyn Tablet,* January 29, 1944; "Catholic Chaplain Praised by Jew," *Ave Maria* 59 (February 1944): 228–229.

35. *Brooklyn Tablet,* January 29, 1944.

36. Drury, *History of the Chaplain Corps,* p. 187; *OSV,* October 29, 1944; Letter of Commendation, William R. O'Neill, n.d., "Five Chaplains Honored," *Navy Chaplain's News Letter* 2 (September–October 1944): 4.

37. *Catholic Courier,* February 22, 1945.

38. Ibid.; Joseph T. Keown to [George J. Collins], November 7, 1944, Keown Papers, ACHS.

39. USMC News Release, March 29, 1945, Frank W. Kelly Papers, PP; Navy News Release, n.d., Frank W. Kelly Papers, box 41, PP.

CHAPTER 5. NORTH AFRICA AND SICILY

1. James MacGregor Burns, *Roosevelt, The Soldier of Freedom* (New York: Harcourt Brace Jovanovich, 1970), pp. 285–292; B. H. Liddell Hart, *History of the Second World War* (G. P. Putnam's Sons, 1970), pp. 310–316; Richard Collier, *The War in the Desert* (Chicago: Time-Life Books, 1977), pp. 140, 154; Samuel E. Morison, *Operations in North African Waters, October 1942–June 1943* (Boston: Little, Brown and Company, 1947), pp. 33, 43–44, 55, 181–188.

2. John Foley, "Haec Olim Meminisse Juvabit" (Manuscript, n.d.), pp. 58–59.

3. L. B. Kines, "Chaplain at Tagaste and the Kasserine Pass," *Woodstock Letters* 89 (February 1960): 31.

4. Foley, "Haec Olim," p. 44.

5. *Denver Catholic Register,* February 18, 1943.

6. *Monitor,* January 2, 1943.

7. [Denis G.] Moore to Marcellus Fortman, November 18, 1942, *Gasparian* 6 (January 30, 1943): 3.

8. *Brooklyn Tablet,* February 6, April 17, November 3, 1943; *Boston Pilot,* December 12, 1942, February 6, 1943; "Letter of Bishop O'Hara Gives Details of Father Falter's Death," *Gasparian* 5 (December 21, 1942): 4; [Denis G.] Moore to Marcellus Fortman, November 18, 1942, *Gasparian* 6 (January 30, 1943): 3; "Provincial Interviews Sergeant in Dayton," *Gasparian* 6 (January 30, 1943): 1, 4; "Chaplain Killed," *Gasparian* 5 (December 6, 1943): 1; *Catholic News,* March 16, 1943; Leigh O. Wright (Manuscript, n.d.), Falter Papers, RG 247, NA; Wright to [William R. Arnold?] (ca. February 17, 1943), RG 247, NA. Chaplain Brown's denominational affiliation is not known.

9. Samuel E. Morison, *Operations in North African Waters, October 1942–June 1943* (Boston: Little, Brown and Company, 1947), p. 65; [Denis G.] Moore to John J. Mitty, November 24, 1942, January 27, 1943, Moore Papers, Personnel Files, Deceased, CAASF.

10. L. B. Kines, "Chaplain at Tagaste and the Kasserine Pass," *Woodstock Letters* 89 (February 1960): 46.

11. Francis X. Murphy, "Redemptorist Chaplains: Lieutenant John S. Wise," *Our Lady of Perpetual Help* (December 1943): 567. One chaplain detested the Arabs: "The Arabs are incredibly dirty. They will steal anything you leave around" (William J. O'Brien to Bub, January 26, 1943, O'Brien Papers, KFC).

12. Joseph M. Clark (Manuscript, n.d.), Clark Papers, file F299a, AMPSJ.

13. *Catholic Courier,* May 3, May 10, 1945; *Catholic Standard and Times,* March 9, 1945.

14. William J. O'Brien to Bub, January 26, 1943, O'Brien Papers, KFC; *Brooklyn Tablet,* February 6, 1943.

15. Collier, *War in the Desert,* pp. 162–167.

16. "Award of Silver Star Medal," June 22, 1943, Orville A. Lorenz, box 120, vol. 1, RG 247, NA. His denomination is not known.

17. John F. Gaffney (Manuscript, n.d.), Gaffney folder, file F299a, AMPSJ; Berkeley [Kines] to [Vincent] Keelan, June 27 and July 14, [1943], Kines Papers, ibid.; L. B. Kines, "Chaplain at Tagaste and the Kasserine Pass, *Woodstock Letters* 89 (February 1960): 52–53, 56–57. It appears that he also suffered a nervous breakdown while in North Africa (Paul A. McNally to [Vincent Keelan], January 9, 1944, Kines Papers, AMPSJ).

18. George F. Howe, *Northwest Africa: Seizing the Initiative in the West* (Washington, D.C.: Office of the Chief of Military History, Department of the Army, 1957), pp. 477–478; Thomas Parrish and S. L. A. Marshall, eds., *Simon and Schuster Encyclopedia of World War II* (New York: Simon and Schuster, 1978), p. 329.

19. *New York Times,* March 19, 1943; Spellman's biographer estimates that he wrote "tens of thousands of letters to Joes [GIs]" (Robert I. Gannon, *The Cardinal Spellman Story* [Garden City, N.Y.: Doubleday and Company, 1962], p. 205). See also Francis J. Spellman, *Action This Day: Letters from the Fighting Fronts* (New York: Charles Scribner's Sons, 1943), pp. 62, 64–65.

20. William J. O'Brien, Diary, November 2, 1943.

21. Morison, *Operations,* p. 260; Collier, *War in the Desert,* pp. 188, 195.

22. *Catholic News,* May 15, 1943; *Denver Catholic Register,* May 13, 1943.

23. Alfred Schneider, *My Brother's Keeper* (Green Bay, Wis.: Alt Publishing Corporation, 1981), p. 39.

24. Patrick J. McGoldrick to [George J. Collins], May 19, 1943, "Letters," *Our Province* 11 (July 1943): 145.

25. Robert Wallace, *The Italian Campaign* (Chicago: Time-Life Books, 1978), pp. 8, 78–79; Albert N. Garland and Howard McGaw Smyth, *Sicily and the Surrender of Italy* (Washington, D.C.: Office of the Chief of Military History, Department of the Army, 1965), pp. 80–81.

26. Patrick J. McGoldrick to [George J. Collins], May 19, 1943, *Our Province* 11 (July 1943): 145; Roger M. Haas, *A History of the American Province of Saint Anthony of Padua of the Order of Friars Minor Conventual, 1906–1983* ([Chicopee, Mass.: no publisher, 1983]), p. 163; *Denver Catholic Register,* July 22, 1943.

27. Joseph D. Barry to Thomas Steiner, August 3, 1943, August 23, 1945, Barry Papers, ACHCIP; Barry to [John F.] O'Hara, January 2, 1944, box 11, Barry folder, O'Hara Papers, AUND; Barry to Thomas Steiner, August 23, 1945, Barry Papers, ACHCIP.

28. *Brooklyn Tablet,* February 12, 1944; James V. Claypool and Carl Wiegman, *God on a Battlewagon* (Philadelphia: John C. Winston Company, 1944), p. 99; Clifford M. Drury, *History of the Chaplain Corps, United States Navy, 1939–1949,* 2 vols. (Washington, D.C.: Bureau of Naval Personnel, 1950), p. 187.

29. James P. Flynn to [John F.] Monahan, January 1, 1942, Flynn Papers, RG 247,

NA; James P. Flynn to William R. Arnold, May 26, 1943, Flynn Papers, ibid.; [John F. O'Hara], Circular Letter No. 34, October 12, 1943, Flynn Papers, ADC.

30. Ralph J. Smith to [William R. Arnold], July 23, 1943, Flynn Papers, RG 247, NA; Jesse F. Gregg to John J. Flynn, August 14, 1943, ibid.; John F. Monahan to Patrick J. Ryan, August 13, 1943, ibid.; John F. O'Hara, Circular Letter No. 33, August 14, 1943, "Circular Letters" file, AAMS.

31. Flynn to Arnold, May 26, 1943, Flynn Papers, RG 247, NA.

32. The version given here of the letter is a conflation of the two best sources: James P. Flynn to Mr. and Mrs. John J. Flynn (ca. June 19, 1943), Flynn Papers, ADC, and Flynn to Dearest Dad and Mother (ca. June 19, 1943), John W. Scannell Papers, RG 247, NA. See also *Brooklyn Tablet*, February 26, 1944.

33. Jesse F. Gregg to Flynn, August 14, 1943, Flynn Papers, RG 247, NA; Ralph J. Smith to [William R. Arnold], July 23, 1943, ibid.

34. [Denis G.] Moore to Thomas Connolly, August 16, 1943, Moore Papers, Personnel Files, Deceased, CAASF.

35. *Brooklyn Tablet*, March 31, 1945.

36. Dwight D. Eisenhower, *Crusade in Europe* (Garden City, N.Y.: Doubleday and Company, 1948), p. 177; Garland and Smyth, *Sicily*, pp. 411–412, 416–417.

CHAPTER 6. ITALY

1. Martin Blumenson, *Salerno to Cassino: The United States Army in World War II* (Washington, D.C.: Office of the Chief of Military History, 1969), p. 28; Robert Wallace, *The Italian Campaign* (Chicago: Time-Life Books, 1978), pp. 54–56, 189; B. H. Liddell Hart, *History of the Second World War* (G. P. Putnam's Sons, 1970), p. 459.

2. Bill Mauldin, *Up Front* (New York: Henry Holt and Company, 1945), pp. 102–103.

3. "Award of the Silver Star," February 12, 1944, Francis J. Keenan, box 120, vol. 2, RG 247, NA; Keenan to John F. O'Hara, September 11, 1943, box 13, "Sicily, Italy" folder, O'Hara Papers, AUND; Keenan to Father Slattery, February 8, 1944, Keenan Papers, ACMP; *Brooklyn Tablet*, February 26, 1944.

4. Liddell Hart, *History of the Second World War*, p. 473; Wallace, *Italian Campaign*, pp. 82–84.

5. Seraph W. Zeitz, "I Was No Hero," *TPC* (June 1947): 27.

6. [Denis G.] Moore to [John J. Mitty], October 16, 1943, Moore Papers, CAASF; Joseph D. Barry to Thomas Steiner, November 1943, Barry Papers, Province Archives Center, ACSCIP.

7. Padre [Karl Wuest], *They Told It to the Chaplain* (New York: Vantage Press, 1953), pp. 99–100.

8. Ibid.

9. Eddie Doherty, "Front-Line Chaplain," *Sign* 24 (October 1944): 121–123.

10. Doherty, "Front-Line Chaplain," p. 123; Jack Alexander, " 'He's Our Guy,' " *Catholic Digest* 9 (June 1945): 88–89; "Helper of the Helpless," *Time* 43 (June 19, 1944): 57–58; Dorothy F. Grant, *War Is My Parish: Anecdote and Comment Collected by Dorothy Fremont Grant* (Milwaukee, Wis.: Bruce Publishing Company, 1944), pp. 63–66; Christopher Cross, *Soldiers of God* (New York: E. P. Dutton and Company, 1945), pp. 140–141.

11. Michael I. English to Nan, May 8, 1944, English Papers, ACHPSJ; English to Mother, January 20, 1944, ibid.; Award of Distinguished Service Cross," March 12,

1944, Albert J. Hoffman, Hoffman file, box 120, vol. 2, RG 247, NA; *Brooklyn Tablet,* February 19, April 15, May 21, 1944; Mark W. Clark to Francis J. Spellman, January 6, 1944, Hoffman Papers, AADU.

12. Grant, *War Is My Parish,* p. 65; *Witness,* May 1, 1983; Gushwa, *Best and Worst of Times,* p. 152; Hoffman to author, March 13, 1981; "Underscorings," *America* 71 (April 22, 1944): 59; "Helper of the Helpless," *Time* 43 (June 19, 1944): 57.

13. William J. O'Brien, Diary, December 31, 1943, January 2 and 8, March 6, 1944, KFC.

14. E. F. Miller, "Two [Christmases]," *Ligourian* 33 (December 1945): 482–484.

15. O'Brien Diary, January 2, 1944.

16. Edward R. Martin to [William R. Arnold], January 10, 1944, Lenaghan Papers, RG 247, NA; *Catholic News,* March 11, 1944; John F. O'Hara, Circular Letter No. 35, January 31, 1944, "Circular Letters to Bishops and Religious Superiors" folder, box 12, John F. O'Hara Papers, AUND; *Catholic Courier,* February 17, 1944; *Catholic Transcript,* March 9, 1944.

17. H[erbert] Bloch, "Monte Cassino, Archabbey of," *New Catholic Encyclopedia* 9 (New York: McGraw-Hill Book Company, 1967): 1080, 1082; Wallace, *Italian Campaign,* pp. 135, 138.

18. Padre, *They Told It to the Chaplain,* pp. 108–109; Zeitz, "I Was No Hero," *TPC* (June 1947): 48–49.

19. O'Brien Diary, January 31, 1944, KFC.

20. William H. Pixley to George J. Collins (ca. January 1944), "Mailbag Perspective," *Our Province* 13 (April 1944): 45; Grant, *War Is My Parish,* p. 17.

21. Denis Moore to John J. Mitty, February 22, 1944, Moore Papers, CAASF.

22. Michael I. English to Mother, April 14, 1944, English Papers, ACHPSJ; Zeitz, "I Was No Hero," p. 49.

23. *Catholic Courier,* October 5, 1944.

24. Denis Moore to [John J. Mitty], April 4, 1944, Moore Papers, CAASF.

25. *Denver Catholic Register,* August 31, 1944.

26. Padre, *They Told It to the Chaplain,* pp. 110–111; O'Brien Diary, May 18, 1944, KFC.

27. Morris Kertzer, *With an H on My Dog Tag* (New York: Behrman House, 1947), pp. 5–6. Walker's denomination is not known.

28. Michael I. English to Mother, April 25, 1945, English Papers, ACHPSJ.

29. Raymond F. Copeland, Monthly Report, February 1944, Copeland Papers, RG 247, NA.

30. Joseph A. Gilmore, Monthly Reports, May 1943 to January 1944, Gilmore Papers, RG 247, NA; Frederick G. Lamb to William R. Arnold, July 1, 1944, ibid. (Lamb was the area's supervising chaplain and a Protestant whose denomination is not known.) Patrick B. Fay to [Donald F.] Crosby, January 6, 1984; Irving Trutt to [Patrick B.] Fay, n.d., copy from Fay to Donald F. Crosby; Gregory Kennedy to John F. O'Hara, n.d., Kennedy folder, box 12, O'Hara Papers, AUND; Francis J. Spellman, *No Greater Love: The Story of Our Soldiers* (New York: Charles Scribner's Sons, 1945), p. 36; Robert L. Gushwa, *The Best and Worst of Times: The United States Army Chaplaincy, 1920–1945* (Washington, D.C.: Office of the Chief of Chaplains, Department of the Army, 1977), p. 153; *New York Times,* August 2, 1944. The Catholic church allows a priest to administer the Last Rites if he believes that some life is left in the body. It does not permit the anointing of bodies clearly dead.

31. Liddell Hart, *History of the Second World War,* p. 473; G. A. Sheppard, *The Italian Campaign, 1943–1945: A Political and Military Reassessment* (New York: Frederick A. Praeger, Publishers, 1968), p. 242.

32. Ausonius, *Ordo Urban Nobilium*, I, 1. On arguments for John Beyenka of Chicago as the first chaplain to enter Rome and Bernard C. Hanna of Rochester as the same, see *Catholic Courier,* July 6, August 17, 1944; *Catholic Review,* June 16, 1944; James Doyle and John Kuhlmey, interviews, August 24, 1983. For evidence supporting the other two claimants—Raymond E. Vint and Thomas F. Nolan—see their questionnaires, December 1983.

33. Michael I. English to Mother, June 23, 1944, English Papers, ACHPSJ.

34. *Denver Catholic Register,* June 29, 1944.

35. Joseph M. Murphy to William R. Arnold, January 1, 1945, Arnold Papers, RG 247, NA; *Chattanooga Times,* April 22, 1945; *Catholic Courier,* August 17, 1944; Michael I. English to Mother, June 23, 1944, English Papers, ACHPSJ.

36. "His Holiness Pope Pius XII to American Catholic Chaplains," Circular Letters to Bishops and Religious Superiors folder, box 12, John F. O'Hara Papers, AUND; *Boston Pilot,* July 8, 1944; Gushwa, *Best and Worst of Times,* p. 153; *The Priest Goes to War* (New York: The Society for the Propagation of the Faith, [1945]), [p. 6]; Bystander, "Side Glances," *Ligourian* 32 (September 1944): 484.

37. Joachim A. Daleidem to [Fathers] Ermine et al., November 4, 1945, Daleiden Papers, AFFPSH; Daniel B. Jorgensen, *The Service of Chaplains to Army Air Units, 1917–1946* (Washington, D.C.: Office of the Chief of Air Force Chaplains, 1961), p. 225.

38. *Catholic Courier,* July 1944; Joseph D. Barry to [Thomas Steiner], July 25, 1944, Barry Papers, ACSCIP.

39. Padre, *They Told It to the Chaplain,* pp. 111–112.

CHAPTER 7. NORMANDY AND FRANCE

1. Charles Messenger, *The Chronological Atlas of World War II* (New York: Macmillan, 1989), p. 198; Samuel Eliot Morison, *Invasion of France and Germany, 1939–1945* (Boston: Little, Brown and Company), p. 67; John Kuenster, "Chaplains Courageous," *Columbia* 33 (June 1954): 5. Chaplain Eugene O'Grady of Baltimore was killed in action on November 29, 1944, by a German shell. In terms of devotion to his men, courage under fire, and leadership abilities, he was surpassed by none in the European theater. He was buried in the American military cemetery at Margraten, in the south of Holland *(Catholic Review,* December 14, 22, 1944, January 12, 1945; John F. O'Hara, Circular Letter No. 41, February 10, 1945, "Circular Letters" file, AAMS).

2. Christopher Argyle, *Chronology of World War II: The Day by Day Illustrated Record, 1939–1945* (New York: Exeter Books, 1980), p. 157; Thomas Parrish and S. L. A. Marshall, eds., *Simon and Schuster Encyclopedia of World War II* (New York: Simon and Schuster, 1978), p. 304; Elmer Heindl, questionnaire, March 24, 1988; *Catholic Courier,* June 14, 1945, and June 6, 1986; *Catholic News,* June 9, 1945.

3. Francis L. Sampson, *Paratrooper Padre* (Washington, D.C.: Catholic University of America Press, 1948), pp. 39, 43.

4. *Catholic Courier,* July 20, 1944, June 14, 1945, June 6, 1986.

5. For the probable location of Maternowski's death, see Gordon A. Harrison, *Cross-Channel Attack* (Washington, D.C.: Office of the Chief of Military History, Department of the Army, 1951), pp. 290–291; Kuenster, "Chaplains Courageous," p. 5; [William J. Heavey?] to [Military Ordinary], November 3, 1944, Ignatius P. Maternowski folder, box 12, John F. O'Hara Papers, AUND; *Holyoke Transcript,* May 8, 1948; Sampson, *Paratrooper Padre,* p. 57; *OSV,* November 19, 1944.

6. John Macdonald, *Great Battles of World War II* (New York: Collier Books, Macmillan, 1986), pp. iii–iv [follow p. 136]; Gordon A. Harrison, *Cross-Channel Attack* (Washington, D.C.: Office of the Chief of Military History, Department of the Army, 1951), pp. 182, 189–190, 196, 302, 319, 329–330, 336, 448.

7. Fabian Flynn, "D-Day and After," *Sign* 24 (September 1944): 62–63.

8. *Catholic Transcript,* June 22, July 13, July 20, 1944; John F. Kelly, Monthly Reports, March, May, June, 1944, Kelly Papers, AAH; Kelly interview, July 25, 1987.

9. *Catholic Transcript,* July 13, 1944.

10. *Catholic Transcript,* June 22, 1944; "Distinguished Service Cross," June 20, 1944, Joseph R. Lacy, box 120, vol. 2, RG 247, NA; *OSV,* February 11, 1945; *Boston Pilot,* August 26, 1944; Joseph R. Lacy, interview, August 7, 1987.

11. Lacy interview, August 7, 1987.

12. Douglas Botting, *The Second Front* (Chicago: Time-Life Books, 1979), pp. 128–129, 131, 304, 328.

13. Sampson, *Paratrooper Padre,* pp. ix, 46–47; "Award of Distinguished Service Cross," n.d., Francis Sampson Papers, RG 247, NA.

14. *Catholic Journal,* June 6, 1986.

15. *Courier Journal,* June 6, 1986.

16. Macdonald, *Great Battles of World War II,* pp. 138, 140.

17. Martin Blumenson, *Liberation* (Chicago: Time-Life Books, 1978), pp. 16, 17, 21.

18. Sampson, *Paratrooper Padre,* p. 48.

19. Ibid., pp. 48–52; "Chaplains Courageous," pp. 17–18; "Award of Distinguished Service Cross," n.d., Francis L. Sampson Papers, RG 247, NA. The Catholic version of the "grace" or blessing before meals, in its World War II version, was "Bless us, O Lord, and these Thy gifts, which we are about to receive through thy bounty, through Christ Our Lord. Amen." Sampson was hardly the first Catholic priest in the service to err in this manner.

20. Henry M. Marusa to Father [?], July 1, 1944, Edelen Papers, ADR; Marusa to [Military Ordinariate?], July 1, 1944, Marusa folder, box 12, John F. O'Hara Papers, AUND; Joseph A. Nee to John F. O'Hara, June 27, [1944], ibid.; Thomas F. O'Connor to William T. McCarthy, August 25, 1944, O'Connor folder, box 12, O'Hara Papers, AUND; *Brooklyn Tablet,* August 12, 1944; Contesse d'Ursely to Mildred W. Edelen, July 25, 1945, "The Edelen Family," *Raleigh Knight* (June 1946): 3. It is not known whether Mrs. Edelen ever visited her son's grave.

21. *Brooklyn Tablet,* August 5, 1944; *America* 71 (August 12, 1944): 467; John F. O'Hara, Circular Letter No. 38, August 1, 1944, "Circular Letters to Bishops and Religious Superiors" folder, box 12, O'Hara Papers, AUND; *Catholic Standard and Times,* August 11, September 29, 1944; *OSV,* February 4, 1945; Daniel A. Poling, "Strong Men of God," *Sign* 24 (May 1945): 548; Citation, Silver Star, Dominic Ternan, October 28, 1944, Ternan Papers, RG 247, NA.

22. Blumenson, *Liberation,* p. 28.

23. [John R. Bradstreet] to [Joseph J. King], May 31, 1945, Bradstreet Papers, ACAPSJ; Leo Weigel to Joseph M. Marling, September 10, 1944, *WLTOC* 49 (September 23, 1944): 49–2.

24. John R. Bradstreet, diary, July 24, 1944, Bradstreet Papers, ACAPSJ.

25. Sampson, *Paratrooper Padre,* pp. 53–54.

26. Ibid., pp. 60–61.

27. Joseph A. Nee to Hugh C. Boyle, June 11, 1945, Nee Papers, HADP; L. Curtis Tiernan to William R. Arnold, August 11, 1944, box 180, vol. 1, RG 247, NA;

Harold F. Donovan, Monthly Report, July 1944, Donovan Papers, ibid.; Donovan to [Joseph M. Nelligan], June 24, 1944, Donovan Papers, AABAL.

28. Blumenson, *Liberation,* p. 57.

29. Stephen P. Kenny to John F. O'Hara, August 23, 1944, box 13, "Somewhere in France, I" folder, O'Hara Papers, AUND; *Brooklyn Tablet,* September 9, 1944; *OSV,* February 4, 1945; Adolph [Thillman] to [Father] Theodosius, December 16, 1944, Thillman Papers, AFFPSH; *Catholic Standard and Times,* August 25, September 1 and 15, 1944. Bonner's hometown Catholic newspaper in Philadelphia reported nothing whatever on either his life or his passing, though it printed a copy of a letter he had written his father shortly before his death in battle. The *Catholic Standard and Times* reflected the attitude of the reigning Archbishop of Philadelphia, Dennis Cardinal Dougherty, who showed not the slightest interest in the chaplains from his archdiocese. A difficult and highly authoritarian figure, it seems that he had experienced difficulties with a chaplain in Manila some thirty years earlier, and for the rest of his life had nothing but contempt for the military chaplaincy.

The memorial Mass held several months later attracted no comment from the paper except a list of names of the priests and other clerics who attended (*Catholic Standard and Times,* August 25, 1944, September 1, 1944). The Catholics of the city, however, erected a shrine to the memory of Bonner and the other five chaplains from the archdiocese who had given their lives in the war (ibid., September 15, 1944).

30. Blumenson, *Liberation,* pp. 80–81.

31. Donald J. Murphy, "Bringing Up Father: Diary of a World War II Chaplain" (Manuscript, n.d.), p. 30.

32. Ibid.

33. Distance figures are based on United States Military Academy, *A Military History of World War II: Atlas* (West Point, N.Y.: Department of Military Art and Engineering, 1956), map 56.

34. *Monitor,* September 30, 1944.

35. *Brooklyn Tablet,* September 16, 1944; *Monitor,* September 30, 1944.

36. *Monitor,* September 30, 1944.

37. Blumenson, *Liberation,* pp. 80, 82–84; Adolph [Thillman] to [Father] Theodosius, December 16, 1944, Thillman Papers, AFFPSH.

38. John [T.] O'Brien to [George J.] Collins, August 16, 1944, O'Brien Papers, ACHS.

39. William S. Gatherwood, September 3, 1944, to [addressee not given], box 180, vol. 1, RG 247, NA.

40. Blumenson, *Liberation,* pp. 109–110. See also Francis J. Spellman, *No Greater Love: The Story of Our Soldiers* (New York: Charles Scribner's Sons, 1945), pp. 42–43; Robert I. Gannon, *The Cardinal Spellman Story* (Garden City, N.Y.: Doubleday and Company, 1962), p. 237.

41. Spellman, *No Greater Love,* pp. 42–43, 45–46.

42. Ibid., pp. 45–46.

43. James A. Martin to John [Matthews?], September 5, 1944, file F35, AMPSJ.

44. Blumenson, *Liberation,* p. 115.

45. Ibid., pp. 140–141.

46. Ibid., p. 156.

47. *Catholic Transcript,* October 19, 1944.

48. Ibid.

49. *Catholic Courier,* September 28, 1944.

50. John A. Strmiska to [George J. Collins], [ca. October 1944], "Mailbag Perspective," *Our Province* 14 (December 1945): 140.

51. Blumenson, *Liberation,* pp. 170–172; Martin Blumenson, *The Patton Papers* (Boston: Houghton Mifflin, 1974), vol. 2, pp. 530–536; Russell F. Weigley, *Eisenhower's Lieutenants: The Campaign of France and Germany, 1944–1945* (Bloomington: Indiana University Press, 1981), pp. 374–375, 390–391. Casualty figures are based on data given in Charles MacDonald, *The Siegfried Line Campaign* (Washington, D.C.: Office of the Chief of Military History, Department of the Army, 1963), p. 617.

52. Clarence R. Ford to John F. O'Hara, September 2, 1944, box 13, "Somewhere in France, I" folder, John F. O'Hara Papers, AUND.

53. Spellman, *No Greater Love,* pp. 106–107.

54. Ibid., p. 107.

55. Blumenson, *Patton Papers,* vol. 2, p. 548.

CHAPTER 8. THE BATTLE OF THE BULGE

1. So-called because the German attack formed a dent (or "bulge") in the American lines. On Germans plans, see William Goolrick and Ogdon Tanner, *The Battle of the Bulge* (Chicago: Time-Life Books, 1980), pp. 21, 32, 34–35, 49; Russell F. Weigley, *Eisenhower's Lieutenants: The Campaign of France and Germany, 1944–1945* (Bloomington: Indiana University Press, 1981), p. 655.

2. Goolrick and Tanner, *Battle of the Bulge,* pp. 49–50, 86–88, 90–91, 93, 95.

3. *Catholic Transcript,* January 4, 1945.

4. Paul W. Cavanaugh, "Chaplain Prisoner," *Woodstock Letters* 90 (February 1961): 20–21.

5. Cavanaugh to [Leo D. Sullivan], July 23, 1945, Cavanaugh Papers, ADPSJ. See also Cavanaugh, Monthly Report, January 1945, ibid.; Gerard F. Giblin, "Jesuits As Chaplains in the Armed Forces, 1917–1960," *Woodstock Letters* 89 (1960): 332. Since the Germans also took three British priests captive, a total of eleven Catholic chaplains had fallen into the enemy in less than one week. On the British, see *Catholic Review,* November 10, 1944.

6. B. H. Liddell Hart, *History of the Second World War* (New York: G. P. Putnam's Sons, 1970), pp. 654–655; Hugh N. Cole, *The Ardennes: The Battle of the Bulge* (Washington, D.C.: Office of the Chief of Military History, Department of the Army, 1965), p. 261.

7. Leo Weigel to Joseph M. Marling, January 16, 1945, *WLTOC* 68 (February 3, 1945): 68–4, 68–5.

8. Forrest Pogue, *Supreme Command* (Washington, D.C.: Office of the Chief of Military History, Department of the Army, 1954), p. 384; Goolrick and Tanner, *Battle of the Bulge,* pp. 148–149.

9. Francis L. Sampson, *Paratrooper Padre* (Washington, D.C.: Catholic University of America Press, 1948), pp. 74–75.

10. *Elmira Star-Gazette,* June 15, 1945.

11. Sampson, *Paratrooper Padre,* p. 77.

12. Maloney's awards included the Distinguished Service Cross, Distinguished Unit Citation with one Oak Leaf, Purple Heart with one Oak Leaf Cluster, and the European Theater Ribbon with four campaign stars (Normandy, the Ardennes, the Rhineland, and Central Europe) (*Catholic Courier,* February 15, June 7 and 14, 1945; *Elmira Star-Gazette,* June 15, 1945; *Catholic Journal,* [June 7, 1945]; *Catholic News,* June 9, 1945).

13. Fred MacKenzie, *Men of Bastogne* (New York: David McKay and Company, 1968), pp. 211–212.

14. George S. Patton, Jr., *War As I Knew It* (Boston: Houghton Mifflin, 1947), pp. 184–185.

15. James H. O'Neill, "The True Story of the Patton Prayer," *Military Chaplain* (October–November 1948): 1, 3, 13; George R. Metcalf, *With Cross and Shovel: A Chaplain's Letters from England, France, and Germany, 1942–1945* (Duxbury, Mass.: [n. pub.], 1957), p. 184; Martin Blumenson, *The Patton Papers* (Boston: Houghton Mifflin, 1974), vol. 2, p. 605.

16. Patton, *War As I Knew It*, pp. 185–186.

17. Paul D. Harkins, *When the Third Cracked Europe* (Harrisburg, Pa.: Army Times Publishing Company, 1969), p. 44; Patton, *War As I Knew It*, p. 186; O'Neill, "True Story of the Patton Prayer," p. 13.

18. Joseph J. Raimondo, questionnaire, December 1983.

19. Aubrey J. O'Reilly to John J. Cantwell, January 1 [1945], O'Reilly Papers, AALA.

20. Joseph N. Couture, "History of the Society of St. Edmund" (Manuscript, n.d.), p. 142, ASSE.

21. Ibid.; *Burlington Daily News,* January 24–25, 1945; *Burlington Free Press,* January 25, 1945; John F. O'Hara, Circular Letters No. 42, March 15, 1945, and No. 43, May 6, 1945, "Circular Letters" file, AAMS; [J. A.] Ulio to Society of Saint Edmund, January 23, 1945, Verret Papers, ASSE; John F. O'Hara to V. F. Nicholle, January 31, 1945, ibid.; Edward F. Witsell to Society of Saint Edmund, July 25, 1945, ibid.; *OSV,* July 24, 1949.

22. John F. O'Hara, Circular Letter No. 43, May 6, 1945, "Circular Letters" file, AAMS; William R. Arnold to John F. O'Hara, February 13, 1945, Anthony E. Czubak Papers, RG 247, NA; Czubak, Monthly Reports, March and October 1943, Czubak Papers, ADPR; Czubak, Monthly Report, January 1945, RG 247, NA; Czubak to John F. O'Hara, December 26, 1942, ibid.; Francis P. Keough to John F. O'Hara, December 26, 1942, ibid.; Czubak to [Francis P. Keough], March 11, 1943, "Military Ordinariate" file, ADPR; O'Hara to Keough, February 10, 1945, ibid.; *Providence Visitor,* February 8, 1945; [Providence] *Evening Bulletin,* February 7, 1945; *Providence Journal,* February 14, 1945; Edward Flannery, interview, November 23, 1987.

23. Leo Weigel to [Joseph M.] Marling, January 16, 1945, *WLTOC* 68 (February 3, 1945): 68–5; Weigel to Marling, *WLTOC* 74 (March 5, 1945): 74–2.

24. John F. O'Hara, Circular Letter No. 43, May 6, 1945, "Circular Letters" file, AAMS; William R. Arnold to John F. O'Hara, February 13, 1945, Czubak Papers, RG 247, NA; "Military Ordinariate" file, ADPR; Raphael H. Hochhaus to Joseph P. Zuercher, February 23, 1945, Hochhaus Papers, JMPA.

25. Gerard J. Cuddy, "The Bulge" (Manuscript, n.d.), p. 33.

26. Edward P. O'Hern, Monthly Report, February 1945, O'Hern Papers, RG 247, NA; Philip C. Breton, Monthly Report, December 1944, Breton Papers, RG 247, NA; Joseph J. Raimondo, questionnaire, December 1983.

CHAPTER 9. THE FALL OF GERMANY

1. L. Curtis Tiernan to [William R. Arnold], March 8, 1945, box 181, vol. 2, RG 247, NA; [Arnold] to Tiernan, February 26, 1945, ibid.

2. Edmond J. Griffin to William D. Cleary, April 23, 1945, John T. O'Brien Papers, ibid.

3. Arnold to John F. O'Hara, February 2, 1945, box 79, vol. 10, ibid.

4. Franklin M. Davis, *Across the Rhine* (Chicago: Time-Life Books, 1980), p. 59. Legend has it that a Protestant chaplain, William Gibble, filmed the whole episode from the top of a hill on the American side of the river, but there is no evidence to support this assertion (William B. Breuer, *Storming Hitler's Rhine* (New York: St. Martin's Press, 1985), pp. 137, 149).

5. "In Memoriam," *Our Mother of Perpetual Help* (June 1945): 179.

6. Ibid., pp. 176–177, 179–180; John B. Wogan to William Arnold, June 18, November 15 and 26, 1943, Clarence A. Vincent Papers, RG 247, NA; Vincent, Monthly Report, May 1944, ibid. W. B. Augur, 1st Indorsement, June 2, 1944, Vincent, Monthly Report, May 1944, ibid.

7. Matthew Meighan to Victor Sabelle, March 14, 1945, Vincent Papers, RPASLP; [Lawrence] H. Keating to Victor Sabelle, March 14, 1945, Vincent Papers, RPASLP; "Chaplain (First Lieutenant) Clarence A. Vincent," Vincent Papers, ibid.; John F. O'Hara, Circular Letter No. 43, May 6, 1945, "Circular Letters" file, AAMS; *Monitor*, March 31, 1945.

8. Arthur J. O'Leary, Monthly Report, April 1945, O'Leary Papers, RG 247, NA; Gerard A. Quinn, Monthly Reports, March and April 1945, Quinn Papers, ibid.

9. Aloys R. Schweitzer, "Shepherding the Timberwolves," *TPC* (June 1947): 57.

10. Alfred J. Kilp to [Joseph J. King], April 2, 1945, Kilp Papers, ACAPSJ; Joseph Hoying to Joseph M. Marling, April 2, 1945, *WLTOC* 78 (April 14, 1945): 78–6; John Hamme to Joseph M. Marling, April 5, 1945, *WLTOC* 79 (April 21, 1945): 79–7.

11. *Union and Echo*, February 16, 1945; Seraph W. Zeitz, "I Was No Hero," *TPC* (June 1947): 114.

12. John Hamme to Joseph M. Marling, April 5, 1945, *WLTOC* 79 (April 21, 1945): 79–7.

13. Francis L. Sampson, *Paratrooper Padre* (Washington, D.C.: Catholic University of America Press, 1948), pp. 90–91; John Toland, *The Last 100 Days* (New York: Bantam Books, 1976), p. 75.

14. Sampson, *Paratrooper Padre*, p. 91.

15. Ibid., pp. 91, 93–95, 97–99.

16. Ibid., pp. 110, 113–116.

17. Ibid., pp. 119–120; Toland, *The Last 100 Days*, p. 74.

18. Paul W. Cavanaugh, "Chaplain Prisoner," *Woodstock Letters* 90 (February 1961): 29.

19. Ibid., pp. 32, 34.

20. Paul W. Cavanaugh, "Itinerary of Chaplain Paul W. Cavanaugh, Prisoner of War" (Manuscript, n.d.), Cavanaugh Papers, ADPSJ; Cavanaugh, Monthly Report, March 1945, ibid.

21. Cavanaugh, "Chaplain Prisoner," p. 39.

22. Ibid., p. 43; Cavanaugh to [Leo D. Sullivan], July 23, 1945, ADPSJ; Cavanaugh, Monthly Report, April 1945, Cavanaugh Papers, ADPSJ; Toland, *The Last 100 Days*, pp. 399–400. The German word *oflag* is a short form replacing the more cumbersome "*offizierenslager*" or prison camp for officers.

23. Cavanaugh to [Leo D. Sullivan], July 23, 1945, Cavanaugh Papers, ADPSJ.

24. Cavanaugh, "Chaplain Prisoner," pp. 49–50; Cavanaugh to [Leo D. Sullivan], June 23, 1945, Cavanaugh Papers, ADPSJ.

25. Frank Laudick to Joseph M. Marling, April 14, 1945, *WLTOC* 81 (May 5, 1945): 81–2; *WLTOC* 85 (June 2, 1945): 85–2.

26. Guy [A. Moews] to Theodore [Hesselbrock], May 7, 1945, Moews Papers, William Faber Franciscana Library.

27. Andrew Pollack to Joseph M. Marling, May 1, 1945, *WLTOC* 83 (May 19, 1945): 83–4.

28. *Catholic Courier,* November 29, 1945.

29. Emmet L. Walsh to Bill Watson, March 22, 1987, Walsh Papers, AMOMIEP; *Monitor,* July 7, 1945; *Providence Visitor,* July 5, 1945; *OSV,* July 8, 1945. For Catholic chaplains at other camps, see Robert L. Gushwa, *The Best and Worst of Times: The United States Army Chaplaincy, 1920–1945* (Washington, D.C.: Office of the Chief of Chaplains, Department of the Army, 1977), p. 183; Alfred J. Kilp to [Joseph J. King], May 2, 1945, ACAPSJ; Edward P. O'Hern, Monthly Report, June 1945, O'Hern Papers, RG 247, NA; *Denver Catholic Register,* June 28, 1944; William Lundy to Joseph McGucken, May 7, 1945, Lundy Papers, AALA.

30. [John D. Duggan] to [Edmund J. Britt], May 12, [1945], Duggan Papers, A&MDB; [Illegible] to John F. O'Hara, June 2, 1945, ibid.; Edward A. McDonough to John F. O'Hara, May 23, 1945, ibid. On the theory that Russian fire downed the aircraft, see [Ralph] H. Schenk to [Joseph P.] Zuercher, August 10, 1945, Schenk Papers, JMPA.

31. On May 3, 1945, Copeland's unit, the 44th Infantry Division, was located nearly 100 miles to the *west* of Berchtesgaden, at the Austrian city of Landeck, where it fought a war's-end skirmish with the rapidly retreating Germans. In addition, Copeland was so severely ill with malaria that it seems highly unlikely he would have attempted the 200–mile round trip (Stanton, *Order of Battle,* p. 132; Macdonald, *The Last Offensive,* p. 442, map XVII; [Raymond F.] Copeland to Joseph J. King, May 3, 1945, Copeland Papers, ACAPSJ).

32. On the total number of dead chaplains, see Matthew Meighan to Victor Sabelle, March 26, 1945, Clarence Vincent Papers, RPALSP; Lewis H. Brereton, *The Brereton Diaries* (New York: W. Morrow and Company, 1946), p. 399.

CHAPTER 10. THE MARIANAS

1. Ronald H. Spector, *Eagle against the Sun: The American War against Japan* (New York: Vintage Books, 1985), pp. 301–303, 312–316; Rafael Steinberg, *Island Fighting* (Chicago: Time-Life Books, 1978) p. 167.

2. Joseph P. Gallagher, interview, June 15, 1987. Gallagher's experiences on Saipan have been described, highly fictionalized, in John Toland's novel, *Gods of War* (Garden City, N.Y.: Doubleday and Company, 1985), under the name of "Jumping Joe" (Joseph Gallagher to Donald F. Crosby, August 18, 1987).

3. Gallagher interview, June 15, 1987.

4. Ibid.

5. Spector, *Eagle against the Sun,* p. 304; Gallagher interview, June 15, 1987.

6. *OSV,* July 30, 1044; *Providence Visitor,* July 27, 1944.

7. The wounded Catholic chaplains were Paul G. Brunet, James F. Cunningham, Ronald J. Dinn, Clarence Duhart, Anthony F. McCabe, Emmet J. Michaels, and John J. Whalen.

8. On Dinn, Duhart, and McCabe, see *Boston Pilot,* August 26, 1944; *Brooklyn Tablet,* August 26, 1944; *Catholic Standard and Times,* August 25, 1944; "Corps Members

Honored," *Navy Chaplain's News Letter* 3 (January–February 1945): 4; *Catholic Transcript*, August 10, 1944; Clifford M. Drury, *The History of the Chaplain Corps, United States Navy, 1939–1949* (Washington, D.C.: Bureau of Naval Personnel, 1950), pp. 188–190.

9. Ronald [Dinn] to Dear Clerics, August 24, 1944, Dinn Papers, AFFPSH; *Catholic Standard and Times*, August 11, 1944; Drury, *History of the Chaplain Corps*, p. 188; [James] P. Rice to John F. O'Hara, July 24, 1944, box 12, Rice folder, O'Hara Papers, AUND; Citation, Bronze Star Medal, Emmet T. Michaels, n.d., "Corps Members Commended," *Navy Chaplain's News Letter* 3 (March–April 1945): 4; Gallagher interview, June 15, 1987; Spector, *Eagle against the Sun*, p. 304; Philip A. Crowl, *Campaign in the Marianas* (Washington, D.C.: Office of the Chief of Military History, Department of the Army, 1960), pp. 95–96.

10. "Honors to Corps Members," *Navy Chaplain's News Letter* 3 (July–August 1945): 4. Brubaker's denomination was Presbyterian Church, USA.

11. Ronald [Dinn] to Dear Clerics, August 24, 1944, Dinn Papers, AFFPSH; *Catholic Herald*, July 27, 1944; *Catholic Transcript*, August 10, 1944. Since the military authorities lost track of Dinn, they first reported him Missing in Action, and the local supervising chaplain had ordered a number of Masses for the "repose of my soul," as Dinn later put it bemusedly ("Military Service Data," Ronald J. Dinn, n.d., Dinn Papers, AFFSH).

12. *Catholic Transcript*, July 20, 1944.

13. Gallagher interview, June 15, 1987.

14. Ibid.

15. Ibid.

16. Charles C. Riedel, "Chaplain's Annual Report of Official Duties for the Year 1943," January 3, 1944, Riedel Papers, ACSV; Charles C. Riedel to [Robert D. Workman], February 16, 1944, ibid.

17. R. Griffin to Charles C. Riedel, July 4, 1944, Riedel Papers, ACSV; Griffin to Riedel, "Punishment—Letter of Instruction 342," July 4, 1944, ibid.

18. Riedel to [Griffin], July 5, 1944, ibid.

19. J. E. Herbold to Riedel, July 7, 1944, ibid.; Award of Bronze Star Medal, H. G. Patrick to Riedel, March 31, 1945, ibid. The award of the Bronze Star Medal was not inconsistent with policy in the armed services, since an officer or enlisted man can earn a decoration but still receive punishment for an improper action.

20. Riedel to Francis J. Spellman, June 10, 1945, ibid.; William T. McCarty to Riedel, June 4 and 21, 1945, ibid.; Riedel to Spellman, June 10, 1945, ibid.; Francis McCarty to Riedel, June 21, 1945, ibid. On Riedel and the navy: F. K. Elder to Riedel, July 5, 1945, ibid.; Riedel to Spellman, n.d. [August 1945], ibid.; [Randall Jacobs] to Riedel, June 23, 1945, ibid. Riedel was lucky to leave the corps in its good graces. Earlier, it had given him a "separation under honorable circumstances" but no "certificate of satisfactory service" (Jacobs to Riedel, September 11, 1944, ibid.). Riedel returned to his order, the Clerics of St. Viator, where he served successfully until his death in 1959.

21. Gallagher interview, June 15, 1987.

22. Ibid.

23. Crowl, *Campaign in the Marianas*, pp. 256–266; Carl W. Hoffman, *Saipan: The Beginning of the End* ([Washington, D.C.]: Historical Division, Headquarters, United States Marine Corps, 1950), pp. 222–230; Samuel E. Morison, *New Guinea and the Marianas* (Boston: Little, Brown and Company, 1953), pp. 335–336; Spector, *Eagle against the Sun*, pp. 316–317.

24. Gallagher interview, June 15, 1987.

25. On chaplains who served in the Tinian campaign, see especially Robert G. Keating, who worked with the wounded after they were evacuated from the island (*Boston Pilot,* September 2, 1944); John V. Loughlin, who gave the Last Rites to seventy-five marines *(New World,* November 3, 1944); Thomas Brady, who was wounded by a sniper but recovered and continued to work (Brady to [John F. O'Hara], September 4, 1944, box 13, "Fleet Post Office—San Francisco" folder, John F. O'Hara Papers, AUND); and Joseph Gallagher, who describes both the constant rains and the story of a marine saved from a sniper's bullet by the buckle on his helmet (Gallagher interview, June 15, 1987).

26. *Brooklyn Tablet,* December 30, 1944.

27. Spector, *Eagle against the Sun,* p. 319; Thomas J. Donnelly, *"Hey Padre": The Saga of a Regimental Chaplain in World War Two* (New York: The 77th Division Association, [1982]), pp. 64, 68–69.

28. *Brooklyn Tablet,* December 30, 1944.

29. *Catholic Transcript,* October 12, 1944; Citation, Bronze Star Medal, Paul J. Redmond, n.d., "Corps Members Commended," *Navy Chaplain's News Letter* 3 (March–April 1945): 4. "Viaticum," from the Latin word *via* meaning "road" or "way," and *cum,* meaning "with," is customarily given to the gravely ill and to those facing the imminent possibility of death. The ritual includes a set of ancient prayers and blessings. It is, of course, Holy Communion, which Catholics believe is the true body and blood of Christ.

30. Anthony Conway to Pop and Mom and Everyone [July 20, 1944], *The Priest Goes to War,* [pp. 54–55]. See also [Anthony J. Conway] to Pop and Mom and Everyone, July 20, 1944, box 13, "Fleet Post Office—San Francisco" folder, O'Hara Papers, AUND.

31. Drury, *History of the Chaplain Corps,* p. 189; Finnigan questionnaire, December 1983; *Catholic Standard and Times,* August 25 and September 1, 1944. The letter was reprinted in virtually all the Catholic publications of the times. His hometown Catholic newspaper in Philadelphia (reflecting Cardinal Dougherty's total disinterest in the military chaplaincy) chose neither to publish it nor to give anything at all on Conway's life, save for the bare facts of his existence. Regrettably, nothing more is known about Conway.

32. Donnelly, *"Hey Padre,"* p. 73.

33. Ibid., p. 74.

34. Henry I. Shaw, Jr., Bernard C. Nalty, and Edwin T. Turnbladh, *Central Pacific Drive* ([Washington, D.C.]: U.S. Marine Corps, 1966), pp. 346, 422, 568; Philip A. Crowl and Edmund C. Love, *Seizure of the Gilberts and Marshalls* (Washington, D.C.: Office of the Chief of Military History, Department of the Army, 1955), p. 446.

CHAPTER 11. THE LIBERATION OF THE PHILIPPINES

1. Ronald H. Spector, *Eagle against the Sun: The American War against Japan* (New York: Vintage Books, 1985), pp. 428, 511; D. Clayton James, *The Years of MacArthur* (Boston: Houghton Mifflin, 1975), p. 556; William Manchester, *American Caesar: Douglas MacArthur, 1880–1964* (Boston: Little, Brown and Company, 1978), pp. 386–387.

2. Rafael Steinberg, *Return to the Philippines* (Chicago: Time-Life Books, 1979), p. 63.

3. Samuel E. Morison, *The Two-Ocean War: A Short History of the United States Navy*

in the Second World War (Boston: Little, Brown and Company, 1963), pp. 462, 472–474.

4. "Honors to Corps Members," *Navy Chaplain's News Letter* 3 (July–August 1945): 4. For the total number of chaplains, see Clifford M. Drury, *The History of the Chaplain Corps, United States Navy, 1939–1949* (Washington, D.C.: Bureau of Naval Personnel, 1950), p. 311; for the attack on the *Suwanee,* see Samuel E. Morison, *Leyte: June 1944–January 1945* (Boston: Little, Brown and Company, 1958), p. 301.

5. Spector, *Eagle against the Sun,* p. 400. The twelve Catholic chaplains killed in the Philippines or at sea were Richard E. Carberry (Portland, Oregon, army); William T. Cummings (Maryknoll, army); William P. Duffy (Holy Spirit Fathers, army); Michael F. Duggan (Buffalo, army); Carl W. Hausmann (Jesuits, army); Joseph V. LaFleur (Lafayette, Louisiana, army); Francis J. McManus (Cleveland, navy); James W. O'Brien (San Francisco, army); Thomas J. Scecina (Indianapolis, army); Henry B. Stober (Cleveland, army); Joseph G. Vanderheiden (Benedictines, army); and Matthias E. Zerfas (Milwaukee, army) ("Honor Roll of deceased chaplains, 1941–1948," Post Locator File, 1940–1949, vol. I, AAMS).

6. NCWC [National Catholic Welfare Conference] News Service Release, September 20, 1943, LaFleur Papers, RG 247, NA; John F. O'Hara to Jules B. Jeanmard, November 21, 1944, LaFleur Papers, ADL; Newell Schindler, *Man among Men: J. Verbis LaFleur, Priest-Soldier* (New Orleans: Alumni Association of Notre Dame and St. Joseph Seminaries, 1965), p. 8.

7. "Chaplain Joseph Verbis LaFleur, 1912–1944" (Manuscript, n.d.), LaFleur Papers, ADL.

8. Daniel B. Jorgensen, *The Service of Chaplains to Army Air Units, 1917–1946* (Washington, D.C.: Office of the Chief of Air Force Chaplains, 1961), p. 86. See also Manny Lawton and George Robinette (Manuscript, n.d.), LaFleur Papers, ADL; Joseph T. Ryan to Mrs. B. H. Delery, April 3, 1989, ibid.; *Catholic Review,* March 9, 1945; Morison, *Leyte,* p. 401.

9. Thomas J. Donnelly, *"Hey Padre": The Saga of a Regimental Chaplain in World War Two* (New York: The 77th Division Association, [1982], p. 98).

10. Ibid., p. 90.

11. Ibid., p. 91.

12. Joseph E. Pohl to Bob, February 7, 1945, Pohl Papers, RPASLP.

13. Chaplain X to [name withheld], December 15, 1944, January 1, 1945, Chaplain X Papers, RG 247, NA.

14. Chaplain X, Monthly Report, July 1942, quoted in Albert N. Corpening to Chief of Army Exchange Service, July 10, 1942, Chaplain X Papers, RG 247, NA.

15. Maurice [Reynolds] to William R. Arnold, May 31, June 24, and July 23, 1943, ibid.; Arnold to Reynolds, June 24, 1943, RG 247, NA; Arnold to Reynolds, August 2, 1943, ibid.; Citation [for Bronze Star], March 28, 1945, Chaplain X Papers, ibid.

16. Chaplain X, questionnaire, December 1983.

17. Ibid.

18. Ibid.

19. Chaplain X to Superior, December 15, 1944, Chaplain X Papers, RG 247, NA. Readers who want to discover the identity of Chaplain X are invited to do what the author did—simply rummage, at random, through the files of the 9,000 World War II army chaplains (of which 2,900 were Catholic) now kept in the Records of the Office of the Chief of Chaplains at the Washington National Records Center in Suitland, Maryland. (The Center is a branch of the National Archives.) The reason for the secrecy is that Chaplain X is still alive at the time of this writing.

20. M. Hamlin Cannon, *Leyte: The Return to the Philippines* (Washington, D.C.: Office of the Chief of Military History, Department of the Army, 1954), p. 361.

21. Morison, *Leyte,* pp. 316, 397; Robert Ross Smith, *Approach to the Philippines* (Washington, D.C.: Office of the Chief of Military History, Department of the Army, 1953), p. 652.

22. John A. Dunn to [Michael J.] Curley, April 13, 1945, Dunn Papers, AABAL; Donnelly, *"Hey Padre,"* pp. 91, 101.

23. Samuel Eliot Morison, *The Liberation of the Philippines: Luzon, Mindanao, the Visayas, 1944-1945* (Boston: Little, Brown and Company, 1959), pp. 210, 325–326; Spector, *Eagle against the Sun,* pp. 519–520.

24. Cornelius O'Brien, interview, July 8, 1987.

25. Ibid.

26. Ibid.

27. Spector, *Eagle against the Sun,* pp. 518–520; William Leonard, interview, August 14, 1987; Leonard to Donald F. Crosby, May 27, 1993. The small number of wartime converts to universal pacifism among the Catholic clergy should occasion no surprise, since the war enjoyed so much popularity with the American public. When the 200 chaplains who responded to our questionnaire were asked, "Did you believe, *while the war was going on,* that this was a 'just war'? In other words, did you believe that the U.S. did the right thing when it entered the war?" Forty-seven percent said, "Very definitely yes"; another 47 percent said, "Yes"; only 5 percent responded, "Don't know"; and 0.5 percent said, "No." Almost none had substantial doubts about the justice of American participation in the conflict. The attack on Pearl Harbor and the government's propaganda machine impressed the clergy as much as the rest of the populace.

28. Sidney Stewart, *Give Us This Day* (New York: W. W. Norton and Company, 1957), pp. 150–151, 164–165; *New York Times,* October 6, 1945.

29. Sidney Stewart, *Give Us This Day* (New York: W. W. Norton and Company, 1956), pp. 168–170; *New York Times,* October 6, 1945; Battle Casualty Report, May 21, 1948, Cummings Papers, RG 247, NA; *Brooklyn Tablet,* August 4. The word "Ghost" in the baptismal formula has since been changed to "Spirit." The total number of prisoners and survivors on the ship is not known, though it is thought that at least 300 perished at Manila and the same number at Formosa *(Brooklyn Tablet,* October 13, 1945).

30. Christopher Cross, *Soldiers of God* (New York: E. P. Dutton and Company, 1945), p. 64.

31. Robert Ross Smith, *Triumph in the Philippines* (Washington, D.C.: Office of the Chief of Military History, 1963), pp. 427–428; John J. Dugan, "Life under the Japs," *Boston Globe,* April 19–21, 1945; Cross, *Soldiers of God,* pp. 59–60, 64; *Boston Pilot,* February 10, April 14, 1945; *Brooklyn Tablet,* February 10, 1945. The exact number of Catholic chaplains freed at Cabanatuan has never been determined.

32. Spector, *Eagle against the Sun,* p. 521; Smith, *Triumph in the Philippines,* pp. 211–236.

33. William Manchester, *American Caesar: Douglas MacArthur, 1880–1964* (Boston: Little, Brown and Company, 1978), pp. 409–413; Spector, *Eagle against the Sun,* pp. 521–523.

34. William Leonard, interview, August 5, 1987.

35. Steinberg, *Return to the Philippines,* p. 136.

36. [William J. Leonard], "From the Same Army Chaplain, Overseas," *Jesuit Seminary News* 15 (June 1945): 12.

37. *Rochester Democrat and Chronicle,* November 11, 1987; Citation, "Distinguished

Service Cross," July 1945, Chaplains' File, ADROCH; "Liberation of Bilibid Prison" (Manuscript, n.d.), Elmer Heindl Papers, ADROCH.

38. Spector, *Eagle against the Sun*, p. 524; Smith, *Triumph in the Philippines*, pp. 306–307.

39. J. Galvin, "The Third Door," *Catholic Digest* 9 (June 1945): 80–82; *Brooklyn Tablet*, May 5, 1945.

40. Galvin, "The Third Door," p. 81.

41. Harold Roth to Joseph M. Marling, March 10, 1945, *WLTOC* 87 (June 16, 1945): 87–4; "Our Chaplains," *Gasparian* 8 (January 1945): 5.

42. Edward M. Starr, Efficiency Report, Aquinas T. Colgan, March 10, 1945, Colgan Papers, RG 247, NA.

43. *Chicago Daily Tribune*, June 23, 1945; William T. McCarty, Circular Letter No. 44, June 26, 1945, "Circular Letters" file, AMA.

44. Spector, *Eagle against the Sun*, p. 527; Smith, *Triumph in the Philippines*, pp. 640–641.

45. John Kuenster, "They Called It Colgan Woods," *Columbia* 35 (May 1955): 18–19.

46. William T. McCarty, Circular Letter No. 44, June 26, 1945, "Circular Letters" file, AMA; *Chicago Daily Tribune*, June 23, 1945; William V. O'Connor to [John F. O'Hara?], May 8, 1945, Colgan Papers, ACFMCP.

47. E. P. Walsh to Military Ordinariate, May 22, 1945, Aquinas Colgan Papers, AMCPCF.

48. Robert L. Eichelberger and Milton MacKaye, *Our Jungle Road to Tokyo* (New York: The Viking Press, 1950), p. 227. Besides Aquinas Colgan on Mindanao, two other Catholic chaplains were lost on Luzon: Myles F. O'Toole (a Franciscan) and Owen Monaghan (a Passionist). Leo G. Rechsteiner (a Benedictine) died on Leyte of non-battle causes.

CHAPTER 12. IWO JIMA

1. Ronald H. Spector, *Eagle against the Sun: The American War against Japan* (New York: Vintage Books, 1985), pp. 493–499, 502; Samuel E. Morison, *Victory in the Pacific* (Boston: Little, Brown and Company, 1960), pp. 69, 72; Allan R. Millet, *Semper Fidelis: The History of the United States Marine Corps* (New York: Macmillan, [1980]), p. 430; George W. Garand and Truman R. Strobridge, *Western Pacific Operations* ([Washington, D.C.: Historical Division, Headquarters, U.S. Marine Corps], 1971), pp. 711, 797.

2. Garand and Strobridge, *Western Pacific Operations*, pp. 475–476, 492; Bill D. Ross, *Iwo Jima: Legend of Valor* (New York: Vanguard Press, 1965), pp. 39–42.

3. Garand and Strobridge, *Western Pacific Operations*, pp. 475, 767, 771; *Catholic News*, March 24, 1945.

4. James Deasy, interview, November 16, 1982.

5. Charles F. Suver, "Iwo Jima" (Manuscript, n.d.), p. 1; James J. Deasy to [Joseph J. King], January 30, 1945, and April 6, 1945, Deasy Papers, ACAPSJ.

6. Deasy to [King], April 6, 1945, ibid.

7. Rosemarian Staudacher, *Chaplains in Action* (New York: Farrar, Straus and Cudahy, 1962), p. 72; T. Grady Gallant, "The Friendly Dead," in Stanley E. Smith, *The United States Marine Corps in World War II* (New York: Random House, 1969), p. 731.

8. Spector, *Eagle against the Sun,* p. 495; Samuel E. Morison, *Victory in the Pacific, 1945* (Boston: Little, Brown and Company, 1960), p. 44.

9. Staudacher, *Chaplains in Action,* p. 72.

10. Suver, "Iwo Jima," p. 2.

11. Ibid., p. 3.

12. Ibid.

13. Ibid., pp. 3–4; Staudacher, *Chaplains in Action,* p. 76.

14. Deasy interview, November 16, 1982.

15. Deasy to [King], April 6, 1945, Deasy Papers, ACAPSJ.

16. Suver, "Iwo Jima," p. 4.

17. Deasy to [King], March 20, April 6, 1945, Deasy Papers, ACAPSJ.

18. Staudacher, *Chaplains in Action,* p. 80.

19. Deasy interview, November 16, 1982.

20. Suver, "Iwo Jima," p. 4; Staudacher, *Chaplains in Action,* p. 76.

21. "Marine Corps Correspondents," *Navy Chaplain's News Letter* 3 (July–August 1945): 6; Deasy to [King], April 6, 1945, Deasy Papers, ACAPSJ.

22. Deasy interview, November 16, 1982; Suver, "Iwo Jima," p. 4. Deasy's burial was common knowledge among the priest-chaplains on the island. (See, for instance, Paul Bradley, interview, February 13, 1987.) Deasy's assistant, Tom Dailey, learned of it from both Deasy and others immediately afterward (Dailey to [James J. Deasy], January 25, 1987).

23. Deasy interview, November 16, 1982.

24. Suver, "Iwo Jima," p. 5. See also Karal A. Marling and John Wetenhall, *Iwo Jima: Monuments, Memories, and the American Hero* (Cambridge: Harvard University Press, 1991), pp. 40–67, 291.

25. Staudacher, *Chaplains in Action,* pp. 78–80; Suver, "Iwo Jima," pp. 5–7; "Mass on Iwo Jima," *Catholic Digest* 11 (July 1947): 10; Gerard F. Giblin, "Jesuits As Chaplains in the Armed Forces, 1917–1960," *Woodstock Letters* 89 (1960): 333; Eugene J. Adams to Donald F. Crosby, January 8, 1983. (Adams witnessed Deasy's burial.) Suver offered Mass under the *first* flag placed on top of the mountain. A *second* flag was the one photographed by Joe Rosenthal (Karal Ann Marling and John Wetenhall, *Iwo Jima: Monuments, Memories, and the American Hero* [Cambridge, Mass.: Harvard University Press, 1991], pp. 40–67).

26. Drury, *History of the Chaplain Corps,* p. 170; James S. Vedder, *Surgeon on Iwo* (Novato, Calif.: Presidio Press, 1984), pp. 125–126, 160–161.

27. Suver, "Iwo Jima," pp. 4, 6, 9; "Mass on Iwo Jima," *Catholic Digest* 11 (July 1947): 10.

28. Deasy to [King], March 1, 20, April 6, May 6, September 14, 1945, Deasy Papers, ACAPSJ; Deasy interview, November 16, 1982.

29. Suver, "Iwo Jima," p. 9.

30. Deasy to [King], March 20, 1945, Deasy Papers, ACAPSJ.

31. Henry Druffel to Joseph M. Marling, March 18, 1945, *WLTOC* 76 (March 31, 1945): 76–1; Deasy to [King], April 6, 1945, Deasy Papers, ACAPSJ.

32. Deasy to [King], April 6, 1945, ibid.

33. Deasy to [King], September 14, 1945, ibid.

34. Deasy to [King], May 21, 1945, ibid.

35. Ibid.

36. "From the Mailbag," *Navy Chaplain's News Letter* 3 (July–August 1945): 8. Nineteen Catholic chaplains served on the island (*Catholic News,* March 24, 1945).

CHAPTER 13. JOSEPH O'CALLAHAN, THE *FRANKLIN*,
AND OKINAWA

1. Keith Wheeler, *The Fall of Japan* (Chicago: Time-Life Books, 1983), p. 98.

2. *America* 73 (June 9, 1945): 193; Adolph A. Hoehling, *The Franklin Comes Home* (New York: Hawthorn Books, 1974), p. 10; Joseph T. O'Callahan to [James H. Dolan], June 23, 25–27, 1940, O'Callahan Papers, ANEPSJ; E. C. Donovan, "He Tasted It," *Extension* 40 (August 1945): 24.

3. Joseph O'Callahan, *I Was Chaplain on the Franklin* (New York: Macmillan, 1956), p. 43.

4. Quentin Reynolds, "Chaplain Courageous," *Collier's* 115 (June 23, 1945): 13. See also O'Callahan, *I Was Chaplain on the Franklin,* pp. 3, 10, 13–14, 17–18. He made the statement in 1956, a full decade after the end of the war. He seemed never to tire of the phrase, using it twenty times in his autobiography and seven times on one page alone (p. 117).

5. Ronald H. Spector, *Eagle against the Sun: The American War against Japan* (New York: Vintage Books, 1985), p. 536; Quentin Reynolds, "Chaplain Courageous," *Collier's* 115 (June 23, 1945): 13; *Boston Globe,* May 18, 1945. On the notion of a "happy death": Traditional Catholic piety emphasized the importance of the believer dying "in the state of grace" (i.e., without having mortal sin on his conscience); he would thus be relieved of the despair that often came at the thought of facing one's Maker.

6. O'Callahan, *I Was Chaplain on the Franklin,* p. 48; *Boston Globe,* May 18, 1945.

7. O'Callahan, *I Was Chaplain on the Franklin,* pp. 33, 38–39, 43, 52; Hoehling, *The Franklin Comes Home,* pp. 18, 21–22, 33.

8. O'Callahan, *I Was Chaplain on the Franklin,* p. 60.

9. Ibid., pp. 57–58.

10. Ibid., p. 111.

11. *Boston Globe,* May 18, 1945; O'Callahan, *I Was Chaplain on the Franklin,* pp. 89, 96.

12. O'Callahan, *I Was Chaplain on the Franklin,* p. 69.

13. Ibid., p. 124.

14. Ibid., pp. 120–121; *Boston Globe,* May 18, 1945; Hoehling, *The Franklin Comes Home,* pp. 102–103; *Catholic Courier,* July 12, 1945.

15. O'Callahan, *I Was Chaplain on the Franklin,* pp. 136–137; *New York Times,* May 22, 1945.

16. Clifford M. Drury, *The History of the Chaplain Corps, United States Navy, 1939–1949* (Washington, D.C.: Bureau of Naval Personnel, 1950), p. 201; *Boston Globe,* May 19, 1945.

17. O'Callahan, *I Was Chaplain on the Franklin,* pp. 133–134. Eleven layers of military or naval authority have to approve the recommendation for the Medal of Honor before it can proceed to the proper cabinet-level secretary (Navy, Army, or Air Force), who alone makes the final decision to award it. Congress does not award it, nor does the president involve himself with the medal, though in recent years he has often awarded it in a ceremony at the White House.

18. Hoehling, *The Franklin Comes Home,* pp. 87–88; O'Callahan, *I Was Chaplain on the Franklin,* pp. 104–105; O'Callahan, "I Was Chaplain on the Franklin," *America* 73 (June 9, 1945): 86.

19. *New York Times,* September 15, 1945; O'Callahan, "I Was Chaplain on the Franklin," *America* 73 (June 9, 1945): 88; Quentin Reynolds, "Chaplain Courageous," *Collier's* 115 (June 23, 1945): 14; *Boston Globe,* May 17, 1945. Plaudits for

O'Callahan came even from the aristocratic and generally uncomplimentary superior of the American Jesuits, Zacheus Maher. He told McEleney that all his men in New England should be deeply "proud . . . at the splendid record made by F[athe]r O'Callahan and of the recognition being given him." This was a remarkable statement, coming as it did from an implacable foe of the military chaplaincy. Maher had an obsessive fear that once his men entered the military and had escaped the control of their superiors, they would become used to their newfound "freedom," abuse it, then give scandal. Most of all, he feared that their freedom from religious supervision might even cause them to become problems for the order after the war ended and they returned home (Zacheus J. Maher to James H. Dolan [sic] [John J. McEleney], May 19, 1945, Provincial's File, ANEPSJ). Maher erred. Among other things, he both overestimated the amount of "freedom" that the men would enjoy in the military service, and he greatly exaggerated the difficulties that they might experience after the war upon reentry into civilian life.

20. Clarence J. Duhart to Doug, May 4, 1945, "Letters, 1940–1946" folder, Lawrence E. Lynch Papers, RPABP; Adolph [Schmitt] to [Carrol Ring], January 19, [1945], Schmitt Papers, APFPNJ.

21. Keith Wheeler, *The Road to Tokyo* (Chicago: Time-Life Books), 1980), pp. 101–102; Appleman, *Okinawa: The Last Battle in the Pacific,* pp. 84–102; Spector, *Eagle against the Sun,* p. 533.

22. Spector, *Eagle against the Sun,* pp. 532–533; John T. Byrne, interview, July 6, 1987.

23. Spector, *Eagle against the Sun,* p. 534.

24. Brian Mahedy to Father Provincial, April 21, 1945, and March 31, 1950, Mahedy Papers, APPCH.

25. Samuel H. Ray, *A Chaplain Afloat and Ashore* (Salado, Tex.: Anson Jones Press, 1962), pp. 60, 84.

26. Morison, *Victory in the Pacific,* pp. 244–245; Walter Karig, et al., *Battle Report: Prepared from Official Sources; Published in Cooperation with the Council on Books in Wartime* (New York: Rinehart and Company, 1944–1948), p. 438.

27. Spector, *Eagle against the Sun,* p. 534.

28. Wheeler, *Road to Tokyo,* pp. 109, 111; Roy E. Appleman, James M. Burns, Russell A. Gugeler, and John D. Stevens, *Okinawa: The Last Battle in the Pacific* (Washington, D.C.: Historical Division, Department of the Army, 1948), pp. 208–248; Spector, *Eagle against the Sun,* pp. 534–535.

29. Daisy Amoury, *Father Cyclone* (New York: Julian Messner, 1958), pp. 32–33, 136–137, 185, 251–253.

30. Clarence Duhart to Doug, May 4, 1945, "Letters, 1940–1946" folder, Lynch Papers, RPABP; Byrne interview, July 6, 1987; Joseph A. Phelan to Philip Lynch, August 16, 1945, Lynch Papers, RPABP; John T. Byrne to [Redemptorist Provincial], June 9, 1945, "Letters, 1940–1946" folder, Lynch Papers, RPABP.

31. Amoury, *Father Cyclone,* p. 110.

32. Byrne interview, July 6, 1987.

33. Amoury, *Father Cyclone,* pp. 32–33, 185; Byrne to [Redemptorist Provincial], August 31, July 32, 1942, "Letters, 1940–1960" folder, Lynch Papers, RPABP; Clarence Duhart to Doug, May 4, 1945, ibid.

34. Byrne to [Redemptorist Provincial], June 9, 1945, "Letters, 1940–1960" folder, Lynch Papers, RPABP; J. A. Phelan to Philip Lynch, August 16, 1945, ibid.

35. J. A. Phelan to Philip Lynch, August 16, 1945, RPABP; John T. Byrne to [Redemptorist Provincial], June 9, 1945, ibid.; Joseph A. Hart to Provincial, May 23,

1945, ibid.; Hart to Henry J. T. McKeever, ibid.; Amoury, *Father Cyclone*, pp. 251–252; *Boston Pilot*, July 28, 1945; *Brooklyn Tablet*, May 26, 1945; *OSV*, August 12, 1945.

36. Byrne interview, July 6, 1987; Marion Budny, interview, July 6, 1983; Byrne to [Redemptorist Provincial], June 9, 1945, "Letters, 1940–1960" folder, Lynch Papers, RPABP.

37. *Brooklyn Tablet*, September 15, 1945. See also Budny interview, July 6, 1983; *OSV*, August 12, 1945; James T. Kenny, "The Memorial Service for Father Lawrence E. Lynch" (Manuscript, n.d.), "Letters, 1947–1950" folder, RPABP.

38. James J. McNeil, "Okinawa to Seoul," *Oblate World* (December 1945): 24; Budny interview, July 6, 1983.

39. Wheeler, *Road to Tokyo*, pp. 192–193.

40. Spector, *Eagle against the Sun,* p. 540; Appleman, *The Last Battle in the Pacific,* pp. 384, 386, 473–474.

CHAPTER 14. THE END OF THE WAR–THE BOMB

1. William F. Frawley to [William T. McCarty], August 5, 1945, Thomas M. Conway Papers, A&MDB.

2. Clifford M. Drury, *The History of the Chaplain Corps, United States Navy, 1939–1949* (Washington, D.C.: Bureau of Naval Personnel, 1950), p. 203; *The Priest Goes to War* (New York: The Society for the Propagation of the Faith, [1945]), [p. 37]; Dan Kurzman, *Fatal Voyage: The Sinking of the USS Indianapolis* (New York: Atheneum, 1990), pp. 9, 52, 56, 66, 100, 128–129; Frawley to [William T. McCarty], August 5, 1945, Conway Papers, A&MDB.

3. Kurzman, *Fatal Voyage*, p. 52.

4. Keith Wheeler, *The Fall of Japan* (Chicago: Time-Life Books, 1983), p. 88; Samuel E. Morison, *Victory in the Pacific, 1945* (Boston: Little, Brown and Company, 1960), pp. 321–322; Kurzman, *Fatal Voyage*, p. 66.

5. Raymond B. Lech, *All the Drowned Sailors* (New York: Stein and Day, Publishers, 1984), p. 126; Kurzman, *Fatal Voyage*, p. 128.

6. Kurzman, *Fatal Voyage*, pp. 128–129. See also Lech, *All the Drowned Sailors,* p. 126; Drury, *History of the Chaplain Corps*, p. 203; *The Priest Goes to War,* [p. 37].

7. Morison, *Victory in the Pacific*, p. 327.

8. James M. Burns, *Roosevelt, Soldier of Freedom* (New York: Harcourt, Brace, Jovanovich, 1970), pp. 249–252; 455–459, 558, 591; Ronald H. Spector, *Eagle against the Sun: The American War against Japan* (New York: Vintage Books, 1985), pp. 554–555; Keith Wheeler, *Fall of Japan* (Chicago: Time-Life Books, 1983), pp. 17, 60, 89, 91.

9. Studs Terkel, *"The Good War": An Oral History of World War Two* (New York: Ballantine Books, 1984), pp. 533–534; "An Interview with a Military Chaplain Who Served the Hiroshima and Nagasaki Bomb Squadrons," *Sojourners* (August 1980): 12; George R. Zabelka to William R. Arnold, June 21, September 13, 1944, January 29, 1945, Zabelka Papers, RG 247, NA; Zabelka, Monthly Reports, February, 1944–May, 1945, ibid.

10. "The Quarter's Polls," *Public Opinion Quarterly* 9 (Summer 1945): 246; *Public Opinion Quarterly* 9 (Fall 1945): 384. Public opinion about the Japanese remained adamantly punitive. A national poll in June 1945 found that 96 percent of the people favored some form of punishment for the emperor, while a survey of August of the same year revealed that 85 percent approved of the dropping of the bomb on Japan.

11. Chaplains' questionnaires, December 1983. For chaplains quoted favoring the dropping of the bomb, see questionnaires of December 1983 for George N. Gilligan, Gerald J. Whelan, and James J. Reddington to [Britt], August 28, 1945, Reddington Papers, A&MDB. For similar views, see questionnaires of Raymond A. Schueth, Edwin J. Casey, Frederick W. Bromham, Leo Kinsella, and John J. Bosa.

12. For chaplains opposed to the dropping of the bomb, see questionnaires, December 1983, of: Joseph T. Hemighaus, Leonard Paprocki, Arthur A. Campbell, and W. Russell Carroll, as well as Stephen P. Kenny to Donald F. Crosby, November 6, 1984. For chaplains with mixed views on the dropping of the bomb—feeling relief that it seemed to end the war, yet disturbed at the mayhem it caused—see questionnaires, December 1983, of: Daniel A. McGuire, Leroy D. Burke, Donald J. Strange, Matthew Nestor, and Cosmas Gerard, as well as John Foley, "Haec Olim," p. 484.

13. Some chaplains changed their minds about the bomb after learning of its effects (radiation sickness, massive and ghastly burns, psychological deterioration and insanity, and death). See questionnaires of Thomas Glynn, Leroy D. Burke, John W. Scannell, David A. McGuire, Matthew Nestor, and Donald J. Strange.

14. Spector, *Eagle against the Sun,* pp. 546–549, 555–559; Morison, *Victory in the Pacific,* pp. 336–353; Toland, *Rising Sun,* pp. 820–855.

15. Sylvester Kleman to Joseph M. Marling, September 18, 1945, *WLTOC* 102 (September 29, 1945): 102–1.

16. Jerome G. Kircher, "Kircher Goes to War," *TPC* (June 1947): 46.

17. Paul L. [O'Connor] to [Leo Sullivan], September 28, 1945, O'Connor Papers, ACHPSJ; Morison, *Victory in the Pacific,* pp. 362–366; Toland, *Rising Sun,* pp. 866–870. See also Drury, *History of the Chaplain Corps,* p. 269; "About Chaplains," *American Catholic Historical Society of Philadelphia, Records* 58 1947): 153; Gerard F. Giblin, "Jesuits As Chaplains in the Armed Forces, 1917–1960," *Woodstock Letters* 89 (1960): 333.

18. Samuel Hill Ray, *A Chaplain Afloat and Ashore* (Salado, Tex.: Anson Jones Press, 1962), pp. 93–94, 96–98; Paul O'Connor to [Zacheus] Maher, September 7, 1945, *Woodstock Letters* 74 (December 1945): 323–324, 326; [O'Connor] to [Leo] Sullivan, September 29, 1945, O'Connor Papers, ACHPSJ.

19. Paul O'Connor to [Zacheus] Maher, September 7, 1945, *Woodstock Letters* 74 (December 1945): 323–324, 326; [O'Connor] to [Leo] Sullivan, September 29, 1945, O'Connor Papers, ACHPSJ; *Chicago Daily News,* September 14, 1945.

20. John A. Wilson to Donald F. Crosby, February 20, 1986.

21. *Dayton Daily News* to Joseph M. Marling, September 15, 1945, *WLTOC* 100 (September 15, 1945): 100–1.

22. *Telegraph Register,* [ca. November 3, 1945]; *WLTOC* 107 (November 3, 1945): 107–1; Joseph M. Marling to Chaplains of the Society of the Precious Blood, November 10, 1945, *WLTOC* 108 (November 10, 1945): 108–1; "Enthusiastic Welcome Given Father Wilson," *Gasparian* 8 (December 20, 1945): 1; "Father Wilson Freed and Return[s] to U.S.," *Gasparian* 8 (October 1945): 5; Paul Wilson to Marling, [ca. September 29, 1945], *WLTOC* 102 (September 29, 1945): 102–2; John Wilson to Marling, September 16, 1945, *WLTOC* 103 (October 6, 1945): 103–1; Aloys Selhorst to Marling, September 22, 1945, *WLTOC* 103 (October 6, 1945): 103–1; *Catholic Telegraph,* August 15, 1980.

23. John P. Foley to [Joseph Foley], September 27, 1945 (copy from John Foley to author).

24. Foley, "Haec Olim Meminisse Juvabit," (Manuscript, n.d.), pp. 550, 577; John P. Foley to [Joseph Foley], September 27, 1945 (copy from John Foley to author).

25. [Clarence] Duhart, "Letter from Yokohama," *Ligourian* 33 (December 1945): 507–508.

26. Foley, "Haec Olim," pp. 553, 577; John P. Foley to [John Foley], September 27, 1945.

27. William Staudt to Marling, October 28, 1945, *WLTOC* 109 (November 17, 1945): 109–2.

28. Ray, *A Chaplain Afloat and Ashore,* pp. 95, 99.

29. Padre [Karl Wuest], *They Told It to the Chaplain* (New York: Vintage Press, 1953), pp. 134–135.

30. Ibid., p. 135.

A NOTE ON SOURCES

This book is limited to the experience of the American Catholic chaplains during World War II. Readers looking for a reliable military history of the war will do no better than Basil H. Liddell-Hart, *History of the Second World War* (New York: G. P. Putnam's Sons, 1970). The Time-Life series on the war, while engagingly written, is of uneven quality. For the Pacific, besides Samuel E. Morison's fourteen-volume work, *History of United States Naval Operations in World War II* (Boston: Little, Brown and Company, 1947–1960), an excellent one-volume work on the subject is Ronald H. Spector, *Eagle against the Sun: The American War against Japan* (New York: Vintage Books, 1985).

For the war in Europe, see any of the many works by Martin Blumenson, such as *Breakout and Pursuit* (Washington, D.C.: Office of the Chief of Military History, Department of the Army, 1961) and *Salerno to Cassino: The United States Army in World War II* (Washington, D.C.: Office of the Chief of Military History, Department of the Army, 1969), and *The Patton Papers,* 2 vols. (Boston: Houghton Mifflin Company, 1967), of which the second volume chronicles the general's war years. Students of the European war will also want to dip into Stephen Ambrose's fine works on Eisenhower (*Eisenhower,* 2 vols. [New York: Simon and Schuster, 1983–1984]), especially volume 1, as well as Russell Weigley's massively detailed but underinterpreted two-volume *Eisenhower's Lieutenants: The Campaign of France and Germany, 1944–1945* (Bloomington: University of Indiana Press, 1981). The best series on the U.S. Army remains its official seventy-volume-plus work, *The U.S. Army in World War II* (Washington, D.C.: Office of the Chief of Military History, 1944–1981).

For a distinctly British view of the war, see the classic six-volume history by Winston Churchill, *The Second World War* (Boston: Houghton Mifflin, 1948–1952), as well as more recent versions of the same theme by such British authors as Martin Gilbert, *The Second World War: A Complete History* (New York: Henry Holt and Company, 1989), and John Keegan, *The Second World War* (New York: Viking Penguin, 1990). Students of Adolph Hitler would do well to start, and then stop, with Joachim Fest's *Hitler* (New York: Random House, 1975).

For a magisterial summation of the attack on Pearl Harbor, see Gordon W. Prange, *At Dawn We Slept: The Untold Story of Pearl Harbor* (New York: Penguin Books, 1981). For the U.S. Marine Corps in the Pacific, see the five-volume *History of U.S. Marine Corps Operations in World War II* (Washington, D.C.: Historical Branch, Headquarters, U.S. Marine Corps, 1958–1971); Frank O. Hough, *The Island War: The United States Marine Corps in the Pacific* (Philadelphia: J. B. Lippincott Company, 1947); and Robert Eichelberger and Milton MacKaye, *Our Jungle Road to Tokyo* (New York: Viking Press, 1950). For more on the Pacific war, see Samuel Milner, *The War in the Pacific* (Washington, D.C.: Office of the Chief of Military History, Department of the Army, 1957), and Robert Sherrod, *On to Westward: War in the Central Pacific* (New York: Duell, Sloan and Pearce, 1945), a classic account by an exceptionally able war correspondent. On Douglas MacArthur, see D. Clayton James, *The Years of MacArthur* (Boston: Houghton Mifflin Company, 1975), and MacArthur's own pompous, but informative, *Reminiscences* (New York: McGraw-Hill Book Company, 1964).

This book is based on a wide range of evidence, much of it never examined before. The Catholic press—the diocesan newspapers and large number of weekly and monthly periodicals—formed the starting point, since the Catholic media followed its chaplains closely during the war (especially those in the Marine Corps). I used the non-Catholic press, above all the *New York Times,* to fill in other parts of the story. Of great value were eleven autobiographies published by the Catholic chaplains during the war and in the years following, of which the most useful are: Joseph O'Callahan, *I Was Chaplain on the Franklin* (New York: Macmillan Company, 1956); Francis L. Sampson, *Look Out Below! A Story of the Airborne by a Paratrooper Padre* (Washington, D.C.: Catholic University of America Press, 1958), and *Paratrooper Padre* (Washington, D.C.: Catholic University of America Press, 1948); and Karl Wuest, *They Told It to the Chaplain* (New York: Vintage Press, 1953). These accounts range in style from the melodramatic (O'Callahan) to the humorous (Wuest) to the grimly realistic (Sampson).

In the course of my research, 300 of the still-living chaplains who served in the war were asked to fill out a questionnaire describing their experiences in the service then. Over 200 responded. In addition, I conducted a series of extensive interviews with 80 of these chaplains, and much of the resulting material can be found in these pages.

I also visited or consulted seventy-two separate archives in order to examine the personal papers of 577 Catholic chaplains as well as those of a small number of Protestant ministers and rabbis. These collections contain valuable information not only on the life of the wartime chaplain but on the larger problem of life in the military both at home and overseas. The most voluminous, and quite the most indispensable group of papers, is the Records of the Chief of Army Chaplains, a vast assemblage of documents in the National Records Center (a branch of the National Archives) in Suitland, Maryland. This collection contains the official records of most of the nearly 9,000 wartime army chaplains, including the monthly reports they sent to the chief of chaplains from all over the world, evaluations of their work, and their correspondence with the Chaplain Corps. Since the army chaplains made up 76 percent of the total American chaplaincy force, this well-preserved compilation proved indispensable.

Unfortunately there is no such group of records for the navy's chaplaincy. The Navy's Chief of Chaplains Office in Washington, D.C., made no attempt to preserve its World War II documents, or anything else for that matter, and indeed, one of the postwar Navy Chief of Chaplains, George Rosso (alas, a Catholic priest) actually had all of the department's personnel records—some of which dated from the American Revolution—burned to provide more space for storage of other documents. Would that the possibility of microfilming them first had occurred to him! On the other hand, the navy had earlier commissioned one of its World War II chaplains (in civilian life a professional historian) to produce an official narrative of its wartime chaplaincy, so at least part of the navy chaplaincy story has been saved. Chaplain Clifford M. Drury (Presbyterian, USA) wrote a two-volume work (*History of the Chaplain Corps: United States Navy, 1939–1949* [Washington, D.C.: Bureau of Naval Pesonnel, 1950]), which not only stands as a model of government-sponsored official history but also puts to shame the army chaplaincy's official history (Robert L. Gushwa, *The Best and Worst of Times: The United States Army Chaplaincy, 1920–1945* [Washington, D.C.: Office of the Chief of Chaplains, Department of the Army, 1977]), which falls far short of professional standards. As fine as Drury's work is, however, it can never replace the tens of thousands of records and letters that have been lost forever.

I also made full use of the archives of the Catholic church's major dioceses, archdioceses, universities, and religious orders. I am sad to say that the archival collections of most Catholic dioceses and archdioceses are in a poor state of preservation, evidence of American Catholicism's lack of interest in its own history. The archives belonging to the religious orders, especially the Redemptorists, Franciscans, and Jesuits, have fared better.

Readers wishing to continue their World War II reading beyond the suggestions made here would do well to consult the bibliographies in the Spector, Blumenson, and Weigley books listed above.

INDEX

291